A Fierce Domain:
Conflict in Cyberspace, 1986 to 2012

Jason Healey, Editor

A CCSA Publication, in Partnership with the Atlantic Council

Executive Editor: Jason Healey

Assistant Editor: Karl Grindal

Copy Editor: David Fletcher

This work is the result of continuing cooperation between the Atlantic Council's Brent Scowcroft Center on International Security and the Cyber Conflict Studies Association. More information on the history of cyber conflict can be found on the websites of those two organizations.

The Rights to republish the "Stalking the Wily Hacker" article were acquired from the magazine, *Communications of the Association for Computing Machinery*.

Note that the Morris Worm piece is a government publication (GAO report) and therefore resides in the public domain.

Books published by the Cyber Conflict Studies Association (CCSA) are available at special discounts for bulk purchases in the United States by corporations, institutions, and other organizations. For more information, please contact CCSA's executive office at info@ cyberconflict.org.

ISBN-10: 0-9893274-0-X

ISBN-13: 978-0-9893274-0-4

LCCN Number: 2013940236

To Akiko

Table of Contents

Preface

History is about stories, and the history of cyber conflict is no different. It is no more about the bits and bytes of malicious Internet packets than military history is about the ballistic characteristics of weapons. These stories deserve to be told in their own right, and more importantly, they matter for policymakers today.

The wake-up call started with a missing 75 cents.[1]

Twenty-five years ago, in 1986, the astronomer at the Lawrence Berkeley National Laboratory sat mystified by what his computer screen was telling him. The billing error was so tiny, less than a dollar, that most people would have simply ignored it. But Cliff was not a typical scientist. Sure, he was driven by curiosity – and more discoveries are prefaced by "that's odd" than announced with "Eureka!" But he was also computer savvy and decided to investigate. He suspected possibly a programming error, or a misbehaving local student poking through his network, but soon uncovered the truth. Intruders were searching for secret information on President Reagan's classified Strategic Defense Initiative (aka Star Wars) plan to intercept Soviet missiles.

The US government was little help: special agents seemed more concerned with "real" crime and counterintelligence than the hard-to-fathom world of networks. This kind of agent would joke for many more years about how they relied on their kids to program their VCR for them. The only exception was a junior Air Force special agent, allowed to investigate the problem not as a counterintelligence case, but as a simple fraud. Together they cast about to figure out what was happening, who was responsible, what should be done, and who should do it.

The astronomer invented counter-measures that are common today, such as creating a honey pot with fake "secret" documents to lure intruders into a trap and trace them. The trail ultimately led back to Hanover, Germany, where hackers transferred their stolen documents to their KGB handlers. Best of all, the astronomer documented his lessons in a best-selling book, The Cuckoo's Egg. The AF special agent is still working cyber issues cases for the Air Force, but few seem to know his story or the lessons that may be derived from it.

---

1   Other than in this preface, the editor does not consider The Cuckoo's Egg to be a "wake-up call," as it did not spur the United States to undertake any new action, such as creating a new organization or major policy. Though this was a very important cyber conflict, the government changed little, except for a few, select law enforcement and counterintelligence agencies. The story is included here to help show similarities between events over time.

The wake-up call started in a flash.

The Internet was still in its adolescence in 1988, connecting only half a million users and 60,000 computers, compared to over 2 billion users and 4 billion computers in 2012. Accordingly, it was relatively easy for a small elite operating within in the largest nodes to collaborate whenever there was a problem — until the evening of 2 November, when a computer worm shot around the Internet, infecting perhaps 10 percent of all computers by the following morning. Such malicious software wasn't new, but never before had any spread so fast and so widely.

Responders experienced difficulties, because their coordination processes depended on the very Internet which was now the problem itself! Together they cast about to figure out what was happening, who was responsible, what should be done, and who should do it. They coped, as determined defenders have ever since, and within days university researchers, with little help from their governments, had fixed the vulnerabilities and eradicated the worm.

Afterwards, they discussed the important lesson. Their response had been informal, and there was no central hub to assist them. To ensure that this would never happen again, by the end of that November, the US military funded a new organization to help Internet technicians to fend off digital attacks.

The wake-up call started in the bathroom.

On Sunday, 1 February 1998, the lieutenant colonel who oversaw all "defensive counter-information" for the US Air Force was interrupted in his shower by a call from the Air Force technical defense team in San Antonio. Ten years after the Cuckoo's Egg and Morris Worm, the Air Force had instituted their lessons — they had created their own Computer Emergency Response Team and had trained computer-smart special agents. Now the geeks and cops at AFCERT had detected sophisticated intrusions, some of which traced back to the Middle East.

The lieutenant colonel knew, of course, that the US military had just sent a third aircraft carrier to the Gulf to help convince Saddam Hussein to cooperate with UN inspection teams. The Department of Defense also had just completed a major exercise, ELIGIBLE RECEIVER, to train for such cyber warfare, which could potentially stop America's vaunted military in its tracks. He quickly raised the alarm, which ultimately reached the President.

Not long after, the Deputy Secretary of Defense sat at the head of a table with his team of generals and senior officials within the most secure conference room in the Pentagon to determine what was happening, whether it was serious, who was responsible, what should be done, and who should do it. "Who's in charge?" he asked, only to be met with awkward silence. All eyes finally steered toward the two-star general responsible for information operations at the Pentagon.

The response that the two-star general supervised, along with the FBI, ultimately determined that two teenage hackers, with an Israeli mentor, were to blame – not Saddam Hussein.

One of the most important lessons was that the Department of Defense had to create a new joint command, which would be in charge, and would possess the authority to issue both orders to fend off digital attacks and resources to follow through. That new unit was set up within a year, had 24 personnel, and was commanded by that same two-star general.

The wake-up call started behind a vault door.

In October 2008, the NSA analyst sitting in his ultra-secure room at Fort Meade spotted something that never should exist: a beacon in SIPRNET. Malicious software had somehow gotten into the secret network that the US military uses for all of its operational purposes and was trying to signal out. If an adversary could disrupt SIPRNET, they might be able to stop America's vaunted military in its tracks. Worse yet, the malware was infecting Central Command, which is responsible for conducting the wars in Iraq and Afghanistan. Like his Air Force predecessors ten years earlier, he raised the alarm.

Within days, the four-star general was briefed. Along with senior military and intelligence leaders, he cast about to figure out what was happening, whether it was serious, who was responsible, what should be done, and who should do it.

One of the most important lessons learned from this case was that the Department of Defense had to create a new joint command, which would be in charge, with authority to issue orders to fend off digital attacks and the resources to follow through. That unit was set up within a year. It contained perhaps 800 personnel and was commanded by that same four-star general.

This book will explore all of these incidents and more in the hope that policymakers will learn from the experiences that their predecessors have already encountered, so that they need no longer be surprised by such jarring wake-up calls.

Introduction

"History does not so much repeat as echo..." Lois McMaster Bujold

Cyber conflict is new, but not so new that it has failed to accumulate its own history. For over twenty-five years, nation states and non-state groups have been using computer networks to strike, spy upon, or confound their adversaries. While many of these dust-ups have been mere nuisances–more playground-pranks than real battles, several incidents have become national security issues, which have placed militaries on alert and prompted warnings to heads of state, the US President included. These conflicts are best understood as issues of international security, not information security.

This book is the first of its kind to address the history of cyber conflict, which started in earnest in 1986, when German hackers searched through thousands of US computer files and sold their stolen materials to the KGB. In 1995, the US intelligence community reported to Congress that incidents involving computers and telecommunications equipment accounted for the "largest portion of economic and industrial information lost by US companies" to espionage.

Cyber espionage cases are among the most prevalent of the many types of stories in this history, but there are also incidents resulting in nations resorting to the use of actual force against one another, or attacking rivals anonymously from the Internet. Patriotic hackers have attempted to disrupt networks, computers, and data controlled by their targets, who were perceived to be somehow insulting the hackers' motherland.

More important than historical cases, of course, is what we can learn from them. An analysis of the first quarter-century of cyber conflict reveals three broad lessons.

1. Cyber conflict has changed only gradually over time; thus, historical lessons derived from past cases are still relevant today (though these are usually ignored).

2. The probability and consequences of disruptive cyber conflicts have often been hyped, while the real impacts of cyber intrusions have been consistently under-appreciated.

3. The more strategically significant a cyber conflict is, the more similar it is to conflicts on the land, in the air, or on the sea – with one critical exception.

Unfortunately, these lessons from the history of cyber conflict largely have been ignored, even though their importance has continued to escalate. Universities are building programs to train thousands of new cyber professionals. Students flow into this field in ever increasing numbers, and as graduates, into new cyber organizations, often with only technical training, a polygraph, and a pat on the back. Senior leaders, such as generals, diplomats, and elected or appointed officials, are seeking or finding themselves assigned to jobs with heavy cyber responsibilities, though they often know little of what this entails, but feel sure that they must be the first to deal with such weighty issues.

In each case, all too often these new entrants are told to forget everything they thought they knew about security and cyberspace. "Don't look back — worry about the future," the flood of the newly hired are told. "History is in front of you."

It is true that closest to the networks, at the most technical and tactical levels, cyberspace does have completely different dynamics from conflicts on the land, in the air, or on the sea. But at the level of international security, the "forget everything" mantra is simply wrong. The technical truths so crucial to network defenders are far less important when abstracted up to commanders and policymakers in charge of handling national security crises.

Admirals don't need to understand details of the ballistics of naval weaponry to plan a naval campaign. Similarly, cyber generals do not need to know the intimate details of TCP/IP packets. One of the most important lessons to be drawn from cyber conflicts thus far is that the fundamental policies of national security and international relations should largely apply in this arena as well.

Another key lesson is that we continue to make the same mistakes, over and over. This type of conflict has become more dangerous and has grown more frequent. But prior cases of cyber conflict are not merely repetitive. They can be seen as echoes. New hires in the cyber field, whether at the junior or senior levels, must learn the lessons of cyber conflict history to avoid repeating the scrambles and improvised efforts of the past. A study of this history is especially important now, because so much of our future security, business, and comfort will depend upon cyber technologies and networks.

Nations and to a lesser degree non-state groups are seizing on cyber conflict tactics and strategies, seeing it as a bloodless and seemingly risk-free way to achieve disruption and conduct espionage. General Robert E. Lee once said, "it is well that war is so terrible, otherwise we should grow too fond of it." Unfortunately, modern cyber warriors, including those in the United States, seem to be increasingly fond of believing that "it is well that cyber war is not so terrible, otherwise we couldn't use it." This philosophy allows them to more eagerly use their new cyber tools for clandestine intelligence and covert disruption.

In cyberspace, however, the future is a jump ball, undecided, and it may be more sensitive to state-sponsored technological disruptions than many governments currently understand. Armed with new cyber capabilities, generals and spymasters may be steering the world toward a much darker cyber future, characterized by unrestrained and unrestrainable attacks. These would be damaging to governments and potentially devastating to the rest of us. These trends, as history, are clear. But what we do about them is not.

As the first account of its kind regarding this history, this book will certainly skip too lightly over countless facts and people and miss enlightening stories. For example, the US government has thousands of pages of material pending in response to filed Freedom of Information Act requests. That trove of potentially useful material was unfortunately made available too late to be included in this book. But it will be available to future researchers. Hopefully, that data will be examined and utilized in future work, to build upon this introduction and provide even more important lessons.

Others will take aim at the lessons of cyber conflict history, as presented here, and well they should. It may be too early to see the lessons clearly, and our research may have been biased by relying only on unclassified information. If there have been important conflicts that are still unclassified, then perhaps the underlying lessons of those will be different. Fortunately, some of the reviewers of this book did have clearances and current knowledge. There has been no feedback yet stating that the lessons from history presented here would be any different if the authors had relied on classified sources. If the reverse does turn out to be true, then the US government should of course declassify the conflicts or at least the lessons.

Part 1 of this book is a chronological narrative of cyber conflict history, mostly from a US perspective. We begin with key lessons. The section titled Realization focuses on the emerging awareness of cyber conflict problems in the 1980s (e.g., the Cuckoo's Egg and Morris Worm). In the section titled Takeoff, the focus is new doctrines concerning information warfare and the creation of military cyber commands in the 1990s. Finally, in Militarization, topics such as Chinese espionage, Estonia, and Stuxnet—all of which became significant in the first decade of the twenty-first century—are examined.

Parts 2, 3, and 4 chronicle some of the most important cyber conflicts over the past twenty-five years and present in-depth case studies, which previously have been surprisingly hard to find. Two case studies are from contemporary sources, but the rest have been created new for this book, including several from former students of mine from Georgetown University. Several others were produced by the Cyber Statecraft Young Professionals group (co-sponsored by the Atlantic Council and Cyber Conflict Studies Association), while another was the winner of a case-study competition held by these groups and the Armed Forces Communications and Electronics Association.

Since so much of cyber history is currently known and seen through a US lens, **Part 5** includes perspectives on key incidents and lessons by analysts from Britain and Japan. In the Concluding Assessment at the end of the book, an analysis is presented concerning which nations seem to be most responsible for some of the conflicts described in the earlier chapters. The Appendices include the sources used for this study and a useful glossary for novices to the field.

While my name appears on the cover and all of the defects of this study are my responsibility, this book is very much the product of a group effort. In addition to the authors of the individual chapters, many people deserve acknowledgment. Early in my career, Greg Rattray helped me to understand the importance of looking back to extract lessons, while James Mulvenon shared his witty wisdom about understanding the present as it unfolds. As fellow board members of the Cyber Conflict Studies Association, they helped to make this book a reality, along with other key people, such as Bob Gourley and Matt Devost. All are cyber heroes and long-time friends. Karl Grindal was the associate editor, who rode hard over all of us to ensure that deadlines were met and the whole operation ran smoothly. Joe Nye, General Michael Hayden, Jeff Moss, and Jeff Lightfoot provided comments to improve the draft.

The Atlantic Council offered never-ending support, not least by hosting unique events so that audiences could hear directly from many of those that created this history over the past few decades. Often, those forums provided the first opportunities for people to ask these heroes to tell their stories. Fred Kempe (CEO of the Atlantic Council), Damon Wilson (Executive Vice President), and Barry Pavel (Director of the Brent Scowcroft Center on International Security) have made mine the perfect job. Thanks also especially go to Samer Khoury and The Morganti Group Inc. for their continuing support of the Cyber Statecraft Initiative and its work on history.

My mother Kathy instilled in me a lifelong love of books and reading, while my father Josh reinforced this, and also encouraged my curiosity about military history and its relevance for today. And of course, my greatest thanks go to my wife Akiko, without whom this book could not have been written, as without her there would be no earth, sun, moon, or stars.

Part 1: A Brief History of US Cyber Conflict

Jason Healey[1]

Introduction

Even in its earliest history, cyberspace had disruptions, caused by malicious actors, which were greater than mere technical or criminal problems. These cyber conflicts occurred in the overlapping area between national security and cyber security, wherein nations and non-state groups used offensive and defensive cyber capabilities to attack, defend, and spy on each other, typically for political or other national security purposes.[2] This book—which is directed toward both national security professionals who should understand cyber conflict and cyber specialists who must learn the context of national security—is the only major attempt in twenty-five years to codify this history.

There have been at least seven major "wake-up calls." Each shocked and surprised the defenders and decision-makers that suffered through them, but their lessons were soon forgotten, until a new wave of cyber leaders were again "awakened" to a similar shock.

In other areas of national security, new military personnel, diplomats, and policymakers are taught to avoid old mistakes through a formal study of history. They thereby vicariously gain the experience of those that have gone before. Just as we teach young cadets and military officers the implications of Gettysburg, Inchon, Trafalgar, and MIG Alley, so too must we pass along the lessons of Cuckoo's Nest, the Morris Worm, and Stuxnet. Yet the opposite has been the case.

Cyber history has been forgotten, ignored as irrelevant, or intentionally falsified, even as a crush of new personnel flood into the field. Even the most historically minded of cyber warriors seem to spend more time wondering how, twenty-two hundred years ago, a southern Mediterranean general could get some elephants across the Alps, rather than seeking lessons to be learned from KGB-associated intrusions into military networks, which happened a mere twenty-five years ago.

The US government and military have almost completely ignored cyber history. Before being interviewed for this book, many of the cyber pioneers had never before been asked about the first cyber organizations and conflicts, or about their ideas concerning lessons for today. A recent search for "cyber" on an official historical site maintained by the Air Force

---

1 Jason Healey is the Director of the Cyber Statecraft Initiative at the Atlantic Council of the United States, a former Vice President at Goldman Sachs, and a former Director of Cyber Policy at the White House.

2 "Cyber conflict" is a term that is meant to be more inclusive than "cyber war," which implies operations that cross a threshold into "armed attack." Cyber conflict excludes most cyber crime, which is conducted for criminal and material gains, but not for political purposes. Cyber conflict can include the largest, malicious Internet disruptions. For more, see Cyber Conflict Studies Association, "Addressing Cyber Instability," 2012, and the glossaries on the next page.

led to only four documents, no images, and a single video (which was from 2012; this hardly counts as historical).[3] Army Cyber Command is now teaching that the main cyber threat which faced the nation prior to 2007 was "Cyber 'Noise' on Networks." This ignores two decades of cases and derivable lessons.[4]

In fact, there is a rich cyber history prior to 2007, which is more than just "noise." This history is not a collection of empty facts, nor trivia for cyber operators to recall for amusement on a long night shift. It yields rich lessons. The most important of these lessons contradict much of which passes for received wisdom in today's cyber community.

By ignoring history, the United States has learned (and is now learning) the wrong lessons. This situation has generated misunderstandings that could prove disastrous. Most cyber conflicts are more than mere, scaled-up hacking attempts, which are often associated with dark and technical mysteries, uncertain attributions, and "speed of light" executions. The reality is that the more strategically significant cyber conflicts of the past have been similar in their dynamics to the more familiar types of conflict that occur on the land, in the air, or on the sea. Significantly, the most important difference between them is regularly ignored. This difference is that the private sector, not governments, plays the primary role in cyber conflicts.

Since today's practitioners rarely look backwards, they may not understand how little progress defenders have made over the last few decades. As the comparative quotes which appear below demonstrate, to a large degree the issues faced today are largely reflected in, or are exactly the same as, those faced by the previous generation. Since twenty-five years of dedicated work has not solved cyber problems, if we continue to approach them with the same old strategies and

Basic Glossary

See Appendix 1 for a more complete glossary.

Cyber conflict: When nations and non-state groups use offensive or defensive cyber capabilities to attack, defend, and spy on each other, typically for political or other national security purposes.

Cyber war: Actions by a nation-state to damage or disrupt another nation's computers or networks, which are heavily damaging and destructive—similar to the effects achieved with traditional military force—and so are considered to be an armed attack. An act of war that is mediated in full or in part through cyberspace

Cyber crime: A criminal act that is mediated through cyberspace, in which computers or networks play an instrumental role. In this book, such crimes are a DDoS or intrusions.

Cyber attack: Geeks, cops, spies, and soldiers all have varying definitions, but in general, this includes any deliberate, illegal, disruptive, or spying attempt against a computer, network, or information. That is, a DDoS or intrusion.

Intrusion: Any deliberate and illegal entry into a computer system, such as to exfiltrate (steal) information or conduct a later disruptive attack.

DDoS: The coordination of a number of computer systems to overwhelm the bandwidth or resources of another computer system, with the intent to disrupt operations.

Malware: Malicious software, such as viruses, worms, or Trojans, used to gain access to or damage a computer, network, or information.

Disruption vs Destruction: Few cyber attacks actually destroy anything physically; they merely disrupt the proper functioning of the software, system, or network.

---

3   The search was conducted on http://www.airforcehistory.af.mil/main/welcome.asp in July 2012.
4   Army Cyber Command. "Army Cyber Command Update," March 8, 2012, slide 3.

techniques, it is unlikely that we will be any more successful.

Why Haven't We Learned?

A number of factors have contributed to hide not just the important lessons of cyber history, but also the fact that there is a history of cyber conflict.

The first and foremost of these factors is the massive influx of new entrants into the field. Each new wave of entrants, every five years or so, feels that they are the pioneers. Since they are not taught any history of their field, many accordingly fail to distinguish between what is actually new versus what is just new to them. In addition, cyberspace not only has many characteristics which are non-intuitive to (older) policymakers, but it seems to be forever changing. Thus, the spirit of cyberspace is to look forward, toward the future and to new technologies. Looking backwards has mistakenly seemed a waste of time and effort. Since cyberspace is still relatively new, the analytical community which views the past twenty-five years as "history" is actually quite small. Admittedly, the field is still emerging rapidly, and we are at the beginning of the "cyber age." But that is no reason to ignore the useful lessons of its current history.

Two other key factors have been instrumental in blocking learning about cyber conflict. Its practitioners largely have been technologists who see cyber conflicts as technical challenges. Though kings and queens in their own field, these technologists have consistently failed to appreciate how different dynamics of national security operate during cyber conflicts. On the other hand, international security specialists don't understand cyberspace, and have been told that cyber is new and different–so their existing theories and approaches do not apply. This mutual misunderstanding between the "geeks" and "wonks" means that the overlaps between the two, which are reflected in history, are perpetually ignored.

The last factor is the pernicious effects of government secrecy. As this book was being developed, many practitioners felt that too much of cyber conflict history was classified for the story to be adequately told (some also felt that many stories perhaps should not be retold). Fortunately there has been no feedback yet that the lessons from history presented here would be any different if it had relied on classified sources. This book is necessarily built upon on media stories, FOIA requested information, interviews, and other non-classified research material, and it does provide a comprehensive overview. But almost certainly, classified conflicts have occurred, which we will not know about for years to come.

Four key recommendations, if implemented, may improve our ability to learn from cyber conflict history.

1. The White House must encourage the military and Intelligence Community to declassify information on past cyber conflicts;

2. The National Intelligence University, Center for Cryptologic History, or Center for the Study of Intelligence should begin a parallel effort to develop a classified history, the lessons of which must be declassified;

3. The DoD, DHS, and others must teach cyber conflict history to both the newer cyber cadres and senior decision-makers. Professional historians need to become more involved. And cyber conflict should be taught in classes in both Cyberspace Engineering and International Security.

4. University history departments, historians, and other researchers must recognize cyber conflict as an area with a rich history, waiting to be mined. (Perhaps this might even offer better prospects for publication than other, long exploited areas of military or national security history. Trust me, you can make far more as a historian if you specialize in cyberspace than in the advantages or disadvantages of the phalanx.)

Hopefully, once more cyber conflict history is revealed, new students, policymakers, and cyber practitioners will learn that the dynamics of cyber conflict are not as mystifying as they have been led to believe.

As shown in Table 1, cyber conflict history can be divided into three very distinct periods. *Realization* started in the mid-1980s, *Takeoff* in 1998, and *Militarization* began in 2003. Each of these periods will be examined in the following pages. In each period, policymakers and technical experts struggled with a few key questions. Are we being too paranoid, or not nearly paranoid enough? How much do we focus on fighting crime, stopping espionage, or defending against catastrophic attacks? What is the right balance between offense and defense? How do we coordinate between different agencies and countries? What is the proper role for the private sector?

This discussion will examine how all of these questions have been answered in the past. But we will start with the conclusions drawn from all of this: the lessons and findings gleaned from an understanding of cyber conflict history.

Table 1: Phases of Cyber Conflict History

	Realization	Takeoff	Militarization
Start Date	1980s	1998-	2003-
Dynamics	O>D: Attackers have advantage over defenders	O>D: Attackers have advantage over defenders	O>D: Attackers have advantage over defenders
Who Has Capabilities?	US and a few others	US, Russia, and Many	US, Russia, China, and many, many more
Adversaries	Hackers	Hacktivists, Patriot Hackers, Viruses, and Worms	Neo-Hacktivists, Espionage agents, Malware, National Militaries, Spies, and their Proxies, Hactivists
Major Incidents	Morris Worm (1988), Cuckoo's Egg (1989), Dutch Hackers (1991), Rome Labs (1994), Citibank (1994)	Maze ELIGIBLE RECEIVER, SOLAR SUNRISE, MOONLIGHT MAZE, ALLIED FORCE, Chinese Patriot Hackers	TITAN RAIN, Estonia, Georgia, BUCKSHOT YANKEE
Driving Policy / Policies	Various covering communications security, command and control warfare	PDD-63	HSPD-7/HSPD-23, NSPD/NSPD-54, CNCI
US Defense Organizations	CERT, NSA, and AF Information Warfare Center (1993), and AF 609 IW Squadron (1995)	JTF-CND, JTF-CNO, USSPACE, NSA, CERT	JTF-GNO, USSTRAT, Cyber Command, DHS/NCSD, NSA, and USCERT
US Offensive Organizations	Special Access Programs	JTF-CNO, USSTRAT	JFCC-NW, USSTRAT, US Cyber Command
Coordination Organizations	IOTC, CERT, JTRB	IOTC, NIPC, and ISACs	NCRCG, SCCs, ISACS, USCERT
US Doctrine	Information Warfare	Information Operations	Cyber
US Governance	Some NSC	J-39, NSC, PCIPB	National Security Council

Doomed to Repeated History

Comparing quotes over thirty years of cyber security and conflict history reveals the continuity over time but also how little progress there has been.

1	"I liken it to the very first aero squadron, when they started with biplanes. We're at the threshold of a new era . . . We are not exactly sure how combat in this new dimension of cyberspace will unfold. We only know that we are the beginning."	"I almost feel like it's the early days of flight with the Wright Brothers. First of all, you need to kind of figure out that domain, and how are we going to operate and maintain within that domain. So I think it will take a period of time, and it's going to be growing."
2	"Few if any contemporary computer security controls have prevented a [red team] from easily accessing any information sought."	[Our red teams] "do get into most of the networks we target."
3	"The market does not work well enough to raise the security of computer systems at a rate fast enough to match the apparent growth in threats to systems."	"We've had market failure when it comes to cybersecurity. Security doesn't come out of voluntary actions and market forces."
4	"[C]omputer intrusions, telecommunications targeting and intercept, and private-sector encryption weaknesses … account for the largest portion of economic and industrial information lost by US corporations."	"Cyber tools have enhanced the economic espionage threat, and the Intelligence Community judges [that] the use of such tools is already a larger threat than more traditional espionage methods."
5	"Espionage over networks can be cost-efficient, offer nearly immediate results, and target specific locations … [while the perpetrators are] insulated from risks of internationally embarrassing incidents."	"Foreign collectors of sensitive economic information are able to operate in cyberspace with relatively little risk of detection by their private sector targets."
6	"The almost obsessive persistence of serious penetrators is astonishing."	[The Advanced Persistent Threat] "successfully evade anti-virus, network intrusion detection, and other best practices."

All the quotes in the first column are nearly twenty years old: (1) Then Lt. Col. "Dusty" Rhoads in 1996, (2) Then Lt. Col. Roger Schell in 1979, (3) National Academy of Science report, Computers at Risk in 1991, (4) NACIC Counterintelligence Report to Congress for FY95, and (5) and (6) Cliff Stoll, "Stalking the Wily Hacker" in 1988.

The second column quotes date from after 2008: (1) Maj. Gen. Webber, Comments at 2009 Air Force National Symposium, (2) NSA Red Teamer, 2008, (3) Deputy Secretary of Defense Ashton Carter at the RSA Conference in 2012, (4) and (5) NCIX Counterintelligence Report to Congress, 2010, and (6) Mandiant M-Trends, 2010.

Lessons and Findings from Our Cyber Past

From the history of cyber conflict, key lessons and findings clearly emerge, and each of these carry significant policy implications for cyber defenders and policymakers today. As with any other indicators, these observations help confirm the long-term trends, but cannot be depended upon to predict the future with accuracy.

1. **Cyber conflict has changed only gradually over time; thus, historical lessons derived from past cases are still relevant today (though these are usually ignored).**

    a. Conflicts today are not exact repetitions of past events, but they are clearly echoes.

    b. There has been no essential discontinuity between the cyber conflicts of twenty-five years ago and those of today. Technologies have changed, but the underlying dynamics of today's conflicts would be familiar to cyber defenders from those early days.

    c. Many of the questions vexing cyber policymakers today were asked in almost exactly the same terms by their predecessors ten and twenty years earlier. Again and again, lessons have been identified and forgotten rather than learned.

2. **The probability and consequences of disruptive cyber conflicts have often been hyped, while the real impacts of cyber intrusions have been consistently under-appreciated.**

    a. Historically, the most important cyber conflicts have not involved war or terror, but rather espionage.

    b   However, it is increasingly clear that nations, including the United States, are engaging in covert "shadow conflicts," which is irregular warfare using proxies and covert sabotage.

    c. Cyber espionage against the United States has been occurring since at least the mid-1980s. But today it is far, far worse—indeed, some say intolerable. Of course, the United States is extremely active in its own, quieter cyber espionage.

    d. While the cost of espionage is high (but difficult to estimate, much less to calculate), there is little evidence that disruptions have caused even blips in national GDP statistics.

    e. We have been worrying about a "cyber Pearl Harbor" for twenty of the seventy years since the actual Pearl Harbor.

f.   No one is known to have died from a cyber attack.

g.   Nations have not sought to cause massive damage to each other outside of larger geo-political conflicts.

h.   Cyber incidents have so far tended to have effects that are either widespread but fleeting, or persistent but narrowly focused. No attacks, thus far, have been both widespread and persistent.

i.   As with conflict in other domains, cyber attacks can take down many targets. But keeping them down over time in the face of determined defenses has thus far been beyond the capabilities of all but the most dangerous adversaries.[5]

j.   Strategic cyber warfare has thus far been well beyond the capabilities of the stereotypical teenaged hackers in their basements.

k.   Adversaries historically have had either the capability to cause significant damage or the intent to do so—but rarely did they possess both dangerous capabilities and truly malicious intent.

3.   **The more strategically significant a cyber conflict is, the more similar it is to conflicts on the land, in the air, and on the sea – with one critical exception.**

a.   The most meaningful cyber conflicts rarely occur at the "speed of light" or "network speed." While tactical engagements can happen as quickly as our adversaries can click the Enter key, conflicts are typically campaigns that encompass weeks, months, or years of hostile contact between adversaries, just as in traditional warfare.

b.   Because the most strategically meaningful cyber conflicts have been part of larger geo-political conflicts, their nature has tended to offer ample warning time to defenders, even without reliance on technical means. A good rule of thumb is that "physical conflict begets cyber conflict."

c.   While some attacks are technically difficult to attribute, it is usually a straightforward matter to determine the nation responsible, since the conflict takes place during an ongoing geo-political crisis.

d.   There have been no digital Pearl Harbors yet. Nations seem generally reluctant to conduct large-scale damaging attacks on one another, outside of traditional

---

5   This will likely change as nations put more physical infrastructure online, such as the Smart Grid.

geo-political conflicts.

e.   To date, no terrorist groups have chosen cyber attack as a primary attack method. There has been no Cyber 9/11 yet, a major attack designed to cause death, destruction, and terror.

f.   Perhaps the biggest difference between cyber conflicts and their traditional equivalents is the one most often overlooked: when defending against cyber conflicts, it is non-state actors, not governments, which typically are decisive in cyber defense. Companies and volunteer groups have repeatedly used their agility and subject matter knowledge to mitigate and prevail in most of the conflicts in this book, while governments are on the side. Only uncommonly are governments able to bring the superior resources of their unwieldy bureaucracies to bear in enough time to decisively defend against attacks.

Despite the popular conception that the nature of cyber "war" must constantly change with every new technology, this book makes the case that the situation is happily much different. The lessons from yesterday are not trivia–they remain eminently useful.

As an analogy, imagine buying a few rounds of drinks for a modern fighter pilot and his predecessors from World Wars One and Two. Despite over a hundred years of technological and doctrinal changes between their respective careers, within five minutes they would be telling breathless tales of dogfights, and how they had zipped through complex aerial maneuvers to lose an adversary or to line up a kill shot. The dynamics of dogfighting, such as the advantages of relative height, speed, and maneuverability, have remained stable over time, even though technology has made dogfights faster, higher in altitude, wider in range, and above all, more lethal. So it is with cyber conflicts.

In addition, these lessons show the underlying continuity of cyber conflict with traditional international relations, national security, and military operations. While there are certainly differences, to date cyber conflicts have not been fundamentally different from conflicts on the land, in the air, or on the sea.

The key historical findings above are different from the common myths about cyber conflict, such as that cyber attacks are like massively disruptive, lightning wars unleashed either by kids in their basements or by nations using surprise attacks which are wholly unrelated to current geopolitical tensions. While not impossible, these scenarios have not yet materialized.

It appears that cyber deterrence, long the subject of theory but usually dismissed, has been operative for some time. This has gone unrecognized, because historical analysis has been focused on quotidian hacking and technical details, rather than on conflicts as nations have actually conducted them.

Despite early fears that nations would strike at each other using surprise, strategic attacks, while relying on anonymity within the Internet, there is no evidence that such conflicts have occurred. Nations seem to be willing to launch significant cyber assaults during larger crises, but not out of the blue. Accordingly, a comparison with nuclear deterrence is extremely relevant, but not necessarily the one that Cold Warriors have recognized.

 Nuclear weapons did not make all wars unthinkable, as some early Cold War thinkers had hoped. Instead, they provided a ceiling under which the superpowers fought all kinds of wars, regular and irregular. The United States and the Soviet Union, along with their allies, engaged in lethal, intense conflicts ranging from Korea to Vietnam, and through proxies in Africa, Asia, and Latin America. Nuclear warheads did not stop these wars, but they did set an upper threshold which neither side proved willing to cross.

Likewise, though the most cyber capable nations (including the USA, China, and Russia) have been more than willing to engage in irregular cyber conflicts, they have stayed well under the threshold of conducting full-scale strategic cyber warfare, and have thus created a *de facto* norm. Nations have proved just as unwilling to launch a strategic attack in cyberspace as they have been to do on the land, in the air, or on the sea.

The failure of the United States to learn from these lessons, or indeed even to notice that there is a history from which they may learn, has critical implications for cyber operations today and tomorrow. For example, cyber conflicts are fast, but by no means do they occur at the "speed of light" or even at "network speed," as is routinely described by US military leaders. As later sections of this history will discuss, MOONLIGHT MAZE, Estonia, Conficker, Stuxnet, and Chinese cyber espionage were all prolonged conflicts.[6]

Tactical engagements in every domain can unfold quickly (for example, aerial dogfights in every war could sometimes be over before an unsuspecting pilot knew he was in one), but successful generals and strategists never allow themselves to obsess over these tactical engagements. Instead, they extrapolate from each action to more strategic levels to plot several moves ahead. This will be difficult if we continue to over-emphasize tactical, rather than strategic, truths.

These popular misunderstandings of cyber conflicts have critical implications, which include the following:

---

6   Since this book is in part a military history, the US military format of writing military exercises and operations in all capital letters has been followed, e.g., MOONLIGHT MAZE.

1. The US cyber community will likely over-invest in capabilities and doctrine to automatically counterattack against surprise attacks.

2. Rules of engagement will allow ever-lower levels of military authority to "shoot back" without seeking authorization—a relaxation of the rules which may not be conducive to long-term US economic or military interests.

3. Response plans will focus on today's incident, with little thought on how to surge and sustain an effort over the weeks and months that it has previously taken conflicts to occur.

4. Defensive actions which make sense in longer campaigns (such as installing new networking capabilities and Internet Exchange Points) will be ignored.

5. The US military will train their new cyber cadres with doctrines and strategies that are focused only on the immediate fight, with little conception of the true nature of the strategic whole.

A reading of today's headlines shows that the US military is barreling down most, if not all of these roads.

Likewise, the US national security community should know it is difficult to have a prolonged strategic effect, even in cyberspace. If Flying Fortresses in World War II could not achieve a strategic victory over Germany after dropping millions of tons of high explosives over several years of operations, why do so many people still believe that a few kids might take down the United States from their garage or basement?

Yet basement-originated strategic warfare is a common theme. As recently as March 2012, the four-star general who oversees Air Force cyber operations said at a conference that deterrence was difficult in cyber conflict since, "[f]or someone with the right brainpower and the right cyber abilities, a cheap laptop and Internet connection is all it takes to be a major player in the domain."[7] These tools might help an adversary to steal data or identities—or even to conduct a major intrusion. But they are not sufficient for a strategic effect that requires deterrence power from the world's most powerful military.

At least as important is the principal difference between cyber and traditional conflicts: the primacy of the private sector. Cyber conflict history clearly shows that nearly every significant incident has been resolved by the private sector, not the government. Yet government response plans, such as the US National Cyber Incident Response Plan, reverse this emphasis and discuss how government bureaucrats and elected officials will make the

---

7   Shelton, remarks at Air Force Association, CyberFutures Conference, March 22, 2012.

key decisions. In cyber conflicts, the private sector is not a "partner" of government, but the "supported command."

It is also becoming apparent that cyber conflicts have not been as universal in scope as has often been thought. Researchers Brandon Valeriano and Ryan Maness used traditional political science methods to find that "Only twenty of 124 active rivals—defined as the most conflict-prone pairs of states in the system—engaged in cyber conflict between 2001 and 2011. And there were only ninety-five total [cyber conflicts] among these twenty rivals." Their more quantified and comprehensive approach confirms that cyber conflicts have not been devastating. Having rated all cyber conflicts with a severity rating "ranging from five, which is minimal damage, to one, where death occurs as a direct result from cyberwarfare… Of all ninety-five [cyber conflicts] in our analysis, the highest score—that of Stuxnet and Flame—was only a three."[8] Their research also counters the myth that cyber conflict is a free-for-all. Instead, they found that conflicts did not take place randomly. Instead, they tend to occur only between existing rivals, who are typically neighbors, and only during ongoing crises. Examples are summarized on the following chart.

---

8   Valeriano and Maness, "The Fog of Cyberwar."

Table 2: Number of Cyberattack Incidents by Country, 2001-11.[9]

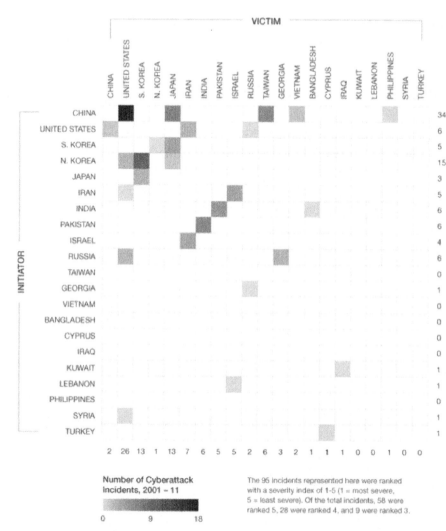

Number of Cyberattack
Incidents, 2001 – 11

0   9   18

The 95 incidents represented here were ranked
with a severity index of 1-5 (1 = most severe,
5 = least severe). Of the total incidents, 58 were
ranked 5, 28 were ranked 4, and 9 were ranked 3.

---

9   Valeriano and Maness, "The Fog of Cyberwar."

The Beginning: Realization (to 1998)

The Earliest Days

Adversaries have always exploited new telecommunications technologies in wartime. Getting into an adversary's networks, intercepting their messages, and disrupting their communications are tactics that are nearly as old as warfare. More recognizable modern forms were already evident during the American Civil War, when Union cavalry captured Confederate telegraph stations and then used them to send false telegraph messages to re-route trains into Union ambushes.[1] Sixty years later, the British cleverly used the intercepted Zimmermann telegram to maneuver the United States closer to entering World War I.[2] And in World War II, signals intelligence became so advanced and critical to the war effort that it pushed forward the development of programmable electronic computers and communications networks.[3]

However, the components of cyber conflict were not mature or interconnected enough for the concept to have real meaning for several more decades. Incidents involving espionage, early computer viruses, and stolen passwords occurred, but these are best understood using existing concepts, such as electronic warfare, signals intelligence, or computer security, rather than cyber conflict.

While there is no universally recognized "Eureka moment" when cyber emerged as something distinctly different from before, the United States and other nations began to realize the national security implications of these new interconnected computer networks by the late 1960s, decades before what we recognize today as "cyber" became a common concept. According to the historian of US Cyber Command, Michael Warner, "West Germany's police caught an East German spy in IBM's German subsidiary in 1968, in what could well have been the world's first case of computer espionage."[4]

Figure 1: The DSB Ware Report of 1970 has similar findings to many reports today

These early incidents did lead to US government action. One of the most significant of these reactions was the report of a

---

1.   "At times, offices were seized so quickly as to prevent telegraphic warnings. General Mitchel captured two large Confederate railway trains by sending false messages from the Huntsville, Alabama office, and General Seymour similarly seized a train near Jacksonville, Florida." Greely, "The Military Telegraph," 360.
2.   See Tuchman, The Zimmermann Telegram for a complete description of how the British cleverly ensured that German telegrams would pass through the United Kingdom, so that they could then be passed to English codebreakers. The decrypted telegram in which German promises were made to Mexico (to encourage Mexico to enter the war) helped to ensure the US entry.
3.   See for example, "Bletchley's code-cracking Colossus."
4.   Warner, "Cybersecurity—A Prehistory," 784.

US Defense Science Board group, chaired by Willis Ware, which was published in 1970. With the advent of "resource-sharing" computers, it was then possible for the first time to access a computer without having to be in the same room. The resulting report, *Security Controls for Computer Systems,* highlighted themes that are still recognizable over forty years later, such as the threat of deliberate penetration: an "attempt to obtain information, cause the system to operate to the advantage of the threatening party or manipulate the system to render it unreliable or unusable."[5] Additionally, because it was originally classified, its valuable findings were not generally available to civilian government agencies or to US companies. This was the start of a trend of classification, which continues to inhibit information sharing today.

Only a few years later, the US military was already conducting "red team" or "tiger team" exercises against itself, looking for vulnerabilities. The findings from one practitioner, writing in 1979, will be recognizable to many red teams today:

- Few if any contemporary computer security controls have prevented a tiger team from easily accessing any information sought.

- It does not take a highly specialized expert to penetrate security.

- The prospect of industry's solving the computer security problem is overestimated by concluding that industry has the same security problem as the military.

- The threat can be minimized by seeking counterintelligence (that is practically unavailable), e.g., actual examples of enemy agents caught in the act.

- Attention to security gimmicks results in overlooking serious weaknesses.[6]

By the 1980s, the earliest computers and computer networks, such as ENIAC and ARPANET, grew into the form recognizable to us today as cyberspace. This was especially true following the creation of MILNET, which split off from ARPANET in 1983, and of the National Science Foundation's NSFNET in 1986.[7]

Technology had now advanced far enough for real national security conflicts to emerge. Similar to the networks in which they were fought, these would be recognizable today. An example is the growing, state-sponsored espionage that occurred over these new networks.

West German intelligence had established Project RAHAB as early as 1981 "to uncover,

---

5   Ware, *Security Controls for Computer Systems.*
6   Schell, "Computer Security, the Achilles' Heel."
7   "The Internet."

develop, and maintain systematic covert BND pathways to foreign computer networks, computers, and databases."[8] Meanwhile, French intelligence had a source in the KGB who provided a full set of documents, known as the FAREWELL dossier, on Russia's efforts to collect Western technologies. This spy in the KGB revealed that thirty years ago, computer intrusions were already being used in more than one-in-fifty Soviet espionage operations.[9] This same dossier appears to have given the US the idea to covertly give to the Soviets industrial software containing intentional flaws, which would make the software certain to fail. This operation may have resulted in a massive explosion, which destroyed a Soviet natural gas pipeline when doctored software was used to construct that pipeline.[10] This may be the only known example of such extensive physical damage resulting from cyber sabotage (but the incident needs more historical examination to determine if it truly happened as reported).

By the 1980s then, all the elements were in place for cyber conflict: a foundation of large-scale computer networks, new conceptions of computer security, and the first glimmers of national security challenges. But it took two malicious cyber incidents to truly launch the phase called Realization and open the age of cyber conflict.

The first of these was an incident in 1986 that came to be known as the Cuckoo's Egg (from the title of the book that popularized the case). A team of German hackers broke into dozens of computers at Lawrence Berkeley National Laboratory, other research institutions, and military commands looking for information on the Strategic Defense Initiative (aka Star Wars), satellites, and other secret information to sell to the KGB.[11] The case was exposed by Cliff Stoll, an astronomer-turned-system administrator, who stumbled on the hack while hunting down a seventy-five cent billing discrepancy, creating new tools and techniques as he went.[12] At first, counterintelligence and law enforcement agencies largely failed to respond, as they did not yet understand cyberspace and how espionage could be conducted there. Fortunately, Stoll was persistent and, with a handful of collaborators, such as special agent Jim Christy of the US Air Force Office of Special Investigations, he tracked down the hackers in Hanover, West Germany. They were arrested and

Figure 2: Cliff Stoll's *The Cuckoo's Egg*, on KGB linked espionage against the US in the 1980s

---

8   Schwiezer, *Friendly Spies*, 160. The quoted passage is from Mark Yanalitis, who has an unpublished paper on RAHAB, which won a CCSA history case study competition in 2013.

9   Madsen, "Intelligence Agency Threats to Computer Security."

10   Reed, *At the Abyss*, 268-270.

11   Stoll, "Stalking the Wily Hacker." For more on this case, please read the case study, edited from Cliff Stoll's own words, in Part 2.

12   *Ibid.*

served time in prison.[13]

But bureaucratic politics had made a mess of the case, just as sometimes happens today. Even though the hackers were looking for classified material and were ultimately linked to a KGB handler, Christy was unable to get his superiors to investigate the case as a counterintelligence operation with a far higher priority for resources: "They denied my request, and [I] had to run the investigation as a larceny by fraud case. The same as a time and attendance" fraud investigation.[14] The Department of Defense, in addition, failed to send anyone to the trial to testify about damages, because of a "disagreement between NSA and OSD [the National Security Agency and the Office of the Secretary of Defense] as to who should go and who should pay" for the trip. This may have resulted in a lighter punishment for the hackers involved.[15]

Sound Familiar?

Espionage over networks can be cost-efficient, offer nearly immediate results, and target specific locations ... insulated from risks of internationally embarrassing incidents.

Cliff Stoll, 1988

There are other lessons as well. Stoll pointed out in 1988 what still passes for fresh wisdom today, that "espionage over networks can be cost-efficient, offer nearly immediate results, and target specific locations ... insulated from risks of internationally embarrassing incidents."[16]

This incident provided the US Government with its first opportunity to tackle key questions that would guide the next decades of cyber conflict, such as how to coordinate with the private sector, within the government, and with foreign governments. Unfortunately, because of the difficulty of the questions, the changing technical nature of the cyber domain, and bureaucratic inertia, US policymakers only made incremental progress in answering these questions—and there would be many more challenges to come.

On the heels of the Cuckoo's Egg incident (and even before the trial of the main hacker involved), a second incident, the Morris Worm of November 1988, rapidly spread over trusted network connections, unintentionally taking down a considerable portion of the fledgling Internet. The Morris Worm "was

Cyber Wake-Up Calls
(so far):
1. **Morris Worm**
2. ELIGIBLE RECEIVER and SOLAR SUNRISE
3. MOONLIGHT MAZE
4. Chinese Espionage
5. Estonia and Georgia
6. BUCKSHOT YANKEE
7. Stuxnet

---

13   Sterling, Crackdown, 194; and Stoll, Cuckoo's Egg, 369.
14   Email from Jim Christy to the author, August 23, 2012.
15   *Ibid.*
16   Stoll, "Stalking the Wily Hacker."

deliberately designed to do two things: infect as many machines as possible, and be difficult to track and stop."[17]

This incident had more far-reaching implications than Cuckoo's Egg, as there had never been such a widespread, fast moving event before. It counts as the first true "wake-up call" for cyber security.[18] Launched as a prank by a college student, the worm caused up to 10 percent of the Internet to rapidly crash and demonstrated how quickly major attacks could cripple cyberspace.[19] The defenders thought themselves lucky: "[h]ad the code been tested and developed further, or had it been coupled with something destructive, the toll would have been considerably higher."[20]

Despite the response being entirely *ad hoc*, it was ultimately successful. This was the first main example of two important historical lessons: widespread, persistent attacks are difficult to maintain in the face of determined defenses, and the private sector, not the government, had the tools and knowledge to solve the problem.[21] Since the private sector responders had the required agility and subject matter knowledge, they quickly traced the source of the worm to the Massachusetts Institute of Technology, where it had been released by Robert Tappan Morris (incidentally, he was the son of an NSA computer security executive). The entire incident was over in days.

Stoll, the mastermind who solved the Cuckoo's Egg incident, estimated that Morris had caused between $100,000 and $10,000,000 in damage, an astonishing range covering two orders of magnitude.[22] More than twenty years later, defenders continue to have tremendous problems assessing how much damage is done by a particular incident or by cyber incidents as a whole, and such huge ranges remain common.[23]

Sound Familiar?

[T]he incident showed that some sites paid insufficient attention to security issues, such as proper password usage, and lacked system management expertise for dealing with technical issues.

From a 1989 GAO Report on the Morris Worm (GAO-IMTEC-89-57)

The Morris Worm was much more of a wake-up call than Cuckoo's Egg, as it led to

---

17 Spafford, "The Internet Worm Program: An Analysis"; Eichin and Rochlis, "With Microscope and Tweezers"; and Markoff, "Computer Intruder Is Put on Probation."

18 For more on the Morris Worm, please refer to Part 2 below.

19 Rhodes, "Information Security."

20 Spafford, "The Internet Worm Program: An Analysis"

21 Eichen and Rochlis, "An Analysis of the Internet Worm of November 1988."

22 Cited in a contemporaneous report: US General Accounting Office, "Computer Security: Virus Highlights Need for Improved Internet Management."

23 In 2009, President Obama quoted a survey which said that "in the past two years alone, cyber crime has cost Americans more than $8 billion." Yet just two years later, another survey said there were direct dollar losses of $32 billion in just one year and another $108 billion in lost time due to the original crimes. The head of US Cyber Command recently quoted reports with even higher numbers, with American companies losing $250 billion—just to theft of intellectual property, and not including credit card fraud or other crimes—which together accounted for a total global annual loss of $1 trillion.

immediate institutional changes. Funded by the Department of Defense, Carnegie Mellon University created the very first Computer Emergency Response Team (CERT). They became the first emergency responders for cyberspace, and provided as a central point to share information and coordinate defenses.[24] Similar centers opened for security problems and response at the Defense Communications Agency (for the unclassified Defense Data Network) and at the Department of Energy (for their unclassified and classified networks, including those for nuclear materials). Before the Morris Worm, defenses were *ad hoc*; afterwards, there were more professional groups to minimize the chances of failures and attacks. These new groups planned for the worst and were ready to respond quickly. Now CERTs (and their equivalents) are nearly universal. But in the late 1980s, they were the most important cyber innovation to that time—and they remain relevant today.

Additionally, as Congress had foreseen the need to bring US law into the computer age, Morris became the first person convicted under the Computer Fraud and Abuse Act of 1986. He was sentenced to three years of probation, several hundred hours of community service, and a fine of over $10,000.[25] Other laws passed during these years were the Electronic Communications Privacy Act of 1986 and Computer Security Act of 1987, which aimed to extend various legal protections into the cyber domain to ensure privacy.

The government was not alone in making changes. Many of the most interesting developments were happening in the private sector. The hacking community was also active. Jeff Moss (aka The Dark Tangent) kicked off an annual DEFCON convention in 1993, one year after the L0pht hacking collective, a "hacker think tank," had formed in Boston.[26] While

> *The market does not work well enough to raise the security of computer systems at a rate fast enough to match the apparent growth in threats to systems.*
>
> Computers at Risk report, 1991

these hackers had technical goals, political activists during this time also came to realize the potential of the Internet. The first hactivist event appears to have occurred in 1994, when a California group calling themselves Zippies conducted a "denial of service attack," which took down UK websites. This was in reaction to the Prime Minister's recent ban on "outdoor raves and festivals."[27] Another group with a potential claim as the first hactivists were the Strano Network (Strano is Italian for strange), formed in 1993 to establish a "permanent seminar on adversarial multimedia communications." It targeted ten agencies of the French government in a 1995 "Net Strike."[28] Over the following years, other hactivists would question these DDoS tactics, as they wanted to be on the side of free

---

24   CERT Coordination Center, "About Us."
25   "U.S. vs. Robert Tappan Morris," F. 2d 504 (1991): 928.
26   "Official DEFCON FAQ v0.95"; and "L0pht on Hackers."
27   "Wikileaks Infowar not the first online protest action."
28   Thomas, "The Ethics of Hactivism."

speech, "not the ones who decided to shackle free speech and the open exchange of ideas," in the words of Oxblood Ruffin of the Cult of the Dead Cow hactivist group.[29] Regardless of whether the first hactivist event was in 1994 or 1995, this was the origin of cyber conflict tactics which inspired the far more aggressive actions of Anonymous more than fifteen years later.[30]

Of course, not all hackers were interested in promoting social goals. Vladimir Levin, from Russia, siphoned $10 million from Citibank before being caught and extradited to the United States.[31] As part of their response, Citibank became the first company to create a specialized Chief Information Security Officer to oversee the security of its networks.[32]

The Gulf War Opens Eyes

These early cyber incidents help to provide some perspective to better understand the first Gulf War of 1991. That war showed how one force with information superiority could dominate an adversary—something which strategic thinkers recognized as a Revolution in Military Affairs. One aspect of this revolution was "information warfare," which examined the direct attack or defense of information and information systems, and also sudden and devastating cyber attacks against an opponents' critical infrastructure. There was a possibility that such an attack might have been aimed at the United States. Testifying before Congress in 1991, Winn Schwartau raised the specter of an "electronic Pearl Harbor," a phrase still used in various forms by the Secretary of Defense and others today.

> ### Twenty+ Years of "Cyber Pearl Harbor"
>
> Optimists will say "No Such Thing."
> Pessimists will say "We're Overdue."
> Realists will backup their data.
>
> *Government and commercial computer systems are so poorly protected today they can essentially be considered defenseless - an Electronic Pearl Harbor waiting to happen.*
>
> Winn Schwartau testimony to Congress, 1991
>
> *Some day we will wake up to find that the electronic equivalent of Pearl Harbor has crippled our computer networks and caused more chaos than a well-placed nuclear strike.*
>
> Jamie Gorelick, Deputy Attorney-General, 1998
>
> *It would virtually paralyze this country [...] And as far as I'm concerned, that represents the potential for another Pearl Harbor, as far as the kind of attack that we could be the target of, using [cyber warfare].*
>
> Leon Panetta, Secretary of Defense, 2012

---

29   Cult of the Dead Cow, "Hactivismo."
30   For more on the history of the hactivists, please read the case study in the section below by Karl Grindal, in Part 2.
31   "Notable Hacks."
32   Field, "The Influencers: Steve Katz."

Also in 1991, the National Academy of Sciences released an extremely influential report, *Computers at Risk*, which discussed technical issues as well as education, awareness, and even the market for insurance. As with nearly every other report from this era, the findings are still germane. For example, the report found that "The market does not work well enough to raise the security of computer systems at a rate fast enough to match the apparent growth in threats to systems."[33]

But the most prescient part of this group's report is Appendix E, which predated by twenty years the current concern over the advanced persistent threat (APT) by warning of cyber adversaries with worrying characteristics:

1. Possessing extensive resources in money, personnel, and technology

2. Patient and motivated

3. Capable of exploiting a successful attack for maximum long-term gain ... taking extraordinary measures to keep the existence of a successful attack secret from the target

4. Adept in circumventing physical and procedural safeguards[34]

Other books and reports by Dorothy Denning, Alan Campen, John Arquilla, Chuck DeCaro, and others fed the demand for new ideas and concepts of Information Warfare.[35] RAND conducted an influential series of exercises, "The Day After ... in Cyberspace," to examine the results of a major cyber conflict. Alongside this work, Schwartau's 1994 book, *Information Warfare,* and Alvin and Heidi Toffler's *War and Anti-War*, which both cast light on the possibilities and dangers of a new phase of warfare, helped drive some in the US military to consider how cyber attacks could fit into their arsenal of kinetic weapons.[36]

Even that long ago, there were sufficient numbers of interconnected computers that the realm of information could be conceived as a separate domain for military operations. This is still a much debated topic. As the United States Air Force highlighted in 1995 in *Cornerstones of Information Warfare*, signed by both the Secretary and Chief of Staff of the Air Force:

> *Information has its own characteristics of mass, motion, and topography ... Before the Wright*

---

33   System Security Study Committee, "Why the Security Market Has Not Worked Well," 3.

34   "Appendix E," in Computers at Risk, 283-284.

35   These books include Dorthy Denning's Information Warfare and Security (1998); Campen's The First Information War. The Story of Computers and Communications in the Persian Gulf War (1993); Campen's Cyberwar: Security, Strategy and Conflict in the Information Age (1996); Arquilla's In Athena's Camp (1997), and Networks and Netwars: The Future of Terror, Crime and Militancy (2001); and DeCaro's work on SOFTWAR, starting with a 1991 piece in the Providence Journal Bulletin.

36   Schwartau, Information Warfare; and Toffler and Toffler, War and Anti-War.

brothers, the air, while it obviously existed, was not a realm suitable for practical, widespread military operations. Similarly, information existed before the Information Age, but the Information Age changed the information realm's characteristics so that widespread operations became practical.[37]

The military services and intelligence community gave form to these new threats, opportunities, and ideas by beginning (or perhaps continuing) highly secretive and compartmented projects to start developing cyber weapons. One of the more visible aspects of these programs was the creation of the Information Operations Technology Center to bring together "highly secret capabilities: NSA's P42 information warfare cell, the CIA's Critical Defense Technologies Division, [and] the Pentagon's 'special technology operations.'"[38]

Another important development for the purpose of exploring these new ideas was the transformation of the Air Force Electronic Warfare Center into the Air Force Information Warfare Center in 1993, with an expanded mission to "explore, apply and migrate offensive and defensive information

The unfortunate part for the 609th was that the offensive side was still classified. You couldn't even discuss it in an open forum.

Lt. Col. "Dusty" Rhoads (Ret.), 1996

warfare capabilities for operations, acquisition, and testing; and provide advanced IW training."[39] The other services followed soon after, with the Navy Information Warfare Activity created in 1994 and the Army Land Information Warfare Activity in 1995.[40]

In addition to the centers of excellence, the military was also exploring the direct integration of cyber power with more traditional military operations, starting with the creation of the first true combat cyber unit in 1995. The 609th Information Warfare Squadron was the first military unit to combine offensive and defensive cyber operations to directly support a war-fighting commander, in this case CENTAF (now AFCENT), the Air Force command conducting combat operations against Iraq.[41] This was a historic moment, the creation of the first dedicated combat cyber unit, which was the predecessor of all such units today—and it undertook similar missions, with similar success, compared to those of today. According to the unit's commander, then Lt. Col. (later Colonel) Walter "Dusty" Rhoads, when exercising with CENTAF, the unit "had control of the blue force Air Tasking Order. They gave us a two-hour window to play in, and we got it within two hours."[42] In another exercise conducted in February 1996, the unit put "all the [operational] commanders in a

---

37 Fogleman and Widnall, "Cornerstones of Information Warfare."
38 Arkin, "A Mouse That Roars?"
39 "Air Force Information Warfare Center."
40 Fredericks, "Information Warfare: The Organizational Dimension."
41 Department of the Air Force, "609 IWS: A Brief History, Oct 1995—Jun 1999."
42 Rhoads, "Lessons from Our Cyber Past, The First Military Cyber Units."

little group talking about how to use cyber effects on the offensive piece, and played the defensive part in the exercise for the first time."[43]

While the 609th pioneered the trend (which is standard today) for offense and defense to be incorporated into the same military unit, the unit was limited by resulting classification concerns. According to its commander, "The unfortunate part for the 609th was that the offensive side was still classified. You couldn't even discuss it in an open forum. You had to be inside a SCIF [an ultra-secure room] to even talk about information warfare." Even though only 30 percent of the unit's staffing was dedicated to offensive operations, these would often take up 70 percent of the unit's attention—a focus that might be familiar to many involved in cyber operations today.[44]

In fact, many of the other early tribulations of this unit would still be recognizable, such as staffing for a new mission:

> [N]obody really understood what information warfare was. There were few commanders and few places that discussed these types of things. But the hardest part was getting everybody familiar with what the mission was.

> [Likewise] nobody knew what a "cyber warrior" was by definition. It was a combination of past war fighters, J-3 [operations] types, a lot of communications people, and a smattering of intelligence and planning people. We threw it all together to make this one particular unit.[45]

These early discussions and experiments were also spurred by two sets of significant computer intrusions that continued to foreshadow the future of cyber conflict.

More Troubling Incidents

The first, an intrusion set, usually called Dutch hackers, involved several teenagers from Holland, who intruded into the networks of thirty-four US military installations between 1990 and 1991.[46] Since this was during the lead up to the first Gulf War—and the group was looking for information on Patriot and other missiles, nuclear weapons, and DESERT SHIELD, the defenders apparently mistakenly thought the group might be selling information to Iraqi intelligence.

Though the Dutch hackers did not have to use sophisticated methods, the affected agencies still never noticed and had to be notified by external parties. That circumstance often still happens today. Verizon found in 2011 that 92 percent of the incidents they investigated at

---

43   *Ibid.*
44   *Ibid.*
45   *Ibid.*
46   Brock, "Computer Security: Hackers Penetrate DOD."

client sites did not involve highly sophisticated methods; 96 percent of the intrusions could have been prevented with simple or intermediate controls; and 86 percent of the intrusions were discovered by a third party.[47]

Though the story of the Dutch hackers is similar to events which occur today, the reporting of that event seems especially quaint, and it highlights the freshness of the Realization phase:

> [The Dutch hackers] have not penetrated the most secure Government computer systems. But they have entered a wide range of computers, including those at the Kennedy Space Center, the Pentagon's Pacific Fleet Command, the Lawrence Livermore National Laboratory, and Stanford University, using an international computer network known as the Internet.[48]

The second incident, in 1994, was an organized intrusion into the Air Force's Rome Labs by young British hackers.[49] Fortunately, some of the lessons from the Cuckoo's Egg had been learned, as "there was a new breed of agent ready to fight back against the infiltrator. These were computer specialists from the Air Force Office of Special Investigations and the Air Force Information Warfare Centre," according to media reports of the incident.[50]

The hackers routed through US military systems and intruded into a Korean nuclear institute. For some harrowing moments, the US military agents and technicians were not sure if the target was in North or South Korea. As the United States was then engaged in difficult nuclear negotiations with North Korea, the military was concerned that the intrusion might be seen as espionage or an attack, and thus invite retaliation.[51] This makes the intrusion an interesting prelude to Stuxnet, when the United States allegedly conducted just such an intrusion into Iranian nuclear facilities fifteen years later.

The fact that these attackers were so young highlighted rather than minimized the danger. If teenagers could cause alarm (but not real damage), policymakers worried, what could be accomplished by professionals backed by a real budget? Moreover, what could *our* spies and soldiers accomplish with these skills?

One of the key government strategies during Realization originated from the Joint Chiefs of Staff in 1996. Joint Vision 2010 was the military's attempt to try to come to grips with the new demands of modern warfare, including how the military services should work together jointly in an information age for "full-spectrum dominance" (i.e., across all kinds of conflict). Key missions involved both offensive and defensive information warfare, to

---

47   Baker, et al., "2011 Data Breach Investigations Report," 3.
48   Markoff, "Dutch Computer Rogues Infiltrate American Systems with Impunity."
49   US Senate Permanent Committee on Investigations, "The Case Study Rome Laboratory, Griffiss Air Force Base, NY Intrusion."
50   Ungoed-Thomas, "How Datastream Cowboy Took U.S. to the Brink of War."
51   Ibid.

achieve "information superiority: the capability to collect, process, and disseminate an uninterrupted flow of information while exploiting or denying an adversary's ability to do the same."[52]

While Joint Vision 2010 encapsulated military thinking, the White House created the President's Commission on Critical Infrastructure Protection (PCCIP) to consider broader policy and to drive an overall national cyber strategy. The Commission found that America's "security, economy, way of life, and perhaps even survival, are now dependent on the interrelated trio of electrical energy, communications, and computers."[53] The report helped set the tone for much of the government's response over the following decades and helped start the next phase of the history of cyber conflict.

Hearing from Cyber Pioneers In Their Own Words

Cyber conflict is mistakenly treated as a technical discipline, divorced from the human dimensions of endeavor. To demonstrate this perspective, several stories told by some of the earliest cyber heroes in their own words are interspersed through Part 1. All of these narratives are derived from their statements made at events hosted by the Atlantic Council. The full transcripts of all of their dialogues can be found online.

---

52   Joint Chiefs of Staff, "Joint Vision 2010," 16.
53   President's Commission on Critical Infrastructure Protection, "Critical Foundations: Thinking Differently."

In Their Own Words: Col. Walter "Dusty" Rhoads, USAF (Ret.)

Founding Commander, 609 Information Warfare Squadron

Colonel Rhoads started his career as a fighter pilot, culminating as a pilot of the then still-secret F-117 stealth fighters. His time in "black" programs opened the door to information warfare and cyber operations, then (as now) considered a similar dark art. This led to his command of the first cyber war-fighting unit, the 609th Information Warfare Squadron of the US Air Force, located at Shaw AFB, South Carolina. With this as a foundation, he moved on to cyber and information warfare jobs with the Joint Staff, where he set up and subsequently was assigned to the Joint Task Force for Computer Network Defense and later to its descendants, the joint task forces for Computer Network Operations and Global Network Operations.

This narrative is adapted from Col. Rhoads' comments given at an event hosted by the Atlantic Council in 2012.[54]

> When we at the 609th Information Warfare Squadron, in South Carolina, started out, the main problem that we were trying to solve was understanding what information warfare was. We really didn't have anybody dedicated to do that type of a mission, as we didn't have anybody that could really define what the mission was. The commander, Air Combat Command, took the proposal up to the Air Staff, in 1994. Then we took the proposal up to the Chief of Staff of the Air Force, who said, "Yeah, it's probably a good idea to put a unit to see what kind of capability we have and how we would play in the information warfare game."

> Some of the complexities in starting the 609th went beyond the logistics things, because back then nobody knew what a "cyber warrior" was by definition. It was a combination of past war fighters, J-3 types, a lot of communications people, and a smattering of intelligence and planning people. We threw it all together to make this one particular unit.

> The unfortunate part for the 609th was that the offensive side was still classified. You couldn't even discuss it in an open forum. You had to be inside a SCIF [an ultra-secure room] to even talk about information warfare. But behind the scenes lay the offensive side of it—getting it integrated into the war-fighters' mentality, understanding the air tasking orders.

> The 609th was an Air Force unit, and we had to understand how to get cyber introduced into the thinking of the commanders. So these issues were fairly sensitive, as we couldn't even talk about it openly. A lot of the publicity that went out about the 609th was on the defensive side.

> There were discussions in the Air Staff to talk about cyberspace as a domain. A lot of the issues

---

54   Rhoads, "Lessons from Our Cyber Past, The First Military Cyber Units."

that are being brought up right now in discussions were discussed way back then. Well, sitting down in South Carolina, we caught a lot of flak for stepping on a lot of people's toes, just like Billy Mitchell did. And we did feel like we were plowing a path. And sometimes your nose gets really beat up when you're plowing a path.

I think probably the best thing we at the 609th did from 1995 ... was to kick-start a lot of stuff in the information operations area, especially during exercises, [such as] in February 1996, when we actually put an IO cell together and got all the commanders in a little group talking about how to use cyber effects on the offensive piece, and played the defensive part in the exercise for the first time.

We got people talking about realizing what information warfare is: it actually was a viable capability. We had control of the blue force Air Tasking Order. They gave us a two-hour window to play in, and we got it within two hours.

The split between defensive and offensive sides—in terms of personnel—at the 609th was approximately 70/30, offensive being 30 percent. However, during mission time it was probably reversed. It was a fledgling outfit, and the operations were all classified. The way we attacked [offense-defense split] at the 609th was we were focused just on one theater, one small area of operations. And we could see the enemy coming. And we had capabilities where we could just kind of play back with them. And it was very limited. It wasn't a strategic event or anything of that sort. And that's how we blended the active defense role.

That was one of the rationales behind having [offense and defense] together, because the defenders would see both offense and defense gather the information. You would actually be doing the reconnaissance, because you're getting hammered. It's the unfortunate way to get intelligence, but then you know where to go back to.

In regard to international partnerships and sharing information with our NATO allies, this was an issue brought up during a trip we took with Deputy Secretary Hamre in the fall of 1997 or early 1998, once we had sort of worked through the ELIGIBLE RECEIVER 97 events and pulled out the lessons and had extracted some of the implications from this cyber exercise. We went to NATO and to several of the partner countries in Europe at very high levels and walked through this whole thing and sort of laid out the way we saw the threat and the opportunities for partnerships going forward for where you have coalition operations.

As Deputy Secretary of Defense, John Hamre, used to say, you know a vulnerability accepted by one is a risk accepted by all. So we clearly saw the need for partnership in information operations with our NATO allies. I left before those took root, but early on, at least at the level of the [Deputy Secretary of Defense] Hamre, there was clearly a realization that this was a coalition activity.

Maturing Organizations and Concepts: Takeoff (1998-2003)

New Strategy, Organizations, and Wake-Ups

Takeoff, a period of rapid ascent, is the best description for the national security response to cyber conflict between roughly 1998 and 2003.[1] New organizations, doctrine, and legal structures were created in reaction to the booming growth of the cyber realm. Rather than the dorm-room hackers of Realization, this period was characterized by large-scale campaigns and the maturation of state-centric, particularly Russian, cyber espionage.

The signature event of the Takeoff period was the release of the first national cyber strategy, Presidential Decision Directive 63 (PDD-63) on 22 May 1998. This document—signed by President Clinton—implemented many recommendations of the PCCIP report, and signaled recognition that America's military and economy were "increasingly reliant upon certain critical infrastructures and upon cyber-based information systems."[2]

Sound Familiar?

[T]he only cyber war raging is inside the US government, where Washington lawyers and policymakers, military leaders, and official hackers battle over the value and legality of network attack.

Washington Post, 1999

Driven by Richard Clarke, the White House's powerful National Coordinator for Security, Infrastructure Protection, and Counter-Terrorism, PDD-63 was the first national-level policy on Critical Infrastructure Protection (CIP) and created key organizations.[3] The Information Sharing and Analysis Centers called for in PDD-63 still mostly exist today to help the private sector's critical infrastructure industries, like finance or electricity, to prepare for and react to cyber attacks. The National Infrastructure Protection Center (NIPC), housed at the Federal Bureau of Investigation, was to be the center of America's cyber defense, to provide "timely warnings of international threats, comprehensive analyses, and law enforcement investigation and response." The Departments of Defense and Commerce (through a newly created organization, the Critical Infrastructure Assurance Office) were ordered "to offer their expertise to private owners and operators of critical infrastructure to develop security-related best practice standards."[4]

Sadly, the government has forgotten the unmet goals for "a reliable, interconnected, and secure information system infrastructure by the year 2003" and "significantly increased security to government systems by the year 2000." Another PDD-63 legacy that is still

---

1   Some of the initiators of the Takeoff phase had existed before, but 1998 is the best cut-off point for the sake of clarity.
2   "Presidential Decision Directive/NSC-63."
3   *Ibid.*
4   *Ibid.*

with us is the notion that government regulation was an option to "be used only in the face of a material failure of the market to protect the health, safety, or well-being of the American people."[5] If the White House and Congress could have known in 1998 that the same problems would extend to 2012, they may have decided then to take stronger steps.

While PDD-63 was the key national policy of Takeoff, there were two key incidents, happening concurrently with its drafting and release, which truly focused the attention of the President and senior decision-makers as they created new policies and organizations. ELIGIBLE RECEIVER in 1997 was a "no notice interoperability exercise" in which NSA red teams—using no inside information—comprehensively intruded into DoD networks.[6] The thirty-five NSA hackers were split into teams, in the United States and on a ship in the Pacific, as if hired by North Korea to disrupt American networks and infrastructure.[7]

According to one senior-level official, "they left what they called a marker file—which basically was 'Kilroy was here'—that was just meant to be a note to prove that they had [gained] access."[8] These markers, and other indicators of the red team's success (only two of their intrusions were detected), were an early "watershed event" that focused the attention of the most senior leadership onto the level of damage that talented intruders, using tools readily available on the Internet, could inflict on the Department.[9]

Cyber Wake-Up Calls
(so far):
1. Morris Worm
2. **ELIGIBLE RECEIVER and SOLAR SUNRISE**
3. MOONLIGHT MAZE
4. Chinese Espionage
5. Estonia and Georgia
6. BUCKSHOT YANKEE
7. Stuxnet

Accordingly, ER97 accelerated plans for a new organizational structure to respond to cyber incidents and implement DoD-wide defensive mechanisms, such as a new organizational structure and an INFOCON, to mirror the more traditional Defense Condition or DEFCON, which would be raised to indicate a higher readiness level, to better defeat a sustained cyber assault.[10]

This exercise was followed in short order by the SOLAR SUNRISE attacks of 1998, which targeted widespread DoD unclassified systems and "demonstrated real world

---

5   White House, "Fact Sheet, Protecting America's Critical Infrastructures: PDD 63."
6   Hildreth, "Cyberwarfare"; "Eligible Receiver"; and Joint Chiefs of Staff, "No-Notice Interoperability Exercise Program."
7   Graham, "US Studies a New Threat: Cyber Attack."
8   Campbell, "Lessons from Our Cyber Past: The First Military Cyber Units"; and a follow up conversation with Col. (Ret.) "Dusty" Rhoads, March 2012.
9   Campbell, "Watershed event" from the "Computer Network Defense" presentation.
10   Campbell, "Lessons from Our Cyber Past: The First Military Cyber Units."

problems predicted in ER 97."[11] Deputy Secretary of Defense John Hamre notified President Clinton early, and said that the incident "might be the first shots of a genuine cyber war, perhaps by Iraq." He suspected this because the attacks coincided with airstrikes against Saddam Hussein's military, and also because many intrusions were initially traced to the Middle East.[12] In an embarrassing lesson on the difficulty of attributing cyber attacks, these intrusions turned out to be the work of California teenagers aided by an Israeli mentor.[13]

The leadership of the Pentagon found itself in another uncomfortable position when Hamre called a meeting to organize the response. John "Soup" Campbell, then the two-star Air Force general in charge of information operations at the Pentagon, described the scene: "Hamre's at the end of the table, looks around the table, we've got probably thirty people in the room … and said, 'Who's in charge?'" Unfortunately, no one was truly in charge, at least not in the strict manner that militaries define command.[14] Put twenty officers of any nations' military in a room, and they'll quickly determine who outranks whom, comparing dates of their last promotion if need be—they will not simply sit and shrug.

Everything we learned in Eligible Receiver, we relearned in Solar Sunrise. In big organizations, you learn things slowly. But there's nothing like a real-world experience to bring the lessons home.

Deputy Secretary of Defense
John Hamre, 1998

At the time, the military responses to major cyber incidents were conducted by the Joint Staff Information Operations Response Cell, which fell under Campbell's purview. The Joint Staff had the only staff at a suitably senior level in the DoD hierarchy to coordinate a response—and they had just responded to a similar scenario only a few days before.[15] But the cell was never meant to be permanent, as the Joint Staff is not supposed to be so directly involved in military operations; that is a role reserved for combatant commands.[16] Moreover, the DoD senior leadership felt they had painfully learned the lesson that there was "No one responsible for [cyber] defense; no one with authority to direct defense."[17]

---

11   Poulsen, "Video: Solar Sunrise"; and "Real world" quote from Campbell's presentation to the DSB Science Board, 2000 (the underlined emphasis is in the original).
12   Graham, "US Studies a New Threat: Cyber Attack."
13   For more on SOLAR SUNRISE, please read the case study by Tim Maurer in Part 3.
14   Campbell, "Lessons from Our Cyber Past: The First Military Cyber Units."
15   Discussion with participants in SOLAR SUNRISE, held at the Atlantic Council on 30 August 2012.
16   Interview with Col. (USAF, Ret.) "Dusty" Rhoads, March 2012; and "DoD Organization for Computer Network Defense: Summary of Proposals" document part of editor's personal collection, to be posted on a future cyber history archive.
17   Campbell, presentation to the Defense Science Board, 2000.

The Military Steps Up

This led to the creation of the first joint cyber war-fighting organization in less than one year, a blistering pace for the Pentagon.[18] Campbell set up the twenty-four person Joint Task Force for Computer Network Defense (JTF-CND) on 30 December 1998. For the first time, someone was able to issue commands to computer defenders elsewhere in the DoD, rather than merely asking for cooperation or providing suggestions.

The mindset of this military command was focused on the war-fighting task of combating America's adversaries, who happened to be contesting the US in cyberspace, rather than on the technical task of securing networks. To match this focus, the JTF-CND was staffed with officers from traditional combatant branches (such as Air Force and Navy combat pilots, a Marine armor officer, and an Army Ranger) to complement the intelligence staff and technical experts. As the commander expressed regarding this fighting spirit, "I grew up as a fighter pilot. My job was to blow things up, make smoking holes, and things of that sort. So I always took it in that direction."[19]

During the creation of the JTF-CND, there were long debates on where it should reside, when it should have the authority to issue commands, and its relationship to offensive cyber operations. Originally, the command was nearly given to the Air Force and co-located with the Joint Command and Control Warfare Center in San Antonio, Texas. At the last minute, however, the commander of the Defense Information Systems Agency (DISA) came forward with a winning proposal to host the JTF, much to the relief of the other services. The JTF would not be captured by the Air Force but would work at DISA alongside the DoD CERT, founded a decade earlier, in the aftermath of a previous cyber wake-

DoD has long recognized that DoD needed an organization to be in charge during computer network attacks. In particular, SOLAR SUNRISE and exercise ELIGIBLE RECEIVER illustrated the lack of centralized control in DoD's response.

Joint Chiefs decided in August 1998 to stand up a strong CND-JTF to be 'in charge' during attacks. The JTF would have authority to direct and coordinate the entire DoD defense. CSAF (the Chief of Staff of the Air Force) stressed the need for a strong, directive, operationally minded CND-JTF.

A CND-JTF Working Group was set up with representatives from CINCs, Services, agencies, and the Joint Staff. The working group has developed a proposed Charter and CONOP to ensure the JTF is set up by the SECDEF's deadline of NLT 30 December 1998.

From HQ Air Force staffwork by the author, October 1998

---

18   Campbell, "Lessons from Our Cyber Past: The First Military Cyber Units."
19   *Ibid.*

up call, the Morris Worm.[20] But, as there was not sufficient space at first, the world's first joint cyber command ignominiously started in a set of temporary trailers in the DISA parking lot.[21]

The unit's charter resolved the second issue, regarding command and control, by authorizing JTF-CND to direct the defense against any strategic cyber attack, defined as an attack that crossed borders between commands and agencies, or with "widespread or critical effects on the Defense Information Infrastructure."[22]

The task force's relationship with cyber offense was not as easy to resolve. Remember, offense was not new. The 609th IW Squadron had been set up several years before. And on 3 March 1997, the Secretary of Defense delegated NSA authority to develop techniques for Computer Network Attack.[23] The *Washington Post* reported at the time that in addition, the Pentagon had its own section for offense, reportedly part of the Joint Staff:[24]

> *[A] little-known Pentagon agency called J-33, or the Special Technical Operations Division (STOD) of the J-3 (Operations) Directorate of the Joint Chiefs of Staff have been trying to figure out how to hack Iraq for a long time and have found the challenge daunting.*
>
> *STOD was set up during the Cold War and is the highest-level military focal point for all matters relating to what is called offensive information warfare. STOD is a covert action broker for the Joint Staff. Unlike other offices in the Pentagon that merely push a lot of paper, it also is charged with providing direct military support to operational missions of the CIA and NSA, and of responding to requests for assistance from the National Security Council. Each US regional command, such as the US Central Command responsible for Iraq, has its own STOD.*

Early drafts of the JTF's founding documents gave it the mission to conduct "active defense," which led to a debate, at least in the Air Force. Headquarters AF lawyers wanted this language removed, as the military lacked definitions for "defensive actions," "offensive actions," and "active defense." Even though the DoD is still keen to take on this mission, the term remains essentially undefined fifteen years later.

To help define the relationship with offense (which during this period became known as Computer Network Attack, or CNA), the founding document of the JTF-CND included a

20 Experience of the author, the Headquarters Air Force action officer responsible for creating the JTF-CND in 1998; and an unclassified presentation for JCS OpsDeps, DoD Organization for Computer Network Defense, Summary of Proposals, June 1998.

21 In a twist on a Navy tradition, pieces of aluminum siding snipped from the trailers' siding were used on plaques for the unit's "plankholders," or founding members.

22 Concept of Operation for the Joint Task Force—Computer Network Defense, December 1998. This document is part of the editor's personal collection, to be posted on a future cyber history archive.

23 Black, Jr., "Thinking Out Loud About IO."

24 Arkin, "Phreaking Hactivists."

special appendix "to discuss how the offense and defense might work together,"[25] though the unit would not initiate any offensive actions itself. This solution did not last long.

Figure 3: Founding members of JTF-CND at the decommissioning of JTF-GNO on 7 September 2010, marking the end of the 12-year JTF era and the start of US Cyber Command. From left to right, Michele Iversen, Bob Gourley, "Soup" Campbell, Bob West, Larry Frank, Marc Sachs, and Jason Healey.

Within a year of its formation, though still associated with DISA, the JTF-CND no longer reported directly to the Secretary of Defense. As of 1 October 2000, it fell under US Space Command, which had both a defensive mission and the responsibility for any "computer network attack, to include advocating the CND and CNA requirements" of combatant commanders and for "conducting CND and CNA operations."[26] According to Air Force Lt. Gen. Harry Raduege, who was later a JTF and DISA commander, the Joint Chiefs of Staff ruled out Strategic Command because "they make big holes" with their traditional nuclear war-fighting mission. Special Operations Command was bypassed, because then they were "quiet professionals," possessing nothing like the celebrity they enjoy today.[27] (This debate continues nearly

The procedures to work CND between JTF-CND and Services and Commands may be rough and acrimonious at first, but should work out, given time.

Author's incorrect prediction in Air Force staffwork, 1998

---

25   Rhoads, "Lessons from Our Cyber Past, The First Military Cyber Units."
26   "Unified Command Plan 99," excerpted from Campbell's presentation to the Defense Science Board, 2000.
27   Lt. Gen. Raduege, Remarks at the FedCyber Conference, Washington, D.C., 15 November 2012.

fifteen years later: Strategic Command now owns the cyber mission, as part of their responsibility for global strike, though many believe it should belong to the special operations commandos, since cyber conflict is so irregular, like their other operations.)

In addition to determining the best parent command, putting offense and defense in the same command led to the same questions of priority that "Dusty" Rhoads encountered when creating the 609th IWS five years earlier. Now the JTF's Chief of Staff, Col. Rhoads helped balance the equation, and there was a much clearer top-down direction. As Lt. Gen. Campbell, the first JTF commander recalls, early on DepSecDef Hamre made it very clear that the philosophy of JTF-CND was defense first: without offense "you're probably not going to lose a war. [But] if you don't do the defense right, you can be in big trouble."[28] However, with this dual mission, JTF-CND would be renamed as the Joint Task Force for Computer Network Operations (JTF-CNO) in the fall of 2000

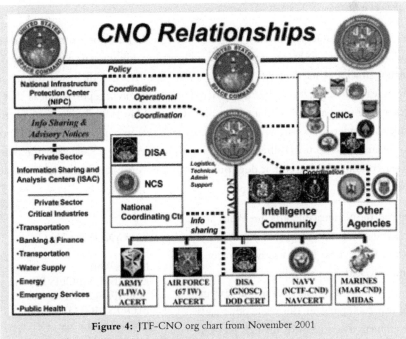

Figure 4: JTF-CNO org chart from November 2001

(courtesy of Derek Franklin, then the JTF-CNO/J1)

---

28   Campbell, "Lessons from Our Cyber Past: The First Military Cyber Units."

New Organizations in Action

As much as the military wanted to use cyber capabilities on the battlefield, problems usually lingered. One problem was that concepts seemed to be focused mostly on sudden crippling attacks on infrastructure. General John Jumper, the Commander of Air Forces in Europe during the operation, put it in terms that still seem familiar:

> *When we hear talk of information warfare, the mind conjures up notions of taking some country's piece of sacred infrastructure in a way that is hardly relevant to the commander at the operational and tactical level. I would submit that we are not there with information warfare.*
>
> *I picture myself around that same targeting table where you have the fighter pilot, the bomber pilot, the special operations people and the information warriors. As you go down the target list, each one takes a turn raising his or her hand saying, I can take that target. When you get to the info warrior, the info warrior says, "I can take the target, but first I have to go back to Washington and get a finding."[29]*

There was also considerable interest in using cyber capabilities, not as a battlefield weapon against an adversary's military targets, but as a covert capability to sneak into their systems to disrupt small and selected bits of information. Theorists had discussed this possibility, and in at least one case, it may have been acted upon. *Newsweek* reported a leak that stated President Clinton had approved a covert operation in May 1998 for the CIA to go after Yugoslavian leader Slobodan Milošević's "financial assets in banks throughout Europe."[30] There seems to be no unclassified information to confirm this, or whether the operation was ever conducted. However, it does presage other covert operations which followed in the next decade.

Along with the National Infrastructure Protection Center at the FBI and other parts of the Federal government, the new JTF military operational structure worked on two critical issues during these years. First, they had roles in the lead up to the Year 2000 problem. But while other parts of government tried to remedy the Y2K problem itself, these organizations worried about nations that might attack the United States (and its allies) under cover of a Y2K failure, or who might think their own failures were the opening of a US

Cyber Wake-Up Calls
(so far):
1. Morris Worm
2. ELIGIBLE RECEIVER and SOLAR SUNRISE
3. **MOONLIGHT MAZE**
4. Chinese Espionage
5. Estonia and Georgia
6. BUCKSHOT YANKEE
7. Stuxnet

---

29   Arkin, "A Mouse that Roars?"
30   *Ibid.*

attack and choose to respond. Ultimately, of course, none of this came to pass, unlike the second issue.

The JTF-CND and NIPC coordinated on the first major cyber espionage case, the still largely classified MOONLIGHT MAZE.[31] The incident, which appears to have started around March 1998, was not just a scare, like SOLAR SUNRISE, but a deeply worrying incident. It rapidly became the next "wake-up call for the DoD," and many other organizations. There were intrusions into "hundreds of computers at NASA, the Pentagon, and other government agencies, as well as private universities and research laboratories."[32]

Michael Vatis, who led the government's response as the head of the NIPC, said in Congressional testimony that the intrusions "appear to originate in Russia" and were responsible for stealing "unclassified but still sensitive information about essential defense technical research matters."[33] Russia was suspected because intrusions were traced to Russian ISPs like Citiline.ru, sometimes from locations only miles from Moscow. The intrusions occurred "on weekdays between 8 am and 5 pm Moscow times—but not on Russian holidays."[34] Some media reports went further, saying the intrusions were not just from Russia but traced specifically to the Russian Academy of Sciences, an institution which would indeed have been curious about the science and technology information being stolen.[35]

The main US government response appears to have been a *demarche* to the Russian government to cease the intrusions or to cooperate, providing telephone numbers associated with the intruders. This *demarche* was essentially ignored, as the Russians denied prior knowledge of the attacks and "the numbers were inoperative."[36] In addition to this political action, there were also technical responses. The DoD ordered that all unclassified communications

> ... the kids [responsible for SOLAR SUNRISE] essentially found a well-known vulnerability and came in that way. MOONLIGHT MAZE brings a whole different, much more sophisticated approach. But it also brings another dimension—we are no longer dealing with hackers but with the problem of state sponsored attack.
>
> Art Money, Assistant Secretary of Defense, 1999

would thereafter be routed "through eight large electronic gateways that will be easier to

---

31 For more on MOONLIGHT MAZE, please read the case study by Adam Elkus in Part 3.
32 "Wake-up call" quote attributed to Art Money, ASDC3I, at "Cyber Security "Wake-Up" Calls for the Federal Government" CTOVision, accessed 18 April 2012, http://ctovision.com/cyber-security-wake-up-calls-for-the-federal-government/. "Hundreds of Computers" is from Adams, "Virtual Defense."
33 Suro, "FBI Lagging Behind on Cyber Crime."
34 Drogin, "Russians Seem To Be Hacking into Pentagon."
35 Kimery, "Moonlight Maze." (Link now dead: http://www.infowar.com/class_2/99/class2_120399b_J.shtml .)
36 Adams, "Virtual Defense."

monitor" (similar to the Trusted Internet Communication directive, implemented across the Federal government a decade later). Also, an order from the JTF-CND directed a change of "all administrative and user passwords for all unclassified systems" across the entire DoD.[37]

The new focus at NIPC, JTF-CND, and other government agencies was just in time to respond to ILOVEYOU, Melissa, Code Red, NIMDA, SQL Slammer, and other major Internet worms that caught the public's attention and highlighted the insecurity of cyberspace. The Code Red worm targeted, among other sites, the White House, forcing perhaps the first cyber related White House press briefing.[38] The DDoS attacks in 2000 against Yahoo, eBay, Amazon, CNN, and E★Trade not only made headlines, but President Clinton convened a cybersecurity roundtable just a few weeks later at the White House.[39]

But perhaps more worrisome than these incidents was how they fed the constant drumbeat of cyber security experts, who warned that even more devastating attacks were imminent.[40]

These warnings seemed to be born out during the years from 1999 to 2001, which marked the heyday of Patriotic Hackers. This breed attacked ostensibly for national pride. Whether the conflict involved Indian and Pakistani hackers working against one another, or Israelis and Palestinians, or Americans and Chinese, many of these attacks were labeled "cyber war" or "cyber terrorism" by journalists and headline writers.[41] Of course, they were certainly not examples of war or terrorism, as no one died and there was no lingering damage. However, they can be considered cyber conflicts. While not true conflicts in the way militaries understand that term, patriotic hacking conflicts tend to either become independent national security crises on their own or complicate solutions to other, more traditional crises (such as the border skirmishes between India and Pakistan).[42]

The most serious patriotic hacking cases from a US perspective were the 1999 attacks by Serbs and Russians against the United States and NATO, and Chinese attacks against the United States in 1999 and 2001. The 1999 incidents were all tied to the NATO operation ALLIED FORCE to force Yugoslavian troops from Kosovo. Hacker groups like the Russian Hacker Brigade and the Serbian Black Hand made news with patriotically motivated attacks:

---

37 Drogin, "Russians Seem To Be Hacking into Pentagon"; and Verton, "DOD: Change Passwords."

38 Conversation with Richard A. Clarke, 23 October 2012; and Lemos, "Web worm targets White House."

39 Conversation with Richard A. Clarke, 23 October 2012; and Madsen, "Code Red: A Red Herring."

40 Stephen, "The Changing Face of Distributed Denial of Service Mitigation."

41 For example, see T the the Guardian's story from 2010, "WikiLeaks backlash: The first global cyber war has begun, claim hackers," as well as CNN's story from 1999, "Kosovo cyberwar intensifies Chinese hackers targeting U.S. sites, government says." As a giveaway that CNN did not consider their story on the Kosovo "cyberwar" to be a "real" war, the story was in the Technology section, not in the International section.

42 For more on patriotic hackers, please read the case study by Jon Diamond in Part 3.

NATO spokesman Jamie Shea apologised ... for the erratic service being provided by its Website [which] has often been down or slowed to a crawl since 28 March.

"We have looked at this very carefully and it seems that we have been dealing with some hackers in Belgrade who have hacked into our website and caused line saturation of the server by using 'ping' bombardment strategy," he said.

As well as stifling Nato's propaganda efforts, Net users opposed to the bombing have also been infiltrating and clogging the defence alliance's computer system.[43]

These attacks seemed bad at the time, as they interfered with NATO wartime public relations and disrupted internal systems. But they were mild compared to those a month later, following the accidental US bombing of the Chinese embassy in Belgrade, which killed three journalists.

Within China, there were large-scale riots. The US embassy in Beijing (among other NATO embassies and consulates) had its windows smashed with stones, while in cyberspace, dozens of webpages were defaced. Several US government webpages had "pictures of Asian people and Chinese writing," later determined to be pictures and tributes to those killed in the bombing.[44] The White House website was shut down after intrusion attempts. Much of the graffiti in the defaced websites included significant anti-NATO rhetoric: "Protest U.S.A.'s Nazi Action! Protest NATO's brutal action! We are Chinese hackers who take no cares about politics ... NATO led by U.S.A. must take absolute responsibility."[45]

This was not the first electronic outburst from China, nor would it be the last or the worst. Almost exactly two years later, on 1 April 2001, a Chinese interceptor collided with a US EP-3 naval reconnaissance aircraft. The Chinese pilot died, and the EP-3 had to make an emergency landing on Hainan Island in far southeastern China. US websites in the United States were attacked, including a denial of service attack on the White House, leading the NIPC to release several warnings.[46] US hackers were not passive; they hacked many Chinese sites in response.[47]

In both 1999 and 2001, the attributions for both the physical attacks on the US embassy and the cyber attacks were relatively clear. The Chinese government was clearly to blame: police controlled the area but permitted the stone-throwing; many protesters were transported by bus from state-run universities in organized processions; and to cap it off, Vice-President Hu Jintao made the state's support explicit in a televised statement.[48]

---

43   "Sci/Tech: Kosovo info warfare spreads."
44   "Hackers attack U.S. government Web sites in protest of Chinese Embassy bombing."
45   Barr, "Anti-NATO Hackers Sabotage 3 Web Sites."
46   Weiss, "FBI Warns of More Cyberattacks."
47   Anderson, "US fears Chinese hack attack."
48   For contemporaneous press reports on each of these points, see "Chinese Embassy Bombing Belgrade."

Accordingly, the United States government knew that to reduce these Chinese government-encouraged stone-throwing and cyber attacks, it needed to assuage the Chinese leadership.

In a potentially more serious, but much forgotten incident, it appears the Chinese government itself got involved. After a crackdown in China, in 1999 a Falun Gong website in Canada was attacked by a denial of service which persisted even when the site was mirrored in the US. Some (but not all) of the attacks were traced directly back to China's Ministry of Public Security. This ministry was, as now, under pressure to crack down on the group.[49] This may have been a rogue attack, but the early evidence (and subsequent cover up) clearly points to Chinese government involvement.

To help bring further analytical clarity, the author, while at the intelligence cell at the Joint Task Force for Computer Network Defense, developed a scale to determine how responsible a nation was for any particular cyber incident. This scale has matured into the Spectrum of State Responsibility (see Table 3) published by the Atlantic Council.[50] Chinese hackers seem to be at least state-ignored and perhaps even state-encouraged by their government to attack overseas during times of geopolitical crisis. But there is little public or direct evidence of their being coordinated or ordered to do so. The Chinese use this tactic for physical protests as well, as official tolerance is part of a "long-standing pattern of behavior in which the Chinese government uses mass protests to further its foreign policy goals," according to one analyst.[51]

Table 3:

The Spectrum of State Responsibility

1. **State-prohibited.** The national government will help stop the third-party attack.

2. **State-prohibited-but-inadequate.** The national government is cooperative but unable to stop the third-party attack.

3. **State-ignored.** The national government knows about the third-party attacks but is unwilling to take any official action.

4. **State-encouraged.** Third parties control and conduct the attack, but the national government encourages them as a matter of policy.

5. **State-shaped.** Third parties control and conduct the attack, but the state provides some support.

6. **State-coordinated.** The government coordinates third-party attackers, such as by "suggesting" operational details.

7. **State-ordered.** The state directs third-party proxies to conduct the attack on its behalf.

8. **State-rogue-conducted.** Out-of-control elements of cyber forces of the state conduct the attack.

9. **State-executed.** The state conducts the attack using cyber forces under their direct control.

10. **State-integrated.** The state attacks using integrated third-party proxies and its own cyber forces.

Chinese official tolerance for patriotic hacking dates at least back to the 1997 online and physical protests against Indonesia, during ethnic

---

49   Chase and Mulvenon, You've Got Dissent, 71–76.
50   Healey, "Beyond Attribution: Seeking National Responsibility in Cyberspace."
51   Johnson and Shanker, "Beijing Mixes Messages Over Anti-Japan Protests."

riots targeting Chinese in that country. That tolerance for patriotic attacks continues up until the present day. A recent example involved Chinese hackers defacing Filipino websites during a maritime standoff over the disputed Scarborough Shoals in the South China Sea.[52]

Restraint appears possible, however. The Filipino authorities urged their own hackers not to attack, saying that they "denounce such cyber attacks, regardless from which side they are coming from."[53] This message is similar to one by the NIPC, which warned US hackers in the days leading up to the second Gulf War in 2003: "Regardless of the motivation, the NIPC reiterates such activity is illegal and punishable as a felony. The US Government does not condone so-called 'patriotic hacking' on its behalf."[54] Such statements are a strong signal, both to hackers and any affected nations, that attacks are not ignored or condoned.

Private Sector Response

During these years, the government was certainly "taking off," but the private sector was equally active. For example, L0pht Heavy Industries, a hacker collective in Boston, was founded several years earlier, but by 1998 its members were well known personages, testifying to Congress that they could take down the Internet in just 30 minutes.[55] The video of these seven confident, but long-haired and decided geeky, young men gained worldwide attention, even from the most senior policymakers. It was not rare for senior policymakers or military officers to wonder what Mudge, Space Rogue, or Dildog might think on a particular issue. Shortly thereafter, these hackers became part of one of the best known computer security services companies, @stake, also based in Boston, showing how the previously bizarre was now becoming mainstream. Indeed, by 2011, Mudge had been hired by the original creator of the Internet, DARPA of the Department of Defense, to improve cyber security.[56]

President Clinton's policy to improve critical infrastructure, PDD-63, was meant to spur government action, but he also asked the private sector to improve their own structures and securities. The most important aspect of this push by the White House and government agencies was "to strongly encourage the creation of a private sector information sharing and analysis center."[57] The mission of such an Information Sharing and Analysis Center (ISAC) was to potentially "emulate particular aspects of such institutions as the Centers for Disease Control and Prevention" with operationally relevant information, so as to share information around the sector and potentially also with government. Several ISACs were

---

52   Tang, "China-U.S. cyber war escalates"; and "Government websites attacked by Chinese hackers.'"
53   "Filipinos told: Exercise restraint amid cyber attacks."
54   Leyden, "US Govt. warns script kiddies to stay out of cyberwar."
55   See the video, "Hackers Testifying at the United States Senate, May 19, 1998 (L0pht Heavy Industries)."
56   "Bio, Mr. Peiter 'Mudge' Zatko."
57   "Critical Infrastructure Protection, PDD-63."

set up in the years after PDD-63, though few were long-term successes. Some sectors simply took an existing organization with similar functions and renamed it as an ISAC, such as the National Coordinating Center for Telecommunications.[58]

By far the most successful ISAC has been the one supporting the banking and financial sector, the FS-ISAC, created in 1999 "to help members prepare for Y2K and establish an anonymous information sharing capability within the financial services industry."[59] The FS-ISAC owes its success to a committed membership, a strong degree of trust between its members (facilitated by bi-annual boozy meetings in Florida), the frequent sharing of sensitive information during cyber crises, and an institutional commitment to cyber security.[60] This was complemented by forging good relations with government partners, especially in the Treasury Department, which boosted the FS-ISAC with significant funding in 2003.[61]

58   "Program Information."
59   "Next Generation FS/ISAC: Frequently Asked Questions."
60   Personal experience of the author, the Vice Chairman of the FS-ISAC in 2002 to 2003. Also see "About the FS-ISAC."
61   "Next Generation FS/ISAC: Frequently Asked Questions."

In Their Own Words: Lieutenant General John H. "Soup" Campbell, USAF (Ret.)

Founding Commander, Joint Task Force-Computer Network Defense (1998)

Lt. Gen. Campbell's career began as an F-15 fighter pilot. He eventually logged over 3,600 hours in the cockpit. His first job in cyber was with the Joint Staff at the Pentagon, where as a Deputy Director for Operations in the late 1990s he oversaw the military's information warfare efforts during a very formative time. This was during the period of the key "wake-up calls" ELIGIBLE RECEIVER and SOLAR SUNRISE. He went on to found the first joint cyber command, the Joint Task Force Computer Network Defense, after which he went to the Central Intelligence Agency as Associate Director of Central Intelligence for Military Support.

This narrative is adapted from comments that Lt. Gen. Campbell made at an event with the first cyber commanders at the Atlantic Council in 2012.[62]

I came to the Pentagon in the summer of 1997. I had been an aviator almost my entire career, and so this whole cyber world was fairly new. But I was part of the Joint Staff J-38, which is sort of the cats-and-dogs directorate of the Joint Staff. And one of the things we had was the Special Technical Operations (STO) Division. When I got there, plans were already in motion to spin that off into a separate directorate... [this] became the J-39, which still exists today. So this was the situation in play when I came to the Pentagon to work on JTF-CND, and I owned that.

In the earlier days, playing with [the National Security Agency] was very, very vital. And as a combatant person, I was always at odds with the intelligence community for intelligence gain or loss. I grew up as a fighter pilot. My job was to blow things up, make smoking holes, and things of that sort. So I always took it in that direction.

The main thing that was in play when I got to Washington DC —which really became the whole reason the JTF-CND existed—was something called ELIGIBLE RECEIVER 1997 [ER97] ... a series that are held semi-annually that the Chairman of the Joint Chiefs of Staff, really, the Chairman, owns. In 1997, the subject was cyber defense. In preparation for that, NSA had chartered a "Red Team"—about six months beforehand—to go in, with the permission of the Deputy Secretary of Defense John Hamre, to do a reconnaissance of DoD's networks—including both unclassified and some classified networks—and to penetrate them if they could, while not to doing any damage. But in each place that the Red Team penetrated, they left what they called a marker file, which basically was: "Kilroy was here." That was just meant to be a note to prove that they had [gained] access.

---

62   Campbell, "Lessons from Our Cyber Past, The First Military Cyber Units."

When the exercise started, the Red Teams were restricted, as much as one can restrict NSA smart folks, from using insider information or special knowledge on these networks. So then the Red Teams took the access that they had with the systems that they thought they could logically influence and control, and… built a series of events around the world. They were into PACOM networks and built a series of world events which involved social engineering and rolling blackouts and other activities that would cause social unrest.

And frankly it scared the hell out of a lot of folks, because the implications of what this team had been able to do were pretty far-reaching. So there were lots and lots of lessons learned. You can figure out all the obvious ones. The one that got the ball rolling for what became JTF-CND was the observation that, in all of this play, there was really no one in charge of the DoD response for recognition, assessment, attribution, and reaction.

The one that got me involved took place in the Secretary of Defense's conference room, third floor. Hamre's at the end of the table, looks around the table… we've got probably thirty people in the room, and he said, "Who's in charge?" Well, I was the Joint Staff J-39 STO bubba and sort of got the action to do the after-action piece of this. And again, one of the things as we worked through this was just the obvious observation that somebody really needed to be in charge. There needed to be an operational commander with the mandate to direct action and direct response.

The philosophy behind how my unit was staffed and structured was that if you're going to have any credibility with the war-fighters, you had to have operational people in the JTF. And the question is: do you take computer guys and gals and put them in an operational situation or go the other way? We thought the best approach was the other way, to start with people who had some credibility in the operational, more traditional military side of the house, and then provide them with training and additional help that they needed to be technically proficient enough for cyber operations.

During the early days, I frankly never thought the JTF-CND construct would last. I think we all thought it was going to be a joint mission, clearly. We thought the JTF would probably last for two or three years tops and then be rolled into some kind of a joint structure, a sub-unified command or something like that. And in fact that's what happened, but a decade later.

DepSecDef Hamre made it very clear early on that the philosophy of JTF-CND was defense first. The offensive stuff was neat. We had some really good capabilities. We had some really smart folks working on our offensive capabilities. In the best case, these IO capabilities may prevent a need for kinetic activity, but in most cases they support the kinetic part. And if you don't do them, it's probably going to work just fine. It may take a little longer. It may take more resources. But you're probably not going to fail the operation or lose the war. However, if you don't do the defense right, you can be in big trouble. If you can't organize your forces, deploy them, support them, employ them, communicate, navigate, you've got some big problems.

My personal take on the doctrine of "defense first" or simply defense is: I don't know, because the capabilities are so very classified you never see the successes. You sometimes see the failures. But you rarely see the successes. So it's hard to judge from that uninformed perspective what the balance is. I would hope that we still prioritize the defense; it's sort of the basics. You've got to do that right. And once you get that done, protect your base, then you can build up and do other things.

In Their Own Words: Major General James D. Bryan, USA (Ret.)

Founding Commander, Joint Task Force-Computer Network Operations (2000)

Major General Bryan's career started as a US Army signal officer. Then he moved to special operations and later commanded the 112th Special Operations Signal Battalion and the 35th Airborne Signal Brigade. Afterwards, he also worked with communications and computers for the Pacific Command in Hawaii, where he pioneered development of their cyber organizations. Then he commanded the JTF-CNO, the first joint offense-defense cyber command.

This narrative is adapted from comments that Maj. Gen. Bryan made with the first cyber commanders at the Atlantic Council in 2012.[63]

> *When I showed up at the [JTF-CND], there were a few folks in uniforms, and some of them had on flight jackets, and some of them had on BDUs, and a bunch of civilians with no ties in the parking lot. I looked over and I said, "Is this it? I thought you were bigger, because the JTF had already begun to have an impact on professionalizing this mission area."*

> *I believe that the biggest challenges that we faced from 2000 to 2001, my first year in command, was that we had to take advantage of the momentum that the JTF had managed to establish. There was momentum, but there was so much work to be done. We rattled everybody's cage — they either loved it or they hated it, but they could see it coming.*

> *We had one-third military, one-third government civilian, and one-third contractor. This mix allowed us to really begin to go deep in the technical skills arena. Once we — particularly on the civilian side and contractor side — were able to set up shop, the services began to send us technically deep military officers, because we were the real deal. The Army had gone so far as to create a functional area for information operations. We began to get folks who had graduate degrees in computer science and understood all of this.*

> *But we also had to work with doctrine. As a good policy with a new commander, I wanted to have a meeting with my subordinate commanders to come up with a doctrine. There were military officers in charge of critical functions in the services. So we invited them all. Two Air Force guys showed up, one from San Antonio and one from somewhere else. Three Army guys showed up, one from NETCOM, one from 1st IO command, and one off the Army staff. We had to talk the Navy into sending somebody. They didn't have anybody really in command of their mission. The Marines had, because they had centralized their network. By default they had a single commander who reported.*

---

63   Bryan, "Lessons from Our Cyber Past, The First Military Cyber Units."

But I had no authority over any of them. Basically we got together in the conference room. When we left, we actually had a little huddle. We all understood how important this mission was, how important it was that we all cooperate together, and that there were times that, even though I did not have official command and control authority over them, we were going to have to issue directives—because we were already operating in hours, and we knew we had to get to minutes and to seconds. However, we couldn't go through this inexorably difficult staffing process in the Pentagon to try to get permission, so I must give it to all of them. Somehow we got to write them all into the history, because we all agreed to kind of get along. That was critically important.

Along the transitional journey from CND to CNO, we had really begun to professionalize. Now we had a command change at US Space Command. General Eberhart had taken over. He was really fond of us and was impressed that the JTF was a very professional organization. He had retained responsibility for the offense mission at US Space Command.

So he decided that unified combatant commanders do best when they hand their combatant missions off to sub-unified commands or JTFs. So in March of 2001 ... he said, "I want you to take on the offense mission too." I said, "Well, what's my E-date for assuming that mission?" He said, "How much time do you need?" Literally two weeks later, I called back, and we worked all around the clock for two weeks to get ready for this mission. On April 2nd, 2001, we were designated the Joint Task Force-Computer Network Operations, to recognize that we now had both the defense and the offense mission.

I think in JTF-CNO some really interesting things happened in 2001. First of all, the first of the really sophisticated viruses began to really hammer networks worldwide. I'll just mention one, and everybody's eyes will roll: Code Red was really an eye-opener. It had a huge effect. But we were able to contain it in a couple of hours in terms of its impact on the DoD. [If] the JTF wasn't in place with its relationship with DISA to do that, it would have had a devastating effect on the DoD's networks.

And then of course, just two months later, September 11th occurred. Shortly thereafter the nation was at war. So our support of combatant commands went from spending most of our time talking to the services or wrestling with the services over networks, to actually getting geared up with the combat and commands for a nation at war. And that really changed the dynamics for us.

We were about a 70 /30 split between defense and offense. But what I realized by about 2003 was that by then... we had done a pretty good job on the offensive missions. We'd actually treated cyber offensive missions as a kinetic effect generating thing in terms of process. We actually went out into the combatant commands and asked them for their target list. And we actually went through the drill of weighting them and analyzing them and prioritizing them on a global scale.

But the fact of the matter is that I had realized that it was taking probably 30 percent of my mission, and it was taking up 70 percent of my time, because it was so sensitive and classified. Every time I turned around, somebody wanted to give me another polygraph to read me onto a program. I had begun to realize that we can't talk about the actual missions in here, because they're still extraordinarily sensitive, despite the fact that we'd actually been conducting the missions.

Even when the missions were wildly successful from a cyber perspective, we were still in our infancy in terms of fully appreciating the effects we could achieve. But it still made us think: whether or not we achieve the desired effect on the offensive side, the nation was not at risk. If we fail on the defensive side, the nation would be at risk. I remember the meeting that we had with the Department of Defense General Counsel on this issue. Basically we got **posse comitatus** handed to us—somebody who was equivalent to an Assistant Secretary of Defense points his finger in your face and says, "Listen, Bryan, the dot-mil boundary is your boundary," because we were advancing aggressively.

But it was taking an extraordinary toll on my personal time as a commander, and it was taking a toll on my staff, which was still measured in... literally I think we were up to 150 or so people by that time, from the 20+ that JTF-CND had originally had. I had realized that when we had success in CNA, we couldn't talk about it, and nobody would know. Those who needed to know knew, but it wasn't anything that was going to make the headlines. But if we failed in CND, I don't think I would be overstating if I said the nation would be at risk.

When they decided [to split the offense and defense missions to different commands], then I said, well, the JTF commander who's going to run the CND mission needs to have rank equivalency, and it needs to not be the Vice Director of DISA, but the Director of DISA. This is going to become a three-star-level mission. The defense commander can't be outranked, frankly, at the end of the day, by the attack commander.

In Their Own Words: Steve Chabinsky

Former Deputy Assistant Director, Cyber Division, Federal Bureau of Investigations.

Steve Chabinsky has been working cyber issues for decades and has served in key roles, including heading the FBI's Cyber Intelligence Section, and becoming Director of the Joint Interagency Cyber Task Force before he managed the FBI's Cyber Division. He managed all of the cyber investigations. He is now the Senior Vice President of Legal Affairs and Chief Risk Officer for CrowdStrike, an advanced cybersecurity company.

This section is derived from an event attended by the "first cyber cops," held at the Altantic Council in 2012.[64]

The way I got into the cybersecurity profession is similar to how a lot of young people get into computers. It started out with games. It was 1979 or '80, and my cousin Kim had a TRS-80, and I was at his house. It was an early personal computer for those of you who know, a Radio Shack Tandy. He was signing into a service called "The Source," which was extremely expensive, and he allowed me to play a game called "Adventure."

It was one of those games where there's no graphics, of course, and you played by reading the prompts and typing out your commands to progress. The game would give prompts that said: A nasty elf has come at you; what do you do? And you say: Fight elf. And the screen says: Elf killed you. At the time, I just thought that this was remarkable. It was, to me, a real piece of artificial intelligence.

I decided, after my experience with "Adventure," that I wanted to program just like that. I was in high school at the time, and I was the kid who worked every day after school—not to buy a car, but to buy an Apple II Plus, which cost about 1,200 bucks, and it didn't come with a floppy drive. That was another 400 bucks for a five-and-a-quarter-inch drive. It came with 48K, so I had to buy another 16K just to be able to program in FORTRAN and Pascal.

When I was choosing a career, I ended up joining the FBI. Fast forward to 1998. Something happened, which was that then-President Clinton issued Presidential Decision Directive 63 (PDD 63). The FBI was put into the lead of a group that no longer exists. It was called the National Infrastructure Protection Center. It was an incredible concept then, and today that strategy is still sound.

The concept behind the Center was that the multiple agencies in the federal government and the private sector needed to work together to combat cyber crime and cyber threats facing US networks. The Center needed another lawyer, so I raised my hand immediately, because I saw it

---

64   Chabinsky, "Lessons from Our Cyber Past: The First Cyber Cops."

had to do with cyber. I was very fortunate to be selected, and the first project I was given—per the provisions of PDD 63—was to help the National Infrastructure Protection Center create its own relationship with the private sector to create a public-private partnership.

We didn't know how to do that, but we realized that in 1996 one of our field offices had created something called "InfraGard." InfraGard was probably about 200 people at the time, and meeting in Cleveland, Columbus, and Indianapolis. There was a lawyer already at the NIPC. He would leave me standing there by myself a few months into it, because he got promoted. As soon as I walked in the door he said, "What I could really use your help on is this project that I've been working on. It would mean a lot to me if you did it." This was his way of saying, "this is a real ugly bear." The challenge was to figure out what InfraGard was, and how do you nationalize this program with the private sector for mutual protection?

So this idea that we see now, when we're talking about learning from our past—you can't do this without the government and the private sector working together. This is not a new idea. When InfraGard started out, we only had this group of a couple of hundred people, and today InfraGard has over 50,000 people throughout the United States. When I first started out in the FBI, I never dreamt that I would be part of helping an organization [InfraGard] grow larger than the one I was part of. The FBI only has about 35,000 people.

InfraGard is for our combined protection, both on the cyber side—and after September 11th—it became much more inclusive of physical security as well. By that time, I also started giving legal advice on our intrusion cases.

One of the first cases I recall working on to capture our after-action lessons learned was the SOLAR SUNRISE incident in 1998. A lot of these types of cases were not defined by how bad the intrusions were, but more about the fog of war concept that permeates our understanding of our entry into the new areas that have come upon us. During SOLAR SUNRISE, we saw military computers being intruded upon and that these intrusions were coming from abroad. This particular case happened during a real-world conflict with Iraq. We were seeing the intrusive traffic coming in from another Middle East country. On the receiving side, it really very much looked like the dot-mil environment was under attack from this other nation-state.

SOLAR SUNRISE was playing it out in real time. Keep in mind that this was the first time we really saw [a set of] large-scale, across-the-board cyber intrusions coming from one area. There was obviously the very real possibility that we were under attack from a serious threat like a nation-state or a criminal organization. At that moment, you see the dynamics play out between the agencies in terms of the individual responses to this intrusion. We were asking ourselves questions like: If we are under attack from a nation-state, how are you sure of the attribution? What is the appropriate response? And then you respond symmetrically.

The FBI, is an organization that is schooled in investigating in a constitutionally acceptable manner, and according to the rules and regulations and statutes of the continental United States. The FBI cannot travel easily in ways that might affect the sovereignty of other nations. On top of that, the FBI is an organization very much into notions of probable cause and "beyond a reasonable doubt" and whether or not we have enough evidence for attribution that would make us comfortable to do something, like a military campaign against a third party or another country.

At the time, we were at the table saying we don't think there was enough attributable evidence to say we were under military attack. But we also knew that it might be state-sponsored. During the SOLAR SUNRISE incident, an assessment that we were under military attack turned out to be incorrect, as we now know, because the culprits turned out to be a couple of kids in Cloverdale, California working with another young adult in Israel to direct the intrusions, purposely, by routing through another country to make it look like it's coming from that country.

Now what's the moral of that story? For me, the wake-up call was the fact that cyber intrusions were so complex, [due to] the difficulty of attribution and investigating international incidents like SOLAR SUNRISE. The moral of the story for US policymakers was that our military computers and networks had been intruded upon on a large scale and depth...[There was] potential for our military computers and networks to be used to launch cyber attacks against another country, while the intruders masqueraded as the US.

The same potential applied for other nations as well, given their existing or upcoming cyber power. So the question we pondered at the time was: will our adversaries have the same restraint that we displayed during SOLAR SUNRISE, when they start seeing attacks against their infrastructure [apparently] coming from us? [Before that,] we really weren't thinking about the optics of computer intrusions launched from the continental US that may ratchet up, escalate, and have this possibility.

We also have a lot of tactical wins when it comes to getting the international community to work on addressing cyber crime. When I see where we were in August of 1998, we were having so much more success between government agencies. I saw the private sector working better than ever together. I saw the government and the private sector working better than ever together. I saw more arrests. So tactically, I think you could show a really good chart on how well we've improved.

Strategically, though, I don't think we're winning against the entirety of the problem, because of the growing use and dependence on the Internet for social interactions. We're doing better tactically, but the broader cyber threat is out-pacing our capabilities.

Yesterday's Problems Today: Militarization (2003 to 2012)

More Organizational Changes … and More and More and More

Since 2003, the cyber defense community had grown at a rapid pace. The military and Intelligence Community already had strong roles in the previous stages. After 2003, this trend intensified, during a period of increasing militarization of cyber conflict at the expense of civilian agencies and the private sector—a process which ironically started with the creation of the Department of Homeland Security.

Created in response to the stovepiping of domestic security agencies and functions highlighted by the 9/11 attacks, DHS was responsible for the national cyber security mandate and brought together many existing organizations under a unified structure, including the NIPC, CIAO, and the DoD's National Communication System. Though helped by strong national policy in Homeland Security Presidential Directive 7 (HSPD-7) and the National Strategy to Secure Cyberspace (both published by the White House in 2003), Chabinsky noted that DHS failed to achieve an early leadership role on cyber issues, or even the level of information sharing practiced by NIPC. Stating, "we had senior level management at the time [at NIPC], not only from the FBI and DOJ, but also the CIA and NSA. The Secret Service was there, Transportation -everyone was there. The irony was that the Homeland Security Act actually ended up getting rid of the NIPC. We lost our collaboration and ended up with another agency."[1]

THE NATIONAL STRATEGY TO
SECURE
CYBERSPACE
FEBRUARY 2003

Figure 5: The White House cyber strategy of 2003

Even though protection from terrorism was the main ostensible mission of DHS, there was then—and remains today—little direct use of disruptive cyber attacks by terrorist groups. While they rely heavily on cyber for recruiting, communications, and fundraising, only a few "cyber terrorists" stand out, including "Irhabi007" (arrested by the British in 2006) and Ibrahim Samudra (executed by the Indonesian authorities in 2008 for participation in the Bali terrorist bombings).[2] Both were involved in credit card fraud and other low-level hacking.

DHS helped coordinate important improvements across the critical infrastructure sectors and within government. Some were important but mundane, such as backing National Cybersecurity Awareness Month in 2006 (after this had been started two years earlier by a non-profit group). Other initiatives were more substantive, including the launch of

---

1   Chabinsky "Lessons from Our Cyber Past: The First Cyber Cops."
2   For more details, see Denning, "Terror's Web: How the Internet Is Transforming Terrorism."

the EINSTEIN intrusion detection network to protect Federal systems, and important documents like the National Infrastructure Protection Plan and National Cyber Incident Response Plan. Other departments sometimes played key roles: the Treasury helped set up two committees, representing the finance sector (FSSCC) and financial regulators (FBIIC), to help steer cybersecurity and infrastructure protection, and also to provide oversight for the more operationally oriented information sharing center, the FS-ISAC.[3]

DHS took the lead in this period in working with international partners, though of course the DoD and Intelligence Communities were probably better resourced and had very active programs, especially for sharing information between the traditional "Five Eyes" partners of the United Kingdom, Canada, Australia, New Zealand, and the United States. The DOJ also played a role, especially when the US ratified the Budapest Convention on Cybercrime in 2006, aligning cyber legislation amongst its (mainly European) signatories.

Ultimately, DHS fell behind with so many responsibilities and few resources. The DoD and the Intelligence Community stepped forward to offer their own capabilities.

The DoD decided to improve their focus on offensive and defensive cyber capabilities by splitting the two missions from the existing Joint Task Force for Computer Network Operations. While it was first thought that combining both missions in JTF-CNO would be the most effective, the commander realized that the offensive side was "probably 30 percent of my mission, and it was taking up 70 percent of my time, because it was so sensitive and classified. Every time I turned around, somebody wanted to give me another polygraph to read me onto a program."[4]

The offense mission was transferred first in 2003 to a new Network Attack Support Staff, co-located with the National Security Agency (NSA), but under the operational control of US Strategic Command (USSTRATCOM).[5] Later in 2004, USSTRATCOM built on this further with the Joint Functional Component Command—Network Warfare (JFCC-NW), which was under the actual command of the Director of NSA. NSA got this offensive mission for several reasons, not least because of the depth of their expertise in cyber issues, but also due to their unique "accesses" into foreign cyber systems. NSA was also helped because its Director has regular access to the White House as a senior intelligence official, a privilege not normally extended to generals that ran military networks.[6]

When the offensive mission went to the NSA, the JTF-CND took on the network

---

3   "National Cybersecurity Awareness Month."; Experience of the author, who was Vice Chair of the FS-ISAC during this period.
4   Bryan, "Lessons from Our Cyber Past: The First Military Cyber Units."
5   Madden, "The Cyber Joint Task Forces: A Legacy of Excellence." See Part 4 of this book for an edited version of this paper.
6   Interview with Lt. Gen. (USAF Ret.) Harry Raduege, Director of DISA during the split, 24 April 2012.

operations mission—to run and maintain, as well as to defend the networks—and became the Joint Task Force for Global Network Operations (JTF-GNO) in 2004. In creating the new JTF, Secretary of Defense Donald Rumsfeld significantly clarified its directive to authorities: "Defense agencies will align their global network operations and network defense capabilities to provide USSTRATCOM visibility and insight … Military departments and defense agencies will respond to USSTRATCOM's orders and directions."[7] Since the JFCC-NW was commanded by the Director of NSA, the JTF-GNO was to be commanded by the director of the Defense Information Systems Agency—another three-star general, rather than the two-star deputy who had commanded the JTF-GNO's predecessors—because the "defense commander can't be outranked, frankly, at the end of the day, by the attack commander."[8]

To some degree, these new organizations were a response to the nation's state of war following the 9/11 attacks and to the subsequent invasions of Afghanistan and Iraq. As Major General Dave Bryan, commander of the JTF-CNO and later GNO expressed it, "So our support of combatant commands—it went from spending most of our time talking to the services or wrestling with the services over networks, to actually getting geared up with the combatant commands for a nation at war. And that really changed the dynamics for us."[9]

Figure 6: Memo from Secretary of Defens.e Rumsfeld creating JTF-GNO, 2004

This wartime role gave particular emphasis to the offensive mission. A plan with an aim similar to the reported proposal for a 1998 covert action against Milošević was hatched "to

I can tell you that as a commander in Afghanistan in the year 2010, I was able to use my cyber operations against my adversary with great impact. I was able to get inside his nets, infect his command-and-control, and in fact defend myself against his almost constant incursions to get inside my wire, to affect my operations.

Lt. Gen. Richard Mills, USMC in 2012

freeze billions of dollars in the bank accounts of Saddam Hussein and cripple his government's financial system." However, it was reportedly canceled by the administration of President Bush, which "worried that the effects would not be limited to Iraq but would instead create worldwide financial havoc, spreading across the Middle East to Europe and perhaps to the United States."[10] This concern means that, at

---

7   Rumsfeld, "Memorandum on Assignment and Delegation of Authority to Director."
8   Bryan, "Lessons from Our Cyber Past: The First Military Cyber Units."
9   Bryan, "Lessons from Our Cyber Past: The First Military Cyber Units."
10   Markoff and Shanker, "Halted '03 Iraq Plan Illustrates U.S. Fear of Cyberwar Risk."

least with President Bush, the Secretary of the Treasury had an effective veto over cyber operations affecting the finance sector, according to former cyber czar, Richard Clarke.[11]

Cyber offensive missions may or may not have been useful on the actual battlefield. The *New York Times* reported that the military ruled out using cyber capabilities in 2011 against Libya "to sever military communications links and prevent the early-warning radars from gathering information and relaying it to missile batteries aiming at NATO warplanes."[12] There may be more to the story at the tactical level, however. A senior US Marine Corps officer, Lieutenant General Richard Mills, told a conference audience in 2012 that when commanding forces in Afghanistan, he used offensive cyber capabilities against the Taliban (though given their limited use of computers, this may have been more about mobile phones).[13]

As the commander of the first cyber joint task force had noted, with offensive cyber capabilities, "You sometimes see the failures. But you rarely see the successes." One of the operations that appeared to be a notable failure was a 2008 takedown by JFCC-NW of a website used to recruit violent extremists to fight US troops, and perhaps to execute operations, in the Middle East.[14] Though the site was established by the CIA and Saudi intelligence to collect information on these same extremists, the *Washington Post* reported that it became too successful, and so the military decided it had to be dismantled. This apparently did not go as planned, and "the dismantling of the CIA-Saudi site inadvertently disrupted more than 300 servers in Saudi Arabia, Germany, and Texas."[15]

Until the revelation that the Stuxnet virus was also a US covert operation (see below), this was the biggest revelation about US offensive cyber capabilities.

Since the 1990's, the US government had balanced its cyber defense efforts between two priorities: protecting their own government systems, and protecting the American people and economy. In January 2008, the Bush administration decided to tackle the easier of those two priorities first, launching the President's Comprehensive National Cyber Initiative or CNCI to protect government systems. CNCI, of which only a summary has been declassified, focused almost entirely on cyber security within the US government to help stem the loss of terabytes of information, much of it being sensitive information on military technologies. The Initiative had a massive budget, which has been estimated to have been as high as $40 billion over five years. That funding was largely funneled into the military and Intelligence Community.[16]

---

11   Clarke and Knake, Cyber War, 202-203.
12   Shmitt and Shanker, "U.S. Debated Cyberwarfare in Attack Plan on Libya."
13   Comments by Lt. Gen. Richard P. Mills, USMC, to AFCEA TechNet Land Forces East Conference, 15 August 2012.
14   Nakashima, "Dismantling of Saudi-CIA Web site illustrates need for clearer cyberwar policies."
15   *Ibid.*
16   Chabrow, "White House Partly Lifts CNCI Secrecy."

Wake-Up Calls Yet Again

CNCI was driven by the realization that the MOONLIGHT MAZE espionage intrusions were just the beginning.

In 2007, a unique cyber incident caught the attention of military analysts. In September, warplanes from Israel violated Syrian airspace unchallenged, to destroy a target widely believed to be a nuclear facility under construction (apparently with North Korean assistance). Several months after the attack, it emerged that the Israelis might have combined traditional electronic warfare with cyber intrusions to scramble the Syrian systems. If true, this would be the first major example of the integration of cyber effects on the battlefield.[17]

More directly worrying to the US and foreign governments were a new set of computer espionage cases into government agencies, the Defense Industrial Base, think tanks, other US companies, as well as foreign companies and governments. Over time, Chinese espionage grew even more serious, though the US government only admitted this openly starting around 2011.

China, it appeared, was a major espionage adversary, intent on stealing enough information to boost itself to the world's first rank of world powers.[18] News reports emerged by 2005 of a classified intrusion set that came to be known as TITAN RAIN. This set of intrusions began at least several years earlier, and involved thefts of information from the DoD, the DHS, State, Energy, and defense contractors.[19] Additional reports emerged about other intrusions: GhostNet (involving espionage into the offices of the Dalai Lama), Shadows in the Cloud (hacking into embassies and other targets of interest to China, such as

Chinese actors are the world's most active and persistent perpetrators of economic espionage. US private sector firms and cybersecurity specialists have reported an onslaught of computer network intrusions that have originated in China, but the [Intelligence Community] cannot confirm who was responsible.

Russia's intelligence services are conducting a range of activities to collect economic information and technology from US targets.

Report from US Counterintelligence Executive, 2011

national Olympic committees), Night Dragon (targeting global energy companies), and thefts of information on the F-35 Joint Strike Fighter from Lockheed Martin, BAE Systems, and several other companies.[20] Some of these intrusions seem to be have been

---

17   See Carrol, "Israel's Cyber Shot at Syria"; and Clarke and Knake, Cyber War, Chapter 1.
18   For more on Chinese espionage, please read the case study edited by Adam Segal in Part 4.
19   Graham, "Hackers Attack Via Chinese Web Sites."
20   For a readable summary, see Gross, "Enter the Cyber Dragon." Also, the Center for Strategic and International Studies

enabled by information stolen during a sophisticated intrusion into the company RSA, which makes security gear used by companies and governments around the world to protect themselves. The NSA director (and commander of Cyber Command) uncharacteristically blamed China directly and publicly for this cyber heist.[21]

Cyber Wake-Up Calls
(so far):
1. Morris Worm
2. ELIGIBLE RECEIVER and SOLAR SUNRISE
3. MOONLIGHT MAZE
4. **Chinese Espionage**
5. Estonia and Georgia
6. BUCKSHOT YANKEE
7. Stuxnet

In other nations, Mitsubishi of Japan and Rio Tinto of Australia suffered intrusions linked to China. This is just a partial list, as espionage touched companies in countless fields and countries, including the governments of Canada, France, Germany, and the United Kingdom. Harkening back to language first used in the Computers at Risk report of 1991, Chinese espionage was usually known by the euphemism advanced persistent threat (APT), as the government was too cautious to directly say China was the perpetrator.[22]

All this forced national leaders and corporate executives to take notice and ask how they should respond to the intrusions. While the US government debated internally (not least to find a way to make Chinese espionage unacceptable, while leaving room for America's own spy operations), others took a more direct approach. In August 2007, "German chancellor Angela Merkel reportedly confronted Chinese premier Wen Jiabao after hackers from his country gained access to the computers in her office, as well as those in the German foreign, economic, and research ministries."[23] After a China-linked intrusion, Google went further, with a very public announcement, attracting significant media attention and allowing a crowd-sourced investigation.[24]

Russia, though certainly engaged in cyber espionage like China, is better known for ignoring, encouraging or coordinating its patriotic hackers to conduct cyber conflicts against Estonia in 2007, and Georgia a year later. Each conflict took the nation offline over the course of days and weeks. Like the earlier Chinese incidents of 1999 and 2001, these attacks were serious enough to get the attention of national leaders—but not serious enough to demand any meaningful response.

---

has an excellent chronology of these and other cyber incidents since 2006, available at http://csis.org/publication/cyber-events-2006.

21　Leyden, "NSA Top Spook Blames China for RSA Hack."
22　It appears that then Colonel Gregory Rattray of the US Air Force coined the term APT while organizing the AF response to espionage incidents.
23　Gross, "Enter the Cyber Dragon."
24　Zetter, "Google Hack Attack Was Ultra Sophisticated, New Details Show."

The attacks against Estonia were in response to the movement by that government of a statue of a Soviet soldier, used as a local rallying point for Russian nationalists.[25] Lasting from 27 April to 18 May of 2007, these denial-of-service attacks disrupted government websites, online financial transactions, and national connectivity.[26]

Though it has been portrayed as a cyber disaster, it was actually a tactical and strategic defeat for the ethnic Russian attackers: the Estonian government was not coerced, and the statue was still moved; the attacks did not result in long-term damage or a negative impact to the economy; and in the longer term, Estonia has become a rallying cry for cyber defenders and a stain on the Russian reputation. The statue was still moved, and the incident gave Estonia so much publicity that it helped to guarantee NATO's cyber center would be located there.

Cyber Wake-Up Calls
(so far):
1. Morris Worm
2. ELIGIBLE RECEIVER and SOLAR SUNRISE
3. MOONLIGHT MAZE
4. Chinese Espionage
5. **Estonia and Georgia**
6. BUCKSHOT YANKEE
7. Stuxnet

The incident may have even had a positive overall impact on the Estonian economy and reputation. For example, *The Economist* magazine stated in 2012 that "Estonia is renowned for cybersecurity."[27] In the meantime, the incident caused yet another stain on Russia's international reputation, and warned NATO and other nations what to expect.

Another mistaken notion is that the attacks were a complete surprise. Actually, by watching Russian nationalists and hackers organizing online, the Estonian technical defenders had several weeks of advance notice for these impending attacks.[28] The surprise resulted from these warnings apparently not reaching the highest NATO headquarters in Brussels or other national leaders, who were thus strategically surprised. The subsequent attacks were not massive or technically interesting. They were important *solely* for their international political nature. According to Bill Woodcock, one of the NSP-SEC representatives who helped mitigate the attack,

> *This was not a very large attack relative to the Internet as a whole … Attacks of this size happened about every three weeks at that time. The very largest attacks were about ten times larger than this and would have been about once a year at that time.*[29]

Incidentally, denial of service attacks today are far worse—about "tenfold larger now

---

25   For more on the Estonian cyber conflict, please read the case study by Andreas Schmidt in Part 4.
26   See Tikk, et al., "International Cyber Incidents," 33.
27   "Paper Cuts."
28   Priisalu, "Building a Secure Cyber Future: Attacks on Estonia, Five Years On."
29   Woodcock, "Building a Secure Cyber Future: Attacks on Estonia, Five Years On."

than then," and an attack the size of the one directed against Estonia "wouldn't make the threshold of response," based only on the size of the attack.[30]

As with attacks before and since, neither the Estonian nor allied governments had many direct levers to mitigate the impact of the conflict. Because they owned the networks, the private sector was relied upon for the heaviest lifting. For example, representatives of the non-state group NSP-SEC, comprised of technical experts of various network provider companies, were sent to Estonia to help coordinate defensive efforts with international telecommunication carriers and "mitigated [these] down to fairly low levels over the course of the next seven hours," illustrating the impact of a determined defense.[31] As one of the representatives sent to Estonia expressed the group's role, "If something needs to be taken down, it needs to be taken down, and there isn't time for argument… that's understood up front [within NSP-SEC] … You can argue about it later." By and large, in the absence of a government response, this kind of ability is required and displayed everyday by private sector defenders, though they tend to lack the endurance of government defensive organizations, which possess healthier budgets and more people.

Because of the attack's ties to Russia, the incident became a clear wake-up call, as NATO was not warned ahead of time and was not prepared to consider the implications of such an external attack on a member of the alliance. The Estonian president, Toomas Ilves, made the incident a cause célèbre, ensuring that Estonia, NATO, and other nations were aware of the implications of cyber conflict, the next example of which was not long in coming.

The cyber conflict over Georgia coincided with the Russian invasion of the country in August 2008 over a dispute regarding the breakaway region of South Ossetia. Prior to the invasion, Georgia suffered a ramp-up of attacks which soon intensified. These were originally downplayed by the Georgian president,[32] but this complacency ended quickly.[33]

The assault developed to include large-scale botnet DDoS attacks, targeting the government, news media, and other sites, along with intrusions and defacements. At their height, the Georgian leadership was essentially unable to use the Internet to communicate internally or get the word to the international community about what was happening.[34] Several of the Georgian government sites worryingly were transferred to the United States, apparently without the knowledge of the US government, possibly making those ISPs legitimate targets during a time of war and arguably violating US neutrality.[35] The governments of Poland and Estonia both took even more active roles, authorizing their

---

30 *Ibid.*
31 *Ibid.*
32 Nazario, Interview by Andreas Hagen.
33 For more on the Georgian cyber conflict, please read the case study by Andreas Hagen in Part 4.
34 "Overview of the US-CCU of the Cyber Campaign against Georgia in August of 2008."
35 Korns and Kastenberg, Georgia's Cyber Left Hook, 66-67.

own official servers to disseminate Georgian information.[36]

The ferocity of the cyber assault, its targeting, and its apparent coordination with Russian military forces led some analysts to conclude that Russia was not just ignoring or encouraging its patriotic hackers (as they did in the conflict with Estonia), but were actively coordinating or directing their actions.[37] In addition, the attackers were aided by Russian organized criminals, who made no effort to conceal their involvement.[38]

Part of the story that has emerged about the Estonian and Georgian attacks is that both countries were knocked off the network by the Russian attacks. This is only partly true. While both countries were essentially unreachable from outside, there is a key difference. Estonia had their own Internet Exchange Point (IXP), a key point of Internet geography in which different network carriers interconnect, allowing them to disconnect themselves from receiving outside traffic.[39] While they could not communicate externally, this ability cut off the brunt of the Russian attack, so that they could still communicate domestically through their IXP. Georgia, lacking an IXP, could not avail themselves of the same tactic; there was simply no way to isolate themselves from international attacks without cutting off domestic traffic as well.[40] Estonia made a deliberate sacrifice to jump offline; Georgia was pushed.

The US government had yet another wake-up call in 2008, though the military did not discuss it until later. In a much publicized article in the journal *Foreign Affairs*, then Deputy Secretary of Defense William Lynn went public about Operation BUCKSHOT YANKEE, an incident involving unclassified and classified networks of the war-fighting Central Command. This is the fifth incident deemed a "wake-up call" for the United States government.[41] According to Lynn, the

Cyber Wake-Up Calls
(so far):
1. Morris Worm
2. ELIGIBLE RECEIVER and SOLAR SUNRISE
3. MOONLIGHT MAZE
4. Chinese Espionage
5. Estonia and Georgia
6. **BUCKSHOT YANKEE**
7. Stuxnet

intrusion began when a malicious software called Agent.btz, contained on a flash drive "placed there by a foreign intelligence agency," spread through the command, sending information back to its controllers.[42] As with the MOONLIGHT MAZE incident of

---

36   Clarke and Knake, Cyber War, 19; and Tikk, et al., "Cyber Attacks Against Georgia," 14.
37   US-CCU, 6.
38   *Ibid.*, 4.
39   Discussion with Bill Woodcock, 15 July 2012 at conference on "The Future of Sovereignty in Cyberspace."
40   *Ibid.*
41   For more on BUCKSHOT YANKEE, please read the case study by Karl Grindal in Part 4.
42   Lynn, "Defending a New Domain."

1999, reports emerged that Russia's intelligence services were behind the intrusion.[43] But unlike previous espionage attempts, the BUCKSHOT YANKEE intruders were able to gain access to unclassified military networks, the SIPRNET network—used for passing operational commands, and the JWICS network—used for the highest classification intelligence material.[44]

BUCKSHOT YANKEE stands out from most cyber conflicts, because the US military was the primary target and was at the center of the response. Typically this is not the case, as with the Conficker worm from 2008 and other incidents extending well into 2009. Microsoft led the coordination to defeat this worm, even offering a $250,000 reward for information leading to the arrest of those responsible.[45] The private-sector's Conficker Working Group was called by one participant "the first truly successful effort they were involved in after a decade of attempts to collaborate." Unfortunately, it appears the US government was not part of this collaboration, as the "group as a whole saw little participation from the government. One person put it as 'zero involvement, zero activity, zero knowledge'," according to the official lessons learned.[46]

Though the Conficker incident may not be a true cyber conflict, because the motives appear not to be related to national security and the impact was limited, Conficker created an "all-hands-on-deck" crisis for defenders worldwide. As it infected at least five million computers, and had no clear criminal purpose, it was feared that "Conficker could be turned into a powerful offensive weapon for performing concerted information warfare attacks that could disrupt not just countries, but the Internet itself."[47]

The US Muscular (Military) Response

A tremendous string of separate wake-up calls came one after the other: Chinese espionage, BUCKSHOT YANKEE, Estonia, and Georgia, in addition to Conficker. These incidents spurred the creation of the Comprehensive National Cyber Initiative. They also drove changes within the DoD, most notably the continued centralization and elevation of cyber capabilities into US Cyber Command (USCYBERCOM).

USCYBERCOM is a larger version of organizations that existed before, and a bigger and better answer to DepSecDef Hamre's 1998 question "Who is in charge?" The US joint military cyber command started in 1998 with JTF-CND, which had a staff of twenty-four people commanded by a two-star general. This quickly expanded into JTF-CNO,

---

43   Barnes, "Pentagon computer networks attacked."

44   "Operation Buckshot Yankee: Key players and networks infected."

45   Mills, "Microsoft offers $250,000 reward for Conficker arrest."

46   "Conficker Working Group: Lessons Learned," 34.

47   Markoff, "Computer Experts Unite to Hunt Worm."

with perhaps 150 people responsible for both offensive and defensive missions.[48] The next iteration split the offense (JFCC-NW) and defense (JTF-GNO) missions under two different three-star generals.[49] Each was then folded into, and became the core of, Cyber Command, which had a four-star commander and perhaps 800 people, not counting subordinate commands.[50] This entire evolution took place in nine years and is not yet over. There is serious talk of turning USCYBERCOM into a stand-alone combatant command. It is currently a unified command subordinate to US Strategic Command.

The military services have also developed their own cyber commands, which all report to USCYBERCOM. These had originally been much smaller organizations, tied to the information warfare "centers" and "activities" created between 1993 and 1995. But they became service "cyber components" to the cyber joint task forces and subsequently Cyber Command. Now, these cyber components are equivalent to the largest operational commands within each service, and are usually commanded by a two-star general. They include:

- 24th Air Force;

- Army Cyber Command - 2nd Army;

- Navy Fleet Cyber Command - 10th Fleet; and

- Marine Forces Cyber Command.

Without doubt, Cyber Command has been the biggest organizational change for cyber issues in the United States since the creation of the DHS, though the DHS also continued to improve their cyber team. Important changes at the DHS combined the cyber and communications divisions and focused operational support in the National Cybersecurity and Communications Integration Center (NCCIC). Other departments did not stand still. The Department of Justice (along with the FBI and the Secret Service) made important arrests and prosecutions, such as Operation Phish Phry, which netted 100 people in 2009, and also issued important manuals, including one on prosecuting cyber crimes, to ensure that prosecutors and investigators understand the latest laws and interpretations.[51]

America's diplomats elevated and centralized their own cyber offices under a Coordinator for Cyber Issues, who reports directly to the Secretary of State. Within the Pentagon itself, a new Deputy Assistant Secretary of Defense was named to focus entirely on

---

48   Bryan, "Lessons from Our Cyber Past: The First Military Cyber Units."

49   From "JTF History," an unofficial JTF chronology kept by alumni of the cyber Joint Task Forces. This document captures the evolution of the units, including the approximate number of people at specific milestones. These are facts which are often otherwise difficult to find.

50   Smithson, "Cyber Command combines offense, defense in planning."

51   "Operation Phish Phry." Also see Eltringham, "Prosecuting Cyber Crimes."

national security cyber policy, separately from the more technical work done by the Chief Information Officer. The White House coordinated all of this work through a new cyber office in the National Security Council.

The first crisis for these organizations was not a pure "cyber conflict" like Estonia or Chinese espionage, but the release by the activist organization Wikileaks of hundreds of thousands of stolen classified or sensitive documents. The US government reeled as they tried to determine the damage caused by the revelations. Though it did not start out as a cyber conflict, the nature of the crisis changed over time, as the Anonymous online collective began a series of increasingly damaging attacks in support of Wikileaks, of Internet freedoms, and to redress any number of perceived slights. These attacks often completely dismantled their adversary's networks and personal lives, and damaged the companies Stratfor and HB Gary Federal.[52]

The Rise of National Cyber Attacks

The most important and dangerous trend today is the apparent willingness of nations to engage in covert campaigns against each other, usually more quietly and even more closely than Russia's muscular swatting of Estonia and Georgia. Perhaps the first incident in this trend occured in 2009, when websites in the United States and South Korea were subjected to a large-scale botnet DDoS attack on the 4th of July. Little to date has been released on this event, but it was both then and now widely attributed to North Korea.[53]

Cyber Wake-Up Calls
(so far):

1. Morris Worm
2. ELIGIBLE RECEIVER and SOLAR SUNRISE
3. MOONLIGHT MAZE
4. Chinese Espionage
5. Estonia and Georgia
6. BUCKSHOT YANKEE
7. **Stuxnet**

However, it was the Stuxnet virus in mid-2010 that instilled the deepest alarm to cybersecurity professionals.[54] Not only was Stuxnet "capable of infecting a fully-patched Windows 7 system"; it was also the first malware to target industrial control systems, in this case, those manufactured by Siemens.[55] This was news in itself, but more was to come. The security researcher who discovered its significance, Ralph Langer, felt it was a "guided missile" designed to destroy industrial gear that used Siemens, but only in a very specific

---

52 For an excellent overview of the Anonymous attacks and mindset, read Norton, "How Anonymous Picks Targets, Launches Attacks, and Takes Powerful Organizations Down."
53 See Clarke and Knake, Cyber War, Chapter 1 for an extended discussion.
54 For more on Stuxnet, please read the case study by Chris Morton in Part 4.
55 Krebs, "Experts Warn of New Windows Shortcut Flaw"; and "Malware Affecting Siemens WinCC and PCS7 Products (Stuxnet)."

configuration—one that Langer felt had to be the Iranian nuclear program.[56] He further felt that attribution was simple. It must have been Israel and the United States. But this was a claim taken with caution, since attribution has a reputation for being incredibly difficult.[57]

However, just as with the Russian-encouraged patriotic attacks on Estonia and Georgia, and Chinese espionage, it turns out that attribution was again easier than expected. On 1 June 2012, David Sanger of The *New York Times* revealed that according to White House sources, Stuxnet was part of a covert operation by the United States and Israel, codenamed OLYMPIC GAMES, to disrupt Iranian nuclear ambitions.[58] Though related malware, known as Flame, was apparently not part of OLYMPIC GAMES, later reporting by Ellen Nakashima of the *Washington Post* revealed that it also was a joint operation of the US and Israeli governments.[59] As with the earlier cyber covert actions against Milošević and Hussein, the information did not stay secret for long, opening up a fresh debate on the use of American offensive cyber operations.

By the end of 2012, it appeared that Iran had counter-attacked twice, as payback for sanctions and the Stuxnet, Flame, and other digital attacks it had suffered. These attacks, including the Shamoon malware against oil and gas facilities in the Middle East, and a large and aggressive DDoS against US bank websites, left US defense officials "increasingly convinced" that Iran was supporting hackers' attacks.[60]

Shamoon erased data from 30,000 computers, "replacing all of it with an image of a burning American flag" and forcing the replacement of all the hard drives.[61] Secretary of Defense Panetta called

Legal Difficulties of Offensive Cyber Operations

Because offensive cyber operations have such uncertain effects and can easily affect non-combatant civilian targets, they have been beset with legal complications since the earliest days. Air Force 4-star general John Jumper said it best in 1999:

"I picture myself around [a] targeting table where you have the fighter pilot, the bomber pilot, the special operations people, and the information warriors. As you go down the target list, each one takes a turn raising his or her hand saying, 'I can take that target.' [But the info warrior] says, "I can take the target, but first I have to go back to Washington and get a finding."

This is still largely the case, as military cyber operations (at least for Western armies) must still comply with International Humanitarian Law (aka, the Geneva and Hague Conventions and Laws of Armed Conflict). The best example is a strict set of criteria for fielding cyber capabilities published by Air Force lawyers.

And since cyberspace is unlikely to get more predictable, do not expect cyber weapons to be fired as easily as kinetic weapons. Like StuxNet, they will remain individually tailored and selectively used for some time to come.

56 Clayton, "Stuxnet malware is 'weapon' out to destroy ... Iran's Bushehr nuclear plant?"
57 "US and Israel were behind Stuxnet claims researcher."
58 Sanger, "Obama Order Sped Up Wave of Cyberattacks Against Iran."
59 Nakashima, et al., "U.S., Israel developed Flame computer virus to slow Iranian nuclear efforts, officials say."
60 Shanker and Sanger, "U.S. Suspects Iran Was behind a Wave of Cyberattacks."
61 Perloty, "In Cyberattack on Saudi Firm, U.S. Sees Iran Firing Back."

this attack "probably the most destructive attack that the private sector has seen to date."[62] The Financial Services Information Sharing and Analysis Center (FS-ISAC, formed in 1999 in response to President Clinton's PDD-63 directive) played the lead role in the DDoS against the finance sector.[63] These attacks were significant, making it difficult to access the banks' public webpages. But they did not cause any significant impact on their operations—not least because banks had spent tens of millions of dollars as part of their DDoS mitigation and shared extensively through the FS-ISAC.[64] A trend that started most clearly with Estonia and Georgia, that of nations attacking through proxies or through their own national security organs, appeared to have reached new levels with Stuxnet and the following Iranian attacks.

The US government had a difficult time discussing Stuxnet. On the one hand, even though they could not officially confirm or deny the reports, Stuxnet was a strong statement the US's cyber capabilities, which might deter America's adversaries. Better yet, the attack delayed the Iranian nuclear program, an important US policy goal. On the other hand, it seemed to sit outside existing US policy on cyber conflict, most recently stated in the best cyber strategy described anywhere in the world: the *International Strategy for Cyberspace* of 2011. Though this strategy was announced after the initial development of Stuxnet during the Bush administration, it was apparently being developed while that attack was ongoing. With Stuxnet, Flame, and other incidents apparently conducted as US covert actions, the strategy's claims that the United States wished a future in which "states act as responsible parties in cyberspace" fell flat.[65]

Otherwise, this new strategy was very successful. Whereas previous strategies from the US government (such as PDD-63 of 1998 and the National Strategy for a Secure Cyberspace of 2003) only focused on aspects of cybersecurity, the US government has had varying (and often competing) agendas concerning cyberspace: fighting crime, protecting freedom of expression and intellectual property, promoting innovation, preventing attacks, and enabling military operations. Because there was no overarching vision, the different government departments promoting these agendas were all too often acting at cross purposes. This often led to confusion, for example, about whether the United States primarily considers cyberspace a place for cooperation (for innovation, commerce, and free speech) or a new domain for conflict. This new International Strategy cut across all of these areas, allowing for the first time a better balance between all of these agendas, which enables smarter policy making. For example, though the strategy features important sections on cyber crime and the importance of free speech, it also includes the first declaratory strategy for

---

62   "Text of Speech by Defense U.S. Secretary Leon Panetta."
63   "US Finance Sector Warned of Cyber Attacks."
64   Interviews by the author with government and financial officials who asked to remain anonymous, October 2012.
65   "International Strategy for Cyberspace."

cyber conflict, stating that,

> *When warranted, the United States will respond to hostile acts in cyberspace as we would to any other threat to our country.*
>
> *We reserve the right to use all necessary means—diplomatic, informational, military, and economic—as appropriate and consistent with applicable international law, in order to defend our Nation, our allies, our partners, and our interests.*
>
> *In so doing, we will exhaust all options before military force whenever we can; will carefully weigh the costs and risks of action against the costs of inaction; and will act in a way that reflects our values and strengthens our legitimacy, seeking broad international support whenever possible.*[66]

As the latest in a series of national strategies, this 2011 document did the best job of uniting many aspects of cyberspace, not just cybersecurity; and it was the first to so directly address cyber conflict. But assuredly, there will be more strategies and more conflicts.

---

66   *Ibid.*, 14.

In Their Own Words: Bill Woodcock

Research Director, Packet Clearing House

Bill has been an Internet routing specialist since the late 1980s. He was one of the founders of the Packet Clearing House, which since 1994 has created and maintained much of cyberspace's critical infrastructure, Internet Exchange Points. During the 2007 attacks on Estonia, he was one of two members that deployed there from an informal security-sharing group formed between network service providers, called the NSP-SEC.

This section is adapted from an event commemorating the five-year anniversary of the cyber attacks on Estonia, held at the Atlantic Council in 2012.[67]

Cybersecurity coordination inside Estonia was done primarily by the Estonian CERT, the EE-CERT, under the direction of Hillar Aarelaid. Hillar worked in law enforcement before coming to the CERT and was well known and trusted within the Estonian government and law enforcement. Consequently, he did not have the networking security background that many of his counterparts in other countries had, who had come from ISP careers, but ultimately his law enforcement experience served the EE-CERT well, and complemented the networking expertise of his staff.

At the time of the attack in 2007, there was no one in Estonia who had yet been vetted into NSP-sec, the cyber attack mitigation coordination body. Kurtis Lindqvist, who was the Swedish government's NSP-sec rep, and I went to the EE-CERT to act as liaisons and to help the EE-CERT coordinate with CERT and Internet service providers in other countries to stem the attacks.

Thus I was in the EE-CERT watching the traffic-graphing screens as the attack started to come in and as the sensors were initially overwhelmed and the screens stopped being able to register the traffic. As the sensors were brought back online, the traffic graphs recalibrated, making the previous day's traffic look like a flat line along the bottom of the graph, compared to the vertical spike of the attack. That was all mitigated to undetectably low levels over the course of the next seven hours, between 11 pm of 27 April—the first night of the attack—and 6 am the following morning.

Mitigation relationships are reciprocal responsibilities, and when an attack needs to be shut down, it needs to be shut down immediately; there isn't time for argument. That's understood up front, so there isn't even a mechanism for arguing about it. The difficulty with these relationships is that parties outside of the circle-of-trust of those mitigation relationships haven't yet demonstrated any ability to reciprocate at the time they're attacked. They haven't demonstrated that they're

---

67   Woodcock, "Building a Secure Cyber Future: Attacks on Estonia, Five Years On."

capable of quid pro quo, and they haven't demonstrated that their forensic abilities, for instance, are adequate to correctly identify the traffic that needs to be mitigated, or to correctly attribute the source of the traffic. So that was why two of us went as liaisons to vet the process that was occurring in Estonia, and the practices and expertise of the Estonian CERT—because there's no way, in the midst of an emergency, to develop all of the necessary reciprocal mitigation relationships. Therefore, we watched, we assisted, and afterwards, when there was time, we got those relationships formalized.

Estonia's participation in NSP-sec since being vetted in after that night has been extraordinarily valuable. The EE-CERT has since been able to aid other eastern European countries in times of need, Georgia in particular. The first time is always the rough one, and after that, you have experience to guide you.

In the two weeks of lead-up to the attack, each individual Estonian network was doing what they could to estimate the impact and prepare for it. Two weeks is too little time to order new equipment or train people on new technologies, but it is enough time to make some of the necessary domestic relationships, between the banks, the government, the EE-CERT, and the ISPs.

The relationships that a CERT maintains are the keystone of its function, and they're the thing that cannot be done quickly. You have to have those relationships in advance in order to be able to call upon them when you need them. You can't establish them in the middle of an emergency, so that's what the CERT is for. It's to create and maintain an organizational instantiation of the relationships that you're going to need when you're in an emergency.

The EE-CERT was able to do outreach among the Internet service providers and get access to statistical information from the ISP network equipment, so that the CERT had, in effect a console in front of them displaying an overview of traffic coming into the country across many different Internet service providers. That was immensely valuable. That's something that is not normally possible, because the private sector doesn't generally share that level of detail, but in an emergency like this, that level of access was temporarily accorded to the CERT—and it made perfect sense to do so.

Likewise, the two weeks gave law enforcement time to work. One of the things that was spectacularly successful was that law enforcement was able to apprehend the Nashi agents who were recruiting inside Estonia and trying to drum up support for the attack among ethnic Russians in Estonia. That effort wound up being completely unsuccessful. Had it been successful, the attack would have had a very different character and outcome.

Although this was a large attack relative to Estonia, it was not a large attack relative to the Internet as a whole. Attacks of comparable size happened about once a month at that time. The *largest contemporary attacks would have one order of magnitude larger, and would have occurred about once a yeah, while the smallest attacks that anyone in mitigation circles would have paid attention to were an order of magnitude smaller and were happening two or three times a day. But relative to Estonia, it was a large attack, and its state-on-state nature meant that it got a lot of attention, particularly from governments, relative to the criminal-on-criminal conflicts that constitute the vast majority of attacks.*

In Their Own Words: Christopher Painter

Coordinator for Cyber Issues, US State Department

Chris Painter is perhaps most famous in the cyber community for his prosecution of the case against the most infamous hacker of the 1990s, Kevin Mitnick. But since then, he has become the nation's senior cyber statesman, through his service in many other jobs in government. These roles include Senior Director and Acting Cybersecurity Coordinator at the White House, and the Coordinator of Cyber Issues at the Department of State.

This section is adapted from an event with the "first cyber cops," held at the Atlantic Council in 2012.[68]

> *I'd always been interested in technology since I was in college and in law school. When I joined the US Attorney's Office out in Southern California in 1991, we didn't actually have computers. in the office. The Internet kind of existed, but the World Wide Web didn't really exist yet in its current form. However, a lot of companies used computer systems and relied on them. The same went for governments, the military, and others.*
>
> *Because I was interested in the technology, I sort of gravitated to this idea of cyber crime, which was just then getting more of a profile. I worked with Scott Charney, who was here in D.C. and had just started the computer crime – then I think it was a unit, which was part of a larger group–[it was a] small group of people who were starting to look at these issues.*
>
> *Back then, it was common practice at the US Attorney's Office to allow the rookies to have a chance to strike out into our own areas of interest, after you did the little things, like bank robberies and other things, to get yourself acclimated to how to prosecute cases. My colleagues and I started seeing these intrusions into various companies and theft of various kinds of source code. The victims included various companies–cellular phone companies and some of the other provider companies that we were seeing in the Los Angeles area in our district. And then also, the University of Southern California was being hit, and it looked like people were storing information there.*
>
> *The cyber perpetrator turned out, after a lengthy investigation, to be Kevin Mitnick who was doing this between 1992 and 1995. When we finally caught up with him, no one really wanted to work on theis case, because it were technical and [people] didn't really understand it. But from my perspective cybercrime presented some [very] interesting cases, and I wanted to do them. We also had great FBI agents in the Los Angeles Field Division, some of whom are still working in this area, including Trent Tyma and Ken McGuire and others – all of whom were really interested in following up on these cases.*

---

68 Painter, "Lessons from Our Cyber Past: The First Cyber Cops."

When we started tracking these early cases of cyber crime, the evidence started snowballing into this huge case of Mitnick. He was a fugitive from a prior Federal conviction for hacking into companies around the world. In the course of this investigation, I learned how to use Linux. I've learned how to look at all of these things. We were planning to do sting operations.

I was able to do all of these really fascinating cases and saw the change in this from a niche issue—in which a select group of people would root for the computer hackers—to when most of the public could see how serious these cyber crimes are and how they can really impact us. During Mitnick's sentencing, there was a plane circling the courthouse with a "Free Kevin" banner attached. Now, the public has actually experienced being hacked and understands the importance. They rely so much on these technologies. Understanding cyber crime is something which people can do much more than they ever did before, but [their understanding is still] certainly not enough.

Mitnick was just one of a number of cases that I really was extraordinarily lucky to be a part of due to being in the right place at the right time with the right interests. I got to do that case, [and now] I can tell stories about it for hours. This led to my involvement in working on the first stock manipulation cases involving the Internet, the first eBay case, and the big denial of service case in 2000, which was the "Mafiaboy" case. Actually, that's where Shawn Henry and I started working together.

There was a lot of concern back around Y2K but people calmed down when nothing seemed to happen. But then in February of 2000, so after the turnover, that's when we had these large-scale denial of service attacks that took down lots of different Internet companies and also media companies like CNN - either took them down, slowed them down in the case of some of the trading companies, and a major impact and also got a lot of attention - a lot of media attention, a lot of world attention.

There was a sense that this illustrates how vulnerable we are, this illustrates how vulnerable e-commerce is, this illustrates how we - we are not going to be able to ever find this person, which we did fairly quickly. It took a few months, but we found the person, and it turned out to be a 13 year-old who went by the moniker "Mafiaboy," not his real name.

That illustrates the asymmetric threat. I mean, this is a 13-year-old boy who lives in Canada. We were able to use very quick international processes and work with the Canadians to track this down. You know, and I think that was important and is a lesson that you can have all this damage, you can have this asymmetric threat and it doesn't have be a nation state.

And the same kind of debate went on - this must be a nation state; this is too sophisticated; it couldn't possibly be anything else. And it turns out to be a 13-year-old. But it did show people that we're vulnerable, and I think that idd create a lot of questions about how do you deal with these issues?

I think some of the early concerns about infrastructure attacks were inadvertent. You had these kids who reset an airport telephone switch to control the local airport. People began to think, well this could have effect on infrastructure. And that was another big development and a wake-up call as this can cause damage beyond just the theft of information. It could really cause physical damage.

Conclusion

This has been the history of cyber conflict, at least from a US perspective—a history which highlights three key lessons:

1. **Cyber conflict has changed only gradually over time; thus, historical lessons derived from past cases are still relevant today (though these are usually ignored).** Again and again, cyber history has provided lessons from the experiences of the pioneering cyber warriors and early reports. These lessons were influential in their time and remain relevant. But all too often, they have been forgotten.

2. **The probability and consequences of disruptive cyber conflicts have often been hyped, while the real impacts of cyber intrusions have been consistently under-appreciated.** There have been no known deaths or any major impact to national GDPs from any cyber attack, ever. Still, headlines continue to fret about "cyber wars," when the quiet conflict of cyber espionage regularly commands the attention of the highest elected leaders.

3. **The more strategically significant the cyber conflict, the more similar it is to conflicts on the land, in the air, and on the sea – with one critical exception.** Cyber conflicts have generally not occurred at the "speed of light," and it is usually obvious who the adversaries are. But governments rarely play a central role in mitigating them.

Based on these lessons, it is worthwhile to ask what will come next. The cyber conflicts in this history were very mild compared to other, physical conflicts. No one has yet been killed, and only Stuxnet had a truly destructive payload. But this is unlikely to remain the case. Instead, it is likely that cyber conflicts will become more destructive. As Smart Grid and other technologies interlink the Internet with real infrastructure—made of concrete and steel, not silicon—the consequences of attacks will be far worse, especially from more covert nation-state conflicts.

There is also likely to be an increasing private-sector role in cyber conflicts. Not only will non-state groups like Anonymous, organized crime, and patriotic hackers grow in capability, but companies will likely decide they need to start taking actions to defend themselves. On the defensive, non-state groups will continue to work, often behind the scenes, to respond to major incidents and conflicts. As expressed by cyber expert Bill Woodcock, cyberspace expands exponentially, far faster than governments are likely to cope, even with more budget and expanded responsibilities and authorities. Only non-state groups can expand quickly enough to bear the burden.[1]

One of the emerging trends during the past several years has been for states to take an increasingly vigorous and obvious role in cyber attacks. Expect more disruptive attacks by states, a trend started in 2007, when the Russians used proxies against Estonia and Georgia. Such large-scale disruptions have been uncommon since, but the underlying pool of outraged Chinese and Russian patriotic hackers (not to mention Indian, Pakistani, Israeli, and Palestinian hackers) hints at brewing opportunities for bruising conflicts.

Lately there has been a further trend, which suggests that there will be more covert disruptive conflicts between governments, as each nation realizes its own advantages in disrupting adversaries online. Each government may be separately justified, but given the other trends, this collective effect is worrying. The United States and Israel took the most public steps relating to this concern with Stuxnet, used against Iran. And it seems Iran countered, possibly through proxies, against the US financial sector in late 2012.

Looking Ahead

1. Cyber conflicts will become more destructive
2. Increasing private-sector role in cyber conflicts
3. More disruptive attacks by states
4. More covert cyber conflicts by states
5. More US offensive cyber operations

Likely, this trend will continue, so that future years will see more conflicts with nations encouraging, directing, and conducting disruptive attacks.

Most specifically, it seems likely there will be more US offensive operations in cyberspace, as there are at least four separate lines of thought that are encouraging a move in that direction. Some argue that a "passive" defense is not enough, so a more "active" defense is required; this could involve shooting back under "stringent rules" to "act outside the confines of military-related computer networks to try to combat cyberattacks on private computers."[2] Even though "active defense" is nearly as poorly defined today as when it was first floated in 1998, this is an argument made not only by the US military but also by the private sector. Some private voices are already clamoring for the opportunity to disrupt the operations of those stealing information from them. A separate but related argument is best made by General James Cartwright, that "we've got to talk about our offensive capabilities and train for them; to make them credible so that people know there's a penalty" for espionage against the United States.[3] Here, offensive operations are meant to be seen as a general threat, rather than a specific technical response to a particular incident.

---

1   Woodcock, comments made at a panel discussion, in a conference at the Centre for Excellence in National Security on "The Future of Sovereignty in Cyberspace: Developing a Global Architecture for Cybersecurity," Singapore, 18 July 2012.
2   Nakashima, "Pentagon proposes more robust role for its cyber-specialists."
3   Shalal-Esa, "Ex-U.S. general urges frank talk on cyber weapons."

A third argument is that, just as they do for other nations, offensive cyber capabilities offer attractive, low cost options for traditional national security missions. These include intelligence gathering (note that because of cyber, the present is known in American circles as the "golden age of espionage") and covert or unattributable actions, such as Stuxnet or the Saudi-CIA Islamic extremist website. The last argument is that while US troops continue to face traditional adversaries on the battlefields of Afghanistan, Iraq, or wherever may be next, commanders will want to use every arrow in their quiver, including cyber capabilities.

It is, of course, still not clear whether offensive operations will achieve any of these positive benefits. It is something of a leap of faith to assume that more US attacks will result in a more stable Internet. The revelation that the United States was behind Stuxnet may not ultimately be in America's long-term best interests, as other nations may not be convinced that the United States wants a peaceful cyberspace. Even if other nations were conducting similar operations, the United States got caught, and very publicly.

Policymakers are beginning to understand the importance of cyber security and the implications of conflict in cyberspace. This understanding benefits from the context provided by history—and the seven wake-up calls so far—which is rich with important lessons for newer generations of cyber defenders and policymakers, especially since these lessons contradict most of the myths perpetuated in the popular imagination, by Hollywood, and in the media. The sooner we begin teaching these lessons from the past, the sooner we can hopefully break out of the cycle of repeated "wake-up" calls and start creating new trends for the future.

Part 2: Realization

In first phase of cyber conflict history, early cyber conflicts caught the attention of policymakers and the technical elite. Whereas Part 1 of this book discussed the broad strokes, the authors of the case studies in Part 2 fill in the details regarding two of the most interesting early cases.

We will hear the story of the Cuckoo's Egg, which is about West German hackers who stole and sold secrets to the KGB, directly from Cliff Stoll. He was the astronomer-turned-system-administrator who uncovered the case in 1986, and who invented many of the best cyber defense tactics while investigating this case. His article, "Stalking the Wily Hacker" (included here with permission and edited for length only) appeared in *Communications of the Association for Computing Machinery* in 1988, just after the event. Cliff's first-person account is just as compelling today as it was then.

Today, cyber espionage is considered the worst scourge. Cliff gives us a twenty-five year perspective on what it means and how to fight it. The actions he took and decisions he faced would be familiar to most cyber defenders facing their own cyber espionage incidents today. How do I know I have an intruder? Should we try to lock them out or trap them, to figure out who they are? What can we tell about the intruder, based on when they operate, what they look for, and where they look for it? Will government help or get in the way? How do we tell others that they've also been hacked, and how do we convince others to cooperate with us? Cliff faced all of these challenges, and his actions echo in responses still seen today.

The other early, major cyber incident is the Morris Worm, which disabled a significant portion of the nascent Internet. As with the story of the Cuckoo's Egg, again we will hear the story from a contemporaneous source, a report from the US General Accounting Office (as GAO was known in 1989). Describing the early Internet—and its lack of a central managing authority, this GAO report covers all the highlights of the virus and its effects. Many of the technical details (and the bureaucratic framing of the original report) are edited out. The Morris Worm was the first real wake-up call that caused the US national and technical elite to realize they must take important steps in response. This led to the first Internet security response organization, the Computer Emergency Response Team.

These two case studies provide a broad overview of cyber conflict when it was young. Many of the key contemporaneous findings are just as relevant today as they were twenty years ago, such as the GAO stating that the Morris Worm was so damaging because "some sites paid insufficient attention to security issues, such as proper password usage, and lacked system management expertise for dealing with technical issues." In 1988, Cliff Stoll said something that still sounds familiar: "Espionage over networks can be cost-efficient, offer nearly immediate results, and target specific locations ... insulated from risks of internationally embarrassing incidents."

Cuckoo's Egg: Stalking the Wily Hacker

Clifford Stoll[1]

In August 1986 a persistent computer intruder attacked the Lawrence Berkeley Laboratory (LBL). Instead of trying to keep the intruder out, we took the novel approach of allowing him access while we printed out his activities and traced him to his source. This trace back was harder than we expected, requiring nearly a year of work and the cooperation of many organizations. This article tells the story of the break-ins and the trace, and sums up what we learned.

We approached the problem as a short, scientific exercise in discovery, intending to determine who was breaking into our system and document the exploited weaknesses. It became apparent, however, that rather than innocuously playing around, the intruder was using our computer as a hub to reach many others. His main interest was in computers operated by the military and by defense contractors. Targets and keywords suggested that he was attempting espionage by remotely entering sensitive computers and stealing data; at least he exhibited an unusual interest in a few, specifically military topics. Although most attacked computers were at military and defense contractor sites, some were at universities and research organizations. Over the next 10 months, we watched this individual attack about 450 computers and successfully enter more than thirty.

Lawrence Berkeley National Labs is a research institute with few military contracts and no classified research (unlike our sister laboratory, Lawrence Livermore National Laboratory, which has several classified projects). Our computing environment is typical of a university: widely distributed, heterogeneous, and fairly open. Despite this lack of classified computing, LBL's management decided to take the intrusion seriously and devoted considerable resources to it in hopes of gaining understanding and a solution.

The intruder conjured up no new methods for breaking operating systems; rather he repeatedly applied techniques documented elsewhere. Whenever possible, he used known security holes and subtle bugs in different operating systems. Yet it is a mistake to assume that one operating system is more secure than another. Most of these break-ins were possible because the intruder exploited common blunders by vendors, users, and system managers.

---

1   An astronomer–turned–sleuth in the mid 1980s, Cliff Stoll while working at Lawrence Berkeley National Labs helped track down hackers working for the KGB. Stoll wrote the book The Cuckoo's Egg, which narrates the events described in this case study with more detail and character. Stoll received his Ph.D. in Astronomy from the University of Arizona in 1980. He continues to remain active in the field of Astronomy, but is now also an advocate for education and has a small business, selling Klein Bottles. This paper is a version, edited for length, of his contemporaneous article, "Stalking the Wily Hacker" (reprinted here with permission), from Communications of the Association for Computing Machinery in 1988.

Throughout these intrusions we kept our study a closely held secret. We deliberately remained open to attacks, despite knowing the intruder held system-manager privileges on our computers. Except for alerting management at threatened installations, we communicated with only a few trusted sites, knowing this intruder often read network messages and even accessed computers at several computer security companies. We remained in close touch with law-enforcement officials, who maintained a parallel investigation. As this article goes to press [in 1988], the United States' FBI and its German equivalent, the Bundeskriminalamt (BKA), continue their investigations. Certain details are therefore necessarily omitted from this article.

Recently, a spate of publicity surrounded computer break-ins around the world.[2] With a few notable exceptions,[3] most were incompletely reported anecdotes[4] or were little more than rumors. For lack of substantive documentation, system designers and managers have not addressed important problems in securing computers. Some efforts to tighten security on common systems may even be misdirected [in 1988]. We hope that lessons learned from our research will help in the design and management of more secure systems.

The intruder conjured up no new methods for breaking into operating systems; rather he repeatedly applied techniques documented elsewhere.

Detection

We first suspected a break-in when one of LBL's computers reported an accounting error. A new account had been created without a corresponding billing address. Our locally developed accounting program could not balance its books, since someone had incorrectly added the account. Soon afterwards, a message from the National Computer Security Center arrived, reporting that someone from our laboratory had attempted to break into one of their computers through a MILNET connection.

We removed the errant account, but the problem remained. We detected someone, acting as a system manager, attempting to modify accounting records. Realizing that there was an intruder in the system, we installed line printers and recorders on all incoming ports and printed out the traffic. Within a few days, the intruder showed up again. We captured all of his keystrokes on a printer and saw how he used a subtle bug in the Gnu-Emacs text editor[5] to obtain system-manager privileges. At first, we suspected that the culprit was a student prankster at the nearby University of California. We decided to catch him in the

2   Markoff, "Computer Sleuths Hunt a Brilliant Hacker"; Omond, "Important notice [on widespread attacks into VMS systems]"; and Schmemann, "West German Computer Hobbyists Rummaged NASA's Files."
3   McDonald, "Computer Security Blunders," 35–46; and Brian Reid, "Reflections on Some Recent Widespread Computer Break-Ins," 103–105.
4   Carpenter, "Malicious Hackers," 4.
5   Stallman, Gnu-Emacs Text Editor Source Code.

act, if possible. Accordingly, whenever the intruder was present, we began tracing the line, printing out all of his activity in real time.

Organizing Our Efforts

Early on, we began keeping a detailed logbook, summarizing the intruder's traffic, the traces, our suspicions, and interactions with law-enforcement people. Like a laboratory notebook, our logbook reflected both confusion and progress, but eventually pointed the way to the solution. Months later, when we reviewed old logbook notes, buried clues to the intruder's origin rose to the surface.

Having decided to keep our efforts invisible to the intruder, we needed to hide our records and eliminate our electronic messages about his activity. Although we did not know the source of our problems, we trusted our own staff and wished to inform whoever needed to know. We held meetings to reduce rumors, since our work would be lost if word leaked out. Knowing the sensitivity of this matter, our staff kept it out of digital networks, bulletin boards, and especially, electronic mail. Since the intruder searched our electronic mail, we exchanged messages about security by telephone. Several false electronic-mail messages made the intruder feel more secure when he illicitly read them.

Since the intruder searched our electronic mail, we exchanged messages about security by telephone. Several false electronic-mail messages made the intruder feel more secure when he illicitly read them.

Monitors, Alarms, and Traffic Analysis

We needed alarms to instantly notify us when the intruder entered our system. At first, not knowing from which port our system was being hit, we set printers on all lines leading to the attacked computer. After finding that the intruder entered via X.25 ports, we recorded bidirectional traffic through that set of lines. These printouts proved essential to our understanding of events; we had records of his every keystroke, giving his targets, keywords, chosen passwords, and methodologies. The recording was complete in that virtually all of these sessions were captured, either by printer or on the floppy disk of a nearby computer. These monitors also uncovered several other attempted intrusions unrelated to those of the individual we were following.

What is a Hacker?

The term hacker has acquired many meanings, including a creative programmer, one who illicitly breaks into computers, a novice golfer who digs up the course, a taxicab driver, and a ditch-digger. Confusion between the first two interpretations results in the perception that one need be brilliant or creative to break into computers. This may not be true.

Indeed, the person we followed was patient and plodding but hardly showed creative brilliance in discovering new security flaws.

To point out the ambiguity of the word hacker, this paper uses the term in the title, yet avoids it in the text.

Alternatives for describing someone who breaks into computers are: the English word "Cracker," and the Dutch term "Computerredebrenk"[6] (literally, computer peace disturber). The author's choices include "varmint," "reprobate," "swine," and several unprintable words. The alarms themselves were crude, yet effective in protecting our system as well as others under attack. We knew of researchers developing expert systems that watch for abnormal activity,[7] but we found our methods simpler, cheaper, and perhaps more reliable. Backing up these alarms, a computer loosely coupled into our LAN periodically looked at every process. Since we knew from the printouts which accounts had been compromised, we only had to watch for the use of these stolen accounts.

We chose to place alarms on the incoming lines, where serial line analyzers and personal computers watched all traffic for the use of stolen account names. If triggered, a sequence of events culminated in a modem calling the operator's pocket pager. The operator watched the intruder on the monitors. If the intruder began to delete files or damage a system, he could be immediately disconnected, or the command could be disabled. When he appeared to be entering sensitive computers or downloading sensitive files, line noise, which appeared to be network glitches, could be inserted into the communications link. In general, we contacted the system managers of the attacked computers, though in some cases the FBI or military authorities made the contact. Occasionally, they cooperated by leaving their systems open. More often, they immediately disabled the intruder or denied him access. From the intruder's viewpoint, almost everyone except LBL detected his activity. In reality, almost nobody except LBL detected him.

Throughout this time, the printouts showed his interests, techniques, successes, and failures. Initially, we were interested in how the intruder obtained system-manager privileges. Within a few weeks, we noticed him exploring our network connections—using ARPANET and MILNET quite handily, but frequently needing help with lesser known networks. Later, the monitors showed him leapfrogging through our computers, connecting to several military bases in the United States and abroad. Eventually, we observed him attacking many sites over the Internet, guessing passwords and account names. By studying the printouts, we developed an understanding of what the intruder was looking for. We also compared activity on different dates in order to watch him learn a new system and inferred sites he entered through pathways we could not monitor. We

6   Hartman, "The Privacy Dilemma."
7   Boing and Kirchberg, "L'Utilisation de Systemes Experts dans l'Audit Informatique."

observed the intruder's familiarity with various operating systems and became familiar with his programming style. Buried in this chatter were clues to the intruder's location and persona, but we needed to temper inferences based on traffic analysis. Only a complete trace back would identify the culprit.

Trace Backs

Tracing the activity was challenging, because the intruder crossed many networks, seldom connected for more than a few minutes at a time, and might be active at any time. We needed fast trace backs on several systems, so we automated much of the process. Within seconds of a connection, our alarms notified system managers and network control centers automatically, using pocket pagers dialed by a local modem.[8] Simultaneously, technicians started tracing the networks.[9]

Since the intruder's traffic arrived from an X.25 port, it could have come from anywhere in the world. We initially traced it to a nearby dial-up Tymnet port, in Oakland, California. With a court order and the telephone company's cooperation, we then traced the dial-up calls to a dial-out modem belonging to a defense contractor in McLean, Virginia. In essence, their LAN allowed any user to dial out from their modem pool and even provided a last-number-redial capability for those who did not know access codes for remote systems.

Analyzing the defense contractor's long-distance telephone records allowed us to determine the extent of these activities. By cross-correlating them with audit trails at other sites, we determined additional dates, times, and targets. A histogram of the times when the intruder was active showed most activity occurring at around noon, Pacific time. These records also demonstrated the attacks had started many months before detection at LBL.

Curiously, the defense contractor's telephone bills listed hundreds of short telephone calls all around the United States. The intruder had collected lists of modem telephone numbers and then called them over these modems. Once connected, he attempted to log in using common account names and passwords. These attempts were usually directed at military bases; several had detected intruders coming in over telephone lines, but had not bothered to trace them. When we alerted the defense contractor officials to their problem, they tightened access to their outbound modems, and there were no more short connections.

After losing access to the defense contractor's modems, the still undeterred intruder connected to us over different links. Through the outstanding efforts of Tymnet, the full X.25 calling

---

8 Stoll, "What do you feed a Trojan Horse?"

9 The monitoring and trace-back efforts mixed frustration with excitement if the computer was hit at 4:00 a.m., by 4:02 the author was out of bed, logged into several computers, and talking with the FBI. Telephone technicians in Germany, as well as network controllers in Europe and stateside, awaited the signal, so we had to eliminate false alarms, yet spread the word immediately. Several intimate evenings were spoiled by the intruder setting off the alarms, and a Halloween party was delayed while unwinding a particularly convoluted connection.

addresses were obtained within seconds of an attack. These addresses pointed to sources in Germany: universities in Bremen and Karlsruhe, and a public dial-up modem in another German city. When the intruder attacked the university in Bremen, he acquired system-manager privileges, disabled accounting, and used their X.25 links to connect around the world. Upon recognizing this problem, the university traced the connections to the other German city. This, in turn, spurred more tracing efforts, coordinating LBL, Tymnet, the university, and the German Bundespost.

Figure 7: Simplified Connectivity and Partial List of Penetrated Sites

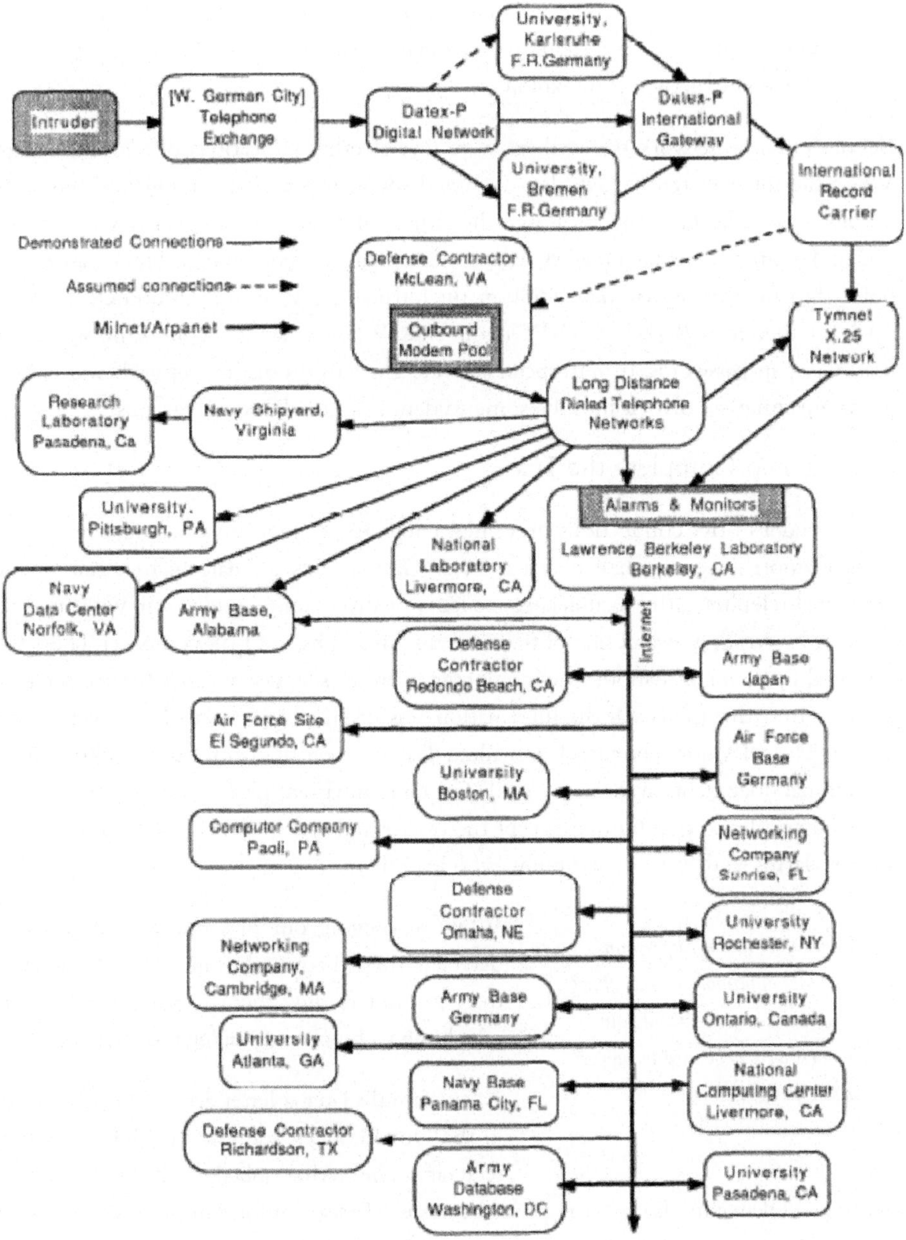

Most connections were purposely convoluted. Figure 7 summarizes the main pathways that were traced, but the intruder used other connections as well. The rich connectivity and redundant circuits demonstrate the intruder's attempts to cover his tracks, or at least his search for new networks to exploit.

Besides physical network traces, there were several other indications of a foreign origin. When the intruder transferred files, we timed round-trip packet acknowledgments over the network links. Later, we measured the empirical delay times to a variety of different sites and estimated average network delay times as a function of distance. This measurement pointed to an overseas origin. In addition, the intruder knew his way around UNIX, using AT&T rather than Berkeley UNIX commands. When stealing accounts, he sometimes used German passwords. In retrospect, all were clues to his origin, yet each was baffling given our mind-set that "it must be some student from the Berkeley campus."

A Stinger to Complete the Trace

The intruder's brief connections prevented telephone technicians from determining his location more precisely than to a particular German city. To narrow the search to an individual telephone, the technicians needed a relatively long connection. We baited the intruder by creating several files of fictitious text in an obscure LBL computer. These files appeared to be memos about how computers were to support research for the Strategic Defense Initiative (SDI). All the information was invented and steeped in governmental jargon. The files also contained a mailing list and several form letters talking about "additional documents available by mail" from a nonexistent LBL secretary. We protected these bogus files so that no one except the owner and system manager could read them, and set alarms so that we would know who read them.

We baited the intruder by creating several files of fictitious text . . . [that] appeared to be memos about how computers were to be used to support research for SDI.

While scavenging our files one day, the intruder detected these bogus files and then spent more than an hour reading them. During that time the telephone technicians completed the trace.

A few months later, a letter arrived from someone in the United States, addressed to the nonexistent secretary. The writer asked to be added to the fictitious SDI mailing list. As it requested certain "classified information," the letter alone suggested espionage. Moreover, realizing that the information had traveled from someone in Germany to a contact in the United States, we concluded we were witnessing attempted espionage. Other than cheap novels, we have no experience in this arena and so left this part of the investigation to the FBI.

The Break-In Methods and Exploited Weaknesses

Printouts of the intruder's activity showed that he used our computers as a way station; although he could become system manager here, he usually used LBL as a path to connect to the ARPANET/MILNET. In addition, we watched him use several other networks, including the Magnetic Fusion Energy network, the High Energy Physics network, and several LANs at invaded sites.

While connected to MILNET, this intruder attempted to enter about 450 computers, trying to log in using common account names like root, guest, system, or field. He also tried default and common passwords, and often found valid account names by querying each system for currently logged-in accounts, using who or finger. Although this type of attack is the most primitive, it was dismayingly successful: In about 5 percent of the machines attempted, default account names and passwords permitted access, sometimes giving system-manager privileges as well.

When he succeeded in logging into a system, he used standard methods to leverage his privileges to become system manager. Taking advantage of well-publicized problems in several operating systems, he was often able to obtain root or system-manager privileges.

In about 5 percent of the machines attempted, default account names and passwords permitted access, sometimes giving system-manager privileges as well.

In any case, he searched file structures for keywords like "nuclear," "sdi," "kh-11," and "norad." After exhaustively searching for such information, he scanned for plain-text passwords into other systems. This proved remarkably effective: Users often leave passwords in files.[10] Electronic mail describing log-in sequences with account names and passwords is commonly saved at foreign nodes, allowing a file browser to obtain access into a distant system. In this manner, he was able to obtain both passwords and access mechanisms into a Cray supercomputer.

This intruder was impressively persistent and patient. For example, on one obscure gateway computer, he created an account with system privileges that remained untouched until six months later, when he began using it to enter other networked computers. On another occasion, he created several programs that gave him system-manager privileges and hid them in system software libraries. Returning almost a year later, he used the programs to become system-manager, even though the original operating-system hole had been patched in the meantime.

This intruder cracked encrypted passwords. The UNIX operating system stores passwords in

---

10   Beals, et al., "Improving VMS security: Overlooked ways to tighten your system."

publicly readable but encrypted form.[11] We observed him downloading encrypted password files from compromised systems into his own computer. Within a week he reconnected to the same computers, logging into new accounts with correct passwords. The passwords he guessed were English words, common names, or place-names. We realized that he was decrypting password files on his local computer by successively encrypting dictionary words and comparing the results to password file entries. By noting the length of time and the decrypted passwords, we could estimate the size of his dictionary and his computer's speed.

Intruder's Intentions

Was the intruder actually spying? With thousands of military computers attached, MILNET might seem inviting to spies. After all, espionage over networks can be cost-efficient, offer nearly immediate results, and target specific locations. Further, it would seem to be insulated from risks of internationally embarrassing incidents. Certainly Western countries are at much greater risk than nations without well developed computer infrastructures.

Some may argue that it is ludicrous to hunt for classified information over MILNET, because there is none. Regulations[12] prohibit classified computers from access via MILNET, and any data stored in MILNET systems must be unclassified. On the other hand, since these computers are not regularly checked, it

Was the intruder actually spying? With thousands of military computers attached, MILNET might seem inviting . . . espionage over networks can be cost-efficient, offer nearly immediate results, and target specific locations.

is possible that some classified information resides on them. At least some data stored in these computers can be considered sensitive,[13] especially when aggregated. Printouts of this intruder's activities seem to confirm this. Despite his efforts, he uncovered little information not already in the public domain, but that included abstracts of US Army plans for nuclear, biological, and chemical warfare for central Europe. These abstracts were not classified, nor was their database.

The intruder was extraordinarily careful to watch for anyone watching him. He always checked who was logged onto a system, and if a system manager was on, he quickly disconnected. He regularly scanned electronic mail for any hints that he had been discovered, looking for mention of his activities or stolen login names (often, by scanning for those words). He often changed his connection pathways and used a variety of different network user identifiers. Although arrogant from his successes, he was nevertheless careful to cover

---

11   Morris and Thompson, "Password security: A Case History," sec 2.
12   Latham, "Guidance and Program Direction Applicable to the Defense Data Network," 1–51.
13   An attempt by the National Security Council to classify certain public databases as "sensitive" met with widespread objections.

his tracks.

Judging by the intruder's habits and knowledge, he is an experienced programmer who understands system administration. But he is by no means a "brilliant wizard," as might be popularly imagined. We did not see him plant viruses[14] or modify kernel code, nor did he find all existing security weaknesses in our system.

Did the intruder cause damage? To his credit, he tried not to erase files and killed only a few processes. If we only count measurable losses and time as damage, he was fairly benign.[15] He only wasted systems staff time, computing resources, and network connection time, and racked up long-distance telephone tolls and international network charges. His liability under California law,[16] for the costs of the computing and network time, and of tracking him, is over $100,000.

But this is a narrow view of the damage. If we include intangible losses, the harm he caused was serious and deliberate. At the least, he was trespassing, invading others' property and privacy; at worst, he was conducting espionage. He broke into dozens of computers, extracted confidential information, read personal mail, and modified system software. He risked injuring a medical patient and violated the trust of our network community. Money and time can be paid back. Once trust is broken, the open, cooperative character of our networks may be lost forever.

Aftermath: Picking Up The Pieces

Following successful traces, the FBI assured us the intruder would not try to enter our system again. We began picking up the pieces and tightening our system. The only way to guarantee a clean system was to rebuild all systems from source code, change all passwords overnight, and recertify each user. With over a thousand users and dozens of computers, this was impractical, especially since we strive to supply our users with uninterrupted computing services. On the other hand, simply patching known holes or instituting a quick fix for stolen passwords[17] was not enough.

We settled on instituting password expiration, deleting all expired accounts, eliminating shared accounts, continued monitoring of incoming traffic, setting alarms in certain places, and educating our users. Where necessary, system utilities were compared to fresh versions, and new utilities built. We changed network-access passwords and educated users about choosing non-dictionary passwords. We did not institute random password assignment, having seen that users often store such passwords in command files or write them on their

---

14   Israel, "Computer viruses: Myth or reality."
15   Stevens, "Who goes there? A Dialog of Questions and Answers about Benign hacking."
16   California State Legislature, "Computer crime law," California Penal Code S. 502, 1986 (revised 1987).
17   D. Morshedian, "How to fight password pirates."

terminals.

To further test the security of our system, we hired a summer student to probe it.[18] He discovered several elusive, site-specific security holes, as well as demonstrated more general problems, such as file scavenging. We would like to imagine that intruder problems have ended for us; sadly, they have not, forcing us to continue our watch.

Remaining Open to an Intruder

Should we have remained open? A reasonable response to the detection of this attack might have been to disable the security hole and change all passwords. This would presumably have insulated us from the intruder and prevented him from using our computers to attack other Internet sites. By remaining open, were we not a party to his attacks elsewhere, possibly incurring legal responsibility for damage?

Had we closed up shop, we would not have risked embarrassment and could have resumed our usual activities. Closing up and keeping silent might have reduced adverse publicity, but would have done nothing to counter the serious problem of suspicious (and possibly malicious) offenders. Although many view the trace back and prosecution of intruders as a community service to network neighbors, this view is not universal.[19]

Finally, had we closed up, how could we have been certain that we had eliminated the intruder? With hundreds of networked computers at LBL, it is nearly impossible to change all passwords on all computers. Perhaps he had planted subtle bugs or logic bombs in places we did not know about. Eliminating him from LBL would hardly have cut his access to MILNET. And, by disabling his access into our system, we would close our eyes to his activities: we could neither monitor him nor trace his connections in real-time. Tracing, catching, and prosecuting intruders are, unfortunately, necessary to discourage these vandals.

Legal Responses

Several laws explicitly prohibit unauthorized entry into computers. Few states lack specific codes, but occasionally the crimes are too broadly defined to permit conviction.[20] Federal and California laws have tight criminal statutes covering such entries, even if no damage is done.[21] In addition, civil law permits recovery not only of damages, but also of the costs to trace the culprit.[22] In practice, we found police agencies relatively uninterested until monetary loss could be quantified and damages demonstrated. Although not a substitute

---

18   Beals, et al., "Improving VMS Security."
19   Lehmann, "Computer Break-Ins," 584–585.
20   Slind-Flor, "Hackers Access Tough New Penalties."
21   U.S. Congress, The Federal Computer Crime Statute. 18 U.S.C.A. 1030, 1986.
22   California State Legislature, "Computer Crime Law," California Penal Code S. 502, 1986 (revised 1987).

for competent legal advice, spending several days in law libraries researching both the statutes and precedents set in case law proved helpful.

[N]o one agency had clear responsibility to solve it. A common response was, "That's an interesting problem, but it's not our bailiwick."

Since this case was international in scope, it was necessary to work closely with law-enforcement organizations in California, the FBI in the United States, and the BKA in Germany. Cooperation between system managers, communications technicians, and network operators was excellent. It proved more difficult to get bureaucratic organizations to communicate with one another as effectively. With many organizational boundaries crossed, including state, national, commercial, university, and military, there was confusion as to responsibility: Most organizations recognized the seriousness of these break-ins, yet no one agency had clear responsibility to solve it. A common response was, "That's an interesting problem, but it's not our bailiwick."

Overcoming this bureaucratic indifference was a continual problem. Our laboratory notebook proved useful in motivating organizations: When individuals saw the extent of the break-ins, they were able to explain them to their colleagues and take action. In addition, new criminal laws were enacted that more tightly defined what constituted a prosecutable offense.[23] As these new laws took effect, the FBI became much more interested in this case, finding statutory grounds for prosecution.

---

23   California State Legislature, "Computer Crime Law," California Penal Code S. 502, 1986 (revised 1987); Slind-Flor,
      "Hackers"; and U.S. Congress, The Federal Computer Crime Statute. 18 U.S.C.A. 1030, 1986.

Figure 8: Simplified Communications Paths between Organizations

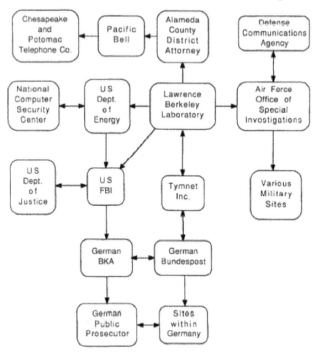

The FBI and BKA maintained active investigations. Some subjects have been apprehended but, as yet, the author does not know the extent to which they have been prosecuted. With recent laws and more skilled personnel, we can expect faster and more effective responses from law-enforcement agencies.

Errors and Problems

In retrospect, we can point to many errors we made before and during these intrusions. Like other academic organizations, we had given little thought to securing our system, believing that standard vendor provisions were sufficient, because nobody would be interested in us. Our scientists' research is entirely in the public domain, and many felt that security measures would only hinder their productivity. With increased connectivity, we had not examined our networks for crosslinks where an intruder might hide. These problems were exacerbated on our UNIX systems, which are used almost exclusively for mail and text processing, rather than for heavy computation.

Lessons

As a case study, this investigation demonstrates several well-known points that lead to some knotty questions. Throughout this, we are reminded that security is a human problem that cannot be solved by technical solutions alone.[24]

The almost obsessive persistence of serious penetrators is astonishing. Once networked, our computers can be accessed via a tangle of connections from places we had never thought of. An intruder, limited only by patience, can attack from a variety of directions, searching for the weakest entry point. How can we analyze our systems' vulnerability in this environment? Who is responsible for network security? The network builder? The managers of the end nodes? The network users? The security weaknesses of both systems and networks, particularly the needless vulnerability due to sloppy systems management and administration, result in a surprising success rate for unsophisticated attacks. How are we to educate our users, system managers, and administrators?

Social, ethical, and legal problems abound. How do we measure the harm done by these penetrators? By files deleted or by time wasted? By information copied? If no files

The almost obsessive persistence of serious penetrators is astonishing.

are corrupted, but information is copied, what damage has been done? What constitutes unreasonable behavior on a network? Attempting to illicitly log-in to a foreign computer? Inquiring who is currently logged in there? Exporting a file mistakenly made world readable? Exploiting an unpatched hole in another's system?

Closing out an intruder upon discovery may be a premature reflex. Determining the extent of the damage and cooperating with investigations argue for leaving the system open. How do we balance the possible benefits of tracking an intruder against the risks of damage or embarrassment? Our technique of catching an intruder by providing bait and then watching what got nibbled is little more than catching flies with honey. It can be easily extended to determine intruders' interests by presenting them with a variety of possible subjects (games, financial data, academic gossip, military news). Setting up alarmed files is straightforward, so this mechanism offers a method to both detect and classify intruders. It should not be used indiscriminately, however.

Passwords are at the heart of computer security. Requirements for a quality password are few: Passwords must be non-guessable, not in a dictionary, changed every few months, and easily remembered. User-generated passwords usually fail to meet the first three criteria, and machine-generated passwords fail the last. Several compromises exist: forcing

24   Whitten, "Computer (in)security: Infiltrating Open Systems."

"pass phrases" or any password that contains a special character. Despite such obvious rules, we (and the intruder) found that poor-quality passwords pervaded our networked communities. How can we make users choose good passwords? Should we?

Vendors usually distribute weakly protected systems software, relying on the installer to enable protections and disable default accounts. Installers often do not care, and system managers inherit these weak systems. Today, the majority of computer users are naive; they install systems the way the manufacturer suggests or simply unpackage systems without checking. Vendors distribute systems with default accounts and backdoor entryways left over from software development. Since many customers buy computers based on capability rather than security, vendors seldom distribute secure software. It is easy to write procedures that warn of obvious insecurities, yet vendors are not supplying them. Capable, aware system managers with plenty of time do not need these tools—the tools are for novices who are likely to overlook obvious holes. When vendors do not see security as a selling point, how can we encourage them to distribute more secure systems?

Patches to operating-system security holes are poorly publicized and spottily distributed. This seems to be due to the paranoia surrounding these discoveries, the thousands of systems without systems administrators, and the lack of channels to spread the news. Also, many security problems are specific to a single version of an operating system or require systems experience to understand. Together, these promote ignorance of problems, threats, and solutions. We need a central clearinghouse to receive reports of problems, analyze their importance, and disseminate trustworthy solutions. How can we inform people wearing white hats about security problems, while preventing evil people from learning or exploiting these holes? Perhaps zero-knowledge proofs[25] can play a part in this.

Operating systems can record unsuccessful log-ins. Of the hundreds of attempted log-ins into computers attached to the Internet, only five sites (or 1–2 percent) contacted us when they detected an attempted break-in. Clearly, system managers are not watching for intruders, who might appear as neighbors, trying to sneak into their computers. Our networks are like communities or neighborhoods, and so we are surprised when we find unneighborly behavior.

Does security interfere with operational demands? Some security measures, like random passwords or strict isolation, are indeed onerous and can be self-defeating. But many measures neither interfere with legitimate users nor reduce the system's capabilities. For example, expiring unused accounts hurts no one and is likely to free up disk space. Well thought out management techniques and effective security measures do not bother ordinary users, yet they shut out or detect intruders.

---

25   Landau, "Zero Knowledge and the Department of Defense," 5–12.

Conclusions and Comments

Perhaps no computer or network can be totally secure. This study suggests that any operating system will be insecure when obvious security rules are ignored. From the intruder's widespread success, it appears that users, managers, and vendors routinely fail to use sound security practices. These problems are not limited to our site or the few dozen systems that we saw penetrated, but are networkwide. Lax system management makes patching utility software or tightening a few systems ineffective.

We found this intruder to be a competent, patient programmer, experienced in several operating systems. Alas, some system managers violate their positions of trust and confidence. Our worldwide community of digital networks requires a sense of responsibility. Unfortunately, this is missing in some technically competent people.

Some speak of a "hacker ethic" of not changing data.[26] It is astounding that intruders blithely tamper with someone else's operating system, never thinking they may destroy months of work by systems people, or may cause unforeseen system instabilities or crashes. Sadly, few realize the delicacy of the systems they fool with or the amount of systems staff time they waste.

The foreign origin of the source, the military computers entered, and the keywords searched suggest international espionage. This author does not speculate as to whether this actually was espionage, but does not doubt that someone took the opportunity to try.

Break-ins from abroad seem to be increasing. Probably this individual's intrusions are different from others only in that his efforts were noticed, monitored, and documented. LBL has detected other attempted intrusions from several European countries, as well as from the Orient. Individuals in Germany[27] have claimed responsibility for breaking into foreign computers. Such braggadocio may impress an unenlightened public; it has a different effect on administrators trying to maintain and expand networks. Indeed, funding agencies have already eliminated some international links due to these concerns. Break-ins ultimately destroy the network connectivity they exploit. If this is the object of such groups as the German Chaos Club, Data Travelers, Network Rangers, or various contributors to *2600 Magazine*, it reflects the self-destructive folly of their apparent cleverness.

Tracking down espionage attempts over the digital networks may be the most dramatic aspect of this work. But it is more useful to realize that analytic research methods can be fruitfully applied to problems as bizarre as computer break-ins. It seems that everyone wants to hear stories about someone else's troubles, but few are willing to write about

---

26   Schmemann, "West German Computer Hobbyists."
27   *Ibid.*

their own. We hope that in publishing this report we will encourage sound administrative practices. Vandals and other criminals reading this article will find a way to rationalize breaking into computers. This article cannot teach these people ethics; we can only hope to reach those who are unaware of these miscreants.

An enterprising programmer can enter many computers, just as a capable burglar can break into many homes. It is an understandable response to lock the door, sever connections, and put up elaborate barriers. Perhaps this is necessary, but it saddens the author, who would rather see future networks and computer communities built on honesty and trust.

Morris Worm: Virus Highlights
Need For Improved Internet Management

A Report by United States General Accounting Office, June 1989[1]

In November 1988, a computer program caused thousands of computers on the Internet–a multi-network system connecting over 60,000 computers nationwide and overseas–to shut down. This program, commonly referred to as a computer virus or worm, entered computers and continuously recopied itself, consuming resources and hampering network operations.

Within hours after it appeared, the Internet virus had reportedly infected up to 6,000 computers, clogging systems and disrupting most of the nation's major research centers. After two days, the virus was eradicated at most sites, largely through the efforts of university computer experts. After the virus incident, multiple intrusions (not involving viruses) at several Internet sites added to concerns about security.

These incidents highlighted such vulnerabilities as (1) the lack of an Internet focal point for addressing security issues, (2) security weaknesses at some sites, and (3) problems in developing, distributing, and installing software fixes (i.e., repairs to software flaws).

While agencies and groups have taken actions to enhance security, GAO believes that many of the vulnerabilities highlighted by the virus and subsequent intrusions require actions transcending those of individual agencies or groups. For this reason, GAO believes a security focal point should be established to fill a void in the Internet's management structure.

Several factors may hinder successful prosecution of virus-type incidents. For example, since there is no federal statute that specifically makes such conduct a crime, other laws must be applied. In addition, the technical nature of such cases may hinder prosecution.

The Internet Evolves from an Experimental Network

The Internet began as an experimental, prototype network called ARPANET, established in 1969 by the Department of Defense's Defense Advanced Research Projects Agency (DARPA). Through ARPANET, DARPA sought to demonstrate the possibilities of computer networking based on packet-switching technology.[2] Subsequently, DARPA

---

1   This is an edited version of the GAO report, "Computer Security:Virus Highlights Need for Improved Internet Management," GAO-IMTEC-89-57, June 1989.

2   Packet switching is a technique for achieving economical and effective communication among computers on a network. It provides a way to break a message into small units, or packets, for independent transmission among host computers on a network, so that a single communication channel can be shared by many users. Once the packets reach their final destination, they are reassembled into the complete message.

sponsored several other packet-switching networks. In the 1970s, recognizing the need to link these networks, DARPA supported the development of a set of procedures and rules for addressing and routing messages across separate networks. These procedures and rules, called the "Internet protocols," provided a universal language allowing information to be routed across multiple interconnected networks.

From its inception, ARPANET served as a dual-purpose network, providing a testbed for state-of-the-art computer network research as well as network services for the research community. In the 1980s, the number of networks attached to ARPANET grew as technological advances facilitated network connections. By 1983 ARPANET had become so heavily used that Defense split off operational military traffic onto a separate system called MILNET, funded and managed by the Defense Communications Agency. Both ARPANET and MILNET are unclassified networks. Classified military and government systems are isolated and physically separated from these networks.

Building on existing Internet technology, the National Science Foundation (NSF), responsible for nurturing US science infrastructure, fostered the proliferation of additional networks. In 1985, NSF made the Internet protocols the standard for

The Internet began as an experimental, prototype network called Arpanet, established in 1969 by the Department of Defense's Defense Advanced Research Projects Agency (DARPA).

its six supercomputing centers and, in 1986, funded a backbone network—NSFNET—linking the six centers[3] NSF also supported a number of regional and local area campus networks whose network connections were facilitated through NSF funding.[4] As of September 1988, there were about 290 campus networks connected to NSFNET through about thirteen regional networks. Many of these networks also connect to ARPANET.

Other federal agencies fund research networks. The Department of Energy, the National Aeronautics and Space Administration (NASA), and the Department of Health and Human Services (HHS) operate networks on the Internet that support their missions.

This loosely organized web of interconnected networks—including ARPANET, MILNET, NSFNET, and the scores of local and regional networks that use the Internet protocols—make up

The Internet's transition from a prototype network to a large-scale multi-network has been rapid, far exceeding expectations.

---

3   A backbone network is a network to which smaller networks are attached. Arpanet and Milnet are also backbone networks.
4   Regional networks include partial-statewide networks (e.g., Bay Area Regional Research Network in northern California), statewide networks (e.g., New York State Educational Research Network), and multi-state networks (e.g., Southern Universities Research Association Network).

the Internet. The Internet supports a vast, multidisciplinary community of researchers, including not only computer scientists but physicists, electrical engineers, mathematicians, medical researchers, chemists, and astronomers.

Researchers use the Internet for a variety of functions; electronic mail, which provides a way of sending person-to-person messages almost instantaneously, is the most frequent use. Using electronic mail, researchers separated by thousands of miles can collaborate on projects, sharing results and comments daily. Other uses of the Internet include file transfers and remote access to computer data banks and supercomputers. Access to supercomputers has had a dramatic impact on scientific endeavors; experiments that took years to complete on an ordinary computer can take weeks on a supercomputer. Currently, use of the Internet is generally free-of-charge to individuals engaged in government-sponsored research.

The Rapid Growth of the Internet

The Internet's transition from a prototype network to a large-scale multi-network has been rapid, far exceeding expectations. In the past five years, its growth has been particularly dramatic. For example,

- in late 1983, the Internet comprised just over fifty networks; by the end of 1988, the number had grown to over 500;

- in 1982, about 200 host computers were listed in a network data-base; by early 1987, there were about 20,000, and by early 1989, the number exceeded 60,000.[5]

- an October 1988 NSF network publication estimated that there were over half-a-million Internet users.[6]

Funding for Internet operations comes from the five agencies (DARPA, NSF, Energy, NASA, and HHS) involved in operating research networks and from universities, states, and private companies involved in operating and participating in local and regional networks. A 1987 Office of Science and Technology Policy (OSTP) report estimated federal funding to be approximately $50 million. A national information technology consortium officially estimated that university investments in local and regional networks are in the hundreds of millions of dollars; state investments are estimated in the millions and rapidly growing.[7]

Management in a Decentralized Environment

Management of the Internet is decentralized, residing primarily at the host site and

---

5   Host computers, which include supercomputers, mainframes, and minicomputers, are the machines attached to the networks that run application programs.

6   NSF Network News, No. 5, NSF Network Service Center, October 1988.

7   Industry also invests in local and regional networks; however, the amount of that investment could not be determined.

individual network levels. Early in the Internet's development, responsibility for managing and securing host computers was given to the end-users—the host sites, such as college campuses and federal agencies, that owned and operated them. It was believed that the host sites were in the best position to manage and determine a level of security appropriate for their systems. Further, DARPA'S (ARPANET's developer and the major federal agency involved in the Internet in its early years) primary function was fostering research in state-of-the-art technology rather than operating and managing proven technology. At each host site, there may be many host computers.[8] These computers are controlled by systems managers who may perform a variety of security-related functions, including:

- establishing access controls to computers through passwords or other means;

- configuration management, enabling them to control the versions of the software being used and how changes to that software are made;

- software maintenance to ensure that software holes (flaws) are repaired; and

- security checks to detect and protect against unauthorized use of computers.

Operational Management at the Network Level

Each of the Internet's more than 500 networks maintains operational control over its own network, be it a backbone network (such as NSFNET), a regional network, or a local area network. Distributed responsibility allows for use of different technologies as well as different types of administration. Each network is autonomous and has its own operations center that monitors and maintains its portion of the Internet. In addition, some of the larger networks maintain information centers that provide information on network use and resources.

No Internet-Wide Management

No one agency or organization is responsible for overall management of the Internet. According to a DARPA official, decentralization provided the

No one agency or organization is responsible for overall management of the Internet.

needed flexibility for the Internet's continuing growth and evolution. Within the Internet, networks operated by government agencies serve as backbones to connect autonomous regional and local (campus) networks. Agency backbone networks were established with agency missions in mind, and their structures and modes of operation generally reflect individual agency philosophies.

---

8   For example, at the University of California, Berkeley, there are over 2,000 host computers.

In the fall of 1987, representatives of the five federal agencies–DARPA, NSF, Energy, NASA, HHS–that operate Internet research networks joined forces to form the Federal Research Internet Coordinating Committee (FRICC). The objectives of this informal group include coordinating network research and development, facilitating resource sharing, reducing operating costs, and consolidating requirements for international connections of the participating agencies. Currently, FFXC is involved in developing plans to upgrade the Internet and improve services.

The Internet Virus Spread over Networks to Vulnerable Computers

The Internet virus, which entered computers and continuously recopied itself, was not the first virus-type program to infect computers. However, it differed from earlier viruses in several key respects. First, previous viruses were almost always limited to personal computers (PCS), whereas the Internet virus infected larger systems, such as minicomputers, workstations, and mainframes. In addition, the Internet virus was the first to spread over a network automatically (i.e., without requiring other programs or user intervention to transmit it).

The networks themselves (i.e., the communications hardware and software that connect the computer systems) were not infected by the virus; rather, they served as a roadway enabling the virus to spread rapidly to vulnerable computers. In transit, the virus was indistinguishable from legitimate traffic and, thus, could not be detected until it infected a computer. The principal symptoms of the virus were degradation of system response and loss of data storage space on file systems.

How the Virus Spread

The Internet virus spread largely by exploiting security holes in systems software based on the Berkeley Software Distribution UNIX system and by taking advantage of vulnerabilities in host site security policies.[9] UNIX is the most commonly used operating system on the Internet—a University of California, Berkeley, researcher estimated that about three-quarters of the computers attached to the Internet use some version of UNIX. Machines infected were VAX and Sun-3 computer systems.[10]

The virus propagated by using four methods of attack:[11]

- **Sendmail**: A utility program that handles the complex tasks of routing and

---

9   UNIX is a registered trademark of AT&T Laboratories. Berkeley distributes its own version of UNIX, and a number of other systems manufacturers have selected the Berkeley UNIX version as the basis for their own operating systems. The virus did not attack the operating system's "kernel" that manages the system; rather, it exploited flaws in peripheral service or utility programs.

10   VAX and Sun-3 computers are built by Digital Equipment Corporation and Sun Microsystems, Inc. respectively.

11   See Appendix 1 for a more detailed account of the security flaws the virus exploited. [Excluded in A Fierce Domain]

delivering computer mail. The virus exploited a "debug" feature of sendmail that allowed a remote operator to send executable programs. After issuing the debug command, the virus gave orders to copy itself.

- **Fingerd**: A utility program that allows users to obtain public information about other users, such as a user's full name or telephone extension. A hole in the program allowed the virus to propagate to distant machines.

- **Passwords**: The virus tried different methods to guess user passwords. Once the virus gained access through a correct password, it could masquerade as a legitimate user and exercise that user's privileges to gain access to other machines.

- **Trusted hosts**: Trusted host features provide users convenient access to each other's resources. This is not a software hole; it is a convenience sometimes used on local networks where users frequently use services provided by many different computers. By using these features, the virus spread quickly within local networks once one computer had been penetrated.

A Chronology of the Virus

The onset of the virus was extremely swift. The first reports of the virus came from several sites at 9 p.m., Eastern Standard Time, on Wednesday, 2 November. An hour later, the virus was reported at multiple Internet sites, and by early morning, 3 November, the virus had infected thousands of computer systems.

Most of the nation's major research centers were affected, including Energy's Lawrence Livermore National Laboratory; NASA'S Ames Research Center; the University of California, Berkeley; the Massachusetts Institute of Technology (MIT); Carnegie Mellon University; Cornell University; Purdue University; and many others. The virus also affected sites on MILNET and several overseas sites. As noted earlier, the Internet is an open, unclassified network; the virus did not affect classified government or operational military systems.

Once the virus was detected, many sites disconnected their computers from the Internet, leaving only one or two computers running to communicate with other sites and to permit study of the virus's activity. By Thursday, 3 November, the sendmail and fingerd holes had been

Once the virus was detected, many sites disconnected their computers from the Internet, leaving only one or two computers running to communicate with other sites and to permit study of virus activity.

identified, and by late that night, the Computer Systems Research Group at the University of California, Berkeley, had posted patches on network bulletin boards to mend the holes.[12]

By Friday evening, the virus had been eliminated at most sites. At a 8 November virus post-mortem conference, hosted by the National Security Agency's National Computer Security Center (NCSC), attendees concluded that the virus had been analyzed and eradicated by computer science experts located primarily at university research institutions, with US government personnel playing a small role.

The Virus Focuses Attention on Internet Vulnerabilities

Although the virus spread swiftly over the networks to vulnerable computers, it apparently caused no permanent damage. However, the virus highlighted vulnerabilities relating to (1) the lack of a focal point for responding to Internet-wide security problems, (2) host site security weaknesses, and (3) problems in developing, distributing, and installing software fixes. A number of agencies and organizations have taken actions since the virus to address identified problems. However, we believe that these actions alone will not provide the focus needed to adequately address the Internet's security vulnerabilities.

The Impact of the Virus

The virus caused no lasting damage; its primary impact was lost processing time on infected computers and lost staff time in putting the computers back on line. The virus did not destroy or alter files, intercept private mail, reveal data or passwords, or corrupt data bases.

No official estimates have been made of how many computers the virus infected, in part because no one organization is responsible for obtaining such information. According to press accounts, about 6,000 computers were infected. This estimate was reportedly based on an MIT estimate that 10 percent of its machines had been infected, a figure then extrapolated to estimate the total number of infected machines. However, not all sites have the same proportion of vulnerable machines as MIT. A Harvard University researcher who queried users over the Internet contends that a more accurate estimate would be between 1,000 and 3,000 computers infected.

Similar problems exist in trying to estimate virus-related dollar loss. The total number of infected machines is unknown, and the amount of staff time expended on virus-related problems probably differed at each site.

Estimated losses from individual sites are generally not available. However, NASA'S Ames Research Center and Energy's Lawrence Livermore National Laboratory, two major government sites, estimated their dollar losses at $72,500 and $100,000, respectively. These

---

12   A patch is a modification made to an object program. Patches to the sendmail hole had been posted on Thursday
     morning.

losses were attributed primarily to lost staff time.

Although the virus is described as benign, because apparently no permanent damage was done, a few changes to the virus program could have resulted in widespread damage and compromise, according to computer experts. For example, these experts said that with a slightly enhanced program, the virus could have erased files on infected computers or remained undetected for weeks, surreptitiously changing information on computer files.

Vulnerabilities Highlighted by the Virus

In the aftermath of the virus, questions have been raised about how the virus spread, how it was contained, and what steps, if any, are needed to increase Internet security. These questions have been the subject of a number of post-virus meetings and reports prepared by government agencies and university researchers.

On the basis of these assessments, we believe that the virus incident revealed several vulnerabilities that made it easier for the virus to spread and more difficult for the virus to be eradicated. These vulnerabilities also came into play in later intrusions (not involving a virus) onto several Internet sites in November and December. The vulnerabilities—lack of a focal point for addressing Internet-wide security problems; security weaknesses at some host sites; and problems in developing, distributing, and installing systems software fixes—are discussed below.

Actions Taken in Response to the Virus

In response to the Internet virus, MRPA, NIST, NCSC,[13] and a number of other agencies and organizations have taken actions to enhance Internet security. These actions include developing computer security response centers, coordinating meetings, preparing publications to provide additional guidance, and publishing statements of ethics.[14]

Computer Security Response Centers Established

In the wake of the virus, many Internet users, site managers, and agency officials have

---

13 NIST is responsible for developing standards and guidelines for the security of unclassified federal computer systems. It performs these responsibilities with the National Security Agency's technical advice and assistance. The National Security Agency (of which NCSC is a part) is responsible for the security of classified information in the defense and national security areas, including that stored and processed on computers.

14 In addition, agencies are engaged in ongoing research aimed at improving network and computer security. An overview of these activities is presented in Appendix 2.[Excluded in A Fierce Domain]

voiced concerns about problems in responding to and preventing emergencies, such as the Internet virus. To address these concerns, some agencies are developing computer security response centers to establish emergency and preventative measures.

The first center, the Computer Emergency Response Team (CERT), was established by DARPA in mid-November 1988. CERT's mandate is broad; it is intended to support all of the Internet's research users. DARPA views CERT as a prototype effort for similar organizations in other computer communities. Also, CERT is seen as an evolving organization whose role, activities, and procedures will be defined as it gains experience responding to Internet security problems.

> [T]he Computer Emergency Response Team (CERT), was established by DARPA in mid-November 1988 ...it is intended to support all of the Internet's research users [and] is a prototype effort for similar organizations in other computer communities.

According to DARPA, CERT's three main functions are to provide:

- mechanisms for coordinating community response in emergencies, such as virus attacks or rumors of attacks;

- a coordination point for dealing with information about vulnerabilities and fixes; and

- a focal point for discussion of proactive security measures, coordination, and security awareness among Internet users.

CERT has no authority, although it can make recommendations. CERT officials recognize the need to establish credibility and support within the Internet community, so that its recommendations will be acted upon.

CERT's nucleus is a five-person coordination center located at the Software Engineering Institute at Carnegie Mellon University in Pennsylvania.[15] CERT has enlisted the help of over 100 computer specialists who are on call when problems arise in their areas of expertise. In addition, CERT is developing working relationships with government organizations, including NCSC, NIST, Energy, and the Federal Bureau of Investigation, and with vendor and user groups. CERT expects to rely on DARPA funding until its value is recognized by the Internet community and alternate funding mechanisms are established—probably within three to five years.

The Department of Energy began setting up a center at Lawrence Livermore National

---

15   The objective of the institute, which is a Federally Funded Research and Development Center, is to accelerate the movement of software technology into defense systems.

Laboratory in February 1989. This center is to focus on proactive preventive security and on providing rapid response to computer emergencies within the agency. The center plans to develop a data base of computer security problems and fixes, provide training, and coordinate the development of fixes. In addition, the center is considering developing software to assist in network mapping and to assure proper system configuration.

Meetings Held and Guidance Issued

NIST is coordinating interagency meetings to (1) draw on agency experience and develop a model for agencies to use in setting up response/ coordination centers and (2) educate others on the model that is developed. NET has also set up a computer system that may be used as a data base for computer problems and fixes and as an alternate means of communication in case the Internet's electronic mail system becomes incapacitated. In addition, NIST is planning to issue guidance this summer that will discuss threats inherent to computers and how such threats can be reduced.

NCSC plans to distribute three security-related reports discussing (1) viruses and software techniques for detecting them, (2) the role of trusted technology in combating virus-related programs, and (3) security measures for systems managers. NCSC is also providing an unclassified system to serve as an alternate means of communications in case the Internet's electronic mail system is not working.

Ethics Statements Released

The Internet Activities Board, a technical group comprising government, industry, and university communications and network experts, issued a statement of ethics for Internet users in February 1989. Many Internet users believe there is a need to strengthen the ethical awareness of computer users. They believe that a sense of heightened moral responsibility is an important adjunct to any technical and management actions taken to improve Internet security.

The Board endorsed the view of an NSF panel that characterized any activity as unethical and unacceptable that purposely:

- seeks to gain unauthorized access to Internet resources;

- disrupts the intended use of the Internet; or

- wastes resources, destroys the integrity of computer-based information, or compromises users' privacy.

The Computer Professionals for Social Responsibility and various network groups have also issued ethics statements encouraging (1) enforcement of strong ethical practices, (2) the teaching of ethics to computer science students, and (3) individual accountability.

Conclusions

In the twenty years in which it evolved from a prototype DARPA network, the Internet has come to play an integral role in the research and development community. Through the Internet, researchers have been able to collaborate with colleagues, have access to advanced computing capabilities, and communicate in new ways. In providing these services, the Internet has gone beyond DARPA's original goal of proving the feasibility of computer networking and has served as a model for subsequent public data networks.

Since there is no lead agency or organization responsible for Internet-wide policy-making, direction, and oversight, management on the Internet has been decentralized. We believe this is because, at least in part, Internet developments were driven more by technological considerations than by management concerns and because decentralized authority provided the flexibility needed to accommodate growth and change on an evolving network. However, we believe that the Internet has developed to the point where a central focus is necessary to help address Internet security concerns. These concerns will take on an even greater importance as the Internet evolves into the National Research Network, which will be faster, more accessible, and have more international connections than the Internet.

The Internet virus and other intrusions highlighted certain vulnerabilities, including:

- lack of a focal point in addressing Internet-wide security issues, contributing to problems in coordination and communications during security emergencies;

- security weaknesses at some host sites; and

- problems in developing, distributing, and installing systems software fixes.

Since the virus, various steps have been taken to address concerns stemming from the incident, from creating computer security response centers to issuing ethics statements to raise the moral awareness of Internet users.

We support these actions and believe they are an important part of the overall effort required to upgrade Internet security. Host sites may need to take additional actions to heighten security awareness among users and to improve identified host-level weaknesses, such as lax password management.

However, many of the vulnerabilities highlighted by the virus require actions beyond those of individual agencies or host sites. For this reason, we believe that a security focal point should be established to fill a void in the Internet's management structure and provide the focused oversight, policy-making, and coordination necessary at this point in the Internet's development.

For example, we believe that concerns regarding the need for a policy on fixes for software holes would be better addressed by a security focal point representing the interests of half-a-million Internet users than by the *ad hoc* actions of host sites or networks. Similarly, a security focal point would better ensure that the emergency response teams being developed by different Internet entities are coordinated and that duplication is lessened.

There are no currently available technical security fixes that will resolve all of the Internet's security vulnerabilities while maintaining the functionality and accessibility that researchers believe are essential to scientific progress. Similarly, there is no one management action that will address all of the Internet's security problems. However, we believe concerted action on many fronts can enhance Internet security and provide a basis for security planning on the National Research Network.

FRICC, an informal group made up of representatives of the five agencies that operate Internet research networks, is attempting to coordinate network research and development, facilitate resource sharing, and reduce operating costs. However, no one agency or organization has responsibility for Internet-wide management and security. The Office of Science and Technology Policy, through its Federal Coordinating Council on Science, Engineering and Technology, has, under its mandate to develop and coordinate federal science policy, taken a leadership role in coordinating development of an interagency implementation plan for the National Research Network. Therefore, we believe that the Office would be the appropriate body to coordinate the establishment of a security focal point.

Recommendation

We recommend that the President's Science Advisor, Office of Science and Technology Policy, coordinate the establishment of an interagency group to serve as an Internet security focal point. This group should include representatives from the federal agencies that fund Internet research networks.

As part of its agenda, we recommend that this group:

- Provide Internet-wide policy, direction, and coordination in security related areas to help ensure that the vulnerabilities highlighted by the recent incidents are effectively addressed.

- Support efforts already underway to enhance Internet security and, where necessary, assist these efforts to ensure their success.

- Develop mechanisms for obtaining the involvement of Internet users; systems software vendors; industry and technical groups, such as the Internet Advisory Board; and NET and the National Security Agency, the government agencies with responsibilities for federal computer security.

- Become an integral part of the structure that emerges to manage the National Research Network.

Part 3: Take Off

One of the seminal events in the next phase of cyber history was the SOLAR SUNRISE set of incidents, which primarily affected the US Department of Defense, as described by Tim Maurer, a member of the informal Cyber Statecraft Young Professionals group. While for years the US government and military had worried about cyber conflict, and had developed initial policy and operational responses, this 1998 event was a true catalyst. The incident itself started small: Air Force cyber defenders noticed something was not quite right. But soon, the incident escalated to involve the Pentagon and the President. This was thought to have been the first cyber war, and it led to tight cooperation between the Pentagon and law enforcement. Within a year, the Pentagon created a new command, based on the lessons from SUNRISE.

The next major challenge emerged soon after. While it turned out that SOLAR SUNRISE did not have critical national security implications, the MOONLIGHT MAZE intrusions heralded the start of essentially unceasing, major cyber espionage intrusions. Though much of this case remains classified, Adam Elkus, also a Cyber Statecraft Young Professional, discusses what we know and the implications. The response to MOONLIGHT MAZE was characterized by intense cooperation between the military and law enforcement, building further on the cooperation initiated during SOLAR SUNRISE.

While espionage arguably remains the most critical type of cyber conflict, the scourge of patriotic hackers is also dangerous. Their activities are both obvious and unclassified, and usually get more coverage in the news. These hackers, who strike at perceived enemies overseas, generally have not caused strategically important damage themselves. But their headline-grabbing, jingoistic attacks can inflame tensions and potentially escalate crises out of control. Jonathan Diamond, another Cyber Statecraft Young Professional, discusses some of the most important, early patriotic-hacker conflicts, such as the cases of Russian and Yugoslav hackers working against NATO during 1999 operations, Chinese hackers working against the US in 1999 and 2001, Israelis vs. Palestinians in 1999, and Indians vs. Pakistanis in 2000.

These kinds of conflicts are still with us today, and these three Cyber Statecraft Young Professionals have each written lively accounts containing rich lessons.

SOLAR SUNRISE: Cyber Attack from Iraq?

Tim Maurer[1]

On 6 February 1998, some 2,000 marines were deployed to the Persian Gulf, and a third aircraft carrier arrived in the region, bringing force levels to a peak of 45,000 troops.[2] Tensions between the United States and Iraq had been rising during the previous few months, as Iraq defied the UN Security Council and denied UN weapon inspectors access to weapons facilities. While diplomats were busy trying to avert a military escalation, inside the Pentagon officials worried that war had already broken out.

"I was in the shower when my wife told me I had a call from work," recalls John Levy, then the Director of Air Force Defensive Info Warfare.[3] It was Sunday, 1 February, when the US Air Force discovered that their systems had been hacked in an attack with links to the United Arab Emirates (UAE). This region possessed one of the few Internet gateways into Iraq.

Deputy Secretary of Defense, Dr. John Hamre, would later call the hack "the most organized and systematic attack the Pentagon has seen to date."[4] The intrusions lasted over three weeks, from 1-26 February, and have become known as Operation SOLAR SUNRISE.

> *The most organized and systematic attack the Pentagon has seen to date.*
>
> Deputy Secretary of Defense,
> Dr. John Hamre

The Pentagon feared that Iraq was behind SOLAR SUNRISE. Only a few months earlier, in June 1997, the US government had conducted the first military, large-scale exercise to test their ability to respond to a cyber attack.

> *We had in Solar Sunrise a real-world event that we thought for several days might be the real thing.*
>
> Lieutenant General John "Soup" Campbell

Exercise ELIGIBLE RECEIVER revealed "significant vulnerabilities in the US Defense Information Systems" and "deficiencies in responding to a coordinated attack." The structures in place were "unresponsive to the speed of attacks," the warning process "inadequate," and capabilities to detect or assess cyber attacks were lacking, making the attribution and characterization thereof "very difficult."[5] The attack pattern of SOLAR SUNRISE was "indicative of preparation for a coordinated attack on Defense Information

---

1   Tim Maurer focuses on the international aspects of Internet policy at the New America Foundation's Open Technology Institute and is an adjunct fellow with the Technology and Public Policy Program at the Center for Strategic and International Studies. His work has been published by Foreign Policy and Harvard University, and has been featured in PRI's The World, the Russian Kommersant, and in other media outlets. He holds a Master in Public Policy degree from Harvard Kennedy School.
2   Poulson, "Video: 'Solar Sunrise.'"
3   Atlantic Council event on August 30, 2012 with John Levy.
4   "FBI Eyes Teens in Pentagon 'Attacks.'"
5   GPO, "Critical Information Infrastructure Protection: The Threat is Real."

Infrastructure."[6] Inside the Department of Defense (DoD), officials were asking themselves, had Iraq launched a war, using cyber-warfare? According to Senator John Kyl, Chair of the Senate Subcommittee on Terrorism at the time, "SOLAR SUNRISE was serious enough that our top defense department people described it as the most serious intrusion into the United States up to that point. It went all the way up to the President of the United States; it was that serious."[7]

> *It went all the way up to the President of the United States; it was that serious.*
>
> Senator John Kyl

A few weeks later, investigations revealed that two teenagers in California and an Israeli hacker were behind the intrusions. SOLAR SUNRISE is therefore an important reminder of the potentially devastating consequences of the attribution problem and lack of evidence. It was also a wake-up call for the US government and showcased the vulnerabilities of their system. Unlike ELIGIBLE RECEIVER, SOLAR SUNRISE had not been an exercise. This was a real situation, in the midst of a political crisis. In the words of Lieutenant General John "Soup" Campbell, "we had just been through an exercise [Eligible Receiver] that simulated what we thought it was possible for a very plausible attacker to do, and now we had in Solar Sunrise a real-world event that we thought for several days might be the real thing."[8] Solar Sunrise therefore deserves special attention in the history of cyber attacks, because of its lessons that are still useful today.

The Geopolitical Context during SOLAR SUNRISE: Rising Tensions with Iraq

In February, when SOLAR SUNRISE took place, military intervention in Iraq seemed imminent. On 4 February, Secretary of Defense Cohen announced additional troop deployments to the Gulf, including some 2,000 marines. Three US aircraft carriers were now present in the region—the USS *Independence*, the USS *Nimitz*, and the USS *George Washington*. This brought the total number of troops in the region to a high of nearly 45,000. Troop strength remained at over 35,000 from March through May. The British government also sent troops to the region.[9]

These rising tensions were the result of Baghdad's increasing efforts to obstruct the work of UN weapons inspectors. These inspectors had been searching Iraqi locations for weapons of mass destruction and were overseen by a UN Special Commission (UNSCOM). Their mission was part of a sanctions regime put in place after Iraqi forces had been expelled

---

6   Unclassified PowerPoint presentation on Eligible Receiver and Solar Sunrise, declassified on 11 December, 2006.
7   Panorama, "CYBER ATTACK."
8   Discussion with "Soup" Campbell on SOLAR SUNRISE, held at the Atlantic Council on 30 August 2012.
9   Prados, "Iraq: Post-War Challenges and US Responses 1991-1998."

from Kuwait during the First Gulf War in 1991. Between 1993 and 1996, UN weapons inspectors were relatively unobstructed by the Iraqi government. But in 1997, the Iraqi government's refusal of access to certain sites prompted the UN Security Council to call for Iraq's compliance with UN resolutions.[10] The Security Council threatened further sanctions, and the United States started to build up its forces in the Gulf in October of that year. A first climax was reached on 29 October 1997, when Iraq issued a set of demands relating to UNSCOM personnel and expelled US inspectors on 13 November 1997.[11] Military action was only averted after a Russian diplomatic initiative. But the Iraqi government continued to complain about the perceived dominance of American and British citizens participating in the inspection teams.

The lead-up to the renewed crisis in February started on 12 January 1998, when Baghdad declared three sites off limits for inspections. In New York, the "Security Council deplore[d] the statement of the Iraqi official spokesman of 12 January 1998 and Iraq's subsequent failure to fulfill its obligations to provide the Special Commission with full, unconditional, and immediate access to all sites. The Council determine[d] that this failure is unacceptable and a clear violation of the relevant resolutions."[12] Shortly thereafter, on 16 January, a team led by American Scott Ritter was unable to carry out its work for three days and so left Iraq. On the forth day, the situation escalated further, when Saddam Hussein threatened the expulsion of all UN inspectors if the sanctions against Iraq were not lifted within six months.

Once again, a military intervention could only be averted by intensive diplomatic negotiations. The Security Council endorsed a new plan, and the United Nations and Iraq signed a Memorandum of Understanding on 23 February. According to a report by the Congressional Research Service, "there were widespread expressions of relief in the Arab World over the 23 February agreement, which averted retaliatory strikes against Iraq for the time being."[13]

Yet, while the agreement was a sign of easing tensions, Resolution 1154 adopted by the Security Council on 3 March made it clear that "any violation would have severest consequences for Iraq." The United States maintained its pressure, and a day after the resolution, a senior official from the State Department indicated that some twenty countries were willing to participate in a military coalition against Iraq if necessary. This number rose to twenty-five countries in a 17 March statement by Secretary Cohen. By May, the crisis had subsided. The Security Council welcomed their "improved access" and hoped for a

---

10   United Nations Security Council resolution S/RES/1115, 21 June 1997.
11   United Nations Security Council Presidential Statement S/PRST/1997/49, 29 October 1997; and
United Nations Security Council Presidential Statement S/PRST/1997/51, 13 November 1997.
12   United Nations Security Council Presidential Statement S/PRST/1998/1, 14 January 1998.
13   Prados, "Iraq: Post-War."

"new Iraqi spirit,"[14] and the President ordered a troop reduction on 26 May. However, that hope was short-lived, and soon tensions flared up again. In August, the Iraqi government decided to suspend cooperation with UNSCOM, eventually ceasing cooperation on 31 October.[15] This time, the United States, together with the United Kingdom, launched a four-day military campaign against Iraqi targets from 16-19 December.

Figure 9: US Force Levels in the Gulf Region[16]

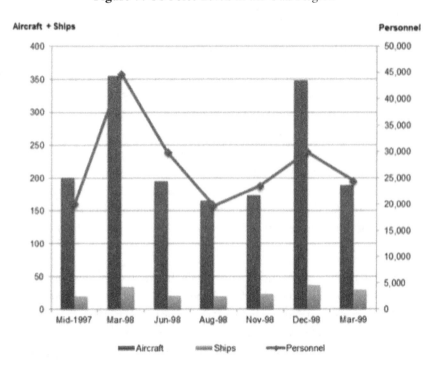

February 1998: Intruder Alert at the Pentagon

SOLAR SUNRISE took place in the midst of this escalating political crisis with Iraq from 1-26 February 1998. The Computer Emergency Response Team of the US Air Force (AFCERT) first detected the intrusions through their Automated Security Incident Measurement system, the first such mechanism to be used by the military branches. A root-level security compromise had been identified on systems at the Andrews Air Force Base in Maryland. The next day, the AFCERT, based at Kelly Air Force Base in San Antonio, Texas, discovered further incidents at Kirtland AFB in New Mexico, Lackland AFB in

---

14   United Nations Security Council Presidential Statement S/PRST/1998/11, 14 May 1998.
15   United Nations Security Council resolution S/RES/1194, 9 September 1998; and
United Nations Security Council resolution S/RES/1205, 5 November 1998.
16   Prados, "Iraq: Post-War."

Texas, and Columbus AFB in Mississippi.[17] The National Military Intelligence Center decided the incident required the establishment of a National Operational Intelligence Watch Officer Network, which allowed secure conference calls to be made between the major intelligence watch centers, including the Pentagon, the State Department, the CIA, the NSA, and the White House. It was the opening response to what turned out to be a three-week long campaign of cyber exploitation, composed of hacks that were designed to spy rather than destroy.

The intrusions were limited to unclassified networks but affected several hundred computer systems (estimates ranged between 500-700).[18] This involved at least eleven military systems at the Air Force, the Navy, NASA, and Lawrence Livermore National Laboratory, and also systems at the Massachusetts Institute of Technology, Harvard University, the University of California-Berkeley, and other universities across the country, as well as commercial sites. It later became clear that computers belonging to the Israeli parliament, Israel's President Ezer Weizman, and Hamas had also been compromised.[19]

SOLAR SUNRISE exploited a single, well-known vulnerability in Sun Microsystems' Unix-based Solaris operating system, versions 2.4 and 2.6 (Sun was the source of the operation's nickname). The hackers used "only moderately sophisticated tools."[20] The attacks resembled the simulation ELIGIBLE RECEIVER, which took place only a few months earlier and was based on actual vulnerabilities using commonly available hacking tools. According to a memo written by Hamre, that exercise had "confirmed our vulnerability to computer attack."[21] The Solaris vulnerability in the rpc.statd subsystem was known, and patches had been made available since December.[22] The attack pattern was the same throughout the three-week campaign. The hackers would probe the servers for the existence of the vulnerability. If present, they would exploit the buffer overflow vulnerability to gain root access and thereby control the system. Once inside, a sniffer malware program was placed in the system to collect passwords and establish a "backdoor" to retrieve the data later. Even though the hackers had root access enabling them to alter, remove, or destroy data, they focused on exploitation and curiously even downloaded a patch for the vulnerability as part of the intrusion, preventing others from copycatting their actions.[23]

---

17   Burrough, "Invisible Enemies."

18   Hildreth, "Cyberwarfare"; and Trounson, "Hacker Case Taps into Fame, Fury."

19   Ridder, "Teen hacker with access to arms lab"; Trounson, "Hacker Case"; and Reed and Wilson, "Whiz-Kid Hacker Caught."

20   Hildreth, "Cyberwarfare"; Poulson, "Video: 'Solar Sunrise'"; and Nichols, "A Perspective on Threats in the Risk Analysis Process."

21   Lardner and Hess, "Pentagon Looks for Answers to Massive Computer Attack."

22   Poulson, "Video: 'Solar Sunrise'"; and CERT, "CERT Advisory CA-1996-09 Vulnerability in rpc.statd."

23   Power, "Joy-Riders: Michief that Leads to Mayhem"; Serabian, Jr., "Cyber Threats and the US Economy"; and Hildreth, "Cyberwarfare."

As part of the campaign, the hackers also targeted the DoD's domain name servers, accessing unclassified systems, including the Global Transportation System, the Defense Finance System, medical logistics, and the official unclassified email system.[24] Though these systems are unclassified, John Serabian, then the Information Operations Issue Manager at the CIA, highlighted in his statement to the Joint Economic Committee on Cyber Threats and the US Economy on 23 February 2000 that they "control our ability to manage and deploy military forces."[25] Scott Charney, Chief of the Computer Crime and Intellectual Property Section at the Department of Justice at the time, added in an 18-minute FBI-made video on SOLAR SUNRISE, "So obviously, people were worried that this might be an information warfare-based attack or some sort of attack designed to disrupt the United States's response to problems in Iraq."[26] That is why military officials at the Pentagon grew increasingly concerned about the origin of the attacks, as the country was preparing itself for possible military intervention in Iraq.

Determining the origin of the hack was a challenge. As John Serabian pointed out, the "intruders hid their tracks by routing their attack through computer systems in the United Arab Emirates."[27] They would also use university websites as their points of entry, due to the typically lax security of these sites.[28] Analysts at the National Security Agency tracked the hacking first to servers at Harvard University, and then discovered a routing pattern that led to Abu Dhabi and the UAE, also linking to seven Air Force and four Navy systems. The links also connected to Gunter Annex in Alabama and the Port Hueneme Air National Guard weather facility in California, in addition to the Air Force bases already mentioned, and Pearl Harbor, the Naval Academy, and two systems in Okinawa.[29] Tyndall Air Force Base and Utah University were also affected, and there were other international links to France, Germany, Israel, and Taiwan.[30]

Due to the discovery of the international links, the threat had escalated. Deputy Secretary of Defense, Dr. John J. Hamre, decided to brief President Clinton, "telling him the attacks could be opening shots of an authentic cyber-war, perhaps launched by Iraq–exactly the kind of 'electronic Pearl Harbor' that Pentagon analysts had been warning of for years."[31] On 25 February, Hamre went public, calling the intrusions "the most organized and systematic ever launched," and he later added in testimony that they "showed a pattern that indicated they might be preparation for a coordinated attack on the Defense Information Structure [...] The attacks targeted key parts of Defense Networks at a time we were preparing for

24   Trounson, "Hacker Case"; and Donelly and Crawley, "Hamre to Hill: 'We're in a Cyberwar'."
25   Serabian, "Cyber Threats."
26   Poulson, "Video: 'Solar Sunrise.'"
27   Serabian, "Cyber Threats."
28   Poulson, "Video: 'Solar Sunrise.'"
29   Lardner and Hess, "Pentagon Looks for Answers."
30   Power, "Joy-Riders"; and Hildreth, "Cyberwarfare."
31   Burrough, "Invisible Enemies."

possible military operations against Iraq."[32]

Figure 10: Solar Sunrise Activity[33]

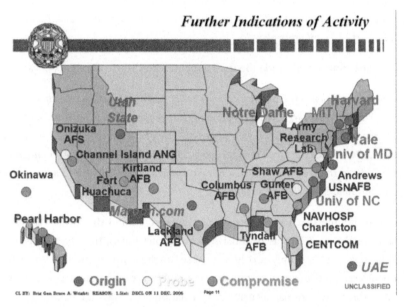

The connections overseas, particularly to the Middle East, were the reason for suspicion among Pentagon officials that they might be witnessing an Iraqi cyber attack, especially during the early days, after the attack had been detected and its nature was unclear.[34] Steve Chabinsky, until recently the Deputy Assistant Director of the Cyber Division at the Federal Bureau of Investigation (FBI), remembers about SOLAR SUNRISE:

> We see military computers, dot-mil computers that are being intruded upon, and it's coming from abroad. And it's during some conflict that was occurring at the same time with Iraq, if I recall correctly. And we're seeing the traffic coming in from another Middle Eastern country. On the receiving side, it really very much looks like the dot-mil environment is under attack at this point from this other nation state.[35]

There was a concern that the cyber exploitation was part of a campaign to prepare for a full-blown, destructive cyber attack in the future, that could potentially disrupt troop deployments to the region.[36] As Richard Power at informIT.com pointed out in his analysis,

---

32   Burrough, "Invisible Enemies"; and Donelly and Crawley, "Hamre to Hill."
33   PowerPoint presentation on ELIGIBLE RECEIVER and SOLAR SUNRISE, declassified on 11 December 2006. This
     document is part of the editor's personal collection, to be posted on a future cyber history archive.
34   Trounson, "Hacker Case."
35   Chabinsky, "Lessons from Our Cyber Past: The First Cyber Cops."
36   Poulson, "Solar Sunrise Hacker 'Analyzer' Escapes Jail."

[a]lthough the targeted systems were not classified, they were all involved in the military build-up being undertaken in regard to the Iraqi weapons inspection crisis. If the targeted systems were damaged, it could impede the flow of transportation, personnel, and medical supplies. If the Iraqis were gathering, aggregating, and analyzing the data from the targeted systems, they could use it to surmise the US military's plans.[37]

One of the questions raised inside the government, according to Chabinsky, was

keeping in mind that this is the first time we really saw a large-scale, across-the-board coming from one area intrusion set – there was obviously the real possibility that we are, quote, unquote, under attack. If we are under attack, how are you sure of attribution? What is the appropriate response? And then you respond symmetrically… Do you have enough here for attribution that would make us comfortable to have you be comfortable to do something as a military campaign against this third party, this other country?[38]

Officials were hoping that some juvenile hackers were behind the intrusions, similar to other hacks in the past. But as national security professionals, they had to assume the worst. "The stakes were simply too high to take anything for granted. It was a time of international crisis and impending military action. Until proven otherwise, it had to be viewed as a threat to national security."[39] If a nation-state was not behind the attacks, another theoretical possibility was that criminals or terrorists were the perpetrators. However, there was no intelligence supporting this scenario. The incident was considered grave enough for Hamre to brief key American allies abroad concerning the topic and to focus on protecting systems of the North Atlantic Treaty Organization (NATO).[40]

According to a report at the time,

information warfare branch security experts at the Pentagon National Security Agency believe the "language" used in the attacks suggests Dutch hackers could be responsible. Allegedly, a group of Dutch hackers stole US military secrets during the Persian Gulf War and offered them to Iraq… US defense officials believe a computer system in the United Arab Emirates served as a 'waypoint' to one of the Navy computers that was attacked. The DoD does not believe the UAE was responsible for the attack, however.[41]

Yet, as Levy recalled, "we never dismissed Iraq until the very end. Nobody stopped focusing on it until it was clear that we were no longer deploying."[42]

---

37 Power, "Joy-Riders."
38 Chabinsky, "Lessons from Our Cyber Past: The First Cyber Cops."
39 Power, "Joy-Riders."
40 Trounson, "Hacker Case."
41 Lardner and Hess, "Pentagon Looks for Answers."
42 Atlantic Council event on August 30, 2012 with John Levy.

Figure 11: Attributing Solar Sunrise Origins[43]

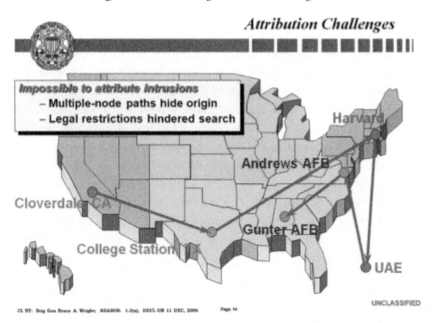

The intrusions caused little direct damage. The hackers browsed through the data without altering or deleting it, though they collected passwords that would allow them to access even more systems.[44] According to a statement by the Department of Justice, dated 18 March 1998, "no classified material was ever compromised."[45] Yet, there was indirect damage. Various IT professionals at the institutions that were hacked had to invest resources to try to block the intrusions. Randall Ballew, at the University of California-Berkeley, said at the time, "these cases are not benign." Poor monitoring systems forced network administrators to check every file that could have been affected by the intrusion for alteration or deletion.[46] "I remember the concern of people who were wondering... if the attackers did not destroy or steal anything, how did we know they had not changed anything? Confidence in the integrity of systems and data is a real issue after an intrusion," General Campbell recalled.[47] Investigators were also particularly worried about the intrusions at Lawrence Livermore National Laboratories. They "asked me if I read any files on it, or if I gave any passwords from it to anyone," one of the hackers said at the time.[48] Seven university computers that were part of a California herbarium plant specimen project were also among the affected systems, showing that the hackers seemed less interested in the content than in the challenge

---

43   PowerPoint presentation on ELIGIBLE RECEIVER and Solar Sunrise, declassified on 11 December 11, 2006.
44   Trounson, "Hacker Case."
45   Reed and Wilson, "Whiz-Kid"; and Hildreth, "Cyberwarfare."
46   Trounson, "Hacker Case."
47   Discussion with "Soup" Campbell on SOLAR SUNRISE, held at the Atlantic Council on 30 August 2012.
48   Ridder, "Teen Hacker with Access to Arm."

of breaking into systems of large institutions.[49]

Solving the Attribution Problem and the Government's Response

Shortly after the intrusions were first detected, a joint task force (led by the Joint Staff Information Operations Response Cell) was set up to begin the investigation. "Dusty" Rhoads, a former senior military officer with the Joint Staff, recalled, "Just the week before, we had finished an exercise including the FBI, so we were able to establish the task force instantaneously within hours."[50] The investigation involved officials from the Joint Staff, the Air Force Office of Special Investigations, the Naval Criminal Investigative Service, the Defense Information Systems Agency, the Defense Intelligence Agency, NASA, the National Security Agency, the CIA, the FBI, and the Department of Justice.[51] Martha Stansell-Gamm, head of the Computer Crime and Intellectual Property section at the Department of Justice at the time, commented that, "[o]ne of the singular aspects of SOLAR SUNRISE was that it was such a multi-agency investigation."[52] That collaboration would pay off over time.

Levy remembered, "When AFCERT called and asked what they should do, the first thing I told them was to block the intrusions."[53] This had the unintended consequence that the DoD started sending pings back to commercial Internet Service Providers (ISPs) from which the intrusions

Just the week before, we had finished an exercise including the FBI, so we were able to establish the task force instantaneously within hours.

Col. "Dusty" Rhoads (Ret.)

were coming. This made it appear to the ISPs that the Pentagon had launched a DDoS attack against them. "We told senior officials about this side-effect, in case someone from the FBI would call," according to Rhoads. Levy added, "This was a fall-out of the actions taken by the AFCERT in defense of the Air Force domain. Accordingly, the side-effects (or unanticipated effects) were briefed to Air Force senior officials."[54] Government officials could also count on the help from the private sector, namely William Zane, who owned an ISP called NetDex, which was based in Santa Rosa, California and operated sonic.net.[55] One day, he started receiving complaints from Harvard University and the Massachusetts Institute of Technology; he then became aware that NetDex had been used as a launch pad to mount the intrusions. He identified the source and started monitoring the two

49   Trounson, "Hacker Case."
50   Discussion with Dusty Rhoads on SOLAR SUNRISE, held at the Atlantic Council on 30 August 2012.
51   Lardner and Hess, "Pentagon Looks for Answers"; and Power, "Joy-Riders."
52   Power, "Joy-Riders."
53   Discussion with John Levy on SOLAR SUNRISE, held at the Atlantic Council on 30 August 2012
54   Discussion with Dusty Rhoads and John Levy on SOLAR SUNRISE, held at the Atlantic Council on 30 August 2012
55   Ridder, "Teen Hacker with Access to Arms."

teenagers' activities. In this activity, he worked with the FBI.[56] This became the crucial link. The sniffer programs planted in the compromised systems were coded to submit their data directly to sonic.net. They then FTPed the data to their home PCs from sonic.net.[57]

The two California 16-year-olds, who were found to be responsible and are known by their online pseudonyms Makaveli and Stimpy[58] (one is a popular rapper and the other a cartoon character), could no longer hide. On 13 February, the same day that additional troops were sent to the Persian Gulf, investigators received the legal authority to wiretap the teens. They monitored their phone lines and employed a keystroke logger to track their activity online. That information was then compared with the results from the on-site surveillance of Makaveli's residence.[59] Ten days later, the 23 February agreement eased tensions in the Gulf, whilst the investigators were busy collecting enough evidence to take a case in court. That is when the story of the hack hit the news. On 25 February, the media learned that the suspected perpetrators were teenagers living in Northern California.[60]

The case was about to become international news overnight. The investigators rushed to obtain and execute search warrants, before the two boys would be warned by the evening news and potentially erase all evidence.[61] As was later revealed, the teenagers actually did hear about it before the warrants were obtained. One of them called John Vranesevich, who ran a website called AntiOnline that was well known among hackers. He recalled receiving a phone call from Makaveli asking, "Are you watching this shit on CNN? J.P., man, they're talking about me!"[62] When FBI agents arrived at Makaveli's home in Cloverdale, California, on 26 February, they found what FBI Special Agent Chris Beeson (who was part of the team) described as a scene "typical of teenagers. Pepsi cans. Half-eaten cheeseburgers."[63]

But the wiretap revealed that the two teenagers were not alone. They had been in touch with a third person, an Israeli hacker known as "The Analyzer," via Internet Relay Chat. The investigation that focused on the intrusions at the Pentagon had already identified another website, which was used to launch the hacks: maroon.com. Maroon.com had a link to Emirnet in the UAE, which was beyond US jurisdiction. But the operator of maroon.net in the United States agreed to allow investigators to monitor the site's traffic.[64] Two days after the arrests in California, The Analyzer boasted about having successfully intruded into over 400 websites, in an interview with Vranesevich posted on AntiOnline.

56   Reed and Wilson, "Whiz-Kid."
57   Power, "Joy-Riders."
58   Poulson, "Video: 'Solar Sunrise"; and Reed and Wilson, "Whiz-Kid."
59   Poulson, "Video: Solar Sunrise."
60   Ibid.
61   Ibid.
62   Burrough, "Invisible Enemies."
63   Power, "Joy-Riders."
64   Poulson, "Video: Solar Sunrise."

The interview included The Analyzer giving a live demonstration of a hack.[65] He was confident that he could not be found and felt comfortable giving the interview, to protect his two "students" in California.[66]

Yet, The Analyzer did not anticipate what would come next. Vranesevich decided to track him down, and after spending twenty seven hours on his computer following The Analyzer's digital footprint through computers in several countries, he eventually arrived at an ISP in Israel. Vranesevich did not stop there, but instead took his hunt into the physical world. He reached out to a journalist in Israel and set up an interview with The Analyzer in Tel Aviv. The journalist's story would become the missing clue that the Israeli police needed to identify 18-year-old Ehud Tenenbaum as The Analyzer. This led to his arrest in Jerusalem on 18 March, along with two other 18-year-old Israeli hackers, with whom he had formed an Israeli hacker group known as "The Enforcers."[67]

The FBI sent agents to Israel in May 1998, to join their Israeli colleagues in the questioning of the hacker. The teenagers in California pleaded guilty and received as a sentence three years of probation, fines, and 100 hours of community service; they were also forced to forfeit their computers and were restricted to accessing the Internet only under adult supervision.[68] A few months later, in February 1999, Tenenbaum was indicted for breaching Israel's computer crime law. As part of a plea agreement, Tenenbaum was eventually sentenced to six months of community service, one year of probation, two years suspended jail sentence, and was fined $18,000.[69]

What had motivated the three teenagers, whose intrusions became one of the first international, high-profile hacker cases? Tenenbaum met the two Californian teenagers through the hacking group, "The Enforcers." Their focus was on hacking racist and pedophile websites. According to the *Los Angeles Times*, Tenenbaum "stumbled into the Pentagon's computers by accident, at least the first time. "I reached the place, the site name of which ended with 'gov,' and I went in without knowing that this was the Pentagon," he said. And, "As far as I'm concerned, the achievement is... breaking into the system. I didn't want to do more than that... I had no intention to destroy or cause damage."[70] Tenenbaum also said he sealed the security gaps that he discovered at the Pentagon and elsewhere. But Tenenbaum was said to "hate" big organizations and considered anarchism a viable alternative to government.[71] He not only hacked US government websites, but was also proud to have hacked the website of the militant Hamas organization. He seemed motivated

65   *Ibid.*
66   Burrough, "Invisible Enemies."
67   Burrough, "Invisible Enemies"; and Power, "Joy-Riders."
68   Poulson, "Video: Solar Sunrise."
69   Poulson, "Solar Sunrise Hacker 'Analyzer,' Escapes."
70   Trounson, "Hacker Case"
71   Warner, "Is The Analyzer Really Back?"

by a desire to teach his knowledge to those younger than him, calling the teenagers in California his students. According to Vranesevich, Makaveli told him he was hacking because "[i]t's power, dude. You know, power."[72]

Yet, unlike the two teenagers in California, Tenenbaum became something like a national hero, according to *Wired*. Prime Minister Benjamin Netanyahu praised the hacker's skills as "damn good," adding they were "very dangerous too."

> *It's power, dude. You know, power.*
>
> 16-year-old hacker "Makaveli"

Tenenbaum received media interview requests, an invitation to appear before an Israeli parliamentary committee (which he could not attend, as he was still under house arrest), job offers, and offers for book and movie deals. A DJ at a club announced, "We are proud of you," when Tenenbaum was on the dance floor. According to *Haaretz'* Dror Feuer, "People see him as the outlaw of our time, and they really like the fact that this little Israeli went up against the big guys – the Pentagon."[73]

Implications

On 18 March 1998, the Department of Justice issued a statement, concluding that "no classified material was ever compromised, and there is no indication that the attacks were part of an organized military or state-sponsored campaign against the United States."[74] It turned out that former Deputy Assistant Secretary of Defense for Command, Control, Communications, and Intelligence, Anthony "Tony" Valletta, had been right when he said (according to a report at the time) that the "DOD may be over-reacting to normal hacker activity."[75] But as Chabinsky pointed out, "this is the first time we really saw a large-scale, across-the-board, coming from one area intrusion set–there was obviously the real possibility that we [were] 'under attack.'"[76] A newspaper at the time quoted a Pentagon official saying, "If we're in the middle of trying to get ready for a military action, it hardly matters who is behind the intrusion...The attacks call into question the integrity of our systems."[77]

> *This is the first time we really saw a large-scale, across-the-board coming from one area intrusion set – there was obviously the real possibility that we are 'under attack'.*
>
> Steve Chabinsky

A review of SOLAR SUNRISE suggested that 75 percent of the intrusions could have been avoided by well-trained network administrators and that $100 million over the

---

72 Ridder, "Teen hacker with access to arms";
73 Trounson, "Hacker Case,"; and Zetter, "Israeli Hacker."
74 Reed and Wilson, "Whiz-Kid."
75 Lardner and Hess, "Pentagon Looks for Answers."
76 Chabinsky, "Lessons from Our Cyber Past: The First Cyber Cops."
77 "Hackers tap into Pentagon Computers."

course of a year would suffice to secure the Pentagon's connection to the Internet.[78] SOLAR SUNRISE therefore underscored that the vulnerabilities in the networks, which had been exposed during the ELIGIBLE RECEIVER exercise, were not only known to people inside the Pentagon but also to outsiders. Outsiders had even succeeded in gaining root access to systems, due to the systems' poor defenses, and lack of warning and monitoring systems.[79] In the aftermath, the Pentagon established the Joint Task Force-Computer Network Defense to coordinate defenses, set up intrusion detectors across the networks, and train its staff in computer network defense. Yet, a year later, the Pentagon's Inspector General Eleanor Hill still judged the improvements inadequate.

> *Audits continue to show lax security measures and inadequate focus by program managers on the threat, despite clear awareness at senior levels of the need for a very high priority of information assurance.*[80]

Apart from technical fixes, SOLAR SUNRISE also highlighted the need for inter-agency coordination. "The meeting took place in the SecDef's 3rd floor conference rooms, and there was a large crowd around the table. At some point, Hamre asked, 'who's in charge?' There was a long silence and a lot of looks around the table," General Campbell later remembered. "As I recall, I got the rose pinned on me, as the J3 Special Technical Operations representative, to take the lead. But the point had been made: organizationally and doctrinally, no one was in charge."[81]

Who's in charge?

Asked Deputy Secretary of Defense, Dr. John Hamre

That is how the joint task force set up for SOLAR SUNRISE became institutionalized as the Joint Task Force-Computer Network Defense (JTF-CND), under the Defense Information Security Agency with Campbell as its first leader. The ILOVEYOU virus would become the JTF-CND's next challenge. The experience of SOLAR SUNRISE also helped mature the National Infrastructure Protection Center, which was an inter-agency entity including the FBI, the Treasury, the Department of Energy, the DoD, and the intelligence community. It raised awareness among government agencies, both domestic and abroad, that they need to coordinate their efforts.

As Michael Vatis, Director of the National Infrastructure Protection Center, pointed out in the SOLAR SUNRISE video, "One of the things that SOLAR SUNRISE demonstrated was that, in cyberspace, the cliché that cyberspace knows no boundaries is absolutely

---

78 Donelly and Crawley, "Hamre to Hill: 'We're in a Cyberwar.'"
79 Dick, "Testimony before the House Energy and Commerce Committee, Oversight and Invesitgation Subcommittee"; Hildreth, "Cyberwarfare"; and Poulson, "Video: 'Solar Sunrise.'"
80 Donelly and Crawley, "Hamre to Hill: 'We're in a Cyberwar.'"
81 Discussion with "Soupl" Campbell on SOLAR SUNRISE, held at the Atlantic Council on 30 August 2012

true, and that we therefore in many investigations have to work closely with our foreign counterparts, because hackers might go through several foreign countries on their way to victims in the US."[82] Moreover, as government officials were busy trying to stop the hacks and track down the perpetrators, they also recognized that many legal questions remained unanswered, including many involving privacy concerns and investigative needs.[83]

A less obvious but important implication was highlighted by Roberta Gross, Inspector General at NASA. She was concerned that:

> *We had teenagers involved, who were being mentored by a foreign citizen, and they don't know why he was mentoring them. They just thought that was cool, somebody sharing tricks, somebody that was one of their kind of people. But they don't know who he is, and they don't know his motives, and they don't know why he wanted them to do certain things or learn certain things.*[84]

Conclusion

SOLAR SUNRISE was ultimately a wake-up call. Key themes of cyber conflict that continue to be central to debates today emerged during this time. The attribution problem; legal challenges; the need for inter-agency, public-private, and international cooperation; and the issue of lag-time between the detection and patching of vulnerability spots have not disappeared. As Steve Chabinsky reflected,

> *this fog of war concept permeates a lot of our entry into the new areas that have come upon us... For me, the moral of the story was that our dot-mil had been intruded upon, meaning our dot-mil could be used therefore to launch attacks against another country, and it will look like it's us. So will our adversaries have the same restraint that we displayed during SOLAR SUNRISE, when they start seeing attacks against their infrastructure coming from us?*

---

82   Poulson, "Video: 'Solar Sunrise.'"
83   Dick, "Testimony"; Serabian, "Cyber Threats"; and Poulson, "Video: 'Solar Sunrise.'"
84   Panorama, "CYBER ATTACK."

Early Patriotic Hacking

Jonathan Diamond[1]

As the Internet came into its own in the late twentieth and early twenty-first century, hacking as a form of activism began to evolve. In place of picket signs and political slogans, hackers took their protests to the web, using tools such as distributed denial of service (DDoS) attacks and website defacements to air their grievances. Though the medium differed, the causes of this early hacktivism were fairly traditional, e.g., human rights violations, political repression, nuclear tests, etc.[2] Around the turn of the twenty-first century, however, a startling new trend emerged as hacktivism exploded in scope and intensity, mirroring very real political and military tensions between nations. Rather than representing specific interest groups, so-called "patriotic hackers" engaged in cyber conflict on behalf of their respective nations.

Though certainly more expansive than previous movements, the incidents of patriotic hacking between 1999 and 2001 were not entirely novel. For one, hackers had plied their craft in the service of governments before, as West German hacker Markus Hess had famously done for the Soviet Union in the late Cold War.[3] It would be a stretch to characterize Hess's work as "patriotic," but hacking in and of itself was not alien to the conduct of international relations. Nor were the early patriotic hackers' means of attack themselves particularly innovative. The vast majority of the attacks in this period were simple website defacements, though some hackers employed distributed denial of service attacks as well. DDoS had already made its first appearance in the "Intervasion" of the UK on Guy Fawkes Day 1994, a response to Prime Minister John Major's bill against outdoor dance festivals.[4] Political website defacements, meanwhile, made their debut with the 1996 hacking of the Justice Department's website, in protest against the controversial Communications Decency Act.[5] Both sorts of attack became common in hacking circles around the world. Yet, until the turn of the century, neither was often viewed as a method of international political activism, as much as a recreational activity. Chinese hackers, now well known for patriotic disruption online, seem to have first emerged in response to anti-Chinese riots in Indonesia during the financial crisis of 1997 and 1998.[6]

Once the potential of these tools was realized, patriotic hacking developed as an added

---

1   Jon Diamond is an International Relations and Linguistics double-major at the University of Pennsylvania. Jon was a research intern at the Center for Strategic and International Studies during the summer of 2012 and worked on issues in Technology and Public Policy. He previously served as a research assistant at the University of Pennsylvania's International Program. Jon is originally from Chattanooga, TN.
2   Paget, "Hacktivism."
3   See Stoll, The Cuckoo's Egg; and "Timeline: A 40-year history of hacking."
4   "Wikileaks Infowar not the first online protest action."
5   "Hackers Deface Website of U.S. Justice Department."
6   Tang, "China-U.S. cyber war escalates"; and "Government websites 'attacked by Chinese hackers.'"

layer to international relations. Netizens of opposing states went head-to-head in what many journalists (but few military officers or international lawyers) called "cyberwars."

Despite the sensational monicker of "war," these cyber *conflicts* in fact lacked many of the features generally associated with war. Crucially, the cyber components of these tensions and conflicts were not officially sanctioned, at least publicly. Rather, the vast majority of the participants in these early cyber conflicts were private hackers, acting alone or in loose coalitions. Accordingly, patriotic hackers were unable to marshal the resources necessary for the sort of high-impact attacks one would expect in war, tending instead to use relatively crude (though nevertheless disruptive) methods, like DDoS and website defacements. These informal and relatively unsophisticated series attacks were ultimately "analogous to stone-throwing"—quite literally in the case of the 1999 Israeli-Palestinian clashes.[7] As with all instances of cyber conflict to that time, patriotic hacking did not result in any major damages to critical infrastructure or loss of life, and thus this activity defies categorization as true "war."

It is nevertheless worth considering these episodes as "the continuation of politics by other means," though not extraordinarily *violent* means.[8] As Valeriano and Maness suggest, the patriotic hacking sort of cyber conflict falls within "the normal relations range" for geo-political rivals and may be tolerated as long as it remains beneath certain thresholds.[9] As such, cyber conflict is but one of many different foreign policy alternatives that are available to national states. However, Patriotic hacking, for all its lack of technical sophistication and kinetic impact, complicates this analysis by introducing into the foreign policy processes a slew of new, less diplomatic actors. Patriotic hacking thus represents an intriguing facet of what Joseph Nye has described as a "diffusion of power," a phenomenon that national states must learn to manage as technology becomes increasingly widespread.

Kosovo: "Web War One"

The smoke had scarcely cleared from the first bombs over Belgrade when the struggle for Kosovo took to the Net. Only three days after Operation Allied Force began, the website whitehouse.gov was reportedly defaced with the text, "Hackers wuz Here." The site was quickly taken offline.[10] Over the next few days, US Navy systems were probed, data erased, and website access blocked, while NATO's official website suffered a distributed denial of service (DDoS) attack and a massive influx of what would be called "Yugospam."[11] This first wave of attacks was only the beginning of a cyber conflict that would earn Kosovo

---

7   Karatzogianna, The Politics of Cyberconflict, 154.
8   Carl von Clausewitz, On War, trans. Michael Howard and Peter Paret (Princeton, NJ: Princeton University Press, 1989), 28.
9   Valeriano and Maness, "Persistent Enemies and Cybersecurity," 8.
10   "White House Web Site Hacked By Anti NATO Hactivists?"
11   "Serb Hackers Reportedly Disrupt US Military Computer"; and "Kosovo Crisis Creates New Roles for Internet Firms."

the title "Web War One" or "The First Internet War."[12] As the campaign wore on, a myriad of "patriotic hackers"—Serbian, Russian, Latvian, Lithuanian, and even Chinese—would emerge to harry Allied forces in cyberspace, ushering in an era of cyber/netwar prophesied by John Arquilla and David Ronfeldt only six years prior.[13] Though the attacks themselves were in no way decisive, they did succeed in drawing attention to the important role networks would play in future conflicts.

As with other instances of patriotic hacking, the anti-NATO hackers were dispersed across a number of different organizations, at times operating independently. Efforts to attribute attacks to specific actors accordingly varied. The initial strains of attack were traced back to systems in Belgrade, and some groups such as the Serbian "Black Hand" claimed responsibility for their attacks, most notably one that wiped the data from a US Navy computer mere days into the conflict.[14] Named after the military secret society implicated in Franz Ferdinand's assassination, this new Black Hand, or *Crna Ruka*, claimed no such infamous assassinations, but focused instead on combating "Albanian lies" spread by news sites such as kosova.com. The group's activity during late 1998 coincided with efforts by the Milošević regime to stifle the independent media and led to some suspicion of official support.[15] Other groups, such as a propaganda cadre under Serbian war hero Captain Dragan Vasiljkovic, were suspected of involvement but publicly denied engaging in what they described as "forbidden" hacking activities. Reported as being over 1,000 strong and composed largedly of student volunteers, "Captain Dragan's Cybercorps," as it was branded in *US News and World Report*, instead vowed to undertake a campaign of information warfare to counter NATO propaganda efforts.[16] Whether this counter-propaganda campaign involved anything more malicious than engaging in online discussion forums and translating English news articles remains unclear, but swathes of Yugospam signed by "students of Serbia" suggested some less-than-fair play on the part of Dragan's men.[17]

After physical communications infrastructure was destroyed in the Belgrade bombings, anti-NATO attacks came increasingly from other Eastern Bloc states, including Russia, Latvia, and Lithuania.[18] One group, known variously as the Russian Hackers Union or the Russian Hackers Brigade, claimed responsibility for a handful of low-level defacements, including the websites of Orange Coast College in California and a paintball course in Indiana. This group also received credit for more high-profile attacks, e.g., on US military sites. Russian news outlet Gazeta.ru speculated about the group's involvement in the

12   Andrews, "The First Internet War"; and Lynch, "Kosovo Being Called First Internet War."
13   Arquilla and Ronfeldt, "Cyberwar is Coming!", 141–165.
14   Geers, "Cyberspace and the Changing Nature of Warfare."
15   Nuttall, "Net warfare over Kosovo."
16   Satchell, "Captain Dragan's Serbian Cybercorps."
17   Pollock and Petersen, "Serbs take offensive in first cyberwar, bombing America."
18   Sheehan, "Serbs hackers fight cyber war."

takedown of whitehouse.gov in the early days of the campaign.[19] These speculations, like others raised during the conflict, remain publicly unsubstantiated, but nevertheless demonstrate the power of networks in cyber warfare. Even though the former Soviet republics were not formal belligerents, the decentralization of the Net allowed their citizens to join in the the fight.

In addition to pro-Serbian hackers, NATO drew a second major line of attack on 7 May, 1999, when US planes bombed the Chinese embassy in Belgrade, killing three Chinese citizens and wounding twenty others. Though the United States officially apologized, claiming they had mistaken the embassy for a Serbian arms warehouse, the Chinese public was nevertheless incensed, and it was not long before China's own band of patriotic hackers joined the fray. Most notably, the Belgrade embassy bombing marked the emergence of the notorious Honkers Union of China (HUC) or Red Hackers Alliance. Chinese hackers had previously taken the name "honkers" (also rendered "Red Hacker"), modifying the Mandarin loanword for hacker, hēikè (黑客,) literally "black visitor," to hóngkè (红客) or "red visitor" in a show of national pride. This moniker in itself was evidence of an emerging patriotic hacking community within China. According to Scott Henderson, their "Union" was in fact the product of earlier patriotic hacking activities during the Jakarta riots of 1998, in which many Chinese nationals were targeted. The Jakarta riots prompted independent Chinese hacking communities to begin networking with one another, but it was not until the 1999 embassy bombing that a central coordinating website was established for the HUC.[20] With their superior experience and organization, the HUC was able to orchestrate a series of attacks against several US government targets, including the Department of the Interior, the National Park Service, and the Department of Energy, whose site remained down for a full day.[21] Attacks launched by the HUC and affiliated hackers made May the most disruptive month of the ALLIED FORCE campaign.[22]

When the media spoke in 1999 of an ongoing "cyberwar," the term often referred to information competition waged over the Internet, or an online "propaganda war."[23] Both pro- and anti-NATO factions jockeyed for advantage in war coverage and propaganda, though anti-NATO hackers ultimately took their efforts one step further with degrading attacks on Allied networks. Ranging from banks to media outlets to Internet Service Providers, the number of targeted systems reached over 170 by the end of the campaign.[24]

---

19 McCullagh, "Did Russians Get Whitehouse.gov?"; and Denning, "Cyber Conflict as an Emergent Social Phenomenon."
20 Henderson, The Dark Visitor, 48.
21 Kellan, "Hackers hit government Web sites after China embassy bombing."
22 Healey, "First Generation CND Activity, 1999" (unclassified presentation, last updated 12 July 2000).
23 Harrison, "NATO Web site holds off cyberattacks"; see also Pollock and Petersen, "Serbs take offensive in first cyberwar, bombing America." For ealier uses of the term in the media, see Brown, "Invasion of the cyber-Members"; and Grier, "Preparing for 21st Century Information Warfare."
24 Jones, et al., Global Information Warfare, 289.

Of these attacks, about twenty were aimed at the US Department of Defense.[25] Figure 12 is a contemporaneous analysis from the US military's Joint Task Force for Computer Network Defense, illustrating the spike in activity against the DoD during ALLIED FORCE, and how this compared to total DoD and Internet defacements.

Spam, DDoS attacks, and most instances of defacement were intended to deny the adversary the ability to communicate and relay their own propaganda. But some defacements allowed enemy websites to be commandeered for friendly uses, e.g., by redirecting traffic to sympathetic news sources.[26] Some spam attacks similarly packed the "Melissa" macro virus, which emailed itself to the first fifty email addresses in a recipient's address book, converting enemy mail systems into additional spam engines.[27]

Figure 12: Jason Healey, 'First Generation CND Activity, 1999'
(unclassified presentation, last updated 12 July 2000)

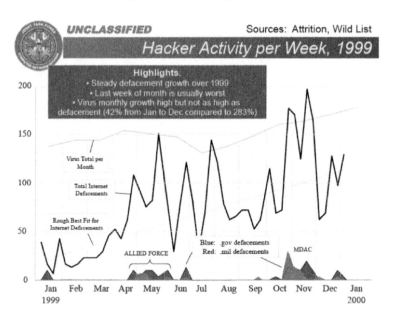

From a technical standpoint, the majority of these attacks were not particularly original, sophisticated, or damaging—certainly by today's standards. Hackers had been defacing websites and blocking access via DDoS since 1994,[28] and though NATO was not always

---

25 Healey, "First Generation CND Activity, 1999."
26 See Dunn, "Battle Spilling Over onto the Internet."
27 CERT, "CERT Advisory CA-1999-04 Melissa Macro Virus."
28 "Wikileaks Infowar not the first online protest action."

prepared for these tactics beforehand, the Allies were able to remediate the damage in a relatively short time span. Defaced websites could be taken down and restored, and spam and DDoS attacks could be averted with proper firewalls. As one *Los Angeles Times* article put it, "the worst appears to be that accessing [pages] has been more difficult."[29] To be sure, each successful attack represented only a marginal gain in the battle for information dominance. But in a war often described in terms of the CNN Effect, ownership of the narrative proved an important asset.

The importance of information dominance is in fact encapsulated in NATO's decision at the outset of the conflict *not* to launch its own cyber attacks on Yugoslav systems, despite its power to do so. State Department spokesman James Rubin explained that "full and open access to the Internet can only help the Serbian people know the ugly truth about the atrocities and crimes against humanity being perpetrated in Kosovo by the Milošević regime."[30] NATO's relative passivity in the conflict was also due to US fears of the legal implications of cyber warfare. At the time, NATO—and in particular US—forces had the capabilities to drain Milošević's bank account and take down Serbian financial systems, yet no such attacks were carried out (or publicly acknowledged in any event). According to a document released in May 1999 by the US Department of Defense (DoD), entitled "Assessment of International Legal Issues in Information Operations," cyber attacks resulting in collateral damage could be classified as war crimes. In keeping with the DoD's guidance, the United States ruled out the use of cyber weapons, despite NATO's calls to "electronically isolate" Milošević.[31] The consequence was a starkly one-sided contest in cyberspace.

Red Visitors: The Hainan Island Incident

Kosovo was certainly not the last time the United States would face patriotic Chinese hackers. In April 2001, a US Navy EP3 signals intelligence aircraft collided with a Chinese J-8II fighter jet off China's southern coast, leading to the death of Chinese pilot Wang Wei and forcing the spy plane to make an emergency landing on the island of Hainan. With the memory of Belgrade still fresh in their minds, Chinese hackers lashed out against American systems in indignation. Groups such as the Honkers Union of China disseminated hacking tools and target lists on popular Chinese web portals, channeling nationalist fury into a series of US government and private sector website defacements. US hackers meanwhile responded in kind, launching a tit-for-tat battle of defacements and a handful of other crude tactics, lasting roughly five weeks in total. The struggle was ultimately notable for its relatively clear trajectory, as the intensity of the conflict built over time, culminating in a

---

29   Dunn, "Battle Spilling Over onto the Internet."
30   Briscoe, "No Winner in Kosovo Propaganda War."
31   *Ibid.*

massive Chinese offensive coinciding with the anniversary of the 1999 Chinese embassy bombing. The conflict similarly revealed stark differences between US and Chinese hackers, with the latter working in what appeared to be close coordination—possibly even with the approval and guidance of Beijing, and the former operating in a fairly decentralized fashion.

In contrast to the earlier attacks over Kosovo, the cyber conflict surrounding the "Hainan Island Incident," as it became known, involved patriotic hackers on both sides of the Pacific. Chinese "honkers" coordinated support through web portals such as sohu.com and sina.com[32] (the precursor to today's popular Sina Weibo microblog service), while also setting up their own sites, such as "USA Kill" and "China Killer."[33] The Honkers Union of China (HUC) played the most powerful role in coordinating China's cyber offensive. The HUC earned a name for itself with a series of attacks, including the targeting of at least nine major websites by 14 April, according to one report.[34] In contrast to US hackers, the HUC coordinated a week-long interval in which to conduct its attacks, beginning on May Day (1 May) and ending with the anniversary of the US bombing of Belgrade on 7 May. The drop in the number of US website defacements in the following weeks suggested that Chinese hackers generally respected the HUC's proposed timeline. This gave the HUC a reputation as a group that could direct the Chinese patriotic hackers' energy toward a single task. Chinese hackers were, however, only loosely organized, and hit a broad range of targets. The scope of these first attacks ranged from small, local businesses to (noncritical) US Navy websites, suggesting a diversity of interests and skill levels.[35] Thus, while the Chinese were, on the whole, better organized than their American counterparts, coordinating groups such as the HUC were ultimately unable to exert *full* control over all Chinese hackers.

---

32   Cha, "Chinese Suspected of Hacking U.S. Sites."
33   Geers, "Cyberspace and the Changing Nature of Warfare."
34   Stenger, "FBI probes pro-China attacks on U.S. Web sites."
35   Cha, "Chinese Suspected of Hacking U.S. Sites"; and Denning, "Cyber Conflict as an Emergent Social Phenomenon."

Figure 13: Navy website defaced by the Honkers Union of China (HUC) in 2001

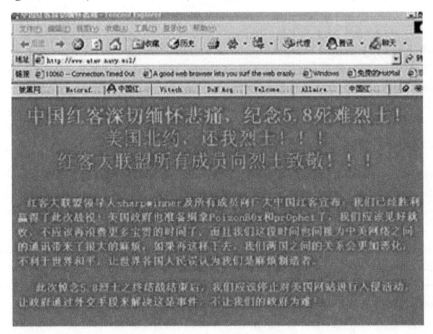

US hackers, on the other hand, arose from the ranks of underground groups, such as HackWeiser and World of Hell, to call for a counter-offensive against early Chinese website defacements.[36] Some American hackers, such as the notorious PoizonB0x, claimed over 300 defacements, and several media reports at the time likewise registered "hundreds" of Chinese website defacements throughout April.[37] Whether the US hackers' "upper hand" during the early weeks of the conflict resulted from superior skills and defenses, or from a lack of Chinese involvement is not altogether clear. The dramatic escalation of the conflict the following month would seem to suggest that the Chinese had either restrained themselves previously, as the number of attempts on US systems increased in fulfillment of the HUC's promises, or simply that they were not as engaged beforehand.[38]

So credible were the threats of Chinese hackers that the National Infrastructure Protection Center (NIPC) at the FBI issued an advisory warning of increased levels of malicious activity during the week of 1 May. The NIPC also released an analysis of a DDoS-facilitating virus by the name of "Lion" (stylized L10n), which it linked to China.[39] Anxieties ran high in the lead up to the May Day attacks, as commentators feared an escalation not only in the quantity of attacks but in their quality as well. While Lion did not play a major role in the

---

36   "China warns of massive hack attacks."
37   See Wagstaff, "The Internet Could Be the Site of the Next China-U.S. Standoff"; and "Virus alert in Hacker War."
38   Krebs, "Chinese Hackers Step Up Attacks On US Web Sites."
39   Evers, "Feds Warn of May Day Hack Attacks."

May Day offensive and subsequent attacks, hackers' tactics did grow increasingly vicious, shifting from simple defacement to outright deletion of data in some cases.[40] Chinese hackers succeeded in defacing a number of more high-profile US government sites, including those of the Department of Health and Human Services and the Department of Labor.[41] US hackers meanwhile scored hits on several Chinese government websites, such as the provincial governments of Yichun and Xiajun.[42] In addition to defacements and file-deletions, Chinese hackers claimed several successful DDoS attacks, e.g., against the US Department of the Interior's National Business Center, the US Geological Survey, and Pacific Bell Internet Services.[43]

As discussed previously, website defacements and DDoS attacks are common tactics, requiring relatively few resources and little technical sophistication, but the patriotic hackers later upgraded their software. Most notably, a self-propagating virus named "sadmind" infected nearly 9,000 servers worldwide in early May, allowing hackers to execute "arbitrary code" on Solaris and Windows systems.[44] Once in control of infected systems, hackers typically defaced the websites associated with them, though CERT noted some reports of file deletions as well.[45] The spread of sadmind underscored the perennial difficulty of collateral damage, as the virus infected systems in Australia, New Zealand, and elsewhere, plastering even non-US sites with anti-US graffiti.[46] South Korea also complained of being caught in the crossfire, with anti-American slogans gracing the site of Seoul National University, and anti-Chinese messages appearing on Samsung and Daewoo's websites.[47]

Not only did the range of targets exceed the immediate belligerents, but so did the hackers themselves. Hackers from Saudi Arabia, Pakistan, India, Brazil, Argentina, and Malaysia reportedly joined the battle on the side of the Americans, while the Chinese received support from South Korea, Indonesia, and Japan.[48] It is difficult to assess the full extent to which the internationalization of the US-China conflict was the result of the Hainan Island incident itself, and to what extent other political factors contributed. Japanese systems were, for example, under attack from both China and South Korea at this time, due to the publication of a nationalist textbook. It is also possible that some systems were added to American and Chinese botnets to fight for one side or another. But the trend toward internationalization was clear.

---

40 Krebs, "Chinese Hackers Step Up Attacks On US Web Sites."
41 Ibid.
42 "Chinese, US hackers' cyber battle goes global."
43 "Vision Of Warfare Future As Us And China Swap Cyber Attacks."
44 Hellaby, "Sadmind Worm Daubs Anti-US Slogans Globally"; and CERT, "CERT Advisory CA-2001-11 sadmind/IIS Worm."
45 Raiu, "One Sad Mind"; and CERT, "CERT Advisory CA-2001-11 sadmind/IIS Worm."
46 Hellaby, "Sadmind worm daubs anti-US slogans globally."
47 "Korea Hit in US, China Crossfire" ; and "Chinese, US Hackers' Cyber Battle Goes Global."
48 Ibid.

Finally on 7 May, the state-run *People's Daily* came out against the ongoing defacement battle, and three days later, the HUC called an official end to its attacks, claiming it had reached its goal of 1,000 defacements.[49] The close proximity of these declarations has led some to infer a connection, albeit informal, between the HUC and the Chinese government.[50] Indeed, according to the Deputy Commander of the Pentagon's Joint Task Force on Computer Network Operations, "We expected another series of attacks from Chinese hackers [in May 2002], but actually the government of China asked them not to do that."[51] Thus, in the framework of the spectrum of state responsibility (see Table 3 on page 50), the patriotic hackers' initial attacks may be considered state-ignored, after which they effectively became state-prohibited. As for the responsibility of the US government, it is not clear whether the relevant authorities took actions against American patriotic hackers. Assuming no concerted action was taken, one might consider US-based attacks state-ignored—or state-prohibited-but-inadequate at best. Viewed in these terms, the United States might appear the more aggressive of the two, yet one should also bear in mind the relative ease with which China is able to censor its citizens' communications, particularly from a legal standpoint.

Although sparked by the original incident over the South China Sea, the cyber conflict ultimately lasted much longer than the diplomatic crisis itself. The crew of the EP3 aricraft was released from Hainan Island on 11 April, following a letter from the United States saying it was "very sorry" for the death of Wang Wei and for entering Chinese airspace without verbal clearance.[52] Despite the resolution of both parties' most immediate grievances, however, tensions lingered, and nowhere was this tension more evident than in cyberspace.

The Birth of E-Jihad: Israel v. Palestine Takes to the Net

To the careful observer, the back and forth between the United States and China over the Hainan Island incident evoked the first major flare up in a different cyber conflict. Less than one year earlier, on 28 September, 1999, the outbreak of the Second Intifada in Israel-Palestine had bled over onto the Internet, unleashing a quickly escalating series of website defacements and DDoS attacks between pro-Israel and pro-Palestine hackers around the world. In many ways, the Israeli-Palestinian conflict resembled other cyber conflicts of the same period, exhibiting broad "horizontal escalation" in the context of relatively low-level website defacements and DDoS attacks. Without altogether abandoning this pattern, however, hackers on both sides ultimately made more sophisticated use of old tools, targeting major e-commerce and financial sites and developing more powerful DDoS

---

49   "Chinese Hackers Halt Web War, Say 1,000 U.S. sites defaced."
50   Henderson, The Dark Visitor, 118–119.
51   Hess, "China prevented repeat cyber attack on the US."
52   "Chinese poker."

programs.[53] Thus did two of the world's oldest rivals turn some of the oldest tools of the trade to new uses, igniting the region in a flurry of cyber attacks that has never truly died out.

Unlike the kinetic intifada which it mirrored, the Israeli-Palestinian cyber conflict of 2000 began with an Israeli, rather than Palestinian offensive. Israeli hackers based on Wizel.com launched a surprise DDoS attack on 6 October against six Hezbollah websites, as well as the official websites of Hamas and the Palestinian National Authority (PNA).[54] Several weeks later, the favor was returned by pro-Palestinian Ummah.net in a counterattack on Wizel.com. Wielding a new DDoS tool by the name of "Defend," Palestinian hackers were able to circumvent the caching mechanisms used to detect and avert ping floods, and thus successfully compromised not only Wizel.com but also the official website of the Israeli Defense Force (IDF).[55] "Defend" and its variants were to become mainstays of the conflict, as the tool was adopted by pro-Israeli hackers and later refined into the Carko DDoS tool, used in the aftermath of the Hainan Island Incident.[56]

The opening moves of the struggle revealed a great deal about the tactics of each side. Pro-Israeli hackers, for instance, overwhelmingly targeted terrorist and extremist websites (e.g., Hezbollah), which comprised approximately 39 percent of all the targets between 28 September and 27 December. The next in popularitiy were government websites (e.g., PNA), which comprised approximately 26 percent of the targets.[57] Pro-Palestinian hackers, in the same period, focused 51 percent of their attacks on corporate websites, especially in the technology and telecommunications sectors, as well as educational institutions (21 percent) and government (10 percent), e.g., the IDF and the Prime Minister's Office.[58]

"Unity," a pro-Palestinian group with connections to Hezbollah, outlined a four-step plan of attack, beginning with government websites, then financial institutions and telecommunications, and finally take-downs of e-commerce sites. The first three phases were faithfully carried out, as seen in the progression of attacks on sites like the IDF, the Knesset, and the Israeli Foreign Ministry, then the Bank of Israel and the Tel Aviv Stock Exchange (TASE), followed by further attempts on ISP NetVision and the telecommunications companies Lucent and AT&T, which had offered NetVision assistance in managing the pro-Palestinian onslaught.[59] Unity threatened a fourth phase, "Attacking Zionist E-Commerce," but there was little evidence of follow-through.

53   Allen and Demchak, "The Israeli-Palestinian Cyber War."
54   iDefense, "Israeli-Palestinian Cyber Conflict (IPCC) Report v2.0PR," 9.
55   Ibid.
56   Geers, "Cyberspace and the Changing Nature of Warfare"; and Allen and Demchak, "The Israeli-Palestinian Cyber War."
57   iDefense, "Israeli-Palestinian Cyber Conflict (IPCC) Report v2.0PR," 8; and Allen and Demchak, "The Israeli-Palestinian Cyber War."
58   Ibid.
59   Ibid.

An Israeli hackers group by the name of the Israeli Internet Underground (IIU) rose to prevent the promised economic doomsday. The IIU was noteworthy for its white-hat membership, and worked in collaboration with Israeli security company X2s to plug the holes in Israeli defenses.[60] Despite their best efforts, the IIU believed that Unity ultimately did unleash phase four and that their attacks on Israeli businesses caused an eight percent drop in the Tel Aviv Stock Exchange.[61] Around this same time, the National Infrastructure Protection Center (NIPC) in the United States issued an advisory to e-commerce and Internet-hosted systems, warning of attempts on customer data and later reporting incidents of extortion.[62] In any event, Unity ultimately did not deliver on its promise of "millions of dollars of losses in transactions," and the Israeli economy remained by-and-large unscathed.[63]

Ultimately, pro-Palestinian hackers were more prolific in their attacks (166 in total, compared with the Israelis' thirty-four). They successfully downed several high-profile targets, such as the Foreign Ministry and the Prime Minister's Office, while compromising access to others, like the IDF.[64] Israeli hackers did manage to attack several important pro-Palestinian sites, but were ultimately limited by the available range. The disparity between Israeli and Palestinian attacks was therefore at least partly a function of Internet penetration within each country.

Although lacking the broad selection of targets which pro-Palestinians attacked, pro-Israeli hackers found plenty of vulnerabilities on sites more tangentially related to the Palestinian cause, including the Qatari Ministry of Awqaf and Islamic Affairs and the Iranian Ministry of Agriculture. Pro-Palestinian hackers similarly targeted websites of Israeli allies, such as the United States, e.g., the American Israel Public Affairs Committee (AIPAC) and the Anti-Defamation League. All the while, third parties were joining in the battle from all around the globe. The most notable among them were the Pakistani Hackerz Club (PHC), Doctor Nuker, and GForce Pakistan, which will be discussed in more detail in connection with a separate cyber conflict in the subcontinent. At length, what had begun as a parallel of the Second Intifada had become an international imbroglio, with hackers from Israel, Palestine, Lebanon, Germany, Saudi Arabia, Pakistan, Brazil, and the United States all becoming involved.[65]

As with other contemporary conflicts, the online struggle between Israel and Palestine was carried out in large part via website defacements and DDoS attacks. As mentioned

---

60   *Ibid.*, 16.
61   Gentile, "Israeli Hackers Vow to Defend."
62   "Timeline of Major Events in Internet Security."
63   iDefense, "Israeli-Palestinian Cyber Conflict (IPCC) Report v2.0PR," 28.
64   *Ibid.*; and Ackerman, "Government sites under cyber-attack."
65   iDefense, "Israeli-Palestinian Cyber Conflict (IPCC) Report v2.0PR," 6.

previously, however, the Palestinians and then the Israelis developed more sophisticated DDoS tools than those used in past conflicts, such as 'Defend' and the forerunner of Carko. A myriad of other DDoS tools were also available for download, bearing names such as EvilPing, WinSmurf, HTTP Bomber 1.001b, FakeMail, MailBomber, Attack 2.5.1, PutDown, and QuickFire—some of which used zombie servers to send thousands and even tens of thousands of pings at once.[66] The explicit targeting of financial institutions like the Bank of Israel and the Tel Aviv Stock Exchange marked another important innovation. Although the idea to target the financial sector was not novel in itself (cf. the US decision on cyber attacks against Milošević), pro-Palestinian hackers were the first do so *en masse*. Hackers on both sides also disseminated and utilized somewhat more sophisticated tools, such as macro viruses—including LoveLetter and Melissa, the latter of which had made its appearance during ALLIED FORCE in 1999. Despite the relative complexity of these macro viruses, the goal remained the same: to take down enemy websites by overwhelming them with traffic, be it spam or pings.

Cyber Conflict on the Sub-Continent: India v. Pakistan

In May of 1999, Pakistani paramilitaries and Kashmiri militants infiltrated the Indian-controlled district of Kargil in the states of Jammu and Kashmir, setting off a short military conflict between the two nuclear states. Under significant pressure from the international community, including China and the United States, Pakistan withdrew its forces to north of the Line of Control, and the short war ended with the *status quo ante bellum*. India declared its Operation Vijay, or "Victory," a success. But over a year later, India would face a different sort of invasion, one which could not be so easily repelled. As talks between India and the Kashmiri militant group Hizbul Mujahideen broke down in August of 2000, a series of Pakistani website defacements hit India, plastering Indian websites with images of alleged atrocities committed by the Indian military in Kashmir.[67] The Indian response was muted at best, in part due to government efforts to limit retaliation.

Editor's Note

The 1999 to 2000 cyber conflict mirrored an earlier incident in 1998, when a teen-aged American hacker, incensed at India's recent nuclear test, intruded into the Bhabha Atomic Research Center in less than a minute.

He shared stolen password files with an online colleague (as it turns out, the colleague was a Serbian immigrant in the US), who extended the intrusion, stealing email and files. All of BARC's passwords were posted online and the site was swarmed by hackers worldwide.

For more, read the excellent contemporaneous coverage by *Forbes*, "Hacking Bhabha" at www. forbes.com/1998/11/16/feat.html.

Although the cyber conflict between India and Pakistan did involve hackers on both sides, Pakistani hackers appeared both more organized and more prolific in their attacks. The

---

66   *Ibid.*, 12; and Allen and Demchak, "The Israeli-Palestinian Cyber War."
67   "Pro-Pakistan hackers invade Indian website, post anti-India messages."

principal Pakistani hacker group was known as "G-Force," which claimed responsibility for many high profile attacks. While G-Force, Doctor Nuker, the Pakistani Hackers Club, and the Pakistan Cyber Army had engaged in attacks prior to the events of 2000, Indian hackers had been relatively passive.[68] The year 2000 is in fact most notable for the entrance of Indian patriotic hackers onto the scene and for their first reciprocal defacements. A group by the name of "Patriotic Indians" claimed a number of Pakistani government website defacements, including pak.gov.pk. No group claimed anything more disruptive than simple defacements, however; and no mention was made of DDoS attacks or macro viruses. According to one Indian network administrator at the time, "Most of the [Pakistani] hackers do nothing more than take the user to a different URL, where they have posted pro-Pakistan messages."[69]

Indian hackers, regardless of their tactics, did not get far. The Cyber Crime Unit of India's Central Bureau of Investigation, also established in 2000, worked to suppress Indian hacking activity, just as much as it sought to mitigate attacks flowing in from Pakistan.[70] Conversely, the Pakistani government, and in particular Inter-Services Intelligence (ISI), was widely suspected of aiding its own patriotic hackers, although many of these allegations were later discredited.[71]

According to statistics from attrition.org, there was an absolute increase in website defacements between the two countries from 1999 to 2000, with India suffering four in 1999 and seventy-two in 2000, while Pakistan suffered seven in 1999 and eighteen in 2000.[72] In other words, India experienced a 1,800 percent rise in attacks, while Pakistan experienced an increase of approximately 250 percent, compared with a global rise of about 180 percent between 1999 and 2000.[73] Even controlling for overall increased levels of defacements worldwide (due to simple technology diffusion, for instance), these figures indicate a clear flare-up in online hostilities in 2000, especially on the part of Pakistani hackers.

Lessons Learned

Patriotic hackers ultimately did not revolutionize the conduct of international conflicts. Their activities were instead symptomatic of the ongoing information revolution. As information technology became increasingly widespread, the number of potential targets and attackers likewise grew, to the point where an international crisis could prompt ordinary civilians to become "warriors" of their own sort. The capability for anything

---

68   Nanjappa, "Cyber wars: Pak has an advantage over India."
69   Joseph, "Both Sides Hacked Over Kashmir."
70   *Ibid.*
71   Shaikh, "The futility of Indo-Pak cyber wars."
72   See Shaikh, "The futility of Indo-Pak cyber wars."
73   Legard, "Web Site Defacements Hit All-Time High."

more than intermittent disruption still lay with state actors. Thus, these early campaigns of patriotic hacking had little effect on state-level decisions. Their impact on public opinion within the opposing states is similarly doubtful, given the often crude nature of website defacements and the ambiguity between DDoS takedowns and simple technical errors.

Peripheral as these early cyber conflicts were, analysis of their dynamics reveals important lessons for today's security and military practitioners. Most notably, the cyber components of these conflicts developed spontaneously outside of governmental control, though typically with government connivance, and often with little coordination among the participants—the HUC being a notable exception.

The diffuse nature of cyber conflict thus poses a challenge for state-level actors accustomed to more centralized decision making. Moreover, how states manage this process will vary according to their technological sophistication and legal institutions. China, and to a lesser extent India, have demonstrated a clear willingness to censor hackers within their borders, in order to help stabilize relations with major geopolitical rivals. The United States, on the other hand, has historically done relatively little to curb patriotic hacking, focusing the lion's share of its attention on domestic cyber criminals.

The decentralization of patriotic hacking likewise allows for a greater degree of collateral damage than direct, state-sponsored or state-integrated cyber attacks. Insofar as patriotic hackers lack the intelligence capabilities and technological sophistication of state actors, they are more likely to unleash indiscriminate attacks, such as the sadmind virus, which risk expanding the conflict beyond the immediate belligerents.

Though none of these attacks were particularly dangerous, there are three reasons for greater concern. These attacks can be escalatory, as the leadership of the nation under attack may feel the need to respond and counter with their own cyber or physical force. Sometimes patriotic hackers seem to rely on networks owned by organized criminals, which can provide greater capabilities (for example, see the chapter of this book on the 2008 Georgian conflict). And of course, sometimes the patriotic hackers may simply get lucky in striking at an important target, as the hackers did against the Indian BARC Atomic Facility in 1998.

Finally, though often cited as one of its greatest difficulties, the attribution problem is not the *sine qua non* of cyber conflict, as early patriotic hacking vividly illustrates. Not only were many attacks self-attributed ("We did this!"), but the cyber conflicts themselves took place in the context of real-world crises, in most cases making the attackers' nationalities all too obvious. Less clear was the extent to which these attacks enjoyed state sponsorship. But the fact remains that these were symptoms rather than the causes of international crises. Accordingly, the cyber component of each crisis proved to be of only secondary importance to the countries involved. The US government did not consider Yugoslav hackers to be a genuine threat to ALLIED FORCE operations, and the India-Pakistan cyber conflict paled in comparison to other perceived slights.

Patriotic hacking therefore complicated but did not revolutionize the conduct of international relations, as so may had hypothesized (and indeed, continue to hypothesize). Instead, foreign policy acquired a new dimension, which nations have thus far found difficult to fully control. The extent to which nations find it necessary to reign in their patriotic hackers is likely to differ according to the circumstances. If patriotic hacking remains low-intensity and low-impact, national governments may see little value in censoring hackers within their borders. But if more sophisticated technologies diffuse outward to non-national actors, governments may need to take more aggressive measures to reassert their sovereignty in cyberspace.

Moonlight Maze

Adam Elkus[1]

One of the enduring frustrations of cyber conflict lies in its tentativeness. Many of the basic events in its history are shrouded in mystery and heavily classified. A paucity of open-source information exists, much of it of limited reliability. Nowhere is this more evident than in the incident known as "MOONLIGHT MAZE."

MOONLIGHT MAZE, a name given to a series of intrusions, is one of many "cyber security wake-up calls" that have highlighted the increasing role of state authorities in generating, sponsoring, or at least passively tolerating sophisticated and far-reaching espionage incidents. Russian involvement has been suspected, but never conclusively proven. Intruders probed computer systems at the Pentagon, the Department of Energy, private universities, and research labs searching for military maps, troop configurations, and military hardware designs.[2] In 1999, the Federal Bureau of Investigation made public that this espionage was ongoing, sending shockwaves throughout the cyber security community.[3]

Even though very little unclassified information is currently available about the incident, the ambiguous and disruptive effects of MOONLIGHT MAZE make it a signal case in cyber history. MOONLIGHT MAZE shaped technical and organizational discourse within the US, and created the perception of a lethal, yet ephemeral and mysterious cyber threat. While earlier cyber espionage had occurred (such as Cuckoo's Egg and RAHAB), these qualities make MOONLIGHT MAZE a useful marker for measuring the growth in widespread awareness of professionalized, state-sponsored threats in cyberspace. Its ambiguity also symbolizes an era of cyber conflict in which few easy answers can be found concerning the origin, dynamics, and/or goals of adversarial espionage threats.

Additionally, the federal government's organizational responses to the incident represented the growing understanding among security executives that defending cyberspace requires different tools, organizations, and concepts. In this, MOONLIGHT MAZE actually dovetailed with a larger focus on adapting the government to fight transnational threats. This focus would take shape immediately before and after the 11 September 2001 terrorist attacks.

---

1   Adam Elkus is an analyst specializing in Foreign Policy and Security Studies. He is currently Associate Editor at Red Team Journal and is a contributor to the ThreatsWatch project. His articles have been published in West Point CTC Sentinel, Small Wars Journal, and other publications. His writing has been cited in essays and monographs published by the Army War College Strategic Studies Institute, the Journal of Information Warfare, US Naval Institute Proceedings, and Studies in Conflict and Terrorism.
2   "Cyberwar!", "The Warnings."
3   Suro, "FBI Lagging Behind on Cyber Crime."

Establishing Context

Before MOONLIGHT MAZE, many high-profile cyber incidents that targeted United States government networks were attributed to non-state actors. The 1994 attacks that targeted the United States Air Force's Rome Labs were the work of two British youngsters—one of whom was motivated by his love of the X-Files.[4] The 1998 SOLAR SUNRISE incident also was carried out by young hackers in California and Israel. Massive, sustained, and state-backed cyber operations were not widespread in the late 1990s. However, this situation was about to radically change.[5]

This is not to say that all or even most pre-MOONLIGHT MAZE incidents were the work of the stereotypical teen-aged hacker. Rather, the point is that the massive state espionage which has characterized cyber incidents in most of the last few years, was not as omnipresent in either public or elite consciousness prior to the late 1990s. In 2001, MOONLIGHT MAZE was considered to be the largest cyber attack on the United States to date. The era of TITAN RAIN and other larger cyber espionage cases, such as Stuxnet, was yet to come.

It is also important to note cybersecurity's interaction with larger trends in American national security during the late 1990s. Natural security policymakers were beginning to recognize that the seductive concepts of the Revolution in Military Affairs (RMA), America's technological superiority in the Gulf War, and the Kosovo conflict disguised a growing threat from state and non-state adversaries determined to play by different rules. American adversaries would not continue to invite the kind of security responses that played best to American strengths. Rather, they would look for cheap tools and target American weaknesses. Information technology, considered a strength in conventional warfare, became a source of weakness within the framework of cyberwarfare and cyber-espionage. Moreover, US policymakers clearly saw similar challenges to inter-agency boundaries and capabilities posed by both cyber opponents and more traditional forms of terrorism.

Presidential Decision Directive 63 (PDD 63) led to the creation of the National Incident Protection Center (NIPC), as an inter-agency body with the power to safeguard the nation's civilian and governmental critical infrastructure from computer-based attack. SOLAR SUNRISE and other thorny cyber incidents prompted the creation of Joint Task Force-Computer Network Defense (JTF-CND), a body trusted with the centralized and coordinated defense of military networks.[6] These agencies were maturing just as MOONLIGHT MAZE became known to the United States government, and played

---

4   Bayuk, et al., Cyber Security Policy Handbook, 213.
5   *Ibid.*, 321.
6   Gourley, "JTF-CND to JTF-CND to Cybercom."

crucial roles in resolving the incident.

MOONLIGHT MAZE's emphasis on Russian espionage also did not occur in a geopolitical vacuum. While geo-strategic competition between the United States and the Soviet Union ended in the early 1990s, Russian espionage has continued largely unabated.

> *There is every reason to be concerned that more damaging spies are still in place, targeting essential secrets about American intelligence and military operations, negating decades of investment and putting American lives at risk. It is a perfect storm. Russian global intelligence operations are a well-resourced and highly developed instrument of state power.*[7]

The MOONLIGHT MAZE incident also occurred in a time of rising American awareness of a growing Russian investment in information warfare capabilities. As adversary cyber doctrine specialist Lieutenant Colonel (Ret.) Timothy Thomas noted, Russian military thinkers incorporated the idea of "system on system" military operations from the early 1990s onwards.[8] Russia, though geopolitically weakened, was energetic in projecting power into cyberspace. Its military doctrine in the period of the late Cold War recognized the importance of command, control, intelligence, and computers (C4I) but lacked the material means to realize this "military-technical revolution." However, cyber-espionage and cyberwarfare capabilities were well within even a greatly weakened Moscow's reach. MOONLIGHT MAZE must be understood within this unique context.

However, some caution should be exercised in pointing toward Russia as the perpetrators of MOONLIGHT MAZE. The evidence of Russian involvement is still circumstantial in the unclassified records. The Russians vigorously denied participation in MOONLIGHT MAZE. This too can be viewed within a larger context. Russia has often been suspected of direct involvement and/or indirect involvement in cyber conflict, but direct proof of Russian involvement has always been frustratingly difficult to assemble. Sorting out official Russian government activity from that of patriotic hackers or the large organized crime sector is also difficult, as all three sectors are both porous and extremely murky.

Lastly, the open-source record does not indicate that there was a strategic or even a tactical warning of the MOONLIGHT MAZE crisis. Network defenders, the Department of Defense, and the FBI struggled to understand the nature of the attack, who carried it out, and why. The fact that these questions are still largely publicly unanswered suggests problems regarding not only cyber early warning efforts but also post-incident damage assessments.

Entering the Maze

---

7   *Ibid.*
8   Thomas, "Nation-State Cyber Strategies," 476-477.

In March 1998, the DoD detected what was then dubbed the most "persistent and serious" computer attack against the United States to date. While no classified networks were targeted, the Non-Classified Internet Protocol Router Network (NIPRNET) was penetrated.[9] Network security specialists at the Defense Information Systems Agency discovered that attackers had entered NIPRNET and other unclassified systems by "tunneling" malicious codes within programs for routine computer operations. This made it more difficult for systems administrators to discover precisely what was occurring.[10]

The intruders broke into computer networks belonging to the National Aeronautics and Space Agency (NASA), the Department of Energy (DoE), the DoD, and other government research agencies and private laboratories. The attackers were after military-technical information on DoD systems.[11] The FBI led the investigation, which was coordinated through the National Infrastructure Protection Center (NIPC), while the newly created Joint Task Force-Computer Network Defense (JTF-CND) took the lead in coordinating a response. The incident was codenamed "MOONLIGHT MAZE."

It is important to understand that MOONLIGHT MAZE was not a one-off incident, but an extended campaign that occurred for at least three years, conducted by multiple actors against defense systems. A Government Accountability Office (GAO) report characterizes MOONLIGHT MAZE as a "stealth" campaign of recurring hacks.[12] It was MOONLIGHT MAZE's massive scale and duration that differentiated the attacks from other cyber incidents during the 1990s. The intruders lifted thousands of files containing information on technical research, contracts, encryption techniques, and unclassified specifications of DoD war-planning systems. In turn, the attack triggered one of the largest and most secretive cybersecurity investigations in the DoD's history.[13]

It is important to understand that MOONLIGHT MAZE was not a one-off incident, but an extended campaign that occurred for at least three years, conducted by multiple actors against defense systems.

Other notable aspects of MOONLIGHT MAZE were its exploitation of the scientific community's access to the DoD and the attackers' operational sophistication. In an interview with PBS Frontline in 2003, former Deputy Security of Defense and later Center for Strategic and International Studies President John Hamre noted that the attacks

9 Drogin, "Russians Seem to Be Hacking into Pentagon."
10 Loeb, "Pentagon Computers Under Assault."
11 Adams, "Virtual Defense," 99-100.
12 Government Accountability Office, "Information Security: Challenges to Improving DOD's Incident Response Capabilities," 5.
13 Adams, "Virtual Defense."

exploited the prevailing norm of openness in the scientific community.

The intruders lifted thousands of files containing information on technical research, contracts, encryption techniques, and unclassified specifications of DoD war-planning systems.

The intrusions were not conducted through the Internet, but instead exploited the Department of Defense's dependence on a scientific-industrial backbone. Hamre emphasized that the perpetrators did not hack from laptops, but rather employed sophisticated hardware with formidable computing power. He also judged that they possessed excellent operational skills, iteratively adjusting their techniques in response to countermeasures. Hamre noted that the broadly DoD-related research community allowed researchers access to large farms of supercomputers. This vulnerability, Hamre argued, could also potentially be exploited again:[14]

> [T]he techniques of penetration were through the very open protocols that exist in the science community. I think that's changed. We certainly ordered changes, at least in the part that DOD controls. But the science community is wide open. Its ethic, its philosophy, is that you make accessible your knowledge and your techniques. So a lot of the penetration occurred through that culture of openness.[15]

Evidence of the sophistication of the attackers can also be found in their use of what was dubbed a "distributed coordination approach" to information extraction. The attackers used thousands of servers to overwhelm a single server. Because many servers are used, each attack can be disguised as a legitimate connection attempt. This makes it difficult for the victim's software to know that it is under assault, and also helps camouflage the identity of the attackers.[16] As will be noted later, DoD audiences also judged that distributed coordination approaches posed a threat to the supposed "perimeter defense" model that dominated DoD information assurance.

Efforts to target the adversaries to disable their operations were considered but were dogged by fears that such self-defense measures might constitute an act of war, if the attackers were state-sponsored.[17] Lack of understanding of the nature of the adversary thus hamstrung what might be considered today an "active" defense against intrusion. However, this did not mean that the DoD did not take steps to secure its networks. The Pentagon also decided that it would reroute its communications through eight large electronic gateways in order to better facilitate monitoring of activities and to cut down the attackers' opportunities.[18]

---

14   Hamre, interviewed in "Cyberwar!", 18 February 2003.
15   *Ibid.*
16   Joyner and Lotrionte, "Information Warfare as International Coercion," 840.
17   Loeb, "Pentagon Computers Under Assault."
18   Cordesman, Cyber Threats, Information Warfare, and Critical Infrastructure Protection, 40.

Passwords also underwent encryption, and a DoD-wide password change was forced by the JTF-CND. The Pentagon responded by investing $200 million to purchase new encryption technology, firewalls, and intrusion detection technologies.[19]

Unfortunately, the response to MOONLIGHT MAZE was also hindered by the fact that the NIPC itself was still unsteady during the time of the intrusions. By October 1999, senior agents were being transferred out of the NIPC to investigate Chinese espionage cases. Congress rejected efforts by the NIPC to expand its stable of agents. All of this occurred as the FBI's load of computer crime cases expanded from 200 in 1997 to 800 in 1999, while the FBI struggled to meet its target of 243 agents pursuing digital crime and espionage cases full time.[20] NIPC Director Michael Vatis said:

> Our bench is thin, very thin… We have put together a good starting lineup. But if we had several major incidents at the same time, we would be severely stretched, to put it mildly.[21]

On 7 October 1999, NIPC director Michael Vatis went public. Though earlier news reports had announced a large cyber campaign against the Pentagon, Vatis' interview and those given by other government officials were the most significant early disclosures. Vatis not only broke the news of a large cyber-espionage campaign, but also explicitly suggested a Russian origin.[22] However, Vatis refused to comment further. Assistant Secretary of Defense for Command, Control, and Communications Arthur Money declared that the scale of the incident was "alarming" and observed that NIPRNET had been compromised. The intensity of the attacks declined after the public announcement, compared to the spring and summer of 1999.

An undisclosed government source noted that the attack had been traced to Internet servers located 20 miles from Moscow. The source also noted that the pattern of the intrusions suggested that the attackers had a regular office-like schedule. The attacks occurred regularly from 8 am to 5 pm and never on Russian holidays.[23] A senior Energy Department official also suggested that it could be a "sponsored" intelligence activity, pointing to the "organized" nature of the activity.[24] Dion Stemfley, an analyst working for the Defense Information Systems Agency (DISA), suggested that the attacks, if not state-conducted, were "state-allowed."[25]

Other circumstantial evidence was offered to the media, which apparently suggested Russian involvement. This included the existence of an unusually high-speed connection,

19   Loeb, "Pentagon Computers Under Assault."
20   Suro, "FBI Lagging Behind on Cyber Crime."
21   Ibid.
22   Drogin, "Russians Seem to be Hacking."
23   Ibid.
24   Ibid.
25   Loeb, "Pentagon Computers Under Assault," quoted in Gelinas, Cyberdeterrence and the Problem of Attribution, 11.

linking research facilities in Moscow to the United States. US government sources speculated that it hid a major offensive command and control network within ostensibly civilian research facilities. Photos of DoD facilities, network maps, and duty rosters were also alleged to be present on these networks.[26] At the time, outside experts began to voice skepticism about foreign state involvement in the hacking attacks. George Smith, editor of the *Crypt Newsletter*, speculated that the attackers were teenagers and accused the DoD of engaging in hysteria. Allan Thompson, a former Central Intelligence Agency analyst, argued that it did not make sense for the Russian intelligence service to "tip its hand" with a massive operation rather than patiently developing its capabilities. Finally, a Russian technology analyst voiced skepticism about the idea that a high-powered connection cable was necessary to steal photographs of DoD facilities or duty rosters.[27] Fred Cohen of Sandia National Labs argued that the attack, while innovative, also owed its success to the DoD's own security deficiencies. The fact that the attacks were recurring, Cohen argued, had more to do with the continued inability of the Department of Defense to protect its networks. Sophisticated attackers, in other words, were not really the problem.[28] However, as is common in cyber conflicts, these commentators were not able to review the government's evidence on the seriousness of the incident, nor why some government voices suggested Russia was responsible.

In 2000, the United States government formally complained to Russia about the hacking and provided the telephone numbers from which the attacks supposedly originated. Russian authorities claimed that the numbers were non-operative and denied any prior knowledge of the attacks.[29] Nonetheless, US officials did travel to Moscow in an effort to reach out to Russia to investigate the source of the espionage.[30] Russia has consistently denied involvement in the MOONLIGHT MAZE incident.

In 2001, a *Foreign Affairs* article revealed that attackers were not only continuing to operate in the system, but had also left in place "backdoors"—code or instructions that easily enable hackers to sneak back into a previously compromised system to exfiltrate more data or inflict damage on a system at a later date. Three years of investigation had produced little information on the source of the attack.[31] In April 2003, PBS Frontline ran a special on MOONLIGHT MAZE and other cyber incidents. Here, it was revealed that network attackers had accessed tens of thousands of files on military maps, troop configurations, and military hardware designs. RAND Corporation analyst John Arquilla, also interviewed, cast doubt on the diagnosis of a Russian attacker, noting that the attacker could have easily

---

26   Verton, "Russia Hacking Stories Refuted."
27   *Ibid.*
28   Loeb, "Pentagon Computers Under Assault."
29   Adams, "Virtual Defense."
30   Verton, "Russia Hacking Stories."
31   Adams, "Virtual Defense."

bounced his traffic off Russian computers to confuse defenders.[32] However, this is a fairly standard rejoinder for most attacks, since it is technically possible, but the response ignores other lines of evidence.

The FBI's investigation ultimately came to center around whether or not the attacks were conducted by Russia's Academy of Sciences.[33] Government officials told *Newsweek* off-the-record that the Russian Academy of Sciences—an entity linked to the Russian military—was behind the attacks.[34] The attacks were ultimately traced back to a mainframe computer in Russia, but the real point of origin remains unknown.[35] No further information has been forthcoming.

Implications

It is difficult to write of MOONLIGHT MAZE's implications while so little is currently known about the incident. However, MOONLIGHT MAZE had a sizable impact on many aspects of cybersecurity and intelligence. As previously noted, it also remarkably originated many ongoing policy issues in cybersecurity.

The United States is upset over what it views as aggressive and unrelenting Russian state-sponsored hacking. Russia continues to deny involvement, while highlighting the risk of what it views as an emerging information warfare arms race. MOONLIGHT MAZE also was a "wake-up call" that aggressive extraction from information resources by state, state-sponsored, or state-sympathetic organizations would be an enduring part of the cyber conflict landscape. It also significantly highlighted the continuing interest of Russia, like China, in American military technology. Michael Vatis said,

> *The greatest potential threat comes from foreign state actors who might choose to engage in information warfare against the United States, because they realize that they can't take us on in conventional military terms and would seek to go after what they perceive as our Achilles heel…which is our reliance on information technology, more than any other country to control our critical operations.[36]*

Lessons Learned

While a distinction is often rightfully made between cyber warfare and cyber espionage, MOONLIGHT MAZE demonstrated to a significant degree that the two feed into each other. Was MOONLIGHT MAZE simply another episode in a long history of spy games? Or did it signal preparation for a possibly imminent war? The attackers ostensibly

---

32   "Cyberwar!", "The Warnings."
33   Armistead, Information Operations, 76.
34   "We're in the Middle of a Cyber War."
35   "Cyberwar!", "The Warnings."
36   Kimery, "Russian Hackers Get Into DOD in the US."

targeted unclassified information, but also allegedly left trapdoors for further infiltration. Without access to the results of the investigation, it is difficult to tell what the ultimate aim of the action was. It very well may have been what Thomas called a "long-range cyber reconnaissance" to prepare the ground for more kinetic actions. But it may also have been an act of espionage.

John Arquilla, one of the early thinkers on information warfare and cyber conflict, put it this way:

> There's an interesting problem here, in that some events, like the Moonlight Maze intrusions, were simply exploitative in nature—gaining access to information. But the means by which access was gained are observationally equivalent to the things that a hacker would do if he wanted to intrude and then engage in vast disruption. So we need to figure out how to deal with these problems that have to do with exploitation of systems, because that's our first basis for defense against attacks designed to take these systems down.[37]

Hence MOONLIGHT MAZE, while an espionage incident, was regarded very much as a hostile military act. Hamre, briefing Congress on the incident, declared that the DoD was in the middle of a "cyberwar." Similarly, militaristic language was consistently used in press accounts. Very few noted that the open-source literature seemed to support the thesis that it was in fact an act of espionage, not warfare or sabotage.[38] The investigation's sheer scale and minuscule results also foreshadowed what would come to be a recurring theme in cyber-espionage investigations. Years of analysis were required to even roughly understand and attribute MOONLIGHT MAZE to Russian actors. These attackers may have had access to DoD networks for years without detection.[39]

While iDefense cybersecurity consultant James Adams highlighted the need for a "deterrent strategy," the US government still struggles with stopping cyber-espionage. If attribution is difficult, and the incidents do not inflict lethal damage, it can be difficult to effectively deter actors from aggressively compromising US networks.[40]

The incident clearly brought the problem of attribution to the fore. The Russian Federation refused to accept responsibility for the incident, and the circumstantial evidence involved was not sufficient to permit the United States to impose any political sanctions upon Moscow. The uncertainty surrounding the incident persists today, as so little information is available on who was responsible for the incident. It is believed that the attack was at least connected with the Russian government, but uncertainties plague even this suspicion.

37 Arquilla and Ronfeldt, "Cyberwar is Coming!"
38 "We're in the Middle of a Cyber War."
39 Gelinas, "Cyber Deterrence and the Problem of Attribution," 11.
40 Abreu, "Cyber Attack Reveals Cracks in US Defense."

Lack of attribution, in turn, leads to paralysis in active defense responses to the attack. If the DoD is not sure precisely who is attacking it, legal implications concerning responses cannot be easily calculated.

Hamre's comments that the attack exploited the open norms of the scientific community also highlighted a problem that continues today in cybersecurity policy. Hamre's point is that attackers exploited an institution with different security norms than the hierarchal and closed world of the DoD. In order to enjoy the benefits of scientific-technical partnerships with research laboratories, however, the military cannot simply dissociate itself from the scientific community. Navigating the organizational and technical implications of continued engagement with communities that employ looser security practices remains a continuing cybersecurity problem.

Technical Innovations

The attack exposed some substantial weaknesses in DoD computer defenses. Those weaknesses were cause for substantial alarm. A 2001 Defense Science Board Task Force report noted that incidents such as MOONLIGHT MAZE constituted a "low and slow" attack that challenged the Department of Defense by exhibiting several characteristics. Low and slow attacks may go undetected for substantial amounts of time, especially if an insider is conducting or abetting the attack. The lack of any apparent outcome in a low and slow attack might blind investigators to the possibility of insertions of logic bombs, Trojan horses, and viruses that could be implemented at the time and place of the attacker's choosing. Attributing motives for the attacks may also be difficult, if not impossible, due to such an undetected insertion not becoming apparent until months or even years after the initial compromise.[41]

The Defense Science Board report similarly raised the issue of "defense-in-depth," which would later become a hot topic among chief technology officers and cyber strategists. The Defense Science Board argued that MOONLIGHT MAZE and similar incidents could partially have occurred because of a prevailing "perimeter defense" mentality, meaning the defense is hard on the outside but soft on the inside. Unfortunately, once the intruders were inside the targeted systems, network defenders had little idea of what was happening within their own networks.[42] Many of these themes will be familiar to cyber policy analysts debating defense-in-depth based approaches, the concept of the "Maginot Line of Information Security," and the idea that network defenders should assume a breach and act to mitigate it.[43]

---

41   Defense Science Board, "Protecting the Homeland," 21.
42   *Ibid.*
43   Gourley, "The Maginot Line of Information Security."

Organizational Innovations

MOONLIGHT MAZE reaffirmed commonly accepted organizational lessons derived from the 1997 ELIGIBLE RECEIVER and the 1998 SOLAR SUNRISE incidents. The multi-dimensional nature of these assaults and the emphasis they put on quick response convinced many that the United States needed an operational organization capable of directing technical changes to DoD computers and networks for cyber defense. The Joint Task Force-Computer Network Defense (JTF-CND), assigned from 1998 to 2004 to a variety of DoD organizations under many different names, played a key role in the MOONLIGHT MAZE incident. Most notably, the JTF-CND issued the first military-wide order to change passwords during the episode.[44] Though the JTF-CND evolved concurrently with the MOONLIGHT MAZE investigation, the incident would only bolster what many viewed as the necessity for unity of command, with one commander being responsible to higher authority.[45]

DoD policymakers also agreed that truly comprehensive incident reporting was needed, with assessors possessing the ability to accept data from both automated systems and qualitative products, such as manual incident reports based on personal observations and analyses. This would speed up and streamline incident response. The DoD's chief organizational response was to institutionalize a four-tiered process of incident response. Military reporting would be handled at the local level through network operations and security centers (NOSCs) under the control of the Defense Information Systems Agency (DISA). The primary purpose of this line of reporting is to report problems. Assessments of the impact from a command control perspective are channeled through individual Service and regional Computer Emergency Response Teams (CERTs). Both kinds of incident reports in turn would be sent to what was then known as the JTF-Computer Network Operations (CNO) and the DISA Global Network Operations and Security Center (GNOSC).[46]

MOONLIGHT MAZE also played an influential role in a government-wide, pre-9/11 effort to create a "counterintelligence czar," who would coordinate inter-agency efforts against terrorists, spies, and cyber intrusions. In an interview with a *National Journal* reporter, Hamre recalled that a conversation about the MOONLIGHT MAZE incident with the FBI's Deputy Director for National Security Robert Bryant in 1998 provided the impetus for a new counterintelligence initiative to respond to unconventional threats. MOONLIGHT MAZE's domestic targets and (alleged) foreign actors prompted this conversation about ways in which organizational stovepipes prevented security agencies

---

44 Nakashima, "An Army of Tech-Savvy Warriors Has Been Fighting Its Battle in Cyberspace."
45 Armistead, Information Operations, 79.
46 *Ibid.*, 78-79.

from countering unconventional threats. The DoD, Hamre noted, cannot investigate inside US borders, and the law enforcement community lacked many tools that the DoD and the CIA possess for operating overseas. Hamre pushed for the Counterintelligence-21 initiative, a call for a national counterintelligence executive, empowered to issue a counterintelligence strategy. Hamre and others' efforts eventually resulted in the founding of the Office of the National Counterintelligence Executive (ONCIX) in 2001.[47]

Conclusion

It remains to be seen whether the public will ever find out what really happened in MOONLIGHT MAZE. Basic elements of the story remain hidden behind classification and a shroud of mystery. Unfortunately, future actions and responses in the cyber world are likely to be more like MOONLIGHT MAZE than not. Only by learning from the incident will we be better prepared for the murky, fast-paced, and organizationally complex cyber campaigns of the future. MOONLIGHT MAZE raised our common awareness of the state-backed attacker and led to far-reaching policy shifts.

---

47 Kitfield, "CIA, FBI, and Pentagon Team to Fight Terrorism."

Part 4: Militarization

During the Militarization phase of cyber history, national militaries and intelligence organizations came to the fore as major cyber players, for espionage and disruptive attacks.

The most worrying trend for the United States has been the rise of Chinese-sponsored espionage. Calling upon his deep background in China studies, Adam Segal, the Maurice R. Greenberg Fellow in China Studies at the Council of Foreign Relations, provides an overview of this espionage, its context, and the response. The result is one of the most concise descriptions of Chinese espionage anywhere, summarizing case after case of linked incidents.

Often, national security organizations do not have to act directly themselves, as patriotic hackers and other groups can be goaded into the necessary attacks. Andreas Schmidt and Andreas Hagen have written case studies of the two best known conflicts of this type, Estonia (2007) and Georgia (2008). Many of their findings disagree with some of the popular understanding of these incidents: for example, it seems the Russian patriotic attack on Estonia did not cause serious disruption. Indeed, the Estonians are now renowned for their cyber security expertise. Rather than being wiped off the network, this incident was a tactical and strategic defeat for the Russians. Andreas Hagen's case study on Georgia was one of the winners of the AFCEA-CCSA-Atlantic Council case-study competition and similarly dives into details to separate facts from fiction.

Karl Grindal provides more detail on yet another incident tied to Russia, operation BUCKSHOT YANKEE, the 2008 intrusion into DoD unclassified and classified systems. These intrusions, initiated by someone inserting an infected thumb-drive into a government computer, were yet another wake-up call for the US government. The first-hand descriptions of those involved in the event and the actions taken afterwards are familiar echoes of previous wake-up calls like the Morris Worm and SOLAR SUNRISE.

A more important global wake-up call was the discovery of the Stuxnet virus. When it was first discovered, it barely registered with the cybersecurity community, until it was found to target industrial control systems—this was the first virus ever to do so. But it didn't make global news until it became clear that it was directed specifically against Iranian nuclear centrifuges, and that the United States and Israel were fairly clearly behind it. Chris Morton, a former student of mine at Georgetown University, has written a clear description of Stuxnet and its related family of malicious software, which the United States called Olympic Games.

As editor of this book, I have added a concluding chapter to help to identify exactly who was behind the Estonian, Georgian, and Stuxnet attacks, based on a "spectrum of state responsibility" published by the Atlantic Council. This analytical tool helps to show that it is unlikely the Russian government directly conducted either the Estonian or the Georgian attacks. But certainly, they ignored and likely encouraged the Estonia attacks, and probably shaped or coordinated those against Georgia.

From TITAN RAIN to BYZANTINE HADES:
Chinese Cyber Espionage

Adam Segal[1]

Over the last decade, cybersecurity has emerged as an increasingly contentious issue in the bilateral relationship between the United States and the People's Republic of China (PRC). Washington and Beijing are both likely to see the other as a, if not the, major actor responsible for frustrating the pursuit of strategic interests in cyberspace. At the same time, the two countries are highly economically interdependent, and they continue to seek broader cooperation on a range of global and regional issues, such as containing the nuclear programs of Iran and North Korea.

While no one policy provides a public framework for China's computer network operations, there is a strategic, political, and economic logic behind much of the behavior emanating from China.[2] In publicly available writings, People's Liberation Army (PLA) analysts frequently talk of the need to seize information dominance early in a conflict through cyber attacks on command-and-control centers.[3] Additional attacks would target transportation, communication, and logistics networks to slow down an adversary. As a result, PRC actors appear to be continually surveilling the networks of US armed forces. Or as Chief Naval Officer Admiral Jonathan Greenert put it in response to a question about Chinese cyber attacks, "We've . . . had a lot of probes on our networks . . . all over the place, both ashore and at sea."[4]

In addition, Chinese defense analysts appear to believe that cyber attacks can have widespread effects and thus are a strong deterrent. In these analysts' view, the United States is much more dependent on banking, telecommunications, and other critical networks than China is, and an attack on these networks might lead to a financial crash or a communications blackout. Chinese intrusions into critical infrastructure, especially when evidence is left behind, act as a warning that the US homeland may not be immune to attack in the case of a conflict over Taiwan or the South China Sea. This situation greatly complicates US decision making.

The Chinese also use computer network operations to shape international political narratives as well as to gather information on agencies, institutions, and individuals who might influence the debates on topics of importance to Beijing. The Gmail accounts of

---

1   Adam Segal is the Maurice R. Greenberg Senior Fellow in China Studies at the Council on Foreign Relations (CFR). An expert on security issues, technology development, and Chinese domestic and foreign policy, Dr. Segal currently leads CFR's Cyberconflict and Cybersecurity Initiative. He thanks Sharone Tobias for research assistance.
2   Segal, "Chinese Computer Games."
3   See for example, Pollpeter, "Controlling the Information Domain: Space, Cyber, and Electronic Warfare."
4   Greenert, "Cooperation from Strength: The U.S., China and the South China Sea."

dozens of activists and journalists have been penetrated in the United States, China, and Europe.[5] The computers of Tibetan activists have been targeted in a global operation, and think-tanks and other non-governmental organizations, media outlets, and academic institutions who deal with China have also had their networks penetrated.[6]

Cyber espionage is also central to efforts to make the Chinese economy more technologically competitive. Chinese policymakers worry that the country is too dependent on foreign technology and desperately want to move the country into higher-value sectors. To do this, China has significantly ramped up R&D spending, but it has also relied on industrial espionage directed at high technology and advanced manufacturing companies. Hackers have also reportedly targeted the negotiation strategies and financial information of energy, banking, law, and other companies.

From TITAN RAIN to BYZANTINE HADES

The first publicly revealed attacks in 2005 were code named TITAN RAIN.[7] Over the course of three or four years, attackers with suspected links to the PLA scanned computers at the Department of Defense and successfully infiltrated the US Army Information Systems Engineering Command, the Defense Information Systems Agency, the Naval Ocean Systems Center, the US Army Space and Strategic Defense installation, and Lockheed Martin, NASA, Redstone Arsenal, and the British Foreign Office. According to DoD officials, the majority of successful hacks gained access to "low risk" computers, containing little to no confidential information.

In 2009, it was reported that hackers broke into networks involved in the Joint Strike Fighter project, also known as F-35 Lightning II, and compromised systems responsible for diagnosing maintenance problems during flight.[8] The attackers took advantage of vulnerabilities in the computer networks of Lockheed Martin, Northrop Grumman, and BAE Systems. Hackers used software that encrypted the data as it was stolen, making it more difficult for investigators to trace the types of information taken. While not naming the attack, then Deputy Defense Secretary William Lynn III said in 2011 that a foreign intelligence agency had victimized a defense contractor, having stolen 24,000 files concerning a developmental system.[9] Hackers also reportedly were on BAE Systems networks for 18 months before they were discovered; during that time, they monitored online meetings and technical discussions of the aircraft.

5   Nakashima, "US Plans to Issue Protest to China over Attacks on Google."
6   Raasch and Johnson, "Think Tanks Hit by Hackers from China, Other Nations."
7   Graham, "Hackers Attack Via Chinese Web Sites"; Norton-Taylor, "Titan Rain - How Chinese Hackers Targeted Whitehall"; and Thornburgh, "Inside the Chinese Hack Attack."
8   Gorman, et al., "Computer Spies Breach Fighter-Jet Project"; Peter, "How Bad Was the Cyber Attack on Lockheed Martin?"; and Tyson and Hedgpeth, "Officials Say Hackers Didn't Steal Critical Data About New Fighter Jet."
9   Lynn, III, Remarks on the Department of Defense Cyber Strategy.

A 2011 attack on the security firm RSA has been linked to the attacks on F-35 networks. These hackers apparently used RSA as a stepping-stone to other targets.[10] RSA specializes in cryptography and security, and helps defend networks at the White House, the Central Intelligence Agency, the National Security Agency, the Pentagon, the Department of Homeland Security, and for most top defense contractors. Hackers gained access to the security tokens RSA produces that let millions of government and private-sector employees, including those of defense contractors, connect remotely to their computers.

While the impact of other attacks remains ambiguous, the outcomes of the attacks on networks involved in developing the F-35 are relatively more suggestive. Several analysts have argued that cost overruns for the fighter jet are in part a response to espionage. After the attacks, contractors were obliged to redesign specialized communications and antenna arrays for stealth aircraft and rewrite software to protect systems vulnerable to hacking.[11] There have also been suggestions that the fuselage of China's second stealth fighter jet, the J-31, resembles that of the F-22 and F-35.

In June 2008, the Information Warfare Monitor, a Canadian research organization, identified a malware-based cyber espionage campaign. Titled GhostNet in a March 2009 report, the campaign appeared to be Chinese in origin and targeted the offices of the Dalai Lama; Tibetan exile centers in India, Brussels, London, and New York; and embassies, foreign ministries, and other government offices of India, South Korea, Indonesia, Romania, Taiwan, Germany, and other countries.[12] Victims in over 100 countries were sent email messages that contained Trojan horse malware, allowing attackers to gain complete, real-time control of computers. Once on the computers, the attackers searched for and downloaded specific files, and covertly operated attached devices, including microphones and web cameras. In a follow up report, *Shadows in the Cloud*, the researchers found evidence that the hackers used Twitter, Google Groups, Blogspot, Baidu Blogs, blog.com, and Yahoo!Mail to coordinate attacks and to direct compromised computers to free web-hosting services, and as these sites were disabled, to command and control servers located in China.[13]

In January 2010, Google announced that it had been the victim of a "highly sophisticated and targeted attack on our corporate infrastructure originating from China that resulted in the theft of intellectual property."[14] The attackers reportedly took advantage of a vulnerability in Microsoft Internet Explorer, and also successfully penetrated thirty other companies, including Yahoo!, Adobe, Symantec, Juniper Networks, Disney, Sony, Johnson & Johnson, General Electric, General Dynamics, the law firm King & Spalding,

---

10 Markoff, "SecurID Company Suffers a Breach of Data Security."
11 Fulghum, et al., "China's Role in Spiraling JSF Costs."
12 Information Warfare Monitor, Tracking Ghostnet.
13 Information Warfare Monitor and Shadowserver Foundation, Shadows in the Cloud.
14 David Drummond, "A New Approach to China."

and DuPont. At Google, attackers stole Google's password management program, Gaia. They also added queries to Google's "law discovery portals," which cooperate with law enforcement officials to provide information, adding many Chinese names. Attackers used Google's internal search engines to search for the company's signing certificates, but were unsuccessful because those were kept offline. Google reportedly traced the attacks to Shanghai Jiaotong University and Lanxiang Vocational School.[15]

The Google attacks, also known as Aurora, may have been related to another operation named Shady RAT by McAfee.[16] Email messages to the victims were linked to a website that automatically downloaded a remote administration tool (RAT) onto the victim's computer. The list of compromised computers was particularly diverse, including fourteen federal, state, and county agencies; eleven defense contractors; Asian and Western national Olympic Committees, the International Olympic Committee, and the World Anti-Doping Agency; the United Nations and the Association of Southeast Asian Nations (ASEAN) Secretariat; and Hong Kong and New York offices of the Associated Press.

The networks of US government agencies, defense contractors, and companies are not the only targets. The espionage campaign targets numerous other countries. As noted above, BAE—Britain's biggest defense contractor—was penetrated, and in 2008, MI5—the UK's internal security and counter-intelligence agency—warned British companies doing business with China that their networks were being targeted by Chinese groups.[17] In 2007, German Chancellor Angela Merkel reportedly complained to former Chinese Premier Wen Jiabao, after Chinese hackers attacked computers in her office and other government ministries. The German domestic security agency, Bundesamt fuer Verfassungsschutz (BVF) has concluded that "the intention of PRC actors is espionage, and the primary attack vector used in their malicious activity is socially engineered email messages containing malware attachments and/or embedded links to hostile websites."[18] Hackers have targeted Canadian firms in the aerospace, agriculture, biotech, oil, military, and communication sectors, and some have linked the collapse of the telecom giant Nortel to an espionage campaign that lasted for a decade.[19] In Japan, Mistubishi Heavy announced that hackers gained access to the networks of companies and research units involved in manufacturing submarines, nuclear power stations, escort ships, guided missiles, and rocket engines, while PRC-based actors allegedly stole documents from the Agriculture, Forestry, and Fisheries

15   Goel, "McAfee Says Microsoft Flaw Was a Factor in Cyberattacks"; Gross, "Enter the Cyber-dragon"; Nakashima, "Google China Cyberattack Part of Vast Espionage Campaign, Experts Say"; and Markoff and Barboza, "2 China Schools Said to Be Tied to Online Attacks."

16   Alperovich, "Revealed: Operation Shady Rat"; Gross, "Exclusive: Operation Shady RAT Unprecedented Cyber-espionage Campaign and Intellectual-Property Bonanza"; and Nakashima, "Report on 'Operation Shady RAT' Identifies Widespread Cyber-spying."

17   Leppard, "China Bugs and Burgles Britain."

18   Welch, "War in the Shadows."

19   Tsukayama, "Chinese Hackers Breach Nortel Networks"; and "Nortel collapse linked to Chinese hackers."

Ministry related to trade negotiations over the Trans-Pacific Partnership.[20]

In the end, dividing attacks on economic and political actors into specific operations is difficult and may not prove particularly useful for analysis. According to a 2009 State Department cable published by WikiLeaks, US counterintelligence officials tracked a massive espionage operation they codenamed BYZANTINE HADES.[21] BYZANTINE HADES had several subsets—BYZANTINE FOOTHOLD, BYZANTINE CANDOR, and BYZANTINE ANCHOR—and may have affected over 750 companies. Aurora and Shady Rat could have been part of these larger operations. In effect, referring to attacks by specific names suggests one-off, narrow independent campaigns. The tally of attacks on over 750 targets, spanning several years, provides a fuller sense of the scope and scale of a systematic espionage effort that is central to Chinese economic policy.

Echoes of the Past

There is a specific political, economic, and strategic logic behind Chinese network operations, but the attacks ascribed to Chinese actors mirror many of the methods and much of the ambiguity surrounding the MOONLIGHT MAZE attacks, as described by Adam Elkus in this volume. Chinese operations appear to be conducted by professional, state-sponsored groups and involve extended campaigns and stealth attacks. Public reports have identified more than a dozen groups, operating from Chinese territory, that are linked with the PLA and with universities and information security enterprises.[22] The cyber security firm Mandiant, for example, reported on the operations of a group they called APT1, conducting cyber espionage against English-language targets from Shanghai. The geographical location of the group; the scale, tactics, and techniques of the attacks; and the target types all suggest that APT1 not only receives government support, but is almost certainly the 2nd Bureau of the People's Liberation Army General Staff Department's 3rd Department, more commonly known in the PLA as Unit 61398.[23]

As with MOONLIGHT MAZE, the public attribution of Chinese attacks has been based primarily on indirect evidence. Some of the code used in the attacks, and the command and control nodes have been traced to China. In the case of the F-35 breach, for example, investigators announced that they traced IP addresses to China with a "high level of certainty," and several Chinese-registered websites were "involved in BYZANTINE HADES intrusion activity in 2006."[24] Hackers were said to log into penetrated computers

---

20   "Japan's Defense Industry Hit by its First Cyber Attack"; and Torres, "Top Secret Trade Documents Stolen from Farm Ministry Computers."
21   Riley and Walcott, "China-Based Hacking of 760 Companies Shows Cyber Cold War."
22   Stokes and Hsiao, "Countering Chinese Cyber Operations"; Riley and Lawrence, "Hackers Linked to China's Army Seen From EU to D.C."; and Barboza, "Hacking Inquiry Puts China's Elite in New Light."
23   Mandiant, "APT1: Exposing One of China's Cyber Espionage Units."
24   Grow and Hosenball, "Special report: In cyberspy vs. cyberspy, China has the edge."

at 9:00 am Beijing time, clock out at 5:00 pm, and take vacations at the time of the Chinese New Year and other national holidays. Perhaps the most suggestive evidence has been the type of information targeted. The information gained from Tibetan activists, defense industries, foreign embassies, and think-tanks is not easily monetized and has little attraction to criminals but is of great use to the Chinese government.

Public understanding and discussions of Chinese attacks have also had to rely on news reports and selective leaks, as was the case with MOONLIGHT MAZE. The inability to get a comprehensive picture of the attacks has been confounded by the unwillingness of most private companies to publicly discuss the type, frequency, and scope of attacks. Google's announcement is the notable exception, but the majority of companies continue to resist disclosing attacks because they fear what may happen to stock prices, and also to their liability and legal responsibilities. They may also worry that Beijing may make it more difficult for them to do business in the China market if they publicly accuse Chinese hackers of being behind attacks.

Actors and Methods

The logic of the attacks is much clearer than either how the attacks are organized or under what authorities. At the top of the policy infrastructure in charge of cyber is the State Informatization Leading Group (SILG), which includes senior representatives of the CCP Central Committee Politburo, State Council, and PLA. The SILG has a Network and Information Security Working Group, which informs and advises senior leaders.[25] At the operational level, Mark Stokes and L.C. Russell Hsiao argue that the "PLA General Staff Department (GSD) Third Department is likely a leading authority for cyber surveillance."[26] The Third Department manages at least twelve operational bureaus and three research institutes.

There is also overlap between state-sponsored attackers and organized cyber criminals. The two groups often "operate in the same environment and sometimes against similar categories of targets."[27] The Information Warfare Monitor argues that evidence of the link between those behind attacks on Tibetan computers and the underground Chinese hacker community can be found in the diffusion of HTran. HTran was developed by a Chinese hacker group in 2003, and, in addition to the attacks on Tibetan activists, was also used in an attack on the Japanese Ministry of Agriculture in 2012.[28]

Government and private security experts have identified between 12 and 20 separate

---

25   Goodrich, "Chinese Civilian Cybersecurity: Stakeholders, Strategies, and Policy."
26   Stokes and Hsiao, "Countering Chinese Cyber Operations."
27   Krekel, et al., "Occupying the Information High Ground."
28   "Cyber-attack Malware Identified."

groups that conduct most of the attacks. Groups appear to specialize, some being responsible for infiltrating networks, and others in exfiltrating data. In public reporting, the attacks are generally described as advanced persistent threat (APT). They have relied on spear phishing, or socially engineered email messages made to look authentic to the recipient. The email messages often included a .PDF or other types of attachments, or a hyperlink which installs a remote access tool when opened. In the case of the RSA attack, for example, an email with the subject line "2011 Recruitment Plan" was sent with an attached Excel file. The spreadsheet contained malware that used a previously unknown, or "zero-day," flaw in Adobe's Flash software to install a backdoor. Operators then gained control of the victim's computers and eventually began exfiltrating encrypted data. In other cases, victims were compromised by visiting an infected website.[29]

Most of these attacks are less advanced and more persistent. That is, the attacks succeed not because of their sophistication, but because of the willingness of the attackers to keep trying. They also succeed because of a lack of security awareness in the target organizations or a lack of defensive resources.[30]

Policy Responses

Beijing, not surprisingly, has consistently denied that it is behind the cyber attacks. The Chinese press often portrays such claims as an effort to poison the bilateral relationship and as evidence of the influence of the "China Threat" school of opinion, which is common among defense contractors and others who hype Chinese strength. Chinese officials are quick to call the accusations "irresponsible and calculating" and to note that Chinese laws prohibit cyber attacks.[31] They also point out that China is the "world's biggest victim" of cyber attacks. According to the National Computer Network Emergency Response Coordination Center of China, the majority of attacks are conducted via IP addresses in Japan, the United States, and South Korea.[32]

Despite these public denials, the United States has slowly ratcheted up a campaign of naming and shaming. In October 2011, House Permanent Select Committee on Intelligence Chairman Mike Rogers called Chinese economic cyber espionage: "A massive and sustained intelligence effort by a government to blatantly steal commercial data and intellectual property."[33] The Office of the National Counterintelligence Executive called Chinese actors the "world's most active and persistent perpetrators of economic espionage."[34] Cybersecurity was on the agenda at the 2012 Security and Economic

---

29   FireWare Malware Intelligence Lab, "CFR Watering Hole Attack Details."
30   Krekel, et al, "Occupying the Information High Ground."
31   See for example, "China Denies Government Links to Cyber Attacks on Google."
32   "Cyber Attacks against China Remain Severe."
33   Rogers, "Opening Statement Open Hearing: Cyber Threats and Ongoing Efforts to Protect the Nation."
34   Office of the National Counterintelligence Executive, "Foreign Spies Stealing US Economic Secrets in Cyberspace."

Dialogue. The topic was raised again that year during US Secretary Hillary Clinton's meeting with Chinese Foreign Minister Yang Jiechi, and in US Secretary Leon Panetta's dialogue with Chinese Defense Minister General Liang Guangjie.

This public diplomacy does not seem to have had much effect, and the United States has experienced difficulty engaging China on the issue. There is a difference between the two sides over the scope of the problem. While US officials talk of promoting "cybersecurity," which is a fairly narrow term that implies protecting communications and other critical networks, Chinese policymakers, like their Russian counterparts, refer to information security, which is a much broader category that also includes controlling content. Moreover, the United States is trying to limit economic espionage, which it does not engage in, though the US maintains the ability and freedom to conduct operations against foreign governments, militaries, and terrorist groups. China, like many other states, makes no distinction and has no prohibition against economic espionage. It also sees itself as highly vulnerable to US computer operations, and so is unlikely to forfeit an important asymmetric advantage.

Domestically, Chinese cyber attacks pose the critical question of what role the government should play in defending commercial enterprises and economic competitiveness. Launched by President George W. Bush, the Comprehensive National Cybersecurity Initiative (CNCI) includes a government-wide cyber counterintelligence plan to "detect, deter, and mitigate the foreign-sponsored cyber intelligence threat to US and private sector information systems."[35]

There have also been administrative and legislative efforts to improve two-way information sharing between the government and industry. The Defense Industrial Base (DIB) Cyber Pilot is an effort to share threat signatures and other information. This effort began with defense contractors and Internet service providers, and has been expanded to other sectors. While government officials have spoken highly of the DIB, a number of companies have complained about the timeliness of the information provided, and a few have dropped out because the program was "too onerous."[36] Sponsored by the NSA, the Enduring Security Framework invites executives from technology companies and defense contractors to provide classified briefings on cyber threats. The *Washington Post* also reported that the NSA signed an agreement with Google to share attack information soon after the Aurora attacks were disclosed.[37]

Several legislative efforts, notably the Cyber Intelligence Sharing and Protection Act (CISPA) introduced by Representative Mike Rogers (R-MI), have tried to improve the

---

35   "The Comprehensive National Cybersecurity Initiative."
36   "Pentagon's Cyber Pilot Dropout Rate Signals Trouble Ahead."
37   Nakashima, "Google to enlist NSA to help it ward off cyberattacks."

information-sharing process. In 2012, CISPA made it through the House but failed to make it to the Senate; opposition revolved around the definition of cyber threats, the protection of individual users' information, liability provisions for the private sector, and the role of intelligence and defense communities in providing information. In 2013, President Obama is expected to introduce an executive order that will introduce a real-time sharing program in coordination with the Secretary of Defense, the Director of the National Security Agency, the Director of National Intelligence, and the Attorney General.

Some private sector victims of cyber attack have grown skeptical of the US government's ability to provide adequate defenses and are pursuing "active cyber defense." However, the concept remains vague, as companies are pursuing a range of responses, such as deception, the creation of fake data, the use of honeypots (decoy networks), and more active efforts, such as taking down botnets and destroying stolen data held on third party servers.

Conclusion

Cyber espionage is by definition an ambiguous threat. Yet part of the problem in responding to Chinese cyber espionage attacks is conceiving of how serious the threat truly is. The scope is reportedly massive. General Keith Alexander, head of the NSA and US Cyber Command, has called cyber espionage attacks on US companies the "greatest transfer of wealth in history" and has estimated that American companies lose $250 billion per year through intellectual property theft.[38]

But if the attacks are so damaging to US economic interests, why has the reaction from the government and the private sector been relatively restrained? For the United States government, do the demands for a positive relationship with Beijing—the need to coordinate with China on a range of global issues from Iran and Syria to climate change and global economic growth—make a potential breach over cyber espionage appear too costly? Is it a problem of attribution, with the United States unwilling to present evidence of Chinese hacking for fear of revealing US intelligence capabilities? For the private sector, perhaps cyber espionage is like the loss of technology through legitimate technology transfer, indigenous innovation and other techno-nationalist policies, and China's failure to protect intellectual property rights. Is that just the cost of doing business in China?

Unless the United States government and the private sector figure out and decide to implement ideas on how to raise the costs for China-based hackers, either through defensive or offensive measures, it should be expected that Chinese operations will continue, and those delegated to keeping the US-China relationship intact will have to learn to accommodate them.

---

38   Rogin, "NSA Chief: Cybercrime constitutes the 'greatest transfer of wealth in history.'"

The Estonian Cyberattacks

Andreas Schmidt[1]

For three weeks from 27 April until 18 May 2007,[2] components of the Estonian Internet infrastructure were subjugated to Distributed Denial of Service (DDoS) attacks, massive e-mail and comment spam, website defacements, and DNS server attacks. These attacks seem to be the first that were possibly directed as a coercive instrument in a political conflict against a nation. At the time of the attacks, Estonia was entrenched in a domestic conflict between the newly elected government and its supporters on the one hand, and an ideologically motivated minority of predominantly ethnic Russians on the other. As a result, the long-standing conflict with Estonia's former occupant power, Russia, had culminated in heated diplomatic exchanges at a time when Russian-US relations approached their post-Cold War bottom.

The incident is noteworthy for more than its geopolitical implications. It also sheds light on organizational aspects of cybersecurity and the role of global technical communities to reestablish the Internet's functionality after an attack.

This chapter offers a descriptive account of the attacks, the damages that they inflicted, and the responses made. The narrative is supplemented by an analysis of the political circumstances of the attacks, the discussions that the attacks spurred, and some recapitulating remarks.

Monument Debates

In January 2007, the Estonian government announced that it would move a World War II monument from the center of Tallinn to a military cemetery in the outskirts of the city. Erected in 1947, when major affairs in the Estonian Socialist Soviet Republic were controlled from Stalin's Kremlin, the "Monument to the Liberators of Tallinn" depicts an unnamed soldier wearing a uniform of the Red Army, with a helmet in is left hand, and his head slightly bowed as if he was mourning his nearly 11 million fallen comrades.[3] After Estonia regained its full political sovereignty in 1991, the monument became a point of conflict in domestic Estonian affairs. Many Estonians regarded the Bronze Soldier, which was located at a busy intersection close to Tallinn's picturesque historic center, as a symbol not of the achievements of the Red Army in WWII, but of its subsequent role as a

---

1   Andreas Schmidt is a researcher at the Faculty of Technology, Policy, and Management at Delft University of Technology. He holds a Masters degree in Political Science and Medieval and Contemporary History. He is currently writing his Ph.D. thesis on the role of technical communities in Internet security governance.

2   At the end, the attacks frayed out a bit, hence the end is not as sharply delineated as the beginning. Therefore, in some descriptions May 23 is given as the end date and 3 ½ or 4 weeks as the overall duration.

3   Hosking, Rulers and Victims, 206.

suppressor of Estonian independence. Russian-Estonians begged to differ. Unsurprisingly, the monument emerged as the site where different interpretations of the role of the Red Army were expressed in demonstrations. The date of May 9, the Russian V-Day,[4] became notorious for verbal clashes between Soviet war veterans and Estonian-Russians on the one side and conservative Estonians on the other. After years of repeated rallies, discussions about the future of the monument and demands for its removal grew more prominent in 2005.[5]

It didn't go unnoticed in Moscow that its former Soviet republic was about to cut ties with the Russian interpretation of Estonia's WWII and post-war history. In January, the Russian Upper-House filed a resolution demanding that their Estonian parliamentary peers prevent the statue from being moved. On 3 April, Russian First Vice Prime Minister Sergei Ivanov made a plea to boycott

Unsurprisingly, the monument emerged as the site where different interpretations of the role of the Red Army were expressed in demonstrations.

Estonian goods and services, though this bullying attitude was not shared by those in Russia's foreign policy circles.[6] The conflict was about Estonian identity, relations between Russia and Estonia, and the perception of World War II.[7] For Russians, it was the Red Army that wrestled down the German war machine in the bloody battles of the "Great Patriotic War," which cost the lives of approximately 27 million Soviet citizens.[8] In the eyes of (some) Estonians, however, the Nazi occupation was only relieved by a five-decade long occupation by the Soviets that continued the suppression of the Estonians, who were striving for autonomy.[9]

After smoldering for a time as a divisive and emotional issue in Estonian politics and public discourses, the monument eventually became one of the core subjects in the lead-up to the Estonian parliamentary elections that were held on 4 March 2007. "War graves are no place for day-to-day politics," warned President Toomas Hendrik Ilves, a Social Democrat, but to no avail.[10] The Union of Res Publica and Pro Patria, a conservative opposition party, lobbied for a bill prescribing the removal of the monument. Trailing in the polls, the incumbent Prime Minister Andrus Ansip and his Reform Party supported the controversial bill in February, fearing an electoral setback for the forthcoming elections.[11] The elections confirmed the Prime Minister's new term, and the Reform Party finished ahead of the

4   The Allied Forces had summoned Wehrmacht General Jodl to Reims, France on May 7, 1945 to sign the capitulation, to be effective on May 8, 23:01 CET, i.e., after midnight in Moscow. In addition, the Soviets held another signing ceremony in Berlin on May 9, close after midnight CET. Kershaw, Hitler, 1073-75.
5   Alas, "May 9 Protestors Call for Removing Bronze Soldier Statue."
6   "Here We Go Again."
7   Myers, "Debate Renewed: Did Moscow Free Estonia or Occupy It?"
8   Kosachev, "An Insult to Our War Dead."
9   Socor, "Moscow Stung by Estonian Ban on Totalitarianism's Symbols."
10   Alas, "Soldier Fails to Sway Elections."
11   *Ibid.*

social-liberal Center Party and its candidate, who preferred a less controversial approach regarding the monument. [12] In March, Ansip's new government immediately laid the legal ground for the removal of the Bronze Soldier.

On 26 April, Estonian authorities fenced off the statue in the center of Tallinn. A day later, they removed the statue, and after several weeks exhumed bodies of Red Army soldiers that had been buried near by, any unclimed remains were transferred to a military cemetery in Tallinn a few kilometers away.[13] Unsurprisingly, the removal angered Russians, Estonia's ethnic minority, and citizens of the Russian Federation alike. On the Russian side, the chorus of outrage was spearheaded by President Putin, who fiercely criticized the Estonian decision. In Tallinn, the streets were filled with protesters, rallying against the decision of the Estonian government. Estonian police forces arrested hundreds of protesters.[14] In the late evening of the day of the monument's removal, on Friday, 27 April,[15] first signs of cyberattacks appeared on the monitoring screens of Estonian IT operators.

Early Attacks

Starting at around 10 pm, Estonian organizations faced several kinds of attack on their servers which were used for e-mail, the Web, domain name resolution, and other Internet services. Systems slackened or stalled under unusually high data traffic. Internet sites suffered from Web defacements. Email inboxes were filled with even more spam and phishing emails.[16]

In the late evening of the day of the monument's removal, on Friday, April 27, first signs of cyberattacks appeared on the monitoring screens of Estonian IT operators.

Political institutions were early targets of the attacks. Estonian Prime Minister Andrus Ansip and other leading politicians were spammed.[17] The email services of the Estonian parliament had to be temporarily shut down, as they were no longer able to handle the

---

12 Alas, "Reformists Pull Off Surprise Victory, Consider Dumping Centrists."
13 "NATO Sees Recent Cyber Attacks on Estonia As Security Issue."
14 Adomaitis, "Estonia Calm After Red Army Site Riots, Russia Angry."
15 In their joint presentation, Gadi Evron, a known ICT security expert who arrived in Tallinn after the attacks had peaked, and Hillar Aarelaid, head of the Estonian CERT, spoke of "Saturday, the 26th of April, 22:00" as the day when the attacks started. But immediately after this, they mentioned "Saturday, the 27th of April, 02:00" as the beginning time. Evron and Aarelaid, "Estonia: Information Warfare and Lessons Learned." However, in 2007, the last Saturday in April was the 28th. In a post-mortem journal article, Evron stated that the attacks started at "10:00 p.m. on 26 April 2007." Evron, "Battling Botnets and Online Mobs," 121-126. Street demonstrations that later led to riots took place on April 26 and April 27. Presentation slides made by Merike Kaeo, a US-based Estonian security expert, contain a graphic of Web traffic between Friday, 0:15 am, and Saturday noon; according to this, traffic first abnormally increased on Friday night around 10:15 pm, but culminated no earlier than late Sunday, April 28. Interviewees confirmed that attacks started on a Friday, i.e., on April 27.
16 For prior descriptions of the Estonian incident, see also Herzog, "Revisiting the Estonian Cyber Attacks," 4; Landler and Markoff, "In Estonia, What May Be the First War in Cyberspace"; and Tikk, et al., "International Cyber Incidents - Legal Considerations."
17 Berendson, "Küberrünnakute Taga Seisavad Profid."

unusual data payload.[18] The Estonian news outlet *Postimees Online* fell victim to two DDoS attacks on its servers and had to close foreign access to its networks, thereby limiting the chances for Estonians to make their voices heard abroad.[19] In addition, discussion forums on *Postimees Online* were spammed by bots with comments badmouthing and insulting the Prime Minister. The president of *Postimees Online* likened the cyberattacks to an "attack on neutral and independent journalism."[20]

While defacements of governmental websites created embarrassment for the sites' owners and symbolically undermined political institutions, they hardly constitute a major blow to the society and its security. The main causes for concern were the DDoS attacks on the Estonian infrastructure, as they endangered the availability and functionality of services crucial to the functioning of Estonian society.

Internet traffic exceeded average-day peak loads by a factor of ten, resulting in malfunctions or non-availability of Internet services.[21] The Estonian government was the most notable among the institutions affected. Its website, valitsus.ee, was not available for eight consecutive hours in the afternoon of 28 April. For the following two days, response times often took an unusually long time, eight seconds and more, if the site was available at all. Statistics from Netcraft.com, a website that gathers information about the up- and down-times of webpages, revealed that the website failed to respond in eight-four of 166 cases until Monday early morning.[22] Among the other affected websites were those of the Prime Minister (peaminister.ee), the Ministry of Economic Affairs and Communication (mkm.ee), the Ministry of Internal Affairs (sisemin.gov.ee), the Ministry of Foreign Affairs (vm.ee), and the Estonian Parliament (riigikogu.ee).[23]

Boot-up of the Estonian Response

18   Finn, "Cyber Assaults on Estonia Typify a New Battle Tactic."
19   "Hansapanka Tabas Küberrünne."
20   Berendson, "Küberrünnakute."
21   Aarelaid, "Overview of Recent Incidents."
22   Hyppönen, "Update on the Estonian DDoS Attacks."
23   Hyppönen, "Unrest in Estonia." Further domains that were attacked included: the Estonian Patent Office (epa.ee), the Estonian Defense Forces (mil.ee), the Estonian Academy of Music and Theatre (ema.edu.ee), Tallinn University (ehi. ee, tpu.ee), the Estonian Business School (ebs.ee), Tallinn University of Technology (est.ttu.ee), a Yellow pages website (infoatlas.ee), and a URL shortening service (zzz.ee). Aarelaid, in "Overview" (confirmed in an interview with the author), said that Berendson mentioned the following additional targets: "the University of Tartu, the Estonian Radio, the Estonian Shipping Company, the Woodman Pärnu furniture company, and a real estate company called Rime." See also Berendson, "Küberrünnakute." However, we have no statistically sound information about the effects on the availability of those websites. Websites marked as available in Hyppönen's brief analysis were: the Party of the Prime Minister (reform. ee), the Ministry of Agriculture (agri.ee), the Ministry of Culture (kul.ee), the Ministry of Defense (mod.gov.ee), the Ministry of Finance (fin.ee), the Ministry of Justice (just.ee), the Ministry of Social Affairs (sm.ee), the Ministry of the Environment (envir.ee), and the Estonian Police (pol.ee). Hyppönen's analysis is ambiguous as to whether the websites marked as reachable had been attacked not at all, before or after the period of time analyzed, i.e., for Saturday, April 28, 2007. In general, there is no consistent, conclusive assessment of the exact downtimes of organizations belonging to the Estonian infrastructure during the entire three weeks of the attacks. It is noteworthy that an attack on the web-services of an organization does not necessarily affect its functionality. E.g., the attacks had "no impact on the Estonian military forces or national security apparatus," as a report by the US-based National Defense University holds. Miller and Kuehl, "Cyberspace and the 'First Battle' in 21st-century War," 3.

The attacks didn't come as a surprise to the Estonian security community. They had seen it coming. "When there are riots in the streets, they will eventually go cyber," was an assessment shared by many in the Estonian security community.[24] But it wasn't only intuition which led to the expectation that some sort of cyberattacks were coming. The message was spreading within both Estonian and international Internet security communities in mid-April that commenters were calling within Russian-language forums for a low-intensity cyber call-to-arms, in an apparent attempt to find comrades who would help to initiate DDoS attacks against organizational pillars of the Estonian society.[25]

Estonia had a well-connected and prepared national ICT security community in place by the time the attacks commenced. As early as the late 1990s, banks had started collaborating and exchanging information on cyber attacks. At first, ICT security departments cooperated, ignoring legal regulations (exchanging information among banks was forbidden by Estonian law). Eventually, executive decrees and later legislation paved the way to legality for the actions of the banks' ICT security staffs. By the early 2000s, the efforts of the banks' information security staffs were supplemented by actions taken by their peers in ISPs, telcos, energy companies and certain major companies from other sectors. "We," an Estonian expert recollected concerning the community's sentiment, "started realizing that we had created a small working group. We were starting to protect the Estonian national critical infrastructure."[26] Not much later, Estonia's informal ICT security community linked up with traditional security institutions. With the advent of Internet-based elections in the early-mid 2000s, a task force consisting of security experts from ISPs, election authorities, police, intelligence services, and others was formed to prepare for potential attacks on national election sites. Exposing the vulnerabilities of electronic voting systems had become a favorite pastime among hackers worldwide, an

---

24   Estonian ICT security expert interviewed by the author. Empirical findings in this chapter are, aside from the literature cited, based on semi-structured one-on-one interviews conducted by the author with persons directly involved in the response activities. Selection criteria for the Interviewees were their roles in the response activities, obviously their willingness to conduct such interviews (not everyone responded, unsurprisingly), and their ability to provide additional explanations of technological, organizational, or political circumstances. Most interviewees worked as security professionals in organizations that were somehow affected by the attacks or were otherwise involved in the response activities. As some interviewees have asked for anonymity, the general policy in this chapter is to not name interviewees, unless they have already become public figures due to previous press coverage. The interviews for the Estonian case were conducted in 2011 and 2012 during research trips to Estonia, California, and various other places in Europe, usually for Internet (security) conferences such as the Internet Governance Forum, TF-CSIRT, GovCERT NL, and FIRST meetings, and also for closed gatherings of the Internet security community. In 2013, I had a few additional background conversations or follow-up interviews.

25   Global network security communities learned about the call-to-arms in the Russian-language forums before the attacks actually commenced, just like their Estonian peers. Priisalu, "Building a Secure Cyber Future." It took these communities some three weeks to establish direct communication channels. Among the reasons for this were unawareness of one another's existence, mutual lack of trust, and issues that appeared to be more important than contacting peer communities. Based on existing links to their Estonian peers, some European technical experts shared their insights on the ongoing scheming within the Russian online forums with Estonian security staff by mid-April; i.e., weeks before the latter were granted access to communication channels of global mailing-list-based communities. Apparently, some Russian web forums are constantly monitored by various Western parties, who are interested in Russia-based cyber-crime, malware, underground economies, espionage, and other suspicious activities.

26   An Estonian interviewee.

activity which severely hurt emerging voting systems businesses. A member of the task force responsible for the security of Internet voting in Estonia admitted that their voting system was as secure or insecure as the PCs of the voters.[27] The task force tried to reduce these risks by continuously monitoring the Estonian Internet during the elections.

The same task force was re-established for the 2007 elections. A good month after the national election was held without major technical security issues, the informal Estonian community was on alert, again. They expected 8 May to be the most likely date for a spill-over of the offsite riots to the digital sphere: "We had everything ready."[28] Persons close to the Ministers of Defense and the Interior were informed about possible DDoS attacks, and Estonian intelligence was also informed, as their operatives were part of the informal Estonian Internet security information exchange system.

Despite the inability to centrally monitor national Internet services, it soon became obvious to technical operators in Estonia that the websites of a number of local institutions had fallen victim to DDoS attacks. In Russia, web forums publichsed descriptions of how to harm Estonian servers, along with respective Windows command shell scripts and pleas to run those scripts at a certain point of time.[29] Thousands of people running these scripts simultaneously can cause web-traffic that over-stretches the capacity of those servers. This brief, initial attack phase, which relied on humans executing the scripts, only lasted for a few days.

Four hours after the attacks had commenced, at 2 am in the early morning of Friday, 27 April, operational teams responsible for governmental servers had realized from mutual updates by telephone that some government websites were being exposed to Internet traffic exceeding normal traffic by 100 to 1,000 times. Servers could not cope with the enormous traffic.

On Russian-language web forums, descriptions of how to harm Estonian servers and Windows command shell scripts were published, along with pleas to run those scripts at a certain point of time.

Hence, the operational teams decided to move websites to "well-defended" web servers, scaled to handle the excessive traffic.[30] What had started as an operational IT security issue (DDoS attacks are almost daily business) turned into a national security situation three hours later, when the chief public relations person of the Estonian Defense Ministry stated around 1 am on 28 April, "We are under cyberattack."[31] His superior, the Estonian Minster

---

27   Sietmann, "22C3: Pro und Kontra e-Voting."
28   An Estonian interviewee.
29   Compare Aarelaid, "Overview." For an example posted in a Russian website, see: http://theologian.msk.ru/thread/list00350.php (last accessed in August 2012).
30   Evron and Aarelaid, "Estonia."
31   Kash, "Lessons From the Cyberattack on Estonia. Interview with Lauri Almann, Estonia's Permanent Undersecretary of Defence."

of Defense Jaak Aaviksso said, "It turned out to be a national security situation."[32]

This "security situation" was subsequently mitigated by the Estonian community of technical experts, who—at the beginning—acted with mild support from their international peers. When the attacks commenced, CERT-EE naturally became the central hub for information exchange and coordinated some of the defensive measures of operational IT units in Estonian organizations. According to Lauri Almann, Estonia's then Permanent Undersecretary of Defense, "we put together a team of experts from our Departments of Commerce and Communications, the military, and the intelligence community, led by Estonian CERT."[33] Hillar Aarelaid, one of the then two full-time staff-members and head of CERT-EE,[34] listed all of the actors involved in the response: the "national crisis committee, DNS / TLD, ISPs, telcos, banks, cyberpolice, intelligence, counterintelligence CERT-EE, [the] community, some friends, [the] Government Communication Office. [the] National Security Coordinator, [the] Ministry of Foreign Affairs, MoD, 'helpers', NATO, DHS, [and the] embassy's [sic]."[35] The most significant role in the technical response activities certainly was handled by the Estonian CERT.[36]

Collaboration with domestic actors was facilitated by previous collaboration and Estonia's unique situation. In a country with 1.4 million inhabitants (about 400,000 of them gathered in the capital, Tallinn), geographic proximity and naturally close social ties facilitate defensive *ad-hoc* collaboration. The Nordic sauna culture, which according to Nokia's then new CEO Stephen Elop had led to the demise of Nokia,[37] came to the rescue for Estonia. Meeting peers in hour-long gatherings of alternating sauna and beer-drinking sessions (which were dubbed the "beer & sauna protocol") helped to formulate a degree of trust among the Estonian experts that allowed them to collaborate seamlessly during the attacks.[38] On 30 April, Estonian experts came together for a joint meeting, representing organizations

> *The most significant role in the technical response activities certainly was handled by the Estonian CERT.*

> *The "beer & sauna protocol" helped to formulate a degree of trust among the Estonian experts that allowed them to collaborate seamlessly during the attacks.*

---

32   Landler and Markoff, "In Estonia."
33   Kash, "Lessons From Cyberattack."
34   Randel, "CyberWar in Estonia 2007 - History, Analysis."
35   Aarelaid, "Overview."
36   Gadi Evron's take on who the decisive actors were in responding to the attacks was: "The heroes of the story are the Estonian ISP and banking security professionals, and the CERT (Hillar Aarelaid and Aivar Jaakson)." Evron, "[NANOG] An account of the Estonian Internet War." Various interviewees criticized the centrality of CERT-EE, as that had established a single-point of failure in the Estonian response. This organizational vulnerability could have been exploited by the attackers.
37   Johnson, "Nokia Crisis Highlights Internal Struggle."
38   Ironically, five years later, the response capacity based upon personal trust among the technical experts responsible for the Estonian ICT infrastructure possibly decreased, as some of the experts had begun to operate from the headquarters of parent companies abroad.

such as ISPs, mobile Telcos, operators of the Estonian TLD and DNS, banks, police, and envoys from the government's Security and Information Boards. This group met only twice in person during the incident, as most of the collaboration was done online via IRC, wikis, email messages, and after-work beer-and-sauna sessions.

The Second Phase

In the second and main attack phase, the coordination of the attacks no longer depended on forum communication and synchronized human actions. Instead, attack coordination was mostly delegated to the command-and-control servers of real botnets. This phase started on 30 April and lasted until 18 May. It ran in four waves of different intensities, focusing on different targets and using different attack techniques. The "first wave" on 4 May included DDoS attacks on websites and DNS systems. Apart from that, the first week of May was relatively calm. The "second wave" on 9-11 May included DDoS attacks against mostly government websites and financial services. The "third wave" on 15 May included botnet-based DDoS attacks against government websites and the financial industry. The "fourth wave" again consisted of attacks against governmental websites and banks.[39]

Among the most significant attacks during this second phase were the attacks on Hansabank. Estonia's largest bank, recently renamed to its parent company's name, Swedbank, owned a 50 percent share of national retail banking, which is almost entirely Internet-based in web-savvy Estonia. Its lending volume in 2007 was close to 7.5 billion EUR, and its net profit in 2007 was 225 million EUR.[40] The web-interfaces for Internet-based services of the two biggest banks in Estonia were offline for about 45-90 minutes.[41] The downtime period and limited availability amounted to losses of about one million USD.[42] On 10 May, a day after the attacks on Estonian systems had reached their highest intensity, Estonian news outlet *Postimees* reported that Hansabank was offline that morning, that customers would encounter problems throughout the day, and that customers from outside Estonia would be denied access to the webpage.[43]

Unlike the attacks in the first phase, the second phase relied on botnets, which are regarded as the main vehicle and platform for cyber crime today. The construction and use of botnets is usually based on divisions of labor. Botnets are created by so-called "bot herders," who often use malware kits created and sold by highly gifted programmers. "Bot herders" then either sell their botnets or rent them out for a certain span of time to other parties, who can then use the botnets to send out spam e-mail, distribute malware, or as in the

---

39   For a more detailed account on these "waves," cf. Tikk, et al, "International Cyber Incidents."
40   Hansabank Group, "Annual Report of Hansabank Group 2007."
41   Ottis, "Conflicts in Cyberspace: Evgeny Morozov on Cyber Myths."
42   Landler and Markoff, "In Estonia."
43   "Hansapanka Tabas Küberrünne."

Estonian case, launch DDoS attacks. The renting hours became visible from sharp rises of DDoS traffic at the beginning, and likewise steep falls at the end of a single attack.[44]

Technical Perspective of the Attacks

As noted before, the cyber attacks on Estonia did not resemble a single, ongoing, steady campaign, but consisted of a number of distinct attacks over the course of almost four weeks. In what constitutes one of the more detailed texts about the actual attack data and patterns, is a long form blog post by José Nazario, then a researcher at Arbor Networks (a vendor for Internet security solutions). Between 3 May and 17 May, 128 unique DDoS attacks on Estonian websites were counted, of which "115 were ICMP floods, four... TCP SYN floods, and nine... generic traffic floods."[45] The attacks were unevenly distributed, with a mere three websites—the Ministry of Finance, the Police and Border Guard, and co-hosted websites of the Estonian government and the Prime Minister—being targeted in 106 of those 128 attacks. Regarding the bandwidths used, twenty-two were located in the range between thirty to seventy Mbps, and twelve were between seventy to ninety-five Mbps. Regarding the duration of distinct attacks, thirty-one of the attacks lasted more than one hour; of these, seven lasted more than ten hours. However, the most telling data on the effectiveness of the attacks is that "10 attacks measured at ninety Mbps, lasting upwards of ten hours."[46] Unfortunately, these local sensors did not catch attacks directed against the banks, which according to Jaan Priisalu, then Head of IT Risk Management at Hansabank, were far more severe having dynamically filled all available chanels and having crested at 3gbps. One botnet that targeted Hansabank was comprised of 82,000 machines.[47]

From a technical perspective, the thrust and sophistication of the attacks directed against government websites was relatively modest, if not low compared to global standards, even in 2007. A survey of ISPs in the US, Europe, and Asia on DDoS attacks conducted by Arbor Networks found: "In 2007, the largest observed sustained attack was twenty-four Gbps, compared to seventeen Gbps in 2006. Thirty-six percent of the surveyed ISPs reported that they had observed attacks of over one Gbps in 2007."[48] In comparison, the Estonian attacks were modest.[49] Some interviewees from affected organizations even described the attacks and the effects on their systems as "boring." Given the overall capacity of the Estonian Internet, which was designed for a population of 1.4 million, these attacks were nevertheless suited to obstruct the Estonian Internet infrastructure.[50] In addition, the

---

44   Frankfurter Allgemeine Zeitung, "Estland Im Visler: Ist Ein Internetangriff Der Ernstfall?"; and Kaeo, "Cyber Attacks on Estonia: Short Synopsis."
45   Nazario, "Estonian DDoS Attacks - A summary to date."
46   *Ibid.*
47   Details from Hansabank come from an email forwarded by Luukas Kristjan Ilves detailing notes by Jaan Priisalu.
48   Arbor Networks, Protecting IP Services from the Latest Trends in Botnet and DDoS Attacks, 2.
49   Clover, "Kremlin-backed Group Behind Estonia Cyber Blitz."
50   A presentation by Merike Kaeo, of doubleshotsecurity.com, provides some details on the topology of the Estonian Internet and government network. Kaeo, "Cyber Attacks on Estonia: Short Synopsis." The Estonian attacks showed that

attacks lasted far longer than typical DDoS attacks—not just hours and days, but weeks, albeit interspersed with periods of no or little malicious traffic.[51]

Despite the lengthy duration, hiring a botnet to generate such malicious traffic would have been cheap. According to advertisements on Russian web forums, the costs to hire a botnet for DDoS services for twenty-four hours and a bandwidth of 100 Mbps was $75, and the price for a week of 1000 Mbps attacks was $600.[52] However, some security professionals involved in the response activities maintain that the attacks were technically and tactically more sophisticated, and required a larger group of knowledgeable persons.[53]

Countering DDoS

At the current stage of technology and legal developments, responding to a technical attack and mitigating DDoS attacks first and foremost requires the application of technical answers. Upscaling servers, offering a temporarily stripped down website, granting or denying access to the website to certain ranges of IP addresses, increasing bandwidth between targets and their ISPs or backbones, routing DDoS traffic to sinkholes—all of these techniques help to keep web services online.

A DDoS attack aimed at overstretching web server capacities can be countered by a reconfiguration of components on the network perimeter of an organization. For attacks flooding the network routes to an organization's infrastructure, a different defense approach is more promising: Malicious packets are dropped by conveying intermediaries located between the attacking and the attacked ends. This approach requires either administrative authority over the networks involved or collaboration with actors controlling parts of the Internet infrastructure that are conveying packets from the attacking systems to the target systems. Given today's ownership structure, the Internet's network configurations, and the absence of central operational control, the only feasible option is globally distributed collaboration.

The second phase of attacks was based on botnets, with bot-infected drones scattered on machines located in numerous countries, emitting innumerable DDoS packets. The short-term response to such an attack is to apply some or any of the aforementioned mitigation techniques. If a botnet is operational for weeks and is dedicated solely to a specific DDoS

the low number and low capacity of international connections contributed to render Estonia's system unavailable. The connection of Georgian networks was even more poorly constructed, and therefore was less resilient to cyber attacks as the attacks in 2008 should prove.

51 Marsan, "How Close Is World War 3.0? Examining the Reality of Cyberwar in Wake of Estonian Attacks."

52 Segura and Lahuerta, "Modeling the Economic Incentives of DDoS Attacks: Femtocell Case Study," 114. A previous version of their article with identical figures was presented at the The Eighth Workshop on the Economics of Information Security in 2009; screenshots in that version of the article captured advertisements published in September 2008. (http://weis09.infosecon.net/files/113/index.html) It is therefore safe to assume that prices for DDoS services were not significantly higher at the time of the attacks.

53 Interviews with the author.

attack, the defending actors would probably want to take down the botnet itself, e.g., by taking over its command-and-control system. Takedowns of sophisticated botnets usually require months of investigation, research, and preparation. In addition, botnet surveillance was only in its infancy in 2007. Nevertheless, two Estonian interviewees from different governmental-administrative authorities stated that they had been able to identify the persons responsible for the DDoS attacks and for providing the botnets used.[54]

International Collaboration

Once the attacks entered the second phase and became botnet-based, international collaboration and coordination became necessary. According to the Estonian Permanent Undersecretary of Defense, the Ministry of Defense was responsible for organizing international support,[55] mainly in the political sphere. This responsibility did not include the self-organized collaboration of operational teams and technical experts. With the Estonian government framing the DDoS attacks as a security issue caused by the Russian government, this attracted close attention from the Western media and governments.

On the international operational level, Estonian Internet security experts collaborated with the global Internet security operations community and CERTs in other countries, mainly in Finland (CERT-FI), Germany (CERTBund) and Slovenia (SI-CERT). CERT-EE, drowning in information and work during the response efforts and operating at the edge of, if not beyond its capacities, welcomed the help offered by their Finnish colleagues. The neighbors from the other side of the Baltic Sea analyzed, processed, and then disseminated attack telemetry data to the operators of those Internet segments, from which some of the attacks possibly originated.

The international collaboration included other contributors in addition to these distinct national CERTs, for they had no operational control over networks and systems in their home countries, nor did they have the staff for such operations. Thus, contributions to the response effort also came from a range of actors, including network companies, vendors of security appliances and network hardware, law enforcement and other security authorities, non-profit Internet security organizations, and a number of individual ICT security professionals from Estonia, Russia, and other places around the world. These participants provided appliances, hardware, and more bandwidth; filtered malevolent traffic; or provided information necessary to understand the scope, nature, and technical details of the ongoing attacks. It is in the nature of these mailing-list-based security communities that tasks emerging from security incidents are picked up by members according to a variety of factors. These include their role within their companies, their company's overall

---

54   Interviews with the author.
55   Kash, "Lessons From Cyberattack."

commercial interests, their personal interests, current workload, and their perceptions of the necessity and self-imposed responsibility to intervene. The lack of a central global Internet security monitoring facility, the distribution of situational knowledge, and the distribution of control over systems requires a loosely coupled networked approach. But it also requires a certain level of trust to share potentially delicate security information. The provider of such information shares details of apparently compromised computers, while the receiver uses such data, for example, to block the Internet traffic of customers with allegedly compromised machines. In early May 2007, there was no deep trust between Estonian security experts on the one hand and the wider global security communities on the other. These are the groups that frequently deal with DDoS attacks on the Internet.

Good luck assisted with the rescue. The cooperation between the international and the Estonian communities was significantly facilitated by the attendance of contact persons at the annual meeting of TF-CSIRT in Prague on 3 May, an annual convention of invited European CERT security experts, and a long-planned RIPE meeting in Tallinn on 7 May.[56] It was at this RIPE meeting that members of the Estonian technical community were eventually introduced to members of the international technical Internet community. With the help of warrantors, who were trusted by the international community and vouched for the integrity of the Estonian newbies, the Estonian technical people were gauged as trustworthy. With this newly achieved status as members of the international technical community, a few Estonians could, for example, send lists with attacking IP addresses to mailing-list-based security communities such as NSP-SEC.[57] Network security professionals around the world that are members of such a list would then help to stop malicious traffic from flowing from their networks towards Estonian systems.

To summarize, the situation was mitigated by a range of technical measures. First, the capacities of the Estonian Internet services and the underlying systems were increased and scaled up. Second, filtering mechanisms were added to the structural layout of the Estonian Internet; these would drop malicious data packets before they would reach their targeted systems. Probably the most effective method was to block access and drop traffic to Estonian servers from outside the country. These measures made systems unavailable from abroad—a situation that was widely reported in the international press, but they also ensured the availability of web services and ICT-based services for the Estonians within

---

56   The Réseaux IP Européens Network Coordination Centre is one of the five global Regional Internet Registries (RIRs) and provides "global Internet resources and related services (IPv4, IPv6 and AS Number resources) to members in the RIPE NCC service region" (http://www.ripe.net/lir-services/ncc). The region encompasses countries on the Eurasian landmass, minus those east of Iran and Kazakhstan.

57   Bill Woodcock, networking professional, and co-founder and Research Director of Packet Clearing House, shared more details on the role of NSP-Sec in mitigating global DDoS attacks during a previous ACUS event. Woodcock, "Building a Secure Cyber Future." Kurtis Erik Lindquist from Swedish Internet Exchange Point operator Netnod, Woodcock, a third mediating person, and Hillar Aarelaid of CERT-EE established a trust-based collaboration between the Estonian technical community and a global community of network operators.

the country. Traffic geographically originating from foreign countries was again routed to Estonian servers, once the ratio of benevolent to malevolent traffic was back to normal levels.[58]

Costs of the Attacks

The influx of DDoS packets had consequences on the quality and availability of Estonian web services—mainly regarding the loss of services for government, communication, and banking.[59] The e-mail and web services of some Estonian organizations were partly unavailable or functioned only at a reduced level. Government officials and journalists had difficulties obtaining access to web services, like email, which inhibited basic administrative actions like sending out a press release .[60] As one would expect for non-physical attacks like DDoS, the information technology structure was left undamaged, but a "leading Estonian information technology expert" claimed that the attacks "were clearly aimed at destroying the Baltic country's Internet backbone."[61] According to security professional and researcher José Nazario, there have been "no apparent attempts to target national critical infrastructure other than Internet resources, and no extortion demands were made."[62]

Despite the press coverage and the political attention that the attacks aroused, a comprehensive post-mortem with a listing of precise downtimes and times of reduced service, aggregated and grouped per organization, and complemented by a rough calculation of estimated financial consequences has yet to be written. The lack of data can be traced to the absence of overall monitoring of the Estonian Internet systems in 2007 and to the omission of systematic reporting by technical staff during the crisis. While the Estonian technical community still has an abundance of data and log files, which could provide these answers (Estonian language skill would be required to read this data), Estonian practitioners and international researchers alike obviously deemed such a study to be unimportant.[63] Existing anecdotal evidence of damages that occurred during the Estonian cyber attacks supports the conclusion that, despite shrill rhetoric heard during the course of the events and in the aftermath, the financial losses more likely were "minimal."[64] According to Rain Ottis, "only a few critical on-line services (like banks) were affected for clients inside Estonia," while "non-critical services (public government websites and

---

58 Goodman, "Cyber Deterrence - Tougher in Theory Than in Practice?"

59 Ashmore, "Impact of Alleged Russian Cyber Attacks," 4, 8.

60 "Estonia Hit by Moscow Cyber War."

61 Arnold, "Russian Group's Claims Reopen Debate on Estonian Cyberattacks." According to a person from Estonia's cyber policy circles, the attackers managed to physically destroy a network component at an Estonian ISP.

62 "Estonian DDoS - a Final Analysis."

63 During the review process of this chapter, sources close to the Estonian MoD informed me that the Estonian Ministry of Defence had indeed written such a report, which was soon to be declassified. There was insufficient time to incorporate that source in this chapter.

64 Ashmore, "Impact of Alleged Russian Cyber Attacks," 8.

news sites, for example) did suffer longer service outage."[65] The costs of the response activities, however, haven't been mentioned anywhere in the existing literature. Nor have the expenses for new hardware to scale-up existing systems or to harden the perimeters of corporate networks. Similarly, no cost figures have been issued for over-time work required of the operational staff. According to an interviewee close to Estonian government circles, some banks accumulated substantial opportunity costs created by lost revenues.[66] One company's executive described the impact of delegating ICT staff to incident response tasks on ongoing ICT projects, and the necessity to both re-plan and re-organize these projects as the most prominent cost factors. Nevertheless, none of these costs should add up to figures creating greater public concern.

It is arguable whether the same can be said for the medium- and long-term effects of the relocation of the Bronze Soldier monument. The Estonian GDP numbers stayed solid during the quarter of the attack, continuing a slow recession that lasted until the Estonian GDP had a brutal (-)14.1 percent nosedive in 2009 .[67] While a small sector of the national economy, the *Baltic Times* reported that Estonia's Transit sector took a sharp hit in 2007, decreasing by 40 percent compared to the previous year. Russia, depending on ice-free Baltic harbors, has since diverted her cargo business from Tallinn's port to Latvia and Lithuania. According to an Estonian report and a Financial Ministry official mentioned in the article, Russia's economic payback aggregated to reductions in the Estonian GDP between 1 and 3.5 percent.[68] However, these reductions were for the Russian response as a whole and not just for the cyber attacks.

On the positive side, Estonia profited from a number of intangible and political gains. The attacks and the respective response turned Estonia into a household brand for all matters cybersecurity, which likely helped to secure the hosting of the NATO Cooperative Cyber Defense Center of Excellence and EU Agency for large-scale IT systems.[69] Its vanguard status was only increased by Estonia's provision of support in some international cyber crime cases. Politically, Estonia managed to secure an increased commitment from NATO and the European Union, thereby advancing its strategic foreign policy goal of strengthening integration into Western institutions, which serve to balance the influence of neighboring Russia.[70] These issues lead to consideration of the international and geopolitical implications of the Estonian cyber attacks, which probably have been more

---

65　Ottis, "Conflicts in Cyberspace."
66　I have not interviewed risk managers or persons with similar roles in banks that could have backed up these claims.
67　Cf. data provided by Statistics Estonia: Eesti Statistika, Statistical Yearbook of Estonia 2009, 26, and Eesti Statistika, Statistical Yearbook of Estonia 2010, 30.
68　"Was It Worth It?"
69　"What We Do - EU Agency for Large-scale IT Systems."
70　On Estonia's foreign policy options and strategies: Danckworth, "Estlands Außenpolitik nach dem Beitritt zur Europäischen Union: Handlungsoptionen eines Kleinstaates." (Doctoral thesis on "Estonia's foreign policy after its accession to the European Union: Courses of action of a small state".)

influential than the effects on Estonian ICT systems.

The Politics of Cyber Attacks

Soon after it had become obvious that problems with the Estonian Internet were caused by malevolent DDoS attacks, officials in Estonia started blaming Russian authorities for being behind it. Ene Ergma, President of the Riigikogu, the Estonian Parliament, likened the attacks to "a nuclear explosion;" the cyber attacks were "the same thing."[71] The Estonian Minister of Justice asserted that some of the data packets in the flood were traced to IP addresses belonging to Moscow offices of the Kremlin.[72] Prime Minister Andrus Ansip blamed the Russian government directly.[73] In an interview with a German daily a good month after the attack, President Ilves used slightly more contained wording regarding the role of Russia. He avoided calling it warfare, but asked how to label such kinds of attacks and said, referring to the potential unavailability of emergency lines, that the attacks also "touched questions of life and death." Furthermore, he referred to the fact that Russian computers were involved in the attacks, and that Russian intelligence service FSB would be able to control the Russian Internet.[74] Ilves also stated that some European states would have gone too far with their appeasement approach toward Russia.[75] Media representatives shared the view of Estonian incumbents. The editor of the Estonian *Postimees* newspaper and website, Merit Kopli, spoke decisively about the responsibilities: "The cyber attacks are from Russia. There is no question. It is political."[76]

The immediate assumption that Russian authorities were involved was soon expressed by Estonian officials, and subsequently by scholars[77] who studied the Estonian incident and interviewed Estonian officials in the months after the attacks. Other researchers have subsequently agreed with that assessment. Bumgarner and Borg emphatically blamed "Russia," but they did not provide details about the specific role of the Russian authorities.[78] Healey stated, "the obvious truth: the attacks were supported or encouraged by the Russian government and… to make the attacks stop, Western decision-makers needed to engage Moscow."[79] Ashmore's detailed account of Russia's role in the attacks concluded that an involvement of Russian authorities had not been proven, but the mere

71   Poulsen, "'Cyberwar' and Estonia's Panic Attack."
72   Rantanen, "Virtual Harassment, but for Real."
73   "Estonia Hit by Moscow Cyber War."
74   "Estland Im Visier."
75   NATO later revised its policy toward the Baltic states in 2009, after Germany dropped its resistance to including the Baltic states into NATO's defense and contingency planning."US Embassy Cables: Germany Behind NATO Proposal for Baltic States."
76   Thomson, "Russia 'hired Botnets' for Estonia Cyber-war."
77   E.g., Blank, "Web War I: Is Europe's First Information War a New Kind of War?"; and Grant, "Victory in Cyberspace."
78   Bumgarner and Borg, "Overview by the US–CCU of the Cyber Campaign Against Georgia in August of 2008." The full report of the US Cyber Consequences Unit has not been released publicly.
79   Healey, "Beyond Attribution: Seeking National Responsibility for Cyber Attacks," 2.

belief of Russian involvement continues to frame Russian-Estonian relations until today.[80] Evron's opinion was typical for a representative of the technical community,[81] and has been shared by many of the operational staff involved in the technical analysis and mitigation in interviews with the author. Evron was reserved about blaming the Russian government, given the lack of direct evidence and a smoking gun. In contrast to the rhetoric used by some politicians and cyberwarfare theorists, technical experts have shied away from calling the incident "cyber warfare."

Historic knowledge of Russian policy during these events remains ambiguous and meager. Gauging the involvement of the Russian government both in the attacks and their termination is difficult, given the lack of sound and first-hand sources, as Russia's governmental records of those months still have the Cyrillic version of the NOFORN stamp or higher. Lacking indisputable facts, assessments concerning Russia's role are therefore mainly based on perceptions of Russian foreign policy strategies, the weight of indications that Russia was involved, and the epistemological threshold that may be reached before pieces of circumstantial evidence add up to a picture "beyond reasonable doubt."

The assumptions concerning involvement by the Russian government and/or their close relationship to the unidentified perpetrators has been based on a number of arguments.[82] These include the arguments that Russian and Kremlin IP addresses were involved in the attacks;[83] that Russian experts had previously executed similar attacks using the same botnets;[84] that online and offline protests were coordinated;[85] that the scale and sophistication of the attacks required a serious organization for coordination;[86] that the Kremlin-directed Nashi youth group was involved;[87] that the attacks required long-

---

80   Ashmore, "Impact of Alleged Russian Cyber Attacks," 8.

81   Evron, "Authoritatively, Who Was Behind the Estonian Attacks?"

82   Partly compiled from Mützenich, "Nutzung Neuer Medien Als Instrument Russischer Außenpolitik," 8-9.

83   "Estonian PM, Justice Minister Insist That Cyber Attacks Came From Kremlin Computers."

84   Grant, "Victory in Cyberspace," 6.

85   According to an interviewee from Estonia's non-technical security circles, some of the organizers of the offline riots had been paid for their services by Russian intelligence services. An IT executive stated that local Estonian-Russians had likely opposed the riots due to their probable negative impact on the Estonian economy, which would be against their personal interests. Interviews with the author. Nevertheless, the Russian minority was highly likely to join in public demonstrations, some of which were decentrally organized by snowballing text messages, which is akin to techniques that later became popular in Iran or during the Arab Spring.

86   An argument for sophistication, advanced by members of Estonian policy circles, is that the attacks focused on a "key network device" in Estonia's Internet infrastructure. The attackers had required detailed knowledge of the Estonian infrastructure, and the attacks resembled a "power demonstration of what can be done." One Estonian security professional described them as "targeted, single-packet router-killing stuff, never seen before." Another dryly stated that there still was the possibility of pure chance that a router and its replacement got broken in quick succession. In addition, some hardware components are known to be vulnerable to so called "Packets of Death." Another example of sophistication that was mentioned was a sample of a bot malware, which foreign security experts and police forces managed to obtain on behalf of the Estonian CERT. However, International malware experts told me that bot malware involved in the attacks was "not far beyond what had already been detected in the wild" back in 2007. All quotes from different interviews with the author.

87   Evron, "Authoritatively, Who Was Behind the Estonian Attacks?"; Grant, "Victory in Cyberspace," 6; and Ashmore, "Impact of Alleged Russian Cyber Attacks," 25.

term planning;[88] that Russia possesses an asymmetric strategy that it employs against its increasingly West-leaning neighbors;[89] that Soviet and Lenin tactics were applied;[90] and that Russian law enforcement agencies refused to cooperate with their Estonian counterparts in identifying the people behind the attacks.[91]

While these arguments carry some weight, they do not add up to evidence "beyond any doubt." The attacks did not have a serious, let alone long-term impact on the Estonian society. More decisive from a political perspective are the long-term implications of the viability and utility of such cyber attacks. The cyber attacks would have fit into Russia's overall foreign policy strategy toward its neighboring countries. Partly because of substantial ethnic Russian diasporas and partly because of security or national interests, Russia seeks to exert influence over the former satellite states that it had annexed during and after WWII and which gained their independence after 1991. Its foreign policy strategy has been aimed at containing both Western influence in its neighboring countries and the advance of NATO facilities toward the Russian border.[92]

What could Russia have gained by the attacks? The actual consequences of the attacks have been rather mild because of the existence of an Estonian cybersecurity community, and because of its ability to timely link-up with cybersecurity communities in neighboring European countries and around the world. If these communities hadn't been in place, things might have turned out differently. Given the still predominant ignorance surrounding the role of global technical communities in Internet security and incident response among Western cyber security pundits, it is safe to assume that the attackers had not been aware of Estonia's response capabilities.

Without these capabilities, domestic politics would have been shaken up in Estonia. Had the attacks been successful, public and economic life in Estonia would have come to a standstill for days. After some time, probably a day or two, the technical experts would have discovered what to do, how, whom to collaborate with, and how to mitigate the

---

88 Interviewees from Estonian policy circles stated that the first signs of the attacks appeared long before the attacks themselves; among these signs were very brief, intense floods of data packages designed to measure the capacity of the Estonian ICT infrastructure. The time span appears to have been interpreted as an indication of strategic long-term planning by Russian authorities, and serves as a counter-argument to the thesis of spontaneous online-riots that were advanced by Russian nationalist "geeks."

89 Blank, "Web War I," 230.

90 Ibid., 230.

91 Evron, "Battling Botnets," 124; and "Venemaa Keeldub Endiselt Koostööst Küberrünnakute Uurimisel." Estonian authorities handed over a list of Russian suspects deemed responsible for the cyber attacks (an interviewee from Estonian policy circles said: "We knew all the names of the criminals, we knew the masters"), and demanded their extradition based on the Estonian-Russian mutual extradition treaty. The request was rejected by Russian authorities. An IT staff member of an Estonian company stated that they had identified the "botmasters" and those "who organized these attacks," and that this information was then passed to the police. But unlike many other cases of cyber crime, the names of the suspects have never been publicized. According to an interviewee, Estonian authorities preferred this affair to remain low-key. Interviews with the author.

92 Mützenich, "Die Nutzung Neuer Medien Als Instrument."

DDoS attacks to bring ICT systems back to life. Much of the blame might have been placed on the Estonian incumbent, for his irreconcilable monument policy. His allegedly more Russia-friendly opponent, one of whose electoral strongholds resided in the Russian minority and who favored a more diplomatic approach to the war memorial problem, might have gained a more favorable image among the Estonian electorate. Presumably more important than such an immediate gain would have been the long-term effects. A successful attack would have left the impression among Estonians that Russia is capable of encroaching on Estonian ICT systems and politics, if Russia feels fundamentally challenged by its neighbor's policies. Such an impression can lead to self-limitations in policy options; Russia would have increased its influence on one of the "near foreign countries."

From a political perspective, the strongest arguments for at least the remote involvement of Russian authorities relate to the overall Russian strategy regarding their neighboring countries, and the tactics applied to decrease their neighbors' collaboration with and leaning towards the West. However, no gains associated with these factors materialized during or after the attacks. Thus, whether the Russian government actually played a role in the attacks is a lesser question. The political lesson is that cyber attacks can potentially be used as an instrument to influence your neighbors domestic politics.

Conclusion

The attacks on the Estonian Internet infrastructure had only a relatively mild direct impact on Estonian society. Certainly, Estonian organizations and their IT departments bore the costs of delegating their staff to handle incident response tasks, and political institutions' cultural capital was diminished by web defacements and other forms of ridicule. But the long-term relevance of the Estonian cyber attacks in 2007 is not that they allegedly constituted the first instance of an cyber war. This was not a war when one applies a serious and sober definition of that term. Yet, the attacks were a watershed event in the history of Internet security for two reasons.

First, the attacks made it seem plausible to a wider public that cyber attacks can be used as a tool in international or bilateral conflicts. This feature is demonstrable irrespective of how one answers the question of who was behind the attacks—whether it was a loosely-connected, *ad hoc* group of feverish Russian nationalist with varying (from little to über-geeky) degrees of IT skills plus some knowledge of how the cyber crime underground economy works; or whether it was a team within the Russian FSB collaborating with befriended cyber criminals of the Russian underground economy, connected with unknown levels up the ladder in Russia's security bureaucracy and administration. Irrespective of the answer, the attacks fitted well into the overall Russian foreign policy strategy developed to influence their neighboring countries at that time. This was characterized by an increasingly hard-line stance of the Kremlin and the drive to increase their cultural, political, and economic influence in countries neighboring Russia's western borders.

The Estonian political response, in concert with their Western allies, was to deter Russia and other countries from attempting future applications of attacks against civil Internet infrastructure in another country. A mix of diverse policy approaches has been implemented. Government representatives have rushed to name-and-shame state-funded or state-tolerated attacks on civil ICT infrastructures, branding this sort of action illegitimate international conduct. Media coverage of the events has emphasized Russia's more dominant foreign policy in the nearer countries to Russia's borders, and has exposed close relationships between Russia's underground economy, intelligence services, and government circles. A long-term endeavor has been to shrink the "grey zone" of arguably just-barely-legal aggressive cyber-conduct. On the technical-operational side, increased alertness and preparedness for such attacks has been a goal of policymakers ever since.

Estonia and its Western security allies have assured their mutual support in the event of future, large-scale attacks on their ICT infrastructures, thereby raising the risks and potential costs for an adversary that tolerates or even utilizes voluntary groups to attack foreign Internet infrastructures. As a result, Estonia has become more embedded than ever into Western security and policy institutions, while Russia's cultural and political influence on Estonia has been further reduced. Whatever Russia's foreign policy circles had defined as strategic goals (if they were involved at all), the Estonian cyberattacks hardly advanced Russia's political causes.

The second reason is less obvious, but nonetheless highly relevant both for future Internet security incidents and regarding questions of democratic governance of communicational infrastructures. This involves the relationship between networks and hierarchies, between operators and owners of communicational infrastructures and traditional security institutions.

The Estonian cyber attacks will go down in history as a rare case in which a Minister of Defence stated that his country was in a "national security situation"—and yet the relevant contribution to straighten out the situation did not come from military staff, but from a community of technical experts, who cooperated in the settings of the "beer & sauna protocol" and fancy conferences that started at 2 pm with a morning pint, and who possessed values favoring effectiveness over procedure and protocol. The response to the Estonian attacks was a wild success for the technical security communities' principles of loose governance, trust-based information-sharing, and technology-facilitated *ad hoc* collaboration. At the same time, however, this marked the end of the community's autonomy from state interference and regulation. Today, the location of briefings for high-level politicians by the security community now routinely takes place at Estonian CERTs headquarters.

Cultural and communication conflicts between the technical community and the political sphere had already emerged during the attacks. Pieces of seemingly contradictory information from different sources of the community added up to an unclear picture of what was going on. Political boards became, at least temporarily, suspicious of information they received from the security community. As a thoughtful member of the technical community put it, "Governments and institutions simply do not know how to communicate with the community. They do not know how to do it. They are not used to it." And therefore, according to another member, "the biggest problem we face in these events is communication between hierarchies and networks."[93] As a consequence, the community was formalized as a legal body (the Cyber Defense League); also, the informal core group of the response team now acts as a formalized technical advisory body to Estonia's National Security Council; and the CERT's hosting organization, RIA, has been granted special executive rights for future national security situations.

In an ideal world, such institutionalization of the technical security communities helps to achieve two goals: to increase democratic control of Internet security governance, and to increase the capacities and abilities of the overall response organization, so that they may successfully counter hostile intruders. Time will tell whether these approaches will serve the Estonian and other societies well, or even better than the self-organized response of technical security communities in 2007.

---

93   Quotes from interviews with the author.

The Russo-Georgian War 2008

Andreas Hagen[1]

The cyber attacks against Estonia in 2007 demonstrated the degree to which nations might persuade patriotic hackers and cyber professionals to exert pressure on a hostile nation. These techniques had yet to be matched with military might. This changed in August 2008 during the South Ossetia War, when traditional Russian forces invaded the Republic of Georgia with the concurrent support of Russian hackers. The conflict between Russia and Georgia centered on a territorial dispute over the independent regions of Abkhasia and South Ossetia in Georgia, which have local independence movements supported by Russia. In 2008, Georgia attempted to reassert its control over South Ossetia, and Russia responded with significant force, invading Georgian territory in conjunction with a strong cyber offensive. Cyber capabilities had been used in conflicts before 2007; however, these actions represent singular operations rather than a campaign of cyber attacks, making 2008 important. It is the length and scope of this cyber attack, and also its effect on the population, which sparked global fears over the potential of future cyber wars.

History and Reasons for War

Russia and Georgia share a long history of differences that reach back to the annexation of Georgia to Russia in the nineteenth century and to the beginning of the Soviet Union in the early twentieth century. These differences have been brewing ever since and have resulted in violent ethnic clashes. After the Soviet Union collapsed in the early 1990s, multiple leaders of ethnic regions in the successor states demanded instant autonomy from the new governments in the former satellite states.[2] Early demands by ethnic regions like South Ossetia and Abkhazia were seen as reasonable at first. But the demands for autonomy soon escalated and turned confrontational, once they were pushing the limits the governments were willing to make. The resulting violent ethnic separatism between Georgia and the regions of Abkhazia and South Ossetia was constantly influenced by Russia.[3] Before 2008, Russia had tried to influence the Georgian economy by blocking trade and by other means of economic pressure.[4] Russia stood on the side of the minorities and supported them, mostly due to a 1992 law that allowed former Soviet Union citizens to apply for Russian citizenship. Many of the people in the neighboring regions had

---

1   Andreas Hagen is an analyst specialized in International Relations and Security Studies with a regional focus on Africa and Asia-Pacific. He holds a Masters degree from the Institute of World Politics in Washington, D.C. and received his Bachelor of Arts with honors in International Relations and Diplomacy from Schiller International University. He has been awarded the second place in the AFCEA/CCSA Cyber History Contest for this case study on the cyber attacks in Georgia in 2012.
2   George, The Politics of Ethnic Separatism in Russia and Georgia, 13.
3   Smith, Interview by Andreas Hagen, 17 September 2012.
4   *Ibid.*

taken advantage of this law.[5] This made Russia a key player in any discourse between the parties, as the nation often invoked the right to intervene for its citizens. To further ensure their constant involvement in any negotiations, Russia aided the regions financially. They also left small military peacekeeping forces in both Abkhazia and South Ossetia after violence broke out in those places in the early 1990s, causing tensions to run high.[6] These disagreements resulted in minor aggressions and occasional posturing.

Saakashvili began to rapidly build up Georgian military capabilities. This build-up only increased the distrust among the regional factions. Georgia implemented several anti-corruption reforms targeted at stopping smuggled imports from Russia, which represent a substantial portion of the economy of South Ossetia.[7] These reforms, combined with heightened rhetoric by senior Georgian officials, caused tense relations that were only worsened by the Russian interest to block Georgian aspirations for NATO membership.[8]

As relations between the parties deteriorated, both Russia and Georgia seem to have taken preemptive measures to ensure their security. Signs of a pending conflict led Russia to hold military exercises (called "Kavkaz-2008") at several points of the border with Georgia.[9] From mid-July to August 2008, Russia had 8,000 soldiers and heavy military hardware in the area, remaining on high alert even after the exercises had ended.[10] One of these exercises involved a hypothetical attack on Abkhazia and South Ossetia (apparently designed as an attack by a country symbolizing Georgia), against which Russian forces practiced a counter-attack to protect their interests (i.e., Russian citizens).[11] In this military exercise, Russian troops received a leaflet indicating exact Georgian troop compositions, strengths and weaknesses, as well as a reminder to be prepared.[12]

These actions suggest that Moscow was intentionally showing force to maintain their traditional regional dominance. In the months leading up to the Georgian incursion, Georgia experienced violent exchanges with South Ossetian militias.[13] While Georgia had hosted a military exercise with troops from the United States and other regional neighbors to increase interoperability between NATO and coalitions forces in Iraq, most of these troops had already left before the fighting with the Russians began.[14]

Finally, in the evening of 7 August 2008, the Georgian military entered the South Ossetian

5   Weir, "Russia-Georgia conflict: Why both sides have valid points."
6   Ibid.
7   George, The Politics of Ethnic Separatism in Russia and Georgia, 183.
8   Weitz, Global Security Watch: Russia, 133.
9   Berryman, "Russia, NATO Enlargement, and 'Regions of Privileged Interests,'" 234.
10   Ibid., 234.
11   Nichol, "Russia-Georgia Conflict in August 2008," 4.
12   Cornell and Starr, The Guns of August 2008: Russia's War in Georgia, xi - xii.
13   George, The Politics of Ethnic Separatism in Russia and Georgia, 181.
14   Nichol, "Russia-Georgia Conflict in August 2008," 4.

capital and several other villages, claiming that they were responding to bombardments by South Ossetian soldiers that were in violation of a previously established cease-fire.[15] On 8 August 2008, Russia responded to the Georgian invasion of South Ossetia with superior military force, because they saw the Georgian actions as a threat. This was the first time that Moscow deployed its military forces outside of its borders since the war in Afghanistan ended in 1989.[16] Though both Russia and Georgia disputed the other side's justifications for intervention, they both entered into this war, which ultimately ended in a show of Russian superiority and the degradation of the long-term effectiveness of the Georgian military.[17]

Cyber Attacks: Their Importance and the Techniques

Prior to and throughout the conflict, Georgia was targeted by intensive and increasing cyber attacks against governmental and civilian online infrastructure. The cyber component in the 2008 South Ossetia War focused largely on the denial and degradation of Georgian communication systems.[18] The most important result was the essential freeze imposed upon the Georgian government's ability to use the Internet to issue any communications to their population or the outside world. Internationally, this meant the Russian version of events tended to predominate.[19] While technically less sophisticated, hackers also infiltrated numerous Georgian websites and defaced them for Russian propaganda purposes.[20]

These attacks were not only designed to control the flow of information or influence people's perceptions. They were also part of information exfiltration activities that were designed to steal and accumulate military and political intelligence from Georgian networks.[21] These activities occurred in waves and featured different techniques that ranged from distributed denial of service (DDoS) attacks to website defacements.[22] Though these attacks utilized simple methods, they were executed in more robust and interesting ways than the similar techniques used against Estonia.

Georgia had a relatively low number of Internet users and a low overall dependence on IT-based infrastructure. However, their access and dependence had been steadily increasing over the years leading up to the conflict.[23]

The coordination for the cyber attacks appeared to have been implemented weeks before

15   George, The Politics of Ethnic Separatism in Russia and Georgia, 182.
16   Ziegler, "Russia, Central Asia, and the Caucasus after the Georgia Conflict," 155.
17   Weitz, Global Security Watch: Russia, 150.
18   Hollis, "Cyberwar Case Study: Georgia 2008," 3.
19   Wentworth, "You've Got Malice."
20   Hollis, "Cyberwar Case Study: Georgia 2008," 3.
21   Menn, "Expert: Cyber-attacks on Georgia websites tied to mob, Russian government."
22   Bumgarner and Borg, "Overview by the US-CCU of the Cyber Campaign against Georgia in August of 2008," 4.
23   Tikk, et al., "Cyber Attacks Against Georgia: Legal Lessons Identified," 5.

any shots were fired between the adversarial parties. Reports suggest that there had been streams of data directed against Georgian government sites and their Internet assets as early as 19 July 2008.[24] Hackers used DDoS attacks against the website of the President of Georgia, Mikheil Saakashvili, and were able to overload the site with requests which made it unavailable. This forced operators to take the site down for twenty-four hours.[25]

This first attack in itself did not raise great suspicion among the international community, mostly because the Georgian President downplayed the significance of the single attack.[26] Only cyber security experts suspected that some of the toolkits used in the attack originated from the Russian regional sphere. This was due to the language used in the code, as well as the obvious statement "win+love+in+Rusia" embedded in some of the messaging.[27] After the initial cyber attack at the end of July, there had not been much activity before the conflict, aside from what in hindsight appears to have been preparations or reconnaissance for the major attacks in August 2008.[28]

Concurrently with the Russian invasion of Georgia, cyber attacks started to increase in number and in sophistication. In addition to the Georgian President's website, cyber attacks targeted the pages of the Parliament, the Foreign Ministry, the Interior Ministry, several news agencies, and a few banks.[29] This disruption of methods of communication denied the Georgian government the ability to effectively communicate with its citizens via the Internet or to deliver their own version of events to the world. Also among the first targeted websites were Georgian hacker forums.[30] These

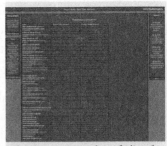

Figure 14: Screenshot of a list of 'potential' targets on StopGeorgia.ru

attacks were not entirely successful, but appear to have been designed as a preemptive strike against any possible retaliatory attacks from Georgian hackers.

The hackers utilized sophisticated DDoS methods against targets, incorporating SQL injections and cross-site scripting (XSS).[31] These methods allow fewer users or smaller botnets to achieve the same results.[32] Besides the distribution of the DDoS tools through various websites, "StopGeorgia.ru" also contained a list of potential target sites to attack,

---

24 Markoff, "Before the Gunfire, Cyberattacks."
25 Danchev, "Georgia President's web site under DDoS attack from Russian hackers."
26 Nazario, Interview by Andreas Hagen, 30 October 2012.
27 Nazario, "Georgia on My Mind – Political DDoS"; and Nazario, Interview by Andreas Hagen, 30 October 2012.
28 Markoff, "Before the Gunfire, Cyberattacks."
29 Wentworth, "You've Got Malice."
30 Keizer, "Russian Hacker 'Militia' Mobilizes to Attack Georgia."
31 Carr, Inside Cyber Warfare, 3.
32 Krebs, "Report: Russian Hacker Forums Fueled Georgia Cyber Attacks."

including sites from governmental institutions (Figure 14).[33] These methods indicate that some basic-level planning and coordination had occurred within Russia's hacker forums.[34]

In addition to DoS attacks, several Georgian websites experienced defacements as well. The online hackers utilized several picture collages that depicted and compared the Georgian President Mikheil Saakashvili with postures of Adolf Hitler (See Figure 15).[35] Defacements of this type and other pro-Russian propaganda were found on the websites of the Georgian President, the National Bank of Georgia, and the Ministry of Foreign Affairs, which later were targeted by DoS attacks.[36]

The cyber aggressors also attempted to sway initial international public opinion concerning the conflict by trying to manipulate non-scientific quick-votes online, on sites like CNN, while blocking access to major international media sites inside Georgia.[37] This helped the Russian bloggers to influence initial perceptions and make Russia's actions appear to be justified as a peacekeeping intervention. Such efforts, in connection with the unreliable communications during the conflict, were no doubt intended to generate initial support for the Russians, at least until the deception was discovered. Such rather minor actions, though not considerably harmful, created nuisances that diverted focus and necessary attention.

The cyber attacks on the banking sector in Georgia had several repercussions that affected everyday life in Georgia and made the period of the invasion more difficult for the population.[38] The persistent attacks on the systems of several banks forced them to shut down their electronic services until the threat had passed.[39] This not only significantly disrupted the connection to foreign banks, but also apparently paralyzed the Georgian payment system, leaving some Georgians without access to money. Due to limited or zero access to financial means, many Georgians could not buy anything in stores. This in turn significantly decreased demand for goods during that time.[40]

Figure 15: Images used comparing Saakashvili to Hitler

33   Danchev, "Coordinated Russia vs Georgia cyber attack Cyber Attack in progress."
34   Krebs, "Report: Russian Hacker Forums Fueled Georgia Cyber Attacks."
35   Danchev, "Coordinated Russia vs Georgia cyber attack Cyber Attack in progress."
36   Tikk, et al., "Cyber Attacks Against Georgia: Legal Lessons Identified," 7.
37   Melikishvili, "The Cyber Dimension of Russia's Attack on Georgia."
38   Schönbohm, Germany's Security - Cyber Crime and Cyber War, 49.
39   Rhodes, Cyber Meltdown, 36.
40   Smith, Interview by Andreas Hagen, 17 September 2012.

Georgian Cyber Defenses

The Georgian government's cyber defense capabilities were very limited and spread thinly, due to the scale of the conflict on the ground as well as the barrage of cyber activities on their systems. The Georgian's first response to the massive amounts of activity in their Internet infrastructure was to establish filtering mechanisms that would lock out any Russian IP-address from accessing Georgian networks.[41] The bulk of attacks originated from servers located in Russia. This method was rather ineffective, because the hackers expected such behavior and adapted quickly by circumventing these filters through accessing the Georgian systems over servers in other countries apart from Russia. The Georgian government also immediately contacted Estonian officials in the hope of gaining access to their vast expertise after the 2007 cyber attacks in Estonia, and also because there was no other international organization they could address for help.[42] The Estonians provided informal access to some of their own cyber security experts and also sent two of their information security experts to Georgia in order to assist locally with the defense.[43] But even with their cooperation, they were unable to mitigate any of the attacks effectively. Thus, these Estonian experts mostly worked on damage control.

Georgia does not have an Internet exchange point (IXP), and they are therefore very dependent on neighboring countries like Turkey, Armenia, and Russia (almost 70 percent).[44] The only really effective defensive countermeasure the Georgians used in order to keep some of their information channels to the public open was the transfer of cyber assets and websites to servers in countries like the United States, Estonia, and Poland.[45] These measures were often undertaken by third parties, such as private businesses, rather than official host countries like the US government.

The Georgian President's website was transferred to Google blog servers in California, the Ministry of Defense website to a private business in Atlanta, the Ministry of Foreign Affairs site to servers in Estonia, and the Office of the President of Poland allowed its website to disseminate information on behalf of the Georgian government.[46] The owner of Tulip Systems in Atlanta offered his services to the Georgian government in order to protect Georgian Internet interests, but without any official approval by the US government.[47] After the conclusion of the conflict, the company reported that it experienced cyber attacks against the website that was taking refuge on their servers.[48] This relocation of cyber

---

41   Bumgarner and Borg, "Overview by the US-CCU of the Cyber Campaign against Georgia in August of 2008," 7.
42   *Ibid.*
43   Tikk, et al., "Cyber Attacks Against Georgia: Legal Lessons Identified," 15.
44   *Ibid.*, 6.
45   *Ibid.*, 14.
46   Clarke and Knake, Cyber War: The Next Threat to National Security and What To Do About It, 19; and Tikk, et al.,
      "Cyber Attacks Against Georgia: Legal Lessons Identified," 14.
47   Korns and Kastenberg, "Georgia's Cyber Left Hook," 66-67.
48   *Ibid.*, 67.

assets could have involved the United States, Poland, or Estonia in the Russo-Georgian conflict politically or militarily.

However, during the attacks on the Georgian Internet infrastructure, the Georgians were not only on the defensive. Once the ramifications and the impact on the Georgian cyber infrastructure were realized, more international support from unlikely places poured in as well. A few German hackers tried to redirect Georgian Internet traffic through a German server to keep the websites up and running. They managed this only for a few hours in the initial stages of the conflict, until their efforts were intercepted and rerouted through servers in Moscow.[49] After the initial attacks and their failure to completely take down local hacker forums, Georgian hackers began to mobilize as well. They retaliated with their own denial of service attacks. The Georgians targeted the website of a Russian news service based in Moscow, called RIA Novosti.[50] According to the US Cyber Consequences Unit report, another counter-attack effort by the Georgians was the distribution of an attack tool designed to be used by Russian sympathizers who would unknowingly attack Russian websites instead of Georgian sites.[51] Retaliations of this kind were very limited and rather ineffective, due to the massive influx of attacks from Russian sources and the apparent "preparedness" of the Russian hackers.

Origin of the Cyber Attacks and Their Possible Connections[52]

Overall, these cyber attacks on Georgian systems and networks spanned over several weeks, from before the conflict had started to after it had ended. However, the main bulk of the attacks coincided–and perhaps were also coordinated–with Russian forces attacking on the ground during the five day Russian incursion that started 8 August and lasted until the ceasefire agreement on 12 August 2008.

After the conflict, there were many accusations, which identified several different groups as perpetrators of the attacks. These groups included the Russian military, their secret intelligence services (i.e., the FSB), Russian nationalists, and even Russian organized crime syndicates. It is likely that all of these groups could have had some (if only limited or indirect) involvement with the cyber attacks.

Despite technical difficulties in attribution, several cyber security analysts concluded that the bulk of the attacks originated from servers that were located in the Russian Federation.[53] There were also signs that an increasing number of pro-Russian sympathizers

---

49   Espiner, "Georgia accuses Russia of coordinated cyberattack."
50   Keizer, "Russian Hacker 'Militia' Mobilizes to Attack Georgia."
51   Bumgarner and Borg, "Overview by the US-CCU of the Cyber Campaign against Georgia in August of 2008," 7.
52   See the Concluding Assessment of this book for additional analysis of the national responsibility for the Georgian attacks.
53   Espiner, "Georgia accuses Russia of Coordinated Cyberattack"; and Bumgarner and Borg, "Overview by the US-CCU of the Cyber Campaign against Georgia in August of 2008," 2.

from other countries, such as the Ukraine and Latvia, soon began participating in some form as well.[54]

In addition, over the past several years, there has been major mobilization in a hacker underground movement located in Russia. Participants often speak out on political issues, and virtually or literally invite involvement by way of nationalistic articles in the Russian media.[55]

Just before the increased volume of the cyber activities were registered, several Russian web forums and hacker sites became active against Georgia. Sites like "xaker.ru" (in English: hacker.ru), "stopgeorgia.ru," and "stopgeorgia.info" began rallying for the Russian cause and encouraged would-be cyber militia members through the use of propaganda. They also distributed of a static list of targets and provided cyber tools with instructions.[56] Security analysts found that many of these sites catered to a specific demographic and nationality, because access from US-based addresses and computers was quickly banned or restricted.[57] At these sites, there was a large cadre of knowledgeable hackers, who assisted beginners with their hacking techniques.

This top-down hierarchy was also the supplier of the instructions and tools that allowed beginners to evade security firewalls and disguise their tracks to circumvent any Georgian countermeasures.[58] Such specialized knowledge and sophistication again suggests some sort of support from the Russian government or military. Some elements could have easily been inside that hierarchy. A Russian defector admitted once that Russian hackers convicted of cyber crimes were often given a choice to work for the intelligence services instead of going to prison.[59]

> *When one considers the forensic evidence, geopolitical situation, timing, and the relationship between the government, the youth, and criminal groups, it is not difficult to conclude that the Kremlin was behind it all.*
>
> David J. Smith, Russian Cyber Operations, Potomac Institute Cyber Center

Such hackers, under the control of the government, could easily direct and give instructions to beginners while completely disguised under a random username in a forum.

Once the targets, tools, and instructions were provided and online for everybody to obtain, the Russian cyber militia began to mobilize themselves like a chain reaction. Many of the hackers began collaborating over well-known social media portals like Twitter and

---

54   Bumgarner and Borg, "Overview by the US-CCU of the Cyber Campaign against Georgia in August of 2008," 3.
55   Danchev, "Georgia President's web site under DDoS attack from Russian hackers."
56   Danchev, "Coordinated Russia vs. Georgia cyber attack in progress."
57   Krebs, "Report: Russian Hacker Forums Fueled Georgia Cyber Attacks."
58   *Ibid.*
59   *Ibid.*

Facebook.[60]

Such a cyber militia, comprised of enthusiastic nationalists and hackers, can be very devastating but also very beneficial for a government. Because there is no "visible" connection between the government and the "voluntary" hackers, deniability is much easier. On the other hand, the actions of the militia cannot be directly controlled unless they are preplanned. Indications for such organization can be found in the specific distribution of targets, tools, and instructions. Therefore, it is still unclear if the cyber militia acted alone or was instigated by the Russian government itself.

Accumulating evidence points to a St. Petersburg-based criminal cyber gang known as the Russian Business Network or RBN.[61] Many of the attackers against Georgia apparently used tools, attack commands, and servers that have been attributed to this Russian organized crime outfit. The RBN has been known to contract its services to third parties, and since there has not been any major attempt by the Russian government to shut down this organization, that absence of action could suggest it is being endured, if not employed, for its services.[62]

Other Russian organized crime groups were involved, such as Stopgeorgia.ru, which has been involved in creating fraudulent passports and credit card scams. The Russian authorities were rather inactive in investigating these activities.[63] A few reports also suggest that the Russian "patriotic hackers" might have been actively hired to perform cyber attacks or reconnaissance under the mantel of a group called Nashi, which has been known to enforce the will of the Kremlin in internal and external matters.[64]

So the role of Russian hackers and organized crime groups seems established. What about the Russian government?

> *Russia is characterized by a unique nexus of government, business, and crime.*
>
> David J. Smith

Ever since the fall of the Soviet Union and the restructuring of the main intelligence service, the KGB, there have been allegations that there are likely ties between the Russian government, organized crime syndicates, and business corporations around Russia. Connections between government, business, and crime are a unique part of Russian society and culture.[65] In Russian society, there occasionally seems to be no clear distinction

---

60   Gorman, "Hackers Stole IDs for Attacks."
61   Markoff, "Before the Gunfire, Cyberattacks."
62   Wentworth, "You've Got Malice."
63   Tikk, et al., "Cyber Attacks Against Georgia: Legal Lessons Identified," 13.
64   Carr, Inside Cyber Warfare: Mapping the Cyber Underworld, 115-117.
65   Smith, Interview by Andreas Hagen, 17 September 2012.

between the government and the criminal underworld, and criminals often share significant contacts with business oligarchs, politicians, and vice versa.[66] Other allegations suggest that the Russian government or parts of the ultra-nationalist Liberal Democratic Party of Russia (LDPR) employ criminal organizations or mafias as an extension of political power, utilizing them in cases in which the government cannot "officially" act.[67]

The involvement of the suspicious Russian Business Network also suggests that this wave of cyber attacks against Georgia was not an unplanned and spontaneous occurrence. There is a strong sense of coordination behind the operation, because they tried to conceal the true origin of the attacks. The Open Source Intelligence report *Project Grey Goose* presented an analysis of the cyber attacks in Georgia; this discusses a piece of Russia's cyber strategy described in a Russian military journal, which emphasizes the need to disguise information warfare or cyber attacks as criminal activities in order to obtain deniability:

> *The practical part of the problem is that the target of a cyberattack, while in the process of repelling it, will not be informed about the motives guiding its source, and, accordingly, will be unable to qualify what is going on as a criminal, terrorist, or military-political act. The more so that sources of cyberattacks can be easily given a legend as criminal or terrorist actions.*[68]

Though there are still a few pieces missing that would establish a concrete connection with the Russian government and military, the coincidence of a coordinated attack from the Russian ground forces and the invisible cyber forces still seems far from random. Both the Russian Business Network (RBN) and Nashi, a Kremlin supported youth group, are known to have cyber capabilities and could have served in an organizing role during the conflict. Either organization might have had a communication link with the Russian military, or even a concrete command and control hierarchy. This seems all the more likely, considering the simultaneous mobilization of Russian forces on the border with Georgia, the reconnaissance work in Georgian networks by hackers, and the first wave of cyber attacks coinciding almost exactly with the first Russian aerial bombing runs.[69]

Outcome and Lessons for the Future

Besides the economic benefits for Russia that resulted from the conflict, the use of the "unofficial" Russian cyber militias has proven to the world the effect that such an instrument can have on a conflict. Not only did these rather crude cyber efforts disrupt vital lines of communications to the people in the crisis, as well as to the international community; they also had a psychological effect that intensified the fears of the public.

---

66   Burton and Burges, Russian Organized Crime.
67   Harding, "WikiLeaks cables: Russian government 'using mafia dirty work.'"
68   Moscow Military Thought (English), Russian Federation Military Policy in the Area of International Information Security, quoted in Greylogic, "Project Grey Goose Phase II Report: The evolving state of cyber warfare."
69   Goodin, "Georgian Cyber Attacks Launched by Russian Crime Gangs."

If such cyber measures increase in sophistication in the future and are applied to a fully developed communications network, then they may have an even more amplified effect compared to the situation in Georgia. The international community, especially the United States, often underestimate the value of such cyber militia groups, whereas countries like Russia, Iran, and China have been encouraging them for a long time, which places the United States at a strategic disadvantage.

These cyber attacks on Georgia have proven to Russia once again that the use of a cyber militia or "independent" hackers like the RBN or Nashi could impact a nation's economy or public perceptions without causing a severe international response.[70] The use of cyber militias has gradually increased over time, giving countries like Russia, China, and Iran, all of whom engage in this tactic, the opportunity to strengthen their cyber warfare capabilities, as seen in the Russian campaigns against Estonia (2007), Lithuania, (2008), and Kyrgyzstan (2009). The Russian government has been benefiting from these situations while always keeping their deniability intact. The use of cyber militias might become a norm for Russian political interaction in the future, since it has been proven useful both in peacetime and in tandem with military operations.

The Russian cyber militia seems to represent a variable which has not been fully explored in the planning of war scenarios by many intelligence and military services. Because of the Russian government's deniability concerning the activities of their civilian cyber force, the militia could be utilized for an array of intelligence functions. Not only can they be called upon in conflict situations; they also could prove useful in intelligence gathering or in denial and deception operations, because their activities in peacetime are still seen as mediocre crimes instead of threats to national security.

---

70   Bumgarner and Borg, "Overview by the US-CCU of the Cyber Campaign against Georgia in August of 2008," 8.

Operation BUCKSHOT YANKEE

Karl Grindal[1]

As the field of cybersecurity has grown and our understanding of the threat has expanded to include highly professionalized foreign intelligence agencies backed with untold millions of dollars, the package by which these threats can be delivered seems more and more humble in comparison. In the summer of 2008, an infected thumb drive, possibly dropped in a parking lot or slipped into a briefcase, was inserted into a US military laptop on a base in the Middle East. The technically advanced virus stored on the USB stick penetrated the air gap that separates the military's secure networks from the Internet at large, infecting both classified and unclassified networks. Once beyond the gap, the malware rapidly replicated throughout the network by infecting additional thumb drives, leading personnel to unintentionally spread the virus further. The virus attempted to beacon back over the Internet for further instructions. Were it not for the diligent work of the NSA employees who disabled the beacon, no one knows what malicious instructions might have been sent. This humble USB stick led to one of the only publicly known cases of classified Department of Defense networks being breached, and the response to this virus was known as operation BUCKSHOT YANKEE.

> *This previously classified incident was the most significant breach of US military computers ever, and it served as an important wake-up call. The Pentagon's operation to counter the attack, known as Operation Buckshot Yankee, marked a turning point in US cyberdefense strategy.*
>
> William Lynn, Former Deputy Secretary of Defense

A Known Surprise

Before infecting government networks, the virus, known as Agent.btz, was circulated months before on the Internet. A Trojan variant of the earlier SillyFDC worm, it was first discovered by the organization F-Secure, a Finnish cyber security firm. Mikko Hypponen, the Chief Research Officer at F-Secure, dubbed it "Agent.btz," as the next name in a sequence used at his company, "Agent.btz," was taken.[2] The virus only became a threat in June 2008, when it was first identified on a NATO computer.[3] It took four months before the virus was discovered in the DoD networks, where the response was rapid and the highest levels of government were briefed. This timeline suggests that the speed of the

---

1   Karl Grindal is an associate at Delta Risk where he provides strategic, policy, and research services for government clients. Mr. Grindal is also the project manager for the Cyber Conflict Studies Association (CCSA) history efforts. His academic background includes a Bachelor of Arts in Government from Wesleyan University and a Master of Public Policy degree with a concentration in Technology Policy from Georgetown University.

2   Nakashima, "Cyber-intruder sparks massive federal response – and debate over dealing with threats."

3   *Ibid.*

threat varied significantly. As a known vulnerability in the cyber security industry, Agent. btz might have sat in DoD networks for weeks before being identified. Once discovered, the threat was rapidly addressed by the NSA and high-level policymakers. While significant steps were taken in the years following, Reuters reported that new variants of Agent.btz were still present in US military networks as late as June 2011.[4]

Attribution

"Almost from the beginning, US officials suspected that Russia's spy service created Agent. btz to steal military secrets."[5] However, the military has not publicly stated this, only going so far as to attribute the virus to, in the words of former Undersecretary of Defense William Lynn, a "foreign intelligence agency."[6] Despite this lack of official attribution, a June 2011 Reuters report stated that "experts inside and outside of the US government strongly suspect that the original attack was crafted by Russian intelligence."[7] A Russian origin to the virus is also suggested by some of the known facts about the case, including the words of an officer interviewed by *Wired Magazine's* Danger Room, which said that Russian hackers had previously used the virus. Despite the strongly supported allegations of attribution, the Russian government was quick to deny these claims in 2008, calling them "groundless" and "irresponsible."[8]

Right after Agent.btz was first reported publicly, there were more alternative theories of origin. The antivirus company Symantec labeled the SillyFDC virus that Agent.btz was based on a "very low" security risk in 2007.[9] Based on this analysis, some experts questioned that an intelligence agency–let alone a Russian intelligence agency–would utilize such an unsophisticated tool. Russia's cybersecurity environment also offered a number of alternative organizations that could have possessed the technical sophistication to construct the virus, either independently or in conjunction with the government.

One notable critic of attributing Russia directly is Jeffrey Carr, who stated that, "[t]he Agent.btz sample that I've seen has indicators that it was created in China," though he added that these indicators "do[n't] exclude Russia" as a possible instigator.[10] Carr went on to hypothesize, "[i] n fact, if I were a Russian hacker running that

The Department of Defense classifies information into five categories: unclassified, confidential, secret, top-secret, and top secret/SCI (specially compartmentalized information).

Richard Clarke in *Cyber War*

---

4   Steward and Wolf, "Old worm won't die after 2008 attack on U.S. military."
5   Nakashima, "Cyber-intruder sparks massive federal response – and debate over dealing with threats."
6   Lynn, III, "Defending a New Domain: The Pentagon's Cyberstrategy."
7   Steward and Wolf, "Old worm won't die after 2008 attack on U.S. military."
8   Nakashima, "Cyber-intruder sparks massive federal response – and debate over dealing with threats."
9   "W32.SillyFDC."
10   Steward and Wolf, "Old worm won't die after 2008 attack on U.S. military."

2008 operation against USCENTCOM, I'd purposefully use malware that was developed in China, Korea, or elsewhere."[11] As William Lynn refused to disclose the specific origins of the attack, Carr's alternative attribution theories remain relevant. However, the overwhelming available evidence suggests both that the US military is confident it knows who is responsible, and that it unofficially attributes a Russian foreign intelligence agency.

The Technical Effect

In the cyber domain, the distinction between intelligence collection and other, more malicious activities in not always clear. A backdoor into a hostile network can be used either to siphon information or to plant a logic bomb that disrupts organizational information. However, the Agent.btz virus, which targeted the Windows operating system, seems indicative of attempted espionage. The military possesses multiple intranets, which are distinct networks that use the TCP/IP protocol, to support differing levels of classification. Agent.btz worked by infecting the intranet where unclassified documents are shared over the Non-classified Internet Protocol Router Network (NIPRNet). BUCKSHOT YANKEE also infected two classified intranets, the Secret Internet Protocol Router Network (SIPRNET) and the Joint Worldwide Intelligence Communications System (JWICS), which are used to share secret and top secret information respectively.[12]

These three networks are supposed to be air-gapped from the Internet, meaning that no computer connected to any of these networks would have Internet access. To get around this security measure, Agent.btz was based on SillyFDC, a virus that replicates itself onto removable and mapped drives. The specific vulnerability that these viruses exploit is the AutoRun feature in Windows, which is designed to allow a configuration where files can be executed when a drive is accessed.[13] The typical recommendation by computer security companies to prevent the virus from spreading is to either stop using thumb drives or to disable Window's AutoRun function. Because of the ease by which this later solution can be implemented, *Wired Magazine* noted that the virus exhibits a particularly low level of sophistication.

The Initial Infection

"It began when an infected flash drive was inserted into a US military laptop at a base in the Middle East," said William Lynn in his 2010 *Foreign Affairs* article.[14] While significant effort was spent trying to track down patient zero, the first USB stick that carried the virus, it remains unidentified. The virus's precise origins within CENTCOM are thus a product

---

11   *Ibid.*
12   Nakashima, "Cyber-intruder sparks massive federal response — and debate over dealing with threats."
13   "W32.SillyFDC"; and Anderson and Anderson, "Seven Deadliest USB Attacks," 86.
14   Lynn, III, "Defending a New Domain: The Pentagon's Cyberstrategy."

of conjecture. As the largest number of infections from Agent.btz occurred in Afghanistan, it is possible that this was the originating country.[15] But, with a concurrent war in Iraq and permanent military bases in Kuwait, Bahrain, and Turkey, Afghanistan is not the only possible origin. While the introduction to this case study infers that the initial thumb drive might have been strategically placed in a parking lot or briefcase, it is possible that the responsible party never held the USB stick. *Wired Magazine* quotes one military official as saying, "[w]e knew fairly confidently that the mechanism had been somebody going to a kiosk and doing something they shouldn't have, as opposed to somebody who had been able to get inside the network."

One of the principal features of the Agent.btz virus was its persistent attempts to beacon over the Internet. While the air-gapping of the networks should have made this impossible, if a connection was made, further instructions could have led the virus to act as a breach head in DoD systems, leading to the mass extraction of highly sensitive data. Intriguingly, the beacon, an innovative technique used by Agent.btz, was also what led to the identification of the virus in the first place. "These signals, or beacons, were first spotted by a young analyst in the NSA's Advanced Networks Operations (ANO) team."[16] The ANO team was formed in 2006, to search for suspect activity on "the government's secure networks."[17] The young team was based in a windowless office in "Ops1, a boxy, low-rise building on the 660-acre campus of the NSA."[18]

The ANO, having identified the virus through the beacon, was now tasked with finding a way to disable the virus across all of the DoD's networks. On 25 October, a Saturday afternoon and the day after senior government officials were notified of the breach, the ANO found a technical solution. With a head-start over the military, ANO staff loaded a server onto a truck headed to the Defense Information Systems Agency. DISA is based in Arlington, Virginia. In 2004, its Director was designated the Commander of JTF-GNO, assigned to defending the Global Information Grid. By 2:20 pm, the ANO team had made significant progress in stopping the spread of Agent.btz. As the beacon requests further instructions, ANO was able to put the malware into a slumber mode by responding to the beacon.

The NSA and military spent months investigating the origins of the attack. Thousands of thumb drives were collected in an effort to find the "patient zero," to no avail. Within the NSA, the Tailored Access Operations (TAO) unit was responsible for investigating "outside the military's networks to look for Agent.btz in a process called 'exploitation' or electronic

---

15   Nakashima, "Cyber-intruder sparks massive federal response – and debate over dealing with threats."
16   *Ibid.*
17   *Ibid.*
18   *Ibid.*

spying."[19] The TAO also took the lead in identifying new variants of the malware. These variants have continued to plague DoD networks.

Notification

On Friday, 24 October, news of the security compromise finally reached senior leadership. Richard Schaeffer, the Director of Information Assurance at the NSA, was in an afternoon briefing with President Bush at the NSA's headquarters, when "[a]n aide handed Schaeffer a note alerting him to the breach."[20] Shaffer walked into the office of the Director of the NSA, General Keith Alexander, around 4:30 pm to alert him to the incident, stating matter-of-factly, "We've got a problem."[21] "That evening, NSA officials briefed top levels of the US government: the Chairman of the Joint Chiefs of Staff, the Deputy Defense Secretary, and senior congressional leaders, telling them about the incident."[22] After the ANO team had tirelessly worked through the weekend to test their technical solutions, plans were formulated to stop the further spread of the virus and to identify its likely origin.[23] On Tuesday, 25 November,

> Gen. Norton A. Schwartz, Air Force Chief of Staff, received a specialized briefing about the malware attack. Officers from the Air Force Network Operations Center at Barksdale Air Force Base in Louisiana outlined their efforts to halt the spread of the malware and to protect military computers from further attack.[24]

That same week, Admiral Mullen, the Chairman of the Joint Chiefs of Staff, took the leadership role in briefing both President George W. Bush and Defense Secretary Robert M. Gates on the incident.[25] While no timeline exists for how long forensics took to attribute the attack, an offensive cyber unit of the Joint Functional Component Command—Network Warfare (JFCC-NW)—proposed offensive techniques that could have "neutralize[d] the malware on non-military networks, including those in other countries."[26]

Technical Implications

On 19 November 2008, Noah Shactman published on the Danger Room blog the first report of BUCKSHOT YANKEE. The US Strategic Command had just released an internal army email that banned the use of "thumb drives, CDs, and flash media cards, and all other removable data storage devices."[27] The ban appears to have been a principally

---

19   Nakashima, "Cyber-intruder sparks massive federal response – and debate over dealing with threats."
20   Ibid.
21   Ibid.
22   Ibid.
23   Ibid.
24   Barnes, "Pentagon computer networks attacked."
25   Ibid.
26   Nakashima, "Cyber-intruder sparks massive federal response – and debate over dealing with threats."
27   Shactman, "Under Worm Assault, Military Bans Disks, USB Drives."

internal decision; neither the President nor Secretary of Defense would be debriefed until the following week. Amongst the military's rank and file, the ban was largely seen as excessive: removable storage devices were commonly being used on the battlefield as a substitute for insufficient bandwidth, to transfer large documents. The ban remained in place up through February 2010, when it was relieved under a set of limited conditions. Deputy Commander of Strategic Command, Vice Admiral Carl Mauney, reported that, "Department-owned drives which have undergone virus scans and checks from network administrators will be made available to troops only when other authorized network resources are not available."[28]

Implications

BUCKSHOT YANKEE was an important wake-up call that shook up the military establishment. This led to dramatic changes within the structure of US cyber policy. The NSA took the lead in responding to Agent.btz, identifying it in the SIPRNET and then devising the technical solution to put the beacon to sleep. However, in 2008, the DoD was technically responsible for defending itself through the Joint Task Force for Global Network Operations (JTF-GNO). JTF-GNO was responsible for both offensive and defensive cyber operations, but without the integration of the NSA's technical proficiency, much of this capability was limited. General Alexander, addressing the House Armed Services Subcommittee in a 2010 hearing, identified BUCKSHOT YANKEE as the event that initiated the integration of the NSA and military operations.

> When we brought that forward, it caused a couple of things to happen. As I mentioned earlier, first it became clear that we needed to bring together the offense and defense capabilities. And so [...] Joint Task Force Global Network Ops was put under my operational control within a month of that happening, and I think that started to change the way we look at this.[29]

In addition to inspiring the concept of merging the NSA and military cyber defense operations, BUCKSHOT YANKEE was also the inspiration for creating Cyber Command. This elevated the role of cyber security within the military. General Alexander went on to say,

> And then the Secretary of Defense set in motion the next step which was to set up Cyber Command as a sub-unified command. And I think both of those are the right things to do. What it does is it gets greater synergy between those who are defending the networks and what they see and those that are operating in the networks abroad and what they see and bringing that together for the benefit of our defense. I think that's exactly what the nation would expect of us.[30]

---

28   Shachtman, "Hackers, Troops Rejoice: Pentagon Lifts Thumb-Drive Ban (Updated)."
29   Alexander, interviewed by House Armed Subcommittee, 2010.
30   *Ibid.*

In addition to these two policy changes, General Alexander identified a broader cultural shift, stating, "we actually hit three parts that came out of that operation BUCKSHOT YANKEE: culture, conduct, and capability."[31] Alexander defined these changes in the context of the understanding of cyber by military commanders. As commanders develop a culture of responsibility for their computer networks, that effects both their conduct and capabilities in defending it. Having commanders be responsible for the integrity of their networks leads them to be invested in having patches frequently updated, and to implementing best practices in security.

31   Ibid.

Stuxnet, Flame, and Duqu – the OLYMPIC GAMES

Chris Morton[1]

Stuxnet emerged on the world stage in the summer of 2010 as the most sophisticated piece of malicious software ever found. Designed to permanently damage Iranian uranium enrichment gas centrifuges, Stuxnet represented a quantum leap in complexity and audacity in cyber conflict. Not only did the malware astonish researchers with its ability to penetrate and cripple a secretive regime's sensitive nuclear enrichment program, it also concerned security experts due to its brash destruction of part of a nation's critical infrastructure. With the emergence of the Duqu and Flame computer viruses, the revelation of a covert American cyber campaign (code-named OLYMPIC GAMES) against Iran, and the recognition of commonality between the three pieces of malware, Stuxnet became known as the centerpiece of a broader campaign, one that might hint at the future of warfare.

The appearance of Stuxnet was like the arrival of an F-35 into a World War I battlefield.

Ralph Langner, 2010

The target of the Stuxnet Worm was Iran's uranium enrichment program at the Natanz nuclear facility, or more specifically, Iran's uranium gas centrifuge tubes. Gas centrifuge tubes are used to enrich uranium, so that it may be used as a fuel for nuclear reactors. If refined highly enough, the uranium be can used in nuclear weapons. Stuxnet's payload only targets systems that meet very detailed specifications, those that perfectly match the gas centrifuges Iran uses at Natanz.

The malware operated for over a year at Natanz completely undetected, destroying gas centrifuge tubes, masking the damage it was causing, and sending data back to the plant operators and digital failsafe systems that the tubes were working perfectly. While sabotaging the enrichment process, Stuxnet was able to replicate itself throughout the system and evolve through updates pushed to it by servers located in two different countries.[2]

In November 2010, four months after the news of Stuxnet went public, the Iranian government acknowledged that a cyber attack damaged its uranium enrichment program at Natanz. In a press conference, Iranian President Mahmoud Ahmadinejad said that, "They

---

1   A 2011 graduate from Georgetown's Public Policy Institute, Chris Morton has spent the past twelve years in public service. His experience ranges from small group leadership to influencing policy at the strategic levels of government. He holds a Masters degree in Policy Management and a Bachelor of Science degree in Chemistry and Life Sciences from the United States Military Academy at West Point. Chris is originally from Muskogee, Oklahoma. The assertions, opinions, or assumptions expressed in this work are solely those of the author and do not reflect the position of any institutions or government agencies with which he is affiliated. The research herein was based on open source information or provided to him from face-to-face interviews.

2   Barnes, "Mystery Surrounds Cyber Missile That Crippled Iran's Nuclear Weapons Ambitions."

succeeded in creating problems for a limited number of our centrifuges with the software they had installed in electronic parts."[3] The Iranian government seemed to downplay the impact Stuxnet had on their systems, but a public admission of interference was out of character for a government known for playing their nuclear program cards close to their chest.

Ultimately, Stuxnet rendered nearly 1,000 of the 9,000 IR-1 type gas centrifuges unusable at the Natanz uranium enrichment facility. While the computer virus did not cripple Iran's ability to enrich uranium, it is unclear how close Iran would be to producing a nuclear weapon without the Stuxnet infection.[4]

Geopolitical Context

On the international stage, Iran was perceived as a destabilizing force, accused of sponsoring terrorist organizations and developing nuclear weapons. Iranian President Mahmoud Ahmadinejad often stoked the fire of conflict, calling for the destruction of Israel, and even suggesting that eradication of the Jewish state was the solution to the Middle East Crisis.[5] Iran flaunted its nuclear technological advancements, claiming they were peaceful in nature, all the while shunning the International Atomic Energy Agency's (IAEA) attempts to inspect its facilities.[6]

As Iran sought to develop its nuclear technology, the United States and Israel were quite vocal in opposition to a nuclear Iran. In the face of this opposition, the United States was engaged in two counterinsurgency conflicts, draining resources and effort that might otherwise be used to curtail Iran's nuclear ambitions. Israel had strong motivation to oppose the development of the nuclear program in Iran, especially because Iran could use ballistic missile technology to strike Tel Aviv. But conventional military strikes, such as Israel's strike on Iraq's Osirak nuclear facility in 1981,[7] were not politically palatable to the United States. On a practical level, Israel would need approval from the United States to traverse Iraqi airspace, and they would require advanced weapons technology to damage the underground facilities.

Iran and Nuclear Weapons

Iran's pursuit of nuclear technology is not a recent development. In fact, it was the United States that gave Iran its first low-enriched uranium (LEU) for use as a research tool under the Atoms for Peace program during the Eisenhower administration. Through this program, the US Atomic Energy Commission leased Iran up to 13.2 pounds of uranium. In

---

3   Clayton, "Stuxnet: Ahmadinejad Admits Cyberweapon Hit Iran Nuclear Program."
4   Albright and Brannan, "IAEA Iran Safeguards."
5   Yoong, "Ahmadinejad: Destroy Israel, End Crisis."
6   Albright and Brannan, "IAEA Iran Safeguards."
7   Neff, "Israel Bombs Iraq's Osirak Nuclear Research Facility."

exchange, Iran agreed to sign the Nuclear Non-Proliferation Treaty (NPT) and established the Tehran Nuclear Research Center.[8]

The United States felt that such a program would open Iranian doors to American commerce and entrepreneurs, while preventing Iran from undergoing its own domestic uranium enrichment research. By the 1970's, France and Germany joined the United States in partnership with the Iranian nuclear power program. Fears of impending energy shortages, combined with Iran's knowledge that their oil supply was limited, encouraged the Shah of Iran, Mohammed Reza Pahlavi, to seek nuclear power as an alternative to fossil fuels. Soon, Germany and France both signed agreements with Iran to assist in building nuclear power plants and to provide the enriched uranium that the plants required.[9] Iran was on its way to becoming a nuclear-powered state.

A 1974 Special National Intelligence Estimate on Nuclear Proliferation indicated that if Iran was able to create a fully sustainable nuclear power program, the Shah could easily decide to procure nuclear weapons. It stated in particular that, if India were to continue with weapons development, Iran would likely follow suit.[10] In May 1974, India detonated its first nuclear weapon.

Concerns about the future of nuclear weapons development led to Germany and France abandoning their plans to assist Iran in building its nuclear power plants. In March 1979, West Germany left the Bushehr nuclear reactor 85 percent complete. Following the Islamic Revolution and the severing of diplomatic ties between the United States and Iran, American leaders grew sour on the idea of supporting a nuclear program in Iran. Throughout the 1980's and 1990's, the United States continued their opposition to Iranian nuclear ambitions. Iran later contracted with Russia to assist in completing the Bushehr nuclear power plant, a project which the United States objected to until 2004. US diplomats changed the focus of their concerns from its nuclear power plants to its enrichment facilities, requesting that Iran answer to the United Nations Security Council.[11]

In 2009, Iran developed the capability to obtain high-enriched uranium (HEU) through the gas centrifuge enrichment process at the Natanz facility. HEU is considered weapons-grade uranium, which is enriched to a point where it consists of 80 percent of the U-235 isotope. Commercial nuclear power reactors only require

Please pay attention and understand that the people of Iran are brave enough that if it wants to build a bomb it will clearly announce it and build it and not be afraid of you.

Iranian President Ahmadinejad

---

8   Bruno, "Iran's Nuclear Program."
9   *Ibid.*
10   Central Intelligence Agency, "Special National Intelligence Estimate."
11   Sarif, "Tackling the Iran-US Crisis," 73-94.

LEU, which is enriched to only 20 percent of U-235. While the IAEA attempted to conduct its inspections as authorized under the NPT, the Iranian government was less than transparent. Perhaps even more disturbing is that Iran developed a 40-megawatt research reactor capable of producing plutonium, a much more efficient fissionable material.[12] These developments have led many western nations, especially the United States and Israel, to condemn Iranian actions, push for sanctions through the United Nations, and make public statements rebuking Iranian nuclear ambitions.

The United States and Iran

The poor relationship between the United States and Iran grew from general discord after the overthrow of the Shah, Iran's monarch and pro-American dictator, into a rage during the hostage crisis of 1979. US President Jimmy Carter agreed to allow the Shah, who was hiding in Mexico following his ouster, to come to New York City for medical treatment of his lymphatic cancer. The Ayatullah Khomeini spurred on anti-American sentiment and called the embassy in Tehran a "nest of spies."[13] Soon thereafter, demonstrations turned into a hostage crisis, with the self-labeled "Students of Khomeini" holding 52 Americans captive, demanding that the United States return the Shah to Iran. The hostage crisis lasted over a year.[14]

Over the next two decades, tensions continued to mount. The United States backed Iraq during the eight-year Iran – Iraq war in the 1980's, when an Iraqi victory became doubtful. Iran responded with its support of radical Islamic terror organizations, such as Hamas and Hezbollah, further increasing tensions. Nation-state support of international terrorism took front stage following the terrorist attacks on the World Trade Center on 11 September 2011.

In his State of the Union Address in 2002, President George W. Bush declared Iran part of an "axis of evil," citing Iran's desires to pursue weapons of mass destruction and to export terror.[15] Part of the new, so-called Bush Doctrine was to not only go after terrorist organizations that posed a threat to the United States, but to also use force against the nations that harbored terror groups. The United States demonstrated its willingness to impose this doctrine through the invasion of Afghanistan and the deposition of its Taliban leadership. The subsequent 2003 invasion of Iraq left Iran with a sizable American military presence to its east and its west, leaving them isolated in the Middle East. In 2003, the Director of National Intelligence, Michael McConnell, said that there was "overwhelming evidence" that Iran was supporting insurgents in Iraq and "compelling" evidence that they

---

12 Kessler, "Nuclear Nonproliferation – Does Iran Want a Nuclear Weapon?"
13 Skow, "The Long Ordeal of the Hostages."
14 *Ibid.*
15 Bush, "President Delivers State of the Union Address."

were doing the same in Afghanistan.[16]

Israel and Iran

As with the United States, outward Iranian dislike of Israel is in-part a byproduct of the overthrow of the Shah. In fact, Iran stayed out of the three Arab-Israeli wars that occurred during the time of the Shah. During the 1970's Arab oil embargo, Iran continued to supply Israel with oil. Iran enjoyed a partnership with Israel against the Sunni-Muslim Arab states. At the same time, Israel benefited from a partnership with Iran, along with the Christian portions of Lebanon and the more secular Turkey.[17] The past thirty years have seen a dramatic change in this relationship.

Current Iranian President Ahmadinejad has made hard-line comments toward the state of Israel, saying that Israel will soon "disappear off of the geographical scene" and should be "wiped off the map."[18] Coinciding with his statements, Iran developed advanced ballistic missile technology capable of reaching Israel. In September 2009, President Obama cited these new capabilities in reference to a European protective missile shield.[19] These new Iranian missiles, combined with their overtly aggressive statements against Israel, seem to position the two nations for a potential head-to-head conflict.

Israeli concerns about the Iranian nuclear program seemed to reach a crescendo in 2008. At the beginning of the year, Israel requested high-tech bunker-busting bombs from the United States, the sort that might destroy underground nuclear facilities. In addition, they sought refueling equipment that would allow their aircraft to reach the Iranian nuclear facilities. They then requested permission to traverse Iraqi airspace. A Pentagon analysis of an Israeli Air Force operation over the Mediterranean Sea in June of 2008 noted that the mission range matched the distance between Israel and the Natanz uranium enrichment facility.[20] Washington rebuffed all of the Israeli requests, while covert operations that the United States were pursuing seemed to satisfy the Jewish state.

Contextually, the Iranian pursuit of nuclear weapons, combined with their involvement in a proxy war against the United States in Afghanistan and Iraq, prepped the grounds for action. Iran's sharp anti-Semitic sentiment stoked Israeli fears that the Persian nation might move from simple financial support of groups like Hamas and Hezbollah to an outright nuclear attack. It seemed to be in the best interest of both the United States and Israel to slow or stop Iran's nuclear weapons ambitions. Conventional attack seemed politically risky, even though the IAEA and the United Nations condemned Iran's efforts

---

16   McConnell, "McConnell Cites 'Overwhelming Evidence' of Iran's Support for Iraqi Insurgents."
17   Weiss, "Israel and Iran: The Bonds that Tie Persians and Jews."
18   Jaseb and Dahl, "Ahmadinejad says Israel will 'disappear.'"
19   Bruno, "Iran's Ballistic Missile Program."
20   Sanger, "U.S. Rejected Aid for Israeli Raid on Iranian Nuclear Site."

to keep their nuclear ambitions under wraps. The best answer might have rested in the dark recesses of cyber sabotage.

The Incident

Stuxnet was designed to destroy Iran's IR-1 centrifuges, rendering them useless for enriching uranium by speeding them up and slowing them down quickly, causing permanent vibrational damage. Damaging these tubes would not just delay the enrichment of uranium; it would also sew internal doubt as to the competence of the Iranian scientists. To accomplish its goal, Stuxnet employed the most sophisticated cyber attack methods seen at the time. It attacked several points of entry to the Natanz nuclear enrichment facility, employed a "dual-warhead" design to deliver its malicious software, and updated itself through peer-to-peer updates to evolve in changing conditions.

> Stuxnet behaved like a lab rat that didn't like our cheese. It sniffed, but didn't want to eat. After we experimented with different flavors of cheese, I realized that this was a directed attack.
>
> Ralph Langner

The Timeline

A Belarusian information technology company called VirusBlokAda discovered Stuxnet on 17 June 2010.[21] While troubleshooting a client's computer, employees discovered not just an encrypted virus using a zero-day vulnerability, but one which boasted a legitimate digital certificate. VirusBlokAda could not ignore the sophistication of the malware. The use of a zero-day vulnerability would permit the virus to gain access to the computer, and a digital certificate would convince the computer that the malware was a trusted piece of software. Therefore, during the first two weeks in July, the small IT company made public what it found.[22]

By 19 July 2010, the computer company Symantec reported that they were investigating malware that infected Siemens SCADA systems. It named the malware W32.Stuxnet, "Stuxnet" being an anagram created from the code of the software.[23] Over the next two months, Symantec conducted an extensive evaluation of the worm, attempting to understand its origin, methodology, and remaining threats. Not until 30 September did Symantec release a comprehensive analysis of the virus.[24]

During the year prior to the release of the Symantec report, problems with gas centrifuge tubes at the Natanz fuel enrichment facility were giving Iranian scientists fits. Until

---

21 Gross, "Stuxnet Worm. A Declaration of Cyber-War."
22 Ibid.
23 Ibid.
24 "W32.Duqu: The Precursor to the Next Stuxnet."

November 2009, things were going smoothly. Then, the facility began having problems. While the detailed actions taken by Iranian scientists at the facility are unknown, by February 2010, Iran removed nearly 1,000 centrifuge tubes from its facility.[25] The number was 984, to be exact—a number frequently found in Stuxnet code.[26] This marked the end of the first version of Stuxnet, and of the first wave of the attack.

On 1 March 2010, the command and control domains pushed an updated version of its code to Stuxnet, creating the second wave of the attack. Only a month and a half later, on 14 April, a third wave was launched. Iran has revealed little evidence of the effects of the second and third waves of attacks.[27] Ostensibly, they were designed to overcome patches and defensive measures that Iranian scientists were able to employ to defeat the virus. They could also be modifications to change the direction of the attack.

One known late change in Stuxnet was its digital signature, that it used to mask its presence. When Symantec found that the malware was using a Realtek digital signature, it notified Realtek, who then revoked the signature. The command and control servers simply pushed a new authentic digital signature, this time held by JMicron, to the virus. This allowed the virus to avoid detection for a time, but by 14 July, when the new digital signature was issued, industry insiders became widely aware of the new threat. Symantec was able to identify this digital signature fairly quickly, and JMicron revoked its signature. A third signature was never sent. On 15 July, a distributed denial of service (DDoS) attack was launched against the websites that contained the mailing lists for two of the top newsletters for industrial control systems security. One of the sites was able to overcome the attack, but the other was shut down, preventing it from responding to requests for information on the new threat.[28]

In August 2010, the Iranians blocked all outbound traffic from infected sites to the command and control servers.[29] By November, the Iranians temporarily halted all enrichment activities at Natanz, perhaps to purge Stuxnet from all of its computer systems.[30] This is the same month that Ahmadinejad admitted that a computer virus infected Iranian nuclear fuel enrichment facilities.[31]

While Stuxnet seems to have only had disabling effects on gas centrifuge tubes at Natanz, it spread worldwide. As of September 2010, it infected over 100,000 hosts in 155 countries.[32] While this infection seemed to spread worldwide, its impact remained isolated in Iran. Iran

25   Markhoff, "Malware Aimed at Iran Hit Five Sites, Report Says."
26   Langner, "Ralph Langner: Cracking Stuxnet, a 21st-Century Cyber Weapon."
27   Falliere, et al., "The Stuxnet Worm."
28   Gross, "Stuxnet Worm. A Declaration of Cyber-War."
29   Falliere, et al., "The Stuxnet Worm."
30   Albright, et al., "Stuxnet Malware and Natanz: Update of ISIS 22 December, 2010 Report."
31   Clayton, "Stuxnet: Ahmadinejad admits cyberweapon hit Iran nuclear program."
32   Falliere, et al., "The Stuxnet Worm."

eventually claimed to have purged its system of the computer virus. By September 2012, two years later, Stuxnet ceased to operate, either by its automatic encoded kill switch, or due to identification and removal tools provided by Symantec.[33] After the shroud was pulled back on Stuxnet in the fall of 2010, little was heard about the complex cyber weapon. Then, two seemingly related pieces of malware emerged—Duqu and Flame. These viruses, combined with the revelations of Stuxnet and of the US OLYMPIC GAMES cyber operation, suggested a multi-phased cyber campaign.

In June 2012, the *New York Times* reported that President Obama ordered the continuation of a complex Bush administration cyber operation against Iran, collectively known as OLYMPIC GAMES.[34] The *Times* citied as its sources current and former American, European, and Israeli officials involved with the program, as well as a number of subject matter experts.[35] OLYMPIC GAMES was a multi-pronged effort to sabotage Iran's nuclear enrichment program at Natanz. Reportedly, it was conceived collaboratively by a team established by then Vice Chairman of the Joint Chiefs of Staff General James Cartwright and the National Security Agency (NSA). According to the *Times*, an initial virus was dropped into the facility to provide a detailed schematic of the Natanz facilities. It then beamed that information back to the NSA, providing the needed intelligence to damage the facility.[36] The initial virus was likely the Flame or Duqu infection, or some combination of the two. Like a blind man describing an elephant, as more parts of the operation are found, Stuxnet's purpose in the context of that operation becomes more clear.

Discovered in October 2011, Duqu is a Remote Access Trojan (RAT), specifically designed to gather intelligence on industrial infrastructure and to acquire design documents, which might enable a future cyber attack against the systems. The RAT gleans its intelligence through executable files that gather system information and by recording computer keystrokes. Once Duqu steals data, it packages it into small files and exfiltrates the data out of the system. In addition, it seems that Duqu has the ability to hide small computer files from the system and disable a computer's security tools, such as antivirus software.[37] Duqu does not propagate as widely as Stuxnet, and it destroys itself after thirty days of functioning.[38] Despite the apparently different functions of Duqu and Stuxnet, two major attributes associate them: they share much of the same computer language in their programming, and they seem to target the Iranian nuclear program.

---

33   "Siemens Industry Online Support"; and Jackson, "Stuxnet Shut Down by its Own Kill Switch."
34   Sanger, "Obama Order Sped Up."
35   *Ibid.*
36   *Ibid.*
37   Venere and Szor, "The Day of the Golden Jackal – The Next Tale in the Stuxnet Files: Duqu Updated."
38   "W32.Duqu: The Precursor to the Next Stuxnet."

Flame, announced to the world by Kaspersky Lab in May 2012, also serves to gather intelligence, but on a much grander scale. Twenty times larger than Stuxnet and more diverse than Duqu, Flame steals documents, takes screen shots from computers, records audio, and even accesses remote Bluetooth devices connected to computers to send and receive information.[39] Recording keystrokes as Duqu did is one thing, but turning on and off microphones, computer cameras, and even extracting a geolocation from an image was off the charts at the time in terms of sophistication. Furthermore, Flame operated undiscovered for more than two years before it was found and revealed in the spring of 2012.[40] It too shared lines of code with Stuxnet, making them brothers, or at least first cousins. Duqu and Flame could gather intelligence and disable security settings, enabling Stuxnet to do its damage.

The Anatomy of the Attack

Stuxnet's attack was simply a quantum leap in terms of the sophistication of its design and effects. Until 2010, most malware focused on other computers—either by overloading networks with DDOS attacks, such as occurred in Estonia during 2007, or by stealing data, such as the operation revealed in 2010 against the Defense Department, which began at the United States Central Command.[41] Stuxnet was different—it damaged infrastructure not directly connected to the Internet. In an interview in 2011, an official from the Department of Homeland Security lauded Stuxnet's elegance. He highlighted the malware's complexity and its ability to perform multiple phases of an attack—infiltration, assumption of control, surveillance, and finally the extraction or destruction of information, all without independent human control or commands.[42]

Upon analysis, researchers found that Stuxnet targets industrial control systems, rewriting the computer code on programmable logic controllers (PLCs), or more specifically, Siemens Supervisory and Control and Data Acquisitions (SCADA) systems. After changing the PLC software to direct industrial systems to operate in a manner that Stuxnet desires, it hides these changes from the operators of the industrial systems.[43] Stuxnet employed an unprecedented four Microsoft Windows vulnerabilities to gain control of the PLCs that dictate the speed at which IR-1 gas centrifuges spin. Once it gained authority over the tubes, Stuxnet sped them up and slowed them down, causing irreversible vibration damage. It also opened and closed valves between groups of centrifuge tubes, called cascades, either to confuse operators or to cause further damage. Once the centrifuges are damaged,

---

39   Kaspersky Lab, "Kaspersky Lab and ITU Research Reveals New Advanced Cyber Threat."
40   Nakashima, et al., "U.S., Israel Developed Flame Computer Virus to Slow Iranian Nuclear Efforts, Officials Say."
41   Nakashima, "Defense Official Discloses Cyberattack"; and "War in the Fifth Domain."
42   Interview by Eric Mann, 26 April 2011. Name withheld as interview was given in an academic context.
43   Falliere, et al., "The Stuxnet Worm."

they become unusable and must be replaced in order for them to enrich uranium.[44] Simultaneously, the malware overrode automated system health indicator monitoring, giving operators indications of normal functioning tubes.[45]

Stuxnet employed a sophisticated dropper software package to deploy its payload. After the initial infection of a computer, Stuxnet went in search of Field Peripheral Gateways (PG). Field PGs are specialized computers that are generally used to control and configure PLCs. The virus would find the Field PGs through one of four methods: a. through a LAN, b. by way of a Windows zero-day vulnerability or a two-year-old unpatched vulnerability, c. through Step 7 projects, or d. through removable drives. Step 7 is the Siemens software that is used to program and configure that company's industrial control systems hardware.[46] Using Step 7 as a vector was especially important for Stuxnet, as the PLCs at Natanz used Siemens software. In addition, because Stuxnet inserted itself into Step 7 projects, cleaned computers would be reinfected with the malware through the hidden software in these project folders.[47]

Stuxnet employed two methods to control the targeted computers and to hide its presence. First, it used a rootkit dropper, which essentially lets the virus act as if it is the administrator of the system—giving Stuxnet persistent, unfettered access to its host.[48] Second, it employed an authentic digital signature to hide its heavily encrypted software, once it found its way to a host. Hackers have used fake digital signatures for some time, but Stuxnet used an actual signature stolen from Realtek, adding to its veracity.[49]

Infection through removable drives likely served as both the initial infection method and as a last hop to the Field PG computer. Normally, Field PGs are not connected to untrusted networks due to security concerns. Propagation through LANs served as intermediate steps, either from a computer that connected to a LAN containing systems with Step 7 projects, or to the Field PGs if they were ever connected to a network that Stuxnet managed to find.[50] Regardless of the method, the malware was constructed with multiple vectors in mind, all of which allowed it to find its way to computers that are normally not part of a network.

Once Stuxnet found its way to a Field PG computer, it then examined the PLCs that the Field PG controlled. It sought a PLC that controlled IR-1 type gas centrifuges, which were spinning at a specific rate. If Stuxnet was unable to find PLCs connected to the

44   Barnes, "Mystery Surrounds Cyber Missile That Crippled Iran's Nuclear Weapons Ambitions."
45   Falliere, et al., "The Stuxnet Worm."
46   Keizer, "Stuxnet worm can re-infect scrubbed PCs."
47   Falliere, et al., "The Stuxnet Worm."
48   Ibid.
49   Gross, "Stuxnet Worm. A Declaration of Cyber-War."
50   Falliere, et al., "The Stuxnet Worm."

Field PG that were running centrifuges with the appropriate configuration, it did nothing, laying dormant as a useless and harmless piece of hidden software.[51] If it found what it was looking for, it contacted home-base.

Stuxnet did not operate completely independently. It communicated with two command and control servers located in Malaysia and Denmark.[52] Stuxnet sent certain bits of information regarding the PLC configuration back to these command and control servers. These servers could then direct the virus to upload whatever code the server controllers wished. It also allowed for updates to Stuxnet, if configurations were changed to combat the infection. More uniquely, Stuxnet could update itself through peer-to-peer updates. If one version of Stuxnet came in contact with another, older version of the virus on another system, it would simply update the older version.[53] Stuxnet's ability to update remotely is the likely cause of its propagation beyond Natanz. US administration officials claimed that an overzealous Israeli update to the virus placed an error in the code, allowing Stuxnet to sneak onto an engineer's laptop when it was connected to the centrifuges. When that laptop was later connected to the Internet, Stuxnet broke free, spilling into an open, unsecure environment.[54] While posing little threat outside of Natanz, its veil of secrecy was gone.

PLCs do not use Windows as an operating system like the Field PGs, so the virus must use the configuring powers of the Field PGs to alter the software residing in the PLCs. The software that it uses to alter the PLCs is the payload of the malware. Ralph Langner, in a presentation at the Technology, Entertainment, and Design (TED) Conference in March of 2011 commented, "If you have heard that the dropper in Stuxnet is complex and high-tech, let me tell you this, the payload is rocket science."[55] The payload would write itself into the software of the PLCs that were controlling the gas centrifuges.

The payload itself consisted of a dual-warhead design. The first, smaller warhead was specifically designed to speed up and slow down individual gas centrifuges within a cascade. A cascade is a grouping of tubes, in the case of Iran's IR-1 tubes, 164 in number. The number 164 appears frequently in the code of the first warhead. The second warhead served to open and close valves connecting Natanz's six centrifuge cascades. Six cascades of 164 tubes totals 984 tubes, a number also frequently found within the code of Stuxnet.[56]

While the malware is speeding up and slowing down centrifuge tubes, it creates reality-blocking software for the operators of the fuel enrichment plant. Much like in Hollywood

---

51   Gross, "Stuxnet Worm. A Declaration of Cyber-War."
52   Ibid.
53   Jackson, "Stuxnet Shut Down"; and Falliere, et al., "The Stuxnet Worm."
54   Sanger, "Obama Order Sped Up Wave of Cyberattacks against Iran."
55   Langner, "Ralph Langner: Cracking Stuxnet, a 21st-century Cyber Weapon."
56   Ibid.

movies, it pre-records normal operating signals, then replays those signals while it is conducting its attack. This gives the operators no indication of any malfunction within the system. Furthermore, it overcomes the digital safety systems employed by the plant. Normally, when anomalies are detected, these automated systems react to prevent damage resulting from system malfunctions. Stuxnet feeds these systems false data, triggering no automatic response.[57]

Adversaries

The Stuxnet attack bears the marks of state involvement. First, the target of the assault seems to have been limited to the uranium enrichment facilities of Iran. While there are groups with motivation to undermine the proliferation of nuclear weapons, simply targeting Iranian gas centrifuge tubes would be a dramatic technological jump for activists, and it would not generate the same sort of publicity that other attacks or methods would bring. As activists rely on graphic images or acts that make a splash in the media, and do not favor subtle, complicated incursions, these attack methods seem not to be the work of activist perpetrators.

In addition, the Stuxnet Worm was specifically designed to attack Siemens-run PLCs, the sort that Iran uses in its enrichment facility. Knowledge of the industrial software that Siemens uses to control its logic controllers is something that would be difficult for the average non-state actor to obtain. Either industrial or nation-state sponsored espionage combined with highly technical engineering would be required to exploit this type of system. Not only is the worm huge, suggesting that it required several man-months of work, it is also highly sophisticated. Only governments wield the resources to produce such malware.[58]

Iran

As of 29 September 2010, Stuxnet infected approximately 100,000 hosts worldwide; of that number, nearly 60 percent were identified to be in Iran.[59] In response, Iran pointed the blame for the attack on the West, and more specifically, at Israel.[60]

Whatever precautions Iran had in place did little to stop the spread of the malware. Stuxnet primarily targeted facilities that would give it the best access to get at its final target. Security firms indicated that there were initially up to five different strains of the virus. These specifically looked for ways to infect systems that were not connected to the

---

57   *Ibid.*
58   *Ibid.*
59   Falliere, et al., "The Stuxnet Worm."
60   Ghajar, "Iran Cites Western Experts to Blame Israel for Stuxnet Virus."

Internet. The virus did this through USB keys.[61] The scenario would be that contractors working at one of a number of infected facilities would transfer the malware from their computers to their USB sticks. Stuxnet would then wait for one of the contractors to plug a removable drive into a computer that is a part of the detached system which Stuxnet targeted. While Iran certainly had basic computer cyber defenses at the Natanz facility, its detachment from the Internet was its best defense. Stuxnet specifically targeted this attribute and had little trouble finding its target, despite Iranian cyber defenses.

In the end, Iran's weak information technology practices at its nuclear facilities and its lack of a stringent cyber defensive structure within its nuclear facility computer network contributed to the attack's success. Iran blamed the attack on Israel and the United States, mostly due to its political mistrust of the two countries rather than because of hard evidence. The private company

Iran's stance has always been clear on this ugly phenomenon [Israel]. We have repeatedly said that this cancerous tumor of a state should be removed from the region.

Ayatollah Ali Khamenei

Symantec conducted the most comprehensive study on the malware.[62] It has avoided outright attribution, but German security expert Ralph Langner revealed at the Long Beach Technology, Entertainment, and Design (TED) Conference that he believes that the Israeli Intelligence Agency Mossad and the United States together are behind the worm.[63] *The New York Times* later specifically attributed the malware to the US and Israel, and claimed this was a part of the OLYMPIC GAMES cyber operation.[64]

Israel and the United States of America

Israel and the United States not only had the motivation to prevent Iran from obtaining highly enriched uranium; they also articulated their intent to prevent Iran from obtaining nuclear weapons. In January 2007, Nicholas Burns, the American Under-Secretary of State, indicated that, "Iran is seeking a nuclear weapon. There's no doubt about it." He further said that, "the policy of the United States is that we cannot allow Iran to become a nuclear state." Burns later commented that, "We are committed to our alliance with Israel. We are committed to being Israel's strongest security partner. I can't remember a time when the relationship between our two countries was stronger than it is today."[65] Mr. Burns made it clear that the United States sought to deny Iran nuclear weapons and that its partnership with Israel was of the utmost importance.

---

61 Fildes, "Stuxnet virus targets and spread revealed."
62 Falliere, et al., "The Stuxnet Worm."
63 Langner, "Ralph Langner: Cracking Stuxnet, a 21st-century Cyber Weapon."
64 Sanger, "Obama Order Sped Up Wave of Cyberattacks against Iran."
65 Lappin, "US Under-Secretary of State: We Won't Allow Nuclear Iran."

In June 2009, the *New York Times* revealed that the United States had hung its hope of preventing the further development of a nuclear Iran on a covert program. After concluding that the sanctions had failed to prevent Iran from enriching uranium, the Bush administration struggled to find another method to intervene. Overt military action, such as the plan that Israel suggested, might ignite a regional conflict, and this was something that Washington desperately wanted to avoid, especially while fighting two wars in the Middle East. The covert operation was an experimental effort to undermine Iran's computers and networks, on which Iran relies to enrich uranium. Some dismissed the efforts as "science experiments," but others said that the covert operations were needed to dissuade Israel from bombing the facility. Secretary of Defense Robert Gates criticized the National Intelligence Estimate (NIE) released in 2007 for under-emphasizing the importance of Iranian enrichment activities.[66] This article reads like a blueprint for the decision to release a covert cyber attack against the Natanz nuclear facility. It was released in January 2009, a full eighteen months before the public or the media knew about Stuxnet.

While both the United States and Israel had the motivation to prevent nuclear advances in Iran, neither nation could accomplish such a feat alone. They would need each other. Richard Clarke, in his book *Cyber War*, asserts that Israeli cyber capabilities were placed on display during a September 2007 attack on secret Syrian nuclear facilities. The Israeli Air Force was able to strike the facility, despite Syria's significant investment of billions of dollars on a new air defense system. Instead of Syrian radar screens lighting up when sorties of F-16 Falcons and F-15 Eagles streaked across the night sky, they remained completely dark. Syrian air defenders were completely blind to the incident.[67]

Although Israel brought cyber expertise to the table, their most valuable asset was more likely their intelligence agency, Mossad. The US and Israel probably needed such an asset, not just to gather intelligence on Iranian facilities and officials, but to plant the virus into a closed computer system not connected to the Internet. Some evidence points to Mossad involvement. In early 2011, retiring Mossad Chief Meir Dagan told the Israeli Knesset that Iran had run into technical difficulties that would delay their construction of a bomb until 2015.[68] Dagan cited "measures that have been deployed against them" when discussing their technical difficulties.[69] Previous estimates of Iranian bomb construction time-frames estimated a date closer to March 2011. Finally, during the retirement of Israeli Defense Forces (IDF) Chief Lieutenant General Gabi Ashkenazi, a commemorative video seemed to allude to the Stuxnet attack while applauding his leadership.[70]

---

66   Sanger, "U.S. Rejected Aid for Israeli Raid on Iranian Nuclear Site."
67   Clarke and Knake, Cyber War, 5.
68   Broad, et al., "Israeli Test on Worm Called Crucial in Iran Nuclear Delay."
69   Gross, "Stuxnet Worm. A Declaration of Cyber-War."
70   Williams, "Israeli security chief celebrates Stuxnet cyber attack."

Israel and the United States both had the ability to test a destructive tool like Stuxnet. In the 1970's, a Pakistani metallurgist, A.Q. Khan, stole the design for the P-1 uranium gas enrichment centrifuge tube from the Dutch (IR-1 centrifuges are the name given to the Iranian version of the same tube). After giving the plans to the Pakistani government, allowing them to go nuclear, he sold the designs on the black market to Libya, North Korea, and Iran. Many nuclear experts believe the secretive Israeli nuclear facility at Dimona houses P-1 gas centrifuges.[71]

I think on the offensive side, the U.S. government invented it [cyber war]. They are probably the best in the world.

Richard Clarke

While it is assumed that Israel possesses P-1 centrifuges, it is known that the United States does. In 2003, Libya abandoned its nuclear program, giving its nuclear enrichment equipment, including P-1 centrifuges, to the United States. They were sent to the Oak Ridge National Laboratory in Tennessee.[72]

In 2008, Siemens teamed up with the Idaho National Laboratory to study the Step-7 software on its programmable logic controllers. The goal of the study was to identify cyber security flaws that might be exploited in a future attack on systems in the United States.[73] The software is the same that Iran uses to control its nuclear enrichment gas centrifuge tubes – Siemens Step-7 software.

There are other pieces of circumstantial evidence pointing to US and Israeli involvement. One string of code in Stuxnet refers to 24 September 2007, the date that Iranian President Ahmadinejad questioned whether the holocaust actually happened.[74] There is also the presence of the file code Myrtus. Myrtus is sometimes an allusion to the biblical book of Esther, in which the Jews preempted a Persian plot to destroy them.[75]

Failsafe mechanisms in the virus, such as its customization to only target software designed to control centrifuge tubes and a "kill switch" that deactivates the virus in June 2012, seem to indicate a Western nation's involvement. Regarding the first of these mechanisms, the virus limits its own ability to spread. Each infected device may only spread Stuxnet to three other systems. This mechanism allows a moderate rate of infection, but does not permit the sort of uncontrolled propagation indicative of other worms. Stuxnet's spillage outside of Iranian systems seems to have been accidental, and due to an error in the code created during an update to the virus.[76] In addition, Stuxnet did not infect computers at

---

71   Broad, et al., "Israeli Test on Worm Called Crucial in Iran Nuclear Delay."
72   *Ibid.*
73   *Ibid.*
74   Gross, "Stuxnet Worm. A Declaration of Cyber-War."
75   Markoff and Sanger, "In a Computer Worm, a Possible Biblical Clue."
76   Sanger, "Obama Order Sped Up Wave of Cyberattacks against Iran."

random. It only affected Siemens SCADA PLC software that matched a complex set of parameters. It would also only infect Windows computers that it believed were connected to these specific PLCs. If these parameters were not found, Stuxnet simply became an inert piece of software.[77] Finally, on 24 June 2012, all copies of the virus ceased to function, due to a command embedded deep in Stuxnet's code. Such efforts to minimize collateral damage and rates of infection indicated a more Western approach to the attack, because of the bureaucratic process that might be involved for approving the assault. In reference to Stuxnet, Richard Clarke commented that, "It just says lawyers all over it."[78] Few places have as many lawyers as the United States government.

In June 2012, the *New York Times* revealed that President Obama had issued an order for OLYMPIC GAMES to be sped up, in an attempt to thwart Iranian nuclear ambitions.[79] Another assertion in the *New York Times*, apparently leaked to them by a high ranking administration official, was that Israel and the National Security Agency (NSA) co-developed the complex virus, which required the expertise of both nations, as well as the sensitive intelligence gathered by Israel's Mossad. Ostensibly, OLYMPIC GAMES would delay Iran's enrichment of uranium, thereby precluding Israel's desire to conduct a conventional strike. The operation was seemingly successful, but the *New York Times* claimed that an Israeli update to the malware caused it to spill outside of Natanz, and thus reveal itself to the world.

Considering their adversarial stance against Iran, and their motives and capabilities to launch such a sophisticated attack, the United States and Israel are likely candidates as participants in the Stuxnet incident. In an interview in 2011, William Marshall, the Managing Director of the Chertoff Group, which is a global security consulting company, noted that non-state actors would not have the ability to bring together all of the elements required to produce Stuxnet— access to Microsoft source code, access to Siemens technology, nuclear engineering expertise, and critical intelligence about the Natanz enrichment facility.[80]

Despite Stuxnet's sophistication, Iran appears to have taken a simple step that may have reduced the impact of a subsequent attack, assuming Iran had not yet discovered the malware on its controllers. It stopped the centrifuges in eleven cascades in module A26, the module that was likely most affected by Stuxnet.

Update of ISIS December 2010 Report

---

77   Falliere, et al., "The Stuxnet Worm."
78   Gross, "Stuxnet Worm. A Declaration of Cyber-War."
79   Sanger, "Obama Order Sped Up Wave of Cyberattacks against Iran."
80   Marshall, interview by Eric Mann, May 5, 2011.

Finally, the lack of significant cyber defenses in the Iranian nuclear facility and the overwhelming strength of American and Israeli cyber offensive tools made Iran a fairly easy target for cyber sabotage. If this imbalance did not exist, the attack might not have been a suitable alternative to an overt kinetic strike.

Response

The government response from Iran occurred both in the technical and political arenas. The immediate response of attempting to identify, control, and eradicate Stuxnet occupied Iranian scientists for some time. Due to the secretive nature of the country, little is known about its inner workings. Politically, Iran has reacted toward the suspected authors of Stuxnet with the usual zeal that emanates from the isolated nation.

Through late summer and early fall, operations at Natanz seemed to be going as planned. The enrichment of uranium fuel and the installation of IR-1 centrifuges had constantly been increasing since the start of the program in 2007. In fact, by September of 2009, nearly 9,000 centrifuge tubes had been installed, and 4,000 of those had been fed with uranium hexafluoride gas. Then something happened. The number of tubes that Iran was installing leveled off, and by February 2010, they had removed nearly 1,000 centrifuge tubes. The number of tubes enriching uranium also stopped rising and leveled off. While Iran managed to install enough tubes to replace the damaged ones, significant growth in capacity did not occur.[81]

Based on these timelines, it seems that between the infections of the Iranian computers in the late summer of 2009 and November 2009, the Iranians were oblivious to what was happening to them and were not reacting. Sometime between November and February 2010, when it was confirmed that Iran removed the 1000 tubes, the country realized that something was causing these gas centrifuge tubes to break. It is unclear whether Iranian scientists thought this was due to the naturally high rate of failure of these types of tubes, or whether something else was causing the problems. At a minimum, Stuxnet was causing the Iranians to question their own competence.

With a rampant computer worm destroying their tubes, and their limited ability to acquire more due to the embargo, replacing these tubes with new ones would have been inadvisable. Between February 2010 and July 2010, when Symantec discovered the virus, it is unknown whether Iranian computer experts understood the problem. That they apparently did not is suggested by the fact that new centrifuge installation as well as utilization remained constant.[82] Likely, they were unwilling to move too quickly until they understood the full nature of their problem. Actual uranium enrichment did still seem to

---

81 Albright, et al., "Stuxnet Malware and Natanz: Update of ISIS December 22, 2010 Report."
82 *Ibid.*

increase, probably because of increased production in their active tubes.

It is also unknown whether the Iranian government understood Stuxnet before the private sector. More likely than not, they spent the bulk of 2010 trying to eliminate Stuxnet from their system. It was not until August 2010 that they finally cut their outbound connections to the command and control servers.[83] While Iran may have eventually stifled the damaging effects of Stuxnet on their nuclear enrichment program, the Flame and Duqu viruses gave the Iranians plenty more to deal with, at least though the summer and fall of 2012.

Iran emphatically blamed Israel and the United States for Stuxnet. President Ahmadinejad's remarks failed to mention any particular country by name, but his anti-Israeli/US rhetoric pointed to those two countries. Ahmadinejad also seemed to downplay the effect of the cyber attack, noting that Iran had the situation under control.[84] With the revelation of Flame, Iran continued to point to Israel, highlighting Flame's similarities to other computer attacks that come from the Jewish State.[85]

Iran also publicly announced the expansion of its militia to include new cyber warriors. The group would be part of Basij, a volunteer military group that is organized within the Iranian Revolutionary Guards. Iranian news specifically mentioned that the unit was being set up to counter-attack those that launched cyber attacks at Iran.[86]

In March 2011, Iranian national news reported that their new cyber warriors in Basij had started operations. General Ali Fazli was quoted as saying, "[a]s there are cyber attacks on us, so is our cyber army of the Basij, which includes university instructors and students as well as clerics, attacking websites of the enemy."[87] Clearly, Iran wanted to flaunt its new capabilities, which are assuredly more complex and capable than what was revealed in public.

Eleven days after this announcement, Comodo, an Internet security group, accused Iran of launching attacks against Google, Microsoft, Yahoo, Mozilla, and Skype.[88] Comodo claimed that they had sold nine digital authentication certificates to fake websites. Their incident report indicated that the Iranian government might have used the certificates to redirect legitimate users of services such as Gmail to a fake site. This would allow the Iranian government to steal usernames and passwords, or install malware to monitor online activities.[89] This sort of activity might have also come from Iran's new cyber police, the creation of which Iran had announced in January 2011. That cyber police force was tasked

---

83   Falliere, et al., "The Stuxnet Worm."
84   Toor, "Ahmadinejad Says Iran's Nuclear Facilities Were Hit by Stuxnet Worm."
85   Erdbrink, "Iran Confirms Attack by Virus That Collects Information."
86   Fogarty, "Iran Responds to Stuxnet by Cyberwar Militia."
87   Berkow, "Iranian Cyber Attacks Against 'Enemies': Report."
88   Couts, "Iran Accused of Attempted Cyber-Attack on Google, Yahoo, Skype."
89   *Ibid.*

with monitoring so-called "foreign-inspired political dissent."[90]

Secretary of State Hillary Clinton and the Israeli Ministry of Defense have noted that Iran's ability to procure nuclear weapons was delayed. Israel indicated that Iran might not become a nuclear-armed state before 2015.[91] Other studies suggest that Stuxnet's effect on Iran's ability to enrich uranium, while problematic, was not catastrophic. The Institute for Science and International Security reported that, although the Iranians were rattled by this attack, their actions in removing the damaged tubes and slowing production likely mitigated further damage. The report also says that since Iran possesses 9000 tubes, the removal of 1000 of them, while damaging, was not ruinous. A larger issue for Iran is that it has a finite amount of material to make more centrifuges, which will eventually limit is ability to expand its program much beyond its 2011 capacity.[92]

Implications[93]

Stuxnet had short-term political effects on both the Iranian government and the potential authors of the malware, which has led to a new state-of-affairs in nation-state conflicts. Stuxnet could prove to be a great equalizer between world powers. If a country can deploy a few lines of computer code and have kinetic effect, countries might choose to stop maintaining their resource-heavy armed forces.

Iranian confidence was certainly shaken. Stuxnet revealed that they were terribly vulnerable to offensive cyber weapons, and that their secrets were not so secret. Some of the techniques employed by the virus required detailed understanding and knowledge of the inner workings of Natanz. This understanding was apparently obtained both through traditional spycraft by Mossad and the CIA, and by modern intelligence operations such as those exemplified by the Flame and Duqu computer viruses. One can imagine the initial paranoia that Iranian government officials experienced when they discovered that their enrichment program was not working properly for unknown reasons. The Iranians most certainly questioned their own ability to maintain an independent nuclear program.

If the destruction of the fuel enrichment plant had been complete, Iran would look different today. Instead, the country took steps that at least limited the damage. Now that Iran has been inoculated with one of the most innovative and capable pieces of malware of our time, they will be on the lookout for the next attack. In this sense, Stuxnet might not have been worth the cost for Israel and the United States. While fuel enrichment was set back, it still continued. Iran publicly acknowledged that it needed stronger cyber defenses, created

90   Dunn, "Iran's Orwellian Cyber-Police Target Dissent."
91   "Report: Iran's Nuclear Capacity Unharmed, Contrary to U.S. Assessment."
92   Albright, et al., "Stuxnet Malware and Natanz: Update of ISIS December 22, 2010 Report."
93   See the Concluding Assessment in this book for additional analysis of national responsibility for the Stuxnet malware.

a militia to conduct cyber operations, and obviously became sensitive to the possibility of further attacks.

Although it is not known with complete certainty that the United States and Israel were behind the attack, it matters not, as most experts agree it was them. The leak by unnamed US administration officials to the *New York Times* about the OLYMPIC GAMES cyber operation was not terribly helpful for an administration trying to maintain at least a shred of attribution ambiguity with respect to Stuxnet. The US and Israel have both revealed what a nation-state created cyber weapon looks like. In addition, they have signaled to the rest of the world what the norms can now be expected to be in this arena, by causing physical damage to another nation's critical infrastructure with a computer attack when faced with a perceived security threat. The toothpaste is out of the tube. William Marshall believes that this might be a blueprint of what is to come—malware intended to influence politics and advance agendas by controlling the cornerstone elements of an industrial civilization. These elements would include critical infrastructure, such as electricity and water distribution systems, financial markets, and transportation networks.[94] Despite Stuxnet's quiet death by self-eradication in June 2012, a message has been sent.

That message might not be all that bad. At the end of World War II, when the United States dropped two atomic weapons on Japan, it sought to end the war and prevent hundreds of thousands of casualties which a land invasion would certainly have caused. The decimation of Hiroshima and Nagasaki also gave the world an in-color, 3D view of American military might. Stuxnet, especially when viewed in the context of the OLYMPIC GAMES cyber operation, could have the same effect. Many in the press have touted the lack of cyber defensive capability and accompanying vulnerability of US critical infrastructure to attack. The message to potential adversaries seeking to exploit this capability could be, "Think twice before you attack us. This is a sample of what we can do. We will do it again."

The most wide reaching implication of the Stuxnet attack stems not from the display of its dazzling engineering, but rather from the potential for reverse engineering. Ralph Langner warned at the TED Conference in 2011 that the problem with the malware is that it is generic.[95] It can be modified to attack any industrial control system. Stuxnet serves as a draft to create a cyber weapon with the capability to attack electrical power grids, oil refineries, nuclear power plants, or hazardous chemical plants. One can only imagine the widespread damages that might be caused by this tool if it fell into the hands of those not so concerned with collateral damage or targeted warfare. Ralph Langer called Stuxnet the first cyber weapon of mass destruction. If Stuxnet is only the beginning of what Albert Einstein predicted concerning World War III, we should start to gather those sticks and stones.

---

94   Marshall, interview by Eric Mann, 5 May 2011.
95   Langner, "Ralph Langner: Cracking Stuxnet, a 21st-century cyber weapon."

Part 5: Other National Perspectives

The United States has been the most influential nation in cyberspace, and much of this history is written from a decidedly US perspective. Fortunately, Yurie Ito, Greg Rattray, and Sean Shank have written a history of how Japan has responded to many of the same challenges as the US, but in markedly different ways. Similarly, Shaun Harvey, of the Royal Air Force, has provided a view of past cyber challenges and responses from a United Kingdom perspective.

Japan's Cyber Security History

Yurie Ito,[1] Greg Rattray,[2] and Sean Shank[3]

Overview

Starting with the Internet's nascent years, cyber security in Japan developed from the interaction between two distinct spheres: 1) the government, in its efforts to develop laws and regulations that govern the security of computerized systems and information, and 2) private industry, in its efforts to limit regulatory burdens and gradually improve the functionality and security of its own networks. Since the beginning, both the Japanese government and private sector have been largely reactive when addressing factors like technological change, transnational criminal activity, and emerging national security threats. From the 1980s until today, the evolution of Japan's approach can be roughly divided into four stages, although each preceding stage partly overlaps with its successor.

During the 1980s, emerging encryption technologies and an increased reliance on computer networks first triggered private research efforts related to cybersecurity,[4] followed by government attempts to set regulatory standards for organizations using this technology. In the 1990s, private research efforts in Japan matured. During this decade, changing technologies would further expose the weakness of governmental approaches, legal structures, and industry practices. In the 2000s, the Japanese government began to focus more on organizational structures and internal capacity for cyber security, while national efforts related to the private sector were led primarily by the Japan Computer Emergency Response Team/Coordination Center (JPCERT/CC), with support from the government. Most recently, beginning with public disclosure of attacks against the Japanese defense industrial base in August 2011, emerging international security threats have targeted government institutions and defense companies. This has forced Japan to look

---

1   Yurie Ito is the Director of Global Coordination for the Japanese Computer Emergency Response Team/Coordination Center (CERT/CC) and previously served for seven years as a technical director for the organization. She has led a number of international collaborative efforts and currently is the Chairperson of the Asia-Pacific Computer Emergency Response Team (CERT) Forum, and was instrumental in the establishment of APCERT and its information sharing mechanisms. Ms. Ito has been an active member of the Forum of Incident Response Security Teams (FIRST), including having served as a board member from 2004-2010. Her Master's thesis at the Fletcher School of Law and Diplomacy, Tufts University was on Managing Global Cyber Health and Security through Risk Reduction.

2   Greg Rattray is a non-resident Senior Fellow of the Atlantic Council, board member of the Cyber Conflict Studies Association, partner at Delta Risk, and full member of the Council on Foreign Relations. His book, Strategic Warfare in Cyberspace (MIT Press, 2001) is a classic in the field. His Ph.D. is from Fletcher and his Masters is from the Kennedy School of Government at Harvard University.

3   Sean Shank is an associate at Delta Risk's Washington, D.C. office. In 2011, he received a JD degree from American University – Washington College of Law, and a Master of Science degree in International Affairs from American University – School of International Service. He is currently a member of the Pennsylvania Bar and helped found American University's National Security Law Brief.

4   The Bright Encryption Research Group (akarui angō kenkyūkai) claims current Yokohama National University scholar Tsutomu Matsumoto as one of its members. This group was established in 1982, and is one of the first examples of a private encryption research group in Japan. "Yokohama National University – Researcher Tsutomu Matsumoto."

beyond its emphasis on cyber hygiene to address cyber espionage and national security risks.[5] Each stage illustrates how the public and private sectors endeavored to implement reforms, only to see new challenges and threats arise.

In attempts to improve cyber security for computer systems and sensitive electronic information, the government's approach has displayed shortcomings. These have usually stemmed from one of three factors: the difficulty of unifying disparate municipal laws under one national domestic law; the complexity of designing a regulatory and assistance framework that will remain applicable to the most current threats and technology; and the difficulty in making certain that laws, regulations, and efforts to collaborate with the private sector adequately enforce or inspire sound practices. Aside from the challenges of developing cyber security practices and standards for the nation as a whole, the Japanese government has also faced challenges in protecting its own information and systems. Developing standard practices within the government, maintaining functionality, avoiding data leaks, and most recently, confronting international security threats have all presented new tests for Japan's cyber security.

The private sector's results in attempting to preserve business functionality and reduce costs have sometimes been achieved at the expense of instituting more meaningful cyber security practices. As the history of Japanese industry from the 1980s to the present day demonstrates, companies have adopted these and other information technology (IT)-related practices when necessary to preserve competitiveness. Japanese industry often has not abided by government guidance on best practices when such guidance was merely voluntary. Examples of this include instances in which the Ministry of International Trade and Industry (or "MITI," now the Ministry of Economy, Trade, and Industry or "METI") issued voluntary guidelines on encryption and the protection of personal information.[6] Additionally, industry standards on information security have sometimes valued certification over concrete security practices and sound procedures for addressing data breaches.

This is not to say that public and private cyber security efforts in Japan have been without success. Though much of the progress in Japanese cyber security has occurred in response to, rather than in anticipation of, major technical and security challenges, this reactive character is not unique to Japan. In fact, Japan has served as an Asia-

The private sector's results in attempting to preserve business functionality and reduce costs have sometimes been achieved at the expense of instituting more meaningful cyber security practices.

Pacific cyber security leader, particularly through the efforts of JPCERT. Additionally, the

---

5   National Information Security Center, "Information Security 2012"; Osawa, "Japan Faces New Cyberwar Era"; and
     Kubota, "Military data possibly stolen in Mitsubishi Heavy hacking: Asahi."
6   Organization for Economic Cooperation and Development, Privacy Online: OECD Guidance on Policy and Practice, 75;
     and Eguchi, "How Have ECOM Guidelines for the Protection of Personal Information Evolved?"

counter-botnet efforts of Japan's Cyber Clean Center (CCC) have strengthened domestic "cyber hygiene," and thus serve as a strong example for the region as a whole.[7] Until recently, national security considerations have not played a significant role in the direction of Japanese cyber security. Since the summer of 2011, however, the government's response to cyber attacks has revealed a significant shift in the Japanese approach to cyber security, as the government and other key players are now pursuing greater domestic capacity building and broader security engagement in cyberspace.

The last section of this paper compares the development of Japan's national cyber security efforts to those of the US, and examines the prospects for joint action by these allies. Given recent developments in Japanese cyber security, the changing regional security environment, and domestic political changes, Japan appears likely to deepen its level of cyber security cooperation with key allies. That next step for Japanese cyber security will likely build upon existing US-Japan collaborative efforts more fully.

We would like to note that to deepen the historical analysis throughout this paper, author Yurie Ito conducted interviews with three expert leaders in Japanese cyber security:

Expert Interviews

Dr. Suguru Yamaguchi: Dr. Yamaguchi is currently a Professor of Information Science at the Nara Advanced Institute of Science and Technology. He led Japan's National Information Security Center (NISC) from 2004 to 2010. His interview was conducted on 11 June 2012.

Mr. Ichiro Murase: Mr. Murase leads the Security Technology Team of the Information Technology Research Department at the Mitsubishi Research Institute. He was interviewed on 13 June 2012.

Ms. Junko Hayakashi: Ms. Hayakashi has served in Japan's Ministry of Justice since 1987, where she led efforts to computerize Japan's legal registration system. She has served as an expert to the Ministry of Foreign Affairs and METI, and as General Manager of the Information Promotion Agency. She became Executive Director of JPCERT/CC in 2006. Ms. Hayakashi was interviewed in June 2012.

---

7   Delta Risk LLC, "International Cyber Engagement: Countries and Organizations" Publication Pending; and
     Yamada, et al., "A Comparative Study of the Information Security Policies of Japan and the United States."

Trial and Error with Encryption and Personal Information Protection Standards in the 1980s and 1990s; Culmination of Legal Reforms in the Early 2000s

During the initial stage of the use of computer networks in government and business, the development of Japanese cyber security was characterized by conflicts over slowly developing government regulations and industry-driven efforts to ease regulatory burdens. In the 1980s, this interaction began with initial encryption regulations promulgated by MITI/METI. These initial encryption regulations were not particularly robust, in that they set forth loose voluntary guidelines which did not provide strong incentives. Through the late 1990s, MITI demonstrated a tendency to avoid strict regulation. This reflected the Ministry's belief that regulation in this arena could dampen free market competition.[8]

Internally, the government's efforts to develop its own encryption capability were also fairly rudimentary. During this decade, the National Police Agency (NPA) and Ministry of Foreign Affairs (MoFA) developed cryptographic capabilities internally, so as to secure their communications.[9] Unlike the US, the Japanese government has never had an agency like the National Security Agency to serve as a leading provider of encryption expertise, technology, and personnel. This difference results from Japanese cyber security's non-military origins, and more broadly, from the historic lack of a clear connection between cyber security and national security.

Although the private sector was slow in adapting to the realities of emerging encryption technology, private research initiatives have driven much of Japan's cyber security progress. One of the earliest examples of these initiatives is the 1982 "Bright Encryption Research Group" (*akarui angō kenkyūkai*), which was Japan's effort to examine and build on the work of Ron Rivest, Adi Shamir, and Leonard Adleman in creating the RSA encryption algorithm. More broadly, this private research effort would examine the application and development of encryption technology in Japan.[10] Japan's financial sector initially helped to lead these efforts, with the Bank of Japan's 1988 creation of its wholesale settlement system, the Bank of Japan Financial Network System (BOJ-NET).[11] However, BOJ-NET was a government institutional mechanism, and thus was unrepresentative of the private sector's comparative slowness to adopt encryption. In general, the Japanese private banking sector was slow to adopt strong encryption approaches until the late 1990s.

As an advanced networking system, BOJ-NET also allowed Japan's central bank to achieve interoperability with the network of the Society for Worldwide Interbank Financial

8   Bar and Murase, "The Potential for Transatlantic Cooperation in Telecommunications Service Trade in Asia."
9   Baker, "Japan Enters the Crypto Wars."
10 "Researcher Details: Tsutomu Matsumoto."
11 Iwashita, "Business Needs for Cryptographic Technology in Japan's Financial Industry."

Telecommunication (SWIFT). To protect confidentiality and provide a mechanism for user authentication, BOJ-NET incorporated the Data Encryption Standard (DES) and Triple DES.[12] Outside of BOJ-NET, the telecommunications sector's Nippon Telegraph and Telephone Corp (NTT) used Fast Data Encipherment Algorithm (FEAL) encryption for its Credit and Finance Information System (CAFIS).[13] For many years after their creation, BOJ-NET and CAFIS were the only two well-known commercial systems that used encryption. This would change gradually, with the growth in public Internet use, cyber crime, and the increasing use of Internet technology in commercial transactions.

The 1980s were also a time of limited progress for Japanese laws protecting private information. In the first half of the decade, policies and laws governing the protection of personally identifiable information were largely dependent on municipal governments throughout Japan. In addition, privacy laws

For municipal governments with laws protecting private information . . . enforcement was problematic, as these laws were not written with computer systems in mind.

enacted during this time period applied legal mandates to government entities only. By contrast, private sector entities were subject to voluntary guidelines. This resulted in insufficient protections for personal information and an uneven enforcement regime in Japan.

In 1983, the Telecommunications Carriers Law, which led to the 1985 privatization of the Nippon Telegraph and Telephone Corporation (NTT), included standards for privacy protection to be imposed on communications and communications facilities.[14] As with other early privacy

Japan's financial sector helped to lead [the adoption of encryption], with the Bank of Japan's creation of its wholesale settlement system, the Bank of Japan Financial Network System (BOJ-NET).

protection laws, this law did not include clear, enforceable mandates for the private sector. For this decade and much of the following decade, the clearest laws protecting personal information and general privacy were based on the post-World War II Japanese Constitution.[15] The Constitution contains protections for secrecy of communications, while post-World War II case law in Japan provides additional guidance on how these standards are applied to government, persons, and corporate entities.[16]

---

12   *Ibid.*
13   *Ibid.*
14   It should be noted that, for matters related to facilities used for the telecommunications business, the Cyber Clean Center [CCC] would gain this authority starting in 2006.
15   Hiramatsu, "Protecting Telecommunications Privacy in Japan," 74.
16   *Ibid.*

For municipal governments with laws protecting private information contained in computer databases, enforcement was problematic, as these laws were not written with computer systems in mind, nor were they consistent throughout Japan. To unify this regulatory landscape, MITI issued the Law on the Protection of Personal Information Held by Administrative Agencies' Computer Systems, which was promulgated in December 1988.[17] However, this law and other existing national standards did not provide means for information security or privacy protections beyond government computer systems. Government computer systems were subject to basic standards and inspection, but the 1988 MITI law gave the government no jurisdiction over the private sector. Thus, in 1989, MITI promulgated the Guidelines for the Protection of Personal Information in the Private Sector.[18] The Guidelines, though similar to the December 1988 law, did not carry the effect of legal mandates, and thus provided insufficient measures for personal information protection. As with encryption regulations, MITI's decision to implement regulations in the form of voluntary guidelines likely reflected an unwillingness to interfere in the free-market development and management of information technology.

Shortcomings in data privacy laws were not only due to the government's unwillingness to regulate the private sector. In 1998, approximately a decade after MITI issued its first administrative data privacy laws and private sector-facing Guidelines, a serious privacy breach occurred within the administrative government of Uji City (Kyoto Prefecture). In

> *As with encryption regulations, MITI's decision to implement . . . voluntary guidelines likely reflected an unwillingness to interfere in the free-market development and management of IT.*

this incident, a city administrative official intentionally leaked personal data entries on 220,000 residents from the city's residence ledger, offering this information for sale on the Internet.[19] Following the leak, three residents sued the city government, and were awarded ¥ 45,000 in 2002, when the suit was concluded. Although the private sector's efforts to protect privacy lagged up to this point, the Uji City leaks showed that government also needed to improve in this area. These events led Japan to finally promulgate the 1995 European Union Privacy Directive 95/46 through domestic legislation in 2003.[20] To honor Japan's commitments as a signatory to Directive 95/46, MITI had previously issued Japanese Industrial Standard JISQ1500 for data privacy protection.[21] Nevertheless, these standards have been criticized as insufficient privacy protections for private IT systems, and would not have applied to management of the Uji City residence ledger. By contrast, the 2003 legislation served as a more broad-sweeping effort to honor Japan's international

17 "Legal Framework."
18 *Ibid.*
19 *Ibid.*
20 See also Purcell, OECD Privacy Guidelines: Thirty Years in the Public Sector
21 Gladstone, "Does the EC Council Directive No. 95/46/EC Mandate the Use of Anonymous Digital Currency?", 1920.

obligations, while more effectively regulating administrative governments' handling of individuals' private information.

Around the same time as the Uji incident, MITI, the Japanese Postal Service, and the National Police Agency (NPA) issued the two-volume *Saneyoshi Survey*, which led to the creation of the Unauthorized Computer Access Law (UCAL), promulgated in Japan in 2000.[22] The UCAL would serve as a major turning point in Japanese cyber law, establishing new privacy protections, as well as criminal penalties for the unauthorized use or alteration of computer systems or databases. Similar to the US Computer Fraud and Abuse Act, passed in 1986, this law would introduce criminal code provisions that would become increasingly difficult to enforce in the face of swift technological change. In instances such as these, where Japan's most sweeping government measures proved inadequate, private sector research initiatives would prove important for developing and protecting a healthy Internet environment.

From the 1990s to the Early 2000s: Collaboration Drives Cyber Security Progress and International Engagement but Cyber Crime Increases

In the 1990s, network managers and communications professionals began to work together through JPCERT/CC to drive cyber security progress. JPCERT/CC began in 1992 as a volunteer task force of the Japan Engineering and Planning Group for IP Networks (JEPG/IP).[23] In 1994, MITI's budget commission recognized JPCERT/CC as a private non-profit organization, furthering JPCERT/CC's role as Japan's leading CERT and funding its activities. Domestically, JPCERT/CC began receiving funding from MITI in August 1996.[24] For its MITI-supported activities, JPCERT/CC activities in Japan initially emphasized incident handling and dissemination of information related to computer security. In 1997, JPCERT published its first security emergency report, which was consistent with its pre-existing mission to serve as a central point of contact for all computer security and incident response teams (CSIRTs) in Japan.

In 1998, JPCERT/CC joined the Forum of Incident Response and Security Teams (FIRST), an international organization that fostered collaboration between CSIRTs from all over the world.[25] With the establishment and recognition of JPCERT/CC, Japan had opened a window to cyber security operations in the international community, and particularly in the Asia-Pacific region. With increasing government support, JPCERT/CC extended Japan's cyber security influence in the new century. In 2002, the Ministry of Education, Culture, Sports & Science provided funding to JPCERT for a number of its

22   "Unauthorized Computer Access Law," Government of Japan, Law No. 128 of 1999.
23   "About JPCERT/CC."
24   Kamata, "JPCERT/CC Activities for Critical Infrastructure Protection."
25   *Ibid.*

initiatives, providing concrete resources for JPCERT/CC's cyber security leadership role in the Asia-Pacific region. In 2003, the Asia-Pacific Computer Emergency Response Team (APCERT) was established, with JPCERT/CC serving as the secretariat. APCERT was established as a coalition of its member nations' Computer Security Incident Response Teams (CSIRTs), to improve computer incident response approaches throughout the region. Up to the present day, JPCERT/CC has served as a major leader in APCERT, acting as a member of the Board of the Directors, maintaining the Secretariat for APCERT, and chairing the organization as of the fall of 2012.[26]

Efforts to harmonize [cyber crime] laws in Japan have moved forward since the [1980s and 1990s], but these national laws, including the UCAL, have not necessarily kept pace with the increasing sophistication of cyber crime.

While JPCERT/CC drove much of Japan's cyber security global engagement in this decade, the government still experienced increasing challenges from growth in Internet use and the resulting surge in cyber criminal activity. As is the case with encryption standardization and data privacy laws, technological and economic progress outstripped developments in the Japanese government's approach to cyber crime. Within Japan, law enforcement has not always targeted cyber criminal activity or the mishandling of private information through one unified approach. Even though Japan had created some basic national encryption and privacy laws in the 1980s and 1990s, law enforcement's approach to cyber crime was largely the domain of Japanese municipal governments during much of this same time period. Efforts to harmonize laws in Japan have moved forward since this time period, but these national laws, including the UCAL, have not necessarily kept pace with the increasing sophistication of cyber crime.

With increasing government support, JPCERT extended Japan's cyber security influence in the new century.

The second half of the 1990s witnessed a significant increase in cyber crime in Japan, based on the growth in public use of the Internet. This increase in crime drove the joint government agency effort behind the *Saneyoshi Survey*, the study which led to the UCAL.[27] Although the UCAL enumerated various forms of activity that involved illegal tampering with private information, its primary goal was to arm the Japanese government with a jurisdictional mechanism for combating new forms of cyber crime.

The UCAL did not significantly deter all cyber criminal activity, however, as financially motivated cyber crime increased in the following decade.[28] While widespread Internet

---

26   *Ibid.*

27   Saka, "Japan's Unauthorized Computer Access Law."

28   Section 2 of this statistics webpage from the NPA shows that financially motivated crimes targeting businesses spiked in 2003 alone, marking an increase in frequency 6.5x larger than the previous year. "Arrests and Consultations of Cybercrime

use increasingly fueled opportunities for cyber crime in Japan, domestic conditions and laws were not solely responsible for cyber criminal trends affecting Japan. It is possible that language barriers between Japanese and other cyber criminal groups delayed the eventual rise in unlawful activity, but this delay was short-lived, highlighting cyber crime's capacity to transcend jurisdiction and undermine the effectiveness of national laws. Although the UCAL incorporated technically vague legal standards,[29] even a more technologically sound domestic law could not have prevented cyber crime's impact, as the increase in crime was also fueled by unlawful activities beyond the Japanese criminal code's limited jurisdiction.

This trend of rising cyber crime reverberated throughout the international community, leading multilateral organizations, particularly the G8 High Tech Crimes Subgroup, to increase pressure to develop laws that could adequately address this issue.[30] Internationally, one of the most significant responses to this increasing criminal trend was the Council of Europe's Convention on Cybercrime. The Convention was first adopted by the Council of Europe in November 2001, and entered into force on 1 July 2004.[31] In the same month that it was adopted, Japan signed the Convention, and not long after, Japan's National Assembly ratified it. However, this accord was not yet fully incorporated into Japan's criminal code, because it required additional enacting laws that reflect the Convention's provisions domestically. In June 2011, a small step forward occurred when the Japanese House of Councillors passed related legislation that outlawed the creation or distribution of a computer virus. Violation of this law carries a maximum sentence of three years; wrongfully and intentionally acquiring or storing an illegal computer virus carries a maximum sentence of two years.[32]

During this time of mounting international concern, cybercrime investigations initiated by the Japanese police showed that inter-governmental cooperation was slow to improve. In response to these trends, the NPA also worked toward a domestic solution, by establishing the Cyber Force Center (CFC). This entity was set up in April 2001 to provide technical support in an arena where, in spite of the existing UCAL, there was little national-level law enforcement presence.[33] Municipal police forces still maintained a great deal of operational influence in this area, but had not placed enough emphasis on building cyber

in 2003."

29   Unlike the US Computer Fraud and Abuse Act (CFAA), the UCAL does not specify what types of domestic computer systems fall under its jurisdiction. Instead, the UCAL broadly prohibits uses of computer systems or data that exceed the authorization of a network administrator. The CFAA, by contrast, specifies prohibited behavior, but also designates US government and financial institutions' computer systems as protected systems. See "Unauthorized Computer Access Law"; Computer Fraud and Abuse Act, 18 U.S.C. Section 1030 (e)(2); and Handerhan, "Japanese and American Computer Crime Policy," 27-28.

30   In June 1997, G8 member countries established the High-Tech Crime Subgroup and issued a communiqué, following the Denver, Colorado G8 summit, which stated member countries' common interests in combating high-tech crime across borders and jurisdictions. Scherrer, G8 Against Transnational Organized Crime, 71.

31   UNESCO, "The Council of Europe Convention on Cyber Crime, Before Its Entry into Force."

32   McMillan, "Japan Criminalizes Cybercrime: Make a Virus, Get Three Years in Jail."

33   "Cyber Force Center."

forensic capacity. The CFC also provides the NPA a means of working around some of the difficulties of trans-national police work—it is a member institution in FIRST, serving as an informational conduit between Japan's government, critical infrastructure operators, and the international cyber security community.

While the NPA improved its capacity for fighting trans-national cyber crime, software trends in Japan demonstrated that transnational influences were not the only source of cyber crime during this period. The Peer-to-Peer (P2P) file-sharing software known as "Winny" became a source of copyright and other legal controversy, highlighting shortcomings and a tendency to overreact in Japanese law enforcement's approach to cyber crime. In 2003, two users of this software program were arrested by the Kyoto Prefectural Police and were charged with copyright violations. The developer, Isamu Kaneko, was also charged at this time. While Kaneko successfully appealed a trial-level guilty verdict, the police investigation of his home, and their subsequent confiscation of the Winny source code triggered greater distrust of law enforcement within the Japanese IT sector.[34] In conjunction with his trial, Kaneko publicly stated that he did not develop Winny with the intent to encourage theft or copyright violation. However, Winny has served as a mechanism for these types of violations, and it has provided a conduit for viruses which have exposed vulnerabilities in government computer systems.

In 2003, widespread use of the Winny program also led to increased exposure to viruses for government computer systems and personal computers alike. These viruses would typically take files contained within a user's computer and leak them via the Winny network, without the authorization of the user. The most notorious example of these viruses, named "Antinny," began to spread throughout the Winny network in August 2003. This data leak problem did not only plague personal computer use. The NPA, the Ground Self-Defense Force, the Maritime Self-Defense Force, and the Air Self-Defense Force were all affected, starting with leaks of internal JSDF documents in November 2002.[35] Lingering problems stemming from Winny network viruses would later lead the Japan Defense Agency (now the Ministry of Defense or MoD) to purchase new computer systems that were less susceptible to infection by Winny and other viruses.[36]

The Japanese Postal Service, prison system, judicial system, nuclear power facilities, and some municipal government agencies were also affected by viruses spread via Winny. In many of these cases, confidential government data under the purview of government officials was uploaded onto the Winny network, demonstrating how everyday personal computer use could produce unintended consequences for vital public institutions.[37]

---

34   Hongo, "File-Sharing: Handle Winny at your own Risk."
35   Kamata and Miyagawa, "Threats of P2P File Sharing Software."
36   "Dell to supply Defense Agency PCs"; and Preatoni, "Japanese Fight against Cybercrime."
37   *Ibid.*

Although these examples are a brief overview, they illustrate how the Winny program and network exposed the broader challenges that the government and the private sector faced in adapting to new technological realities, including those of cyber crime. These incidents also exposed the persistent inadequacy of approaching Internet governance and cyber security challenges with old laws and pre-twenty-first century institutions. To combat these challenges, the Japanese government and public-private groups began to acknowledge distinct cyber security issues more closely, creating new entities and standards, and engaging in capacity building.

2000s: Government Agencies and Public-Private Collaboration Lead to New Cyber Security Organizations, Efforts to Clean the Internet Ecosystem, and Standards; Political Hacking Rises

Following concerns raised by the rise of cyber crime in the 1990s and concerns about what vulnerabilities these trends could expose, Japan's government began more focused efforts to improve domestic cyber security. These efforts were further driven by web attacks against the government in 2000, and by growing interest in protecting critical infrastructure and key resources. As a response, multiple government agencies initiated or reinforced efforts and organizations dedicated to cyber security, including the NPA (within their Security Group), the Japan Self-Defense Force (JSDF) and their respective branches, and agencies regulating industry, including METI. The NPA established the Cyberterror Technical Policy Office within its Telecommunications and Information Analysis Division. Within its Community Safety Bureau, the NPA set up an IT Crimes Analysis Division. Municipal governments followed the NPA's example, and cyber crime offices were established at police headquarters throughout all of Japan. In Tokyo, the Metropolitan Police's High-Tech Crimes Division Integration Center was established.[38] METI also set up an Information Security Policy Office. The Ministry of Internal Affairs and Communications followed suit, establishing an administrative office for information distribution, as well as a division for promoting information sharing.[39] This division similarly included an information security policy office. Within the private sector, communications industry professionals, in collaboration with other research institutions, developed a security information sharing and analysis center, known as the Telecom ISAC.

In 2000, the Cabinet issued the Basic Law Regarding the Development of an Advanced Information and Communications Society (commonly known as the "IT Act").[40] Based on this law, a Strategic Headquarters for Promoting an Advanced Information and Telecommunications Network Society was established.[41] That same year, in May,

---

38   Kitahara, "Information Society Law in Japan."
39   Yamada et al., "A Comparative Study of the Information Security Policies of Japan and the United States."
40   Kitahara, "Information Society Law in Japan," 21.
41   *Ibid.*

the Information Security Policy Council (ISPC) was established with the mission of determining national information security policy and strategy.[42] Over the following two years, the ISPC then issued the Special Action Plan on Countermeasures to Cyber-terrorism for Critical Infrastructure, as well as the Partnership with the Private Sector on Countermeasures against Cyber-terrorism on Critical Infrastructure.[43] In April 2005, the National Information Security Council (NISC) was instituted, with the mission to lead government cyber security activities while serving to ensure the physical and cyber security of national security and emergency response systems.[44] The first Advisor on Information Security was Suguru Yamaguchi.[45]

In addition to these new institutions, METI and the Ministry of Internal Affairs and Communications (MIC) supported the creation of the Cyber Clean Center (CCC), a national initiative aimed at botnet reduction through collaboration with ISPs on malware removal. Beginning in 2006 and operating over an initial five-year-period, the CCC began as a counter-botnet initiative for improving the health of the Japanese cyber environment.[46] The CCC was supported by joint budget contributions from METI and the MIC, as well as private organizations such as JPCERT, the Telecom ISAC, telecommunications companies/ISPs, and antivirus vendor companies. In utilizing the combined resources of these entities, the CCC could address the cost burdens of reporting and assessing information security incidents and botnet infection information. Following its inception, the CCC has disseminated removal tools for infected computer systems throughout Japan, and claims to have served over a million customers within its first three years.[47] The CCC has notified tens of thousands of computer users about botnet infection in Japan, while disseminating disinfection tools and dismantling botnets.[48] This effort correlates with Japan's low malware and botnet infection rates of 2.1 CCM (Computer Cleaned per Mille [thousand]) and .625 CCM, respectively.[49] Despite recent concerns about its future, based on waning government financial support, the CCC has achieved success by developing response mechanisms, and by improving cultures in large Japanese ISPs and the computer security operations community. This effort has improved the health of Japan's Internet environment and aided the international computer security operations community, by initiating broader improvements in the Internet environment as a whole.[50]

---

42 Ibid.
43 "Japanese Government's Efforts to Address Information Security Issues: Focusing on the Cabinet Secretariat's Efforts."
44 Yamada, et al., "A Comparative Study of the Information Security Policies of Japan and the United States," 218.
45 Ibid.
46 "What is Cyber Clean Center?"
47 Krebs, "Talking Bots with Japan's Cyber Clean Center."
48 Ibid., 227.
49 Microsoft uses the term "Computer Cleaned per Mille (Thousand) MSRT Executions" to refer to the number of computers found to have infections, out of every 1,000 computers cleaned by their Malicious Software Removal Tool (MSRT). Microsoft, "Microsoft Security Intelligence Report," Vols. 9 and 11.
50 Ibid.

This period also saw progress in the creation of new industrial standards, as METI issued summary criteria for handling and communicating about software vulnerabilities in 2004.[51] Before METI issued the summary criteria, there were no clear standards for how such vulnerabilities were to be disclosed, leading each company to develop its own unique approach to disclosure. This pre-existing, reactive approach had caused problems, as it left a greater number of companies open to attack. As such, these problems fueled an increasing demand for the enactment of rules under the summary criteria. Following METI's publication of these criteria, the Information Technology Promotion Agency and JPCERT/CC began working together on handling software vulnerability information handling in July 2004, and they soon provided industry with a standardized process for vulnerability information disclosure.[52]

The Information Security Management System (ISMS) and Japanese Industrial Standards (JIS) are Japan's information security certifications, similar to those issued by the International Organization for Standardization (ISO). Many companies in Japan, and particularly the largest, have successfully acquired ISMS and JIS certifications.[53] Additionally, Japanese companies lead internationally in receiving ISO certifications.[54] These facts suggest a strong culture of information security certification within Japanese industry. This focus has created an environment which encourages a costly certification process, disproportionately favoring larger companies. Under this system, smaller organizations cannot easily absorb the cost of the certification, or see adequate returns on the time, money, and effort invested in acquiring such credentials.[55] Even though the increasing compliance with these standards demonstrates that Japanese industry has improved its information security focus since the 1980s, this has not necessarily improved the operational protection of information or networked systems in Japanese industry.

During this period of government-wide capacity building, the MoD established the Ground Self-Defense Force's Systems Protection Corps, as well as the joint-JSDF Command, Control, Communications, and Computer Systems Command. The latter group was established in 2008 with the intent of developing national cyber defense capabilities. The group now houses Japan's developing cyber defense unit.[56] Although these new MoD organizations symbolized significant progress for Japan's military cyber capabilities, steps toward greater military and national security-level readiness would not occur until 2012,

---

51 "Information Security."
52 Information Technology Promotion Agency, "Reporting Status of Vulnerability-related Information about Software Products and Websites."
53 Baker, "Decoding OECD Guidelines for Information Security Policy."
54 The International Register of ISMS certificates lists Japan as the world leader in domestic registrants, with 4152. "Register Search."
55 "An Overview of ISMS Conformity Assessment Scheme in Japan."
56 Lewis and Timlin, "Cybersecurity and Cyberwarfare."

the year in which the cyber defense unit was originally projected to become operational.[57]

In spite of Japan's new cyber security initiatives and organizations launched during this decade, the government did not initially focus on these efforts to address the growing threat of patriot hacking within East Asia. In this decade, pre-existing regional tensions between Japan and its neighbors were aggravated by controversial WWII accounts in Japanese history textbooks. This resulted in acts of patriot hacking against the Japanese government. In March 2001, South Korean hackers crashed the Japanese Ministry of Education's website, after making announcements that the Japanese textbooks diminished the significance of the Nanjing Massacre and described the invasion of the Korean peninsula as an unopposed annexation.[58]

Later, in August 2001, hackers belonging to the Honkers Union of China attacked the servers of multiple Japanese agencies, while issuing statements criticizing Prime Minister Koizumi's visit to the nationalist Yasukuni War Shrine.[59] In 2004, Chinese hackers allegedly belonging to the China Federation of Defending the Diaoyu Islands attacked multiple Taiwanese and Japanese websites.[60] In 2005, Chinese hacktivists again targeted Japanese government websites in response to another of the Prime Minister's visits to Yasukuni.[61]

To counteract this growing friction within cyberspace, the China-Japan-South Korea (CJK) Agreement was established in 2005. This was intended to be a confidence-building measure (CBM) to reduce the potential for cyber conflict in the Asia-Pacific Region. The CJK Memorandum of Agreement, which established this relationship, created links between the member countries' respective CERT groups. Activities supported by the CJK Agreement have since included information sharing, procedures for handling cyber attack incidents, and other approaches for decreasing the likelihood of escalation.[62] The CJK Agreement also delineates specific responsibilities of member nations' national organizations. At the national CSIRT level, parties initiate contact regarding incidents, share cyber threat intelligence, provide information on what resources are targeted by a given attack, and coordinate responses to attacks. At the ISP level in China, Japan, and South Korea, parties would

To counteract this growing friction within cyberspace, the China-Japan-South Korea (CJK) Agreement was established in 2005. This was intended ... to reduce the potential for cyber conflict in the Asia-Pacific Region.

57   *Ibid.*
58   "Japan textbook angers neighbors."
59   "Chinese hackers deface Yasukuni Shrine website…again."
60   These attacks were allegedly in response to previous Japanese attacks on the website of the China Federation of Defending the Diaoyu Islands; the initial Japanese attacks defaced the site with a message asserting that the Diaoyu (or Senkaku) Islands belonged to Japan. "Japan: Organized Chinese hackers hit official Japan Sites."
61   Segal, "Coming this Weekend: A Sino-Japanese Hacking War?"
62   Ito, "Making the Internet Clean, Safe and Reliable."

receive requests for response coordination from CSIRTs, while carrying out response actions, including the disabling of servers and websites responsible for malicious activity. At the government level, parties to the agreement would engage in diplomatic exchanges, so as to enhance political understanding of a cyber incident, and decrease the potential for further conflict.[63]

The CJK agreement was a proactive step toward regional cyber engagement, and helped to eliminate some of the potential for harmful escalation between regional neighbors. Collaboration under this agreement has helped to offset some of the more harmful outcomes of political hacking, even when addressing the underlying historic and diplomatic concerns in this region is a more challenging task. But despite the beneficial impact of the CJK agreement against political hacking, new national security threats have emerged in East Asia, including advanced persistent threats (APT).

Present Day: National Security Threats Emerge in Cyberspace, Affecting Japan's Defense Industrial Base and Government

Beginning with incidents first disclosed in June 2011, APT attacks against Japanese defense industrial base companies, government agencies, and the Japanese Diet, led to the theft of proprietary and other confidential information. In the summer and fall of 2011, Mitsubishi Heavy Industries (MHI) acknowledged that it had been targeted by cyber attacks, leading to the exfiltration of data on military aircraft, air-to-ship missiles, and nuclear power plants.[64] According to subsequent news reports, the MoD indicated that MHI would be required to carry out an internal investigation, and a review of their information control systems.[65] Although Japanese legal codes provided no clear guidelines for Japanese defense industrial base companies to safeguard against or report these types of incidents, it is possible that MHI's failure to report was a breach of its supply agreement with the MoD.[66]

Although the NPA's investigation could not identify a clear culprit behind the attacks, the level of sophistication involved in this data theft led Japanese news sources to suggest that a Chinese adversary was likely involved.[67] From June through October 2011, computer systems in the Japanese Diet and multiple other government agencies were also attacked.[68] Targeted agencies included the Financial Services Agency, the Japan Fair Trade Commission, METI, and the Cabinet Secretariat. These attacks were executed through acts of phishing and infected dozens of computers at each affected institution.[69]

---

63   Ibid.
64   Leyden, "Japan's biggest defense contractor hit by hackers."
65   "Japan defence firm Mitsubishi Heavy in cyber attack."; and "Japan cyber attack silence may breach arms contracts."
66   Ibid.
67   Ibid.
68   "Cyber-attacks target 20 ministries, agencies."
69   Ibid.

Given the severity of the attacks and the sensitivity of the targeted assets, Japanese government and industry leaders have begun to view cyber as a national security issue. Leading up to these attacks, processes for analyzing threat intelligence were insufficient. This delayed analysis and critical response measures. In response to these issues, Japanese industry has embarked on the creation of systems to facilitate threat information sharing, increased research efforts related to APT, and further cooperation with international partners.[70]

In addition to industry's efforts, JPCERT/CC and multiple government agencies have begun initiatives to address APT. In the wake of these attacks, such efforts exemplify the types of international cooperation Japan seeks in order to combat national security-level cyber threats.[71] The NPA, METI, and JPCERT/CC have already developed partnerships with US IT companies and US-CERT/DHS. These efforts regarding APT include a desire to focus on information sharing and to provide clear signs that the Japanese government is paying greater attention to the intersection between national security threats and sophisticated, malicious actors in cyberspace.

Within Japan, Japanese national cyber defense and cyber combat capabilities have also lagged, although significant efforts to establish capabilities are now underway. The rising threat has even led some commentators to suggest the need for Japan to resort to self-help in the form of cyber militias.[72] NISC has recommended in its 2010 "Information Security Strategy for Protecting the Nation," the development of "active" cyber defense capabilities.[73] Depending on how this capability is developed, Japan's own national laws may prohibit capabilities that can "hack back" at a cyberspace adversary.[74]

Additionally, the MoD's efforts to develop a cyber defense unit are still at an early stage as of late 2012.[75] As the *Yomiuri Shimbun* reported in early September 2012, the MoD will develop a unit of approximately 100 personnel dedicated to cyber defense. Currently, cyber defense roles within the JSDF are divided between the Ground, Air, and Maritime branches. In 2013, these roles will be consolidated under the new cyber defense unit.[76] By centralizing these functions under one unit, the MoD will be able to devote greater efforts to researching and defending against cyber threats to military and national critical infrastructure. In conjunction with this shift, the JSDF has also declared that cyberspace, like land, air, sea, and space, will be considered a domain for the purpose of military

---

70   Through their own operational experience in related engagements, authors Greg Rattray and Yurie Ito have both
     contributed to recent counter-APT initiatives supported by METI and involving JPCERT/CC.
71   *Ibid.*
72   Tsuchiya, "Patriotic Geeks Wanted to Counter a Cyber Militia."
73   "The Second National Strategy on Information Security."
74   *Ibid.*
75   Delta Risk LLC, "International Cyber Engagement: Countries and Organizations." Publication Pending.
76   "Ministry to establish cyber defense unit."

operations, following the lead of the United States.[77] Finally, the MoD panel behind these changes has declared that cyber attacks against Japanese critical infrastructure will trigger Japan's right of self-defense, if such attacks are carried out in conjunction with a military attack.[78]

As Japan looks to advance its national security-level cyber defense capabilities, joint statements with friendly nations like the US and Estonia strongly suggest that cyber security will become an avenue for increased international engagement.[79] On 30 April 2012, President Barack Obama and Japanese Prime Minister Yoshihiko Noda issued a joint statement addressing a number of US-Japan security issues, including the realignment of US forces in Japan, China's strategic impact in East Asia, and US-Japan cooperation on cyber security.[80] That same month, Japan's Vice Minister of Defense Hironori Kanazawa and Estonian Permanent Secretary of the Ministry of Defense Mikk Marran met, providing Marran the opportunity to invite Japan's participation in NATO's Cyber Collective Defense Center of Excellence.[81] International engagement on cyber defense will help Japan to address cyber threats more effectively beyond its borders.

Conclusion: Looking Back and Forward

Unlike the US, Japan's cyber security policies and practices are not traceable to military and intelligence-driven origins. For Japan, the commercial origins of cyber security efforts as well as broad constitutional prohibitions and political limitations affected until recently the relatively slow movement to address cyber security as a national security issue. However, despite their differing origins, a number of similarities exist between US and Japanese cyber security efforts at the domestic level. Both nations reflect an aversion to strong government regulation of private industry's cyber security practices. Because of the free market leanings of the political culture in both countries, achieving new and comprehensive cyber security regulations is highly difficult. Despite making gradual progress in enlarging capacity, both Japan and the US have also fallen behind in their efforts to limit cyber crime. Given the benefits of past initiatives shared by the private sector and government, both Japan and the US may consider collaborative public-private initiatives as avenues for addressing national security issues raised by APT and other threats.

Japan has demonstrated leadership in certain aspects of cyber security that focuses on cyber hygiene and international collaboration. The establishment of the Cyber Clean Center was one of the first national-level efforts to focus on malware reduction. It provides an exemplar

---

77 *Ibid.*
78 *Ibid.*
79 "Remarks by President Obama and Prime Minister Noda of Japan at Joint Press Conference"; and "Tallinn, Japan to Strengthen Military Co-Operation."
80 "Remarks by President Obama and Prime Minister Noda."
81 "Tallinn, Japan to Strengthen Military Co-Operation."

of effective public–private collaboration as a government funded, ISP executed operation. JPCERT/CC leadership within APCERT and capacity enlargement efforts with the Asian and Pacific partnership, as well as more broadly, have allowed this organization to develop a regional leadership role and a global posture. The CJK Agreement relating to coordinating responses to politically motivated hacking provides a model for the growing efforts to develop confidence-building measures in the realm of cyberspace.

Looking forward, domestic political factors in Japan will continue to play an important role in driving the direction of cyber security efforts. Following the LDP electoral victory in December 2012, Shinzo Abe has returned as Prime Minister, bringing with him a greater emphasis on specific public sector cyber initiatives, as well a stronger ability to influence administrative officials and private sector experts on cyber security.[82] The LDP's plan is laid out in the Proposal on Information Security, which calls for an official declaration that cyber security is an essential part of national security, and for the provision of significant additional funding for cyber security research and development, as well as for the information security industry.[83]

In addition to an improved domestic focus, the LDP government's renewed focus on cyber will likely stress the importance of international relationships. Given its history of support for close ties with the US, the LDP's re-emergence as Japan's governing party represents an opportunity for significant progress in US-Japan cyber security collaboration. Although it would be politically difficult for the current government to reform the Constitution and provide the Japanese military with greater freedom to respond to cyber threats, current proposals for enhanced national security collaboration with the US, the United Kingdom, and India include cyber cooperation.[84] By revising the current war contingency bill to incorporate provisions for cyber attacks and by passing a bill with requirements for the protection of classified information, the Japanese government can further facilitate its cyber international engagement, while easing allies' concerns about information security.[85]

Given their strategic relationship, Japan and the US are closely tied together in determining their cyber security futures. By understanding the distinct nature and origins of their respective approaches to cyber security, both allies can better address collaborative efforts to move forward. As current engagements suggest, their differences do not necessarily pose obstacles to collaboration. On the contrary, their efforts to share information and to jointly address APT demonstrate ingenuity and political will to confront common strategic threats.

---

82   *Ibid.*
83   *Ibid.*
84   Matsubara, "What the LDP Victory Means for Japan's Cybersecurity Policy."
85   *Ibid.*

Unglamorous Awakenings: How the UK Developed Its Approach to Cyber

Group Captain Shaun Harvey RAF[1]

Britain is quietly proud of its heritage in cyberspace. If evidence is needed, one need only look at the billing given to the inventor of the World Wide Web, Sir Tim Berners-Lee, at the opening ceremony of the London 2012 Olympics. Since the mid-nineteenth century, in producing such British visionaries as Charles Babbage, who conceived of the first computer, or William Fothergill Cooke and Charles Wheatstone, who developed Britain's own telegraph system, the UK has been at or close to the forefront of employing information and its supporting technologies for national ends. Today, Britain has a thriving technology sector, a population that has embraced a parallel digital existence, and even the world's first human cyborg in the shape of Professor Kevin Warwick.[2] The Nation's military power relies heavily on Network Enabled Capability to provide the leverage and flexibility it needs to deliver its international security contribution. The UK's diplomatic prowess is vested heavily in information, via public diplomacy and the soft power projection of national values. Moreover, 21 percent of GDP growth in the UK is attributed to Internet technologies. London is a core hub of Internet connectivity, and with an estimated 6 percent of the nation's GDP resulting from e-commerce,[3] the UK is increasingly alive to both the opportunities and vulnerabilities presented by cyberspace. Thus, Britain can still claim to be at the vanguard of the information revolution.

In 2009, the Cabinet Office produced the first UK National Cyber Strategy,[4] and thereafter, the National Security Strategy in 2010 identified hostile attacks upon UK cyberspace by other states and large-scale cyber crime as a Tier 1 National Threat.[5] The Strategic Defence and Security Review of 2010[6] provided £650 million of investment over four years and established cyber security as a programme at the heart of government.[7] This chapter will describe some of the events that have led to the gentle awakening of the UK's cyber consciousness. It has been written primarily from a UK MOD perspective because of the size, complexity, and cyber-dependency of that organization. Nonetheless, it will be

---

1   Group Captain Shaun Harvey is a serving British Royal Air Force officer and a Chief of the Air Staff Fellow. Over his 23 year career to date, he has served as a communications engineer, satellite operator, military planner, and staff officer including an appointment in the Defence Cyber Security Programme. He has also worked as an Exchange Officer with the United States Air Force, running a Division of the Air Staff in the Pentagon. He has an MBA and an MA in Defence Studies, and has just completed an MPhil with Professor Colin Gray at Reading University, where his thesis was on the application of strategy to the issues of cyber power. The views offered in this chapter are those of the author and do not necessarily represent those of the UK Ministry of Defence or the Royal Air Force
2   The website of Professor Kevin Warwick can be accessed at http://www.kevinwarwick.com/.
3   Cabinet Office. The UK Cyber Security Strategy.
4   Cabinet Office. Cyber Security Strategy of the United Kingdom.
5   A Strong Britain in the Age of Uncertainty: The National Security Strategy
6   Securing Britain in an Age of Uncertainty: The Strategic Defence and Security Review.
7   The UK Cyber Security Strategy.

shown that at each juncture, wider issues than those first apparent were at play, forcing the view of cyberspace to become ever more holistic. The evidence presented in this chapter will show that, rather than employing a deliberate strategy, the UK government's journey through cyber conflict has emerged from a holistic approach to information issues, operational lessons, the exigencies of government reorganization, budget cuts, and the occasional moment of serendipity. Nonetheless, the end result has allowed Britain to take its seat at the international cyber top table, at the right hand of the US.

There is very little in the public domain about UK government cyber security incidents, either concerning evidence that exposes vulnerabilities, current operational techniques, or developing capabilities. This information rightly remains classified. Indeed, the unsung heroes of UK cyber operations are, with little doubt, the men and women of the Government Communications Headquarters (GCHQ) in Cheltenham. Regrettably, recent stories of GCHQ's exploits must remain unsung.[8] However, there is much that we can learn from the approach the UK military has taken to the lower-level problems of cyberspace. These are developments that can be mapped largely to the responses of the burgeoning cyber community to even seemingly innocuous incidents and opportunities.

This chapter will describe a brief history of the UK's involvement in cyberspace. It will chart some of the early pioneering technologies and the uses to which the UK put them, highlighting the historical importance of information to Britain's national interests. It will then show how in the years following the end of the Cold War, Britain attacked the combined challenges of modernizing its Armed Forces and making reductions in its defense budget. Also to be examined are the topics of how this dilemma shaped the approaches of British policymakers; and how a philosophy of pragmatism, broadly inspired innovation, and the ability to "make do" have created the governance structures, practices, and institutions that constitute the UK's response to the cyber security question. It is not yet possible to publish any details relating to major UK operational cyber activities. However, many of the events that have shaped the thinking and approaches of the small cadre of personnel involved in protecting Britain's interests in cyberspace are explored in the chapter. It is important to acknowledge just how much progress has been made in developing a UK Cyber Strategy that is genuinely cross-governmental. This chapter describes some of its key features and alludes to some of the challenges that are most likely to be faced in the next few years.

Before It Had a Name: the Early Evolution of UK Cyber

Long before William Gibson coined the phrase 'cyberspace' in his novel *Neuromancer*,[9] the

---

8   For a comprehensive account of GCHQ's history, see Aldrich, GCHQ: The Uncensored Story of Britain's Most Secret Intelligence Agency.

9   William Gibson, Neuromancer (London: Harper Collins, 1995).

UK understood the value both of information and exploiting technology to maximise its value. The entrepreneurial spirit so crucial to Britain's success throughout the Industrial Revolution also spawned important national information capabilities in intelligence and espionage. The Zimmerman Telegram in 1917, and later the extraordinary and successful efforts to decode the German Ultra ciphers at Bletchley Park, not only pioneered the new world of signals intelligence, but also gave rise to the development of one of the world's first computers, in the form of Colossus.[10] Information was established firmly as a strategic asset. Coincidentally, knowledge was (and still is) viewed as power, and with the 'need to know' principle in full force, the culture was set to establish stove-pipes of excellence across government.

In 1940, the early use of Radar technology and the development of a network of Royal Observer Corps aircraft spotters informing command and control at Group Headquarters were vital contributors to the success of the Royal Air Force in the Battle of Britain.[11] After World War II, Flight Lieutenant Arthur C. Clarke's discovery

> *Long before William Gibson coined the phrase 'cyberspace' in his novel Neromancer, the UK understood the value both of information and exploiting technology to maximise its value.*

of geosynchronous space orbits[12] made possible the global telecommunications revolution that would follow. In the years of the Cold War, Britain developed further capabilities in its military and civilian telecommunications sectors, but the greatest progress was state-led. Then with the privatization of British Telecom in 1984,[13] market-driven commercial pressures were applied to the British Telecommunications industry. This also accelerated the transition to the private sector leading the public in technological development. In 1982, the UK was first surprised and then stretched to the geographical limits of its reach by the Falklands War. Britain's victory was hard fought, but its military success was significantly aided by new "smart" weapons, such as the latest version of the US air-to-air "Sidewinder" heat-seeking missile, secure command and control enabled by military communications satellites, and the availability of space imagery intelligence from the US. These technologies were not physically networked, but the potential advantages in concentration of effort, synchronization of forces, surprise, and lethality whet the appetites of military planners. It was a valuable reminder to the British of the vital importance of information, both to conflict prevention and to the conduct of war itself.

Not a decade later in 1991, by expelling Iraqi forces from Kuwait, the US showed the

---

10   Colossus was built by Tommy Flowers, a brilliant Post Office engineer. It was successful in cracking the Lorenz ciphers of the Nazi High Command. Its first upgrade was working in time to help Eisenhower and Montgomery to be sure that Hitler had swallowed the bait from the deception campaigns prior to D-Day (June 6, 1944). There were eventually ten working Colossus machines at Bletchley Park. Further details can be found at: "Colossus Rebuild Project."
11   Michell, "A History of Networks," 11.
12   "The 1945 Proposal by Arthur C. Clarke for Geostationary Satellite Communications."
13   "Privatisation of British Telecom (1984)."

world what was possible with technological superiority, driven by the microprocessor. Royal Air Force aircraft were controlled from Airborne Warning and Control System (AWACS) aircraft in the air over the Gulf and connected electronically via secure digital data links. UK Royal Navy warships were linked to their Maritime Commander in Theatre and to Headquarters back in the UK via satellite communications. The satellites themselves, the UK's Skynet 4 constellation of three geosynchronous communication satellites, were controlled by the Royal Air Force at 1001 Signals Unit at RAF Oakhanger in Hampshire, England. One of the satellites was re-positioned in orbit to provide better coverage of the Gulf region.

By expelling Iraqi forces from Kuwait, the US showed the world what was possible with technological superiority, driven by the microprocessor.

The British Army headquarters in the field enjoyed 'reach-back' communications to the UK via satellite and was able to employ its Ptarmigan radios to deliver some data, as well as voice communications. Given the media frenzy over the technical wizardry of the Allies, one could be forgiven for thinking that in an instant, Cold-War doctrines had been abandoned and western militaries had all become post-modern manoeuvrists. Yet, as it happened, the UK military in the Gulf was able to achieve its objectives without abandoning the fundamental principles of its most classical doctrine. Continuity was shown to be as important as change. The post-war quest for improvement then centered on the need to synchronize forces electronically, to exploit information to deliver increased precision, surprise and concentration, and also to pay for the investment necessary by reductions in mass elsewhere. The seeds were sown for what became known as the UK's "Network Enabled Capability (NEC)," which was strongly analogous to Network Centric Warfare (NCW) in the US.

British military commanders were becoming ever more reliant on connecting to secure, networked command, control, and intelligence channels. This required connectivity to information systems from the planning headquarters to the foxhole and huge increases in required bandwidth to accommodate the growth in demand for information services. But in the 1990s, the expectation of a post-Cold War peace dividend delivered its own strategic paradox.[14] The goals of modernization and capability uplift would have to be accomplished under increasing pressures both on finances and the front-line strength of the British military.

In terms of conceptual development, the works of American futurists, like Alvin and Heidi

---

14   For an excellent exposition on the paradoxical logic of strategy, see Edward N. Luttwack, Strategy: the Logic of War and Peace (Cambridge, MA: Harvard University Press, 1987).

Toffler's *War and Anti War,*[15] were studied in British Staff Colleges and assisted in a re-evaluation of how Britain's forces were equipped, trained, and directed in battle. Yet, in typical and peculiarly British fashion, the impetus for change resulted far less from the evangelical drive of the new gurus of the information age and much more from the need to craft business cases that would pass rigorous financial scrutiny at the Ministry. Following the introduction of the New Management Strategy in the early 1990s, the government pushed new cost-cutting initiatives, known variously as "Options for Change" and "Front-Line First."[16] These ventures were, in part, designed to adapt UK forces to the needs of a post Cold-War world. They provided for delegated budgets, but also demanded significant efficiency savings including substantial manpower reductions and restructuring. Any proposed increase in capability, such as the networking of systems and functions, had to produce a net reduction in the defense budget.

The works of American futurists like Alvin and Heidi Toffler's War and Anti War were studied in British Staff Colleges and assisted in a re-evaluation of how Britain's forces were equipped, trained, and directed in battle.

This meant the potential cutting of other capabilities and the challenging of traditions of the Services. Moreover, it set the conditions for every budget holder to establish and run separate, stove-piped[17] information networks and systems, without any of the higher governance that would be needed to integrate their functionality.

The British involvement in the Balkans during the mid-1990s was too soon after the Gulf War for the UK to have benefited from a significant growth in its cyber capabilities. However, these operations cemented the British view of the need for expeditionary military capability, with the ability to execute complex operations using a lighter, more agile force structure. This agility and responsiveness would rely on expert intelligence and increasingly, networked command, control, and situational awareness.

Modern, Agile, Capable Forces: Organizing to Exploit Cyber

The 1998 Strategic Defence Review (SDR)[18] provided the policy framework for modernization. It also provided centralization through joint organizations to fund capability from a joint budget at MOD and direct all expeditionary military operations from the new Permanent Joint Headquarters (PJHQ). In some ways, this was a mirroring of the Goldwater Nichols Act in the US (although the US retained Title 10 funding

---

15   The Tofflers were among the first to herald and examine the idea of information wars for an information age. See Toffler and Toffler, War and Anti-War.

16   For useful background on the changes in UK Government Defence Policy in the 1990s, see Taylor, "The Defence White Paper," 7-14.

17   In this chapter, a "stove-pipe" or "stove-piping" refers to a structure, organization, or activity that is pursued in isolation from other activities that could reasonably be expected to be interconnected. This behavior often results in un-coordinated outcomes and problems with interoperability.

18   "Strategic Defence Report."

through individual Service channels). Another trans-Atlantic reflection was the creation of the Defence Communications Services Agency (DCSA) on 1 April 1998. The DCSA was very similar in character and constitution to the Defense Information Services Agency (DISA) in the US. Led by a military two-star, Major General Tony Raper, from the outset the DCSA comprised military, civil service, and contractor staff. One of its most important features was the Global Operations Security and Control Centre (GOSCC), whose mission was to direct and control end-to-end information services for defense users worldwide, 24/7.

Within the GOSCC, the Defence Computer Incident Response Team (DCIRT) was formed to execute the Computer Network Defense (CND) mission for the MOD. This joint, military-led team included engineers, computer technicians, military police, and an active duty Major exchange officer from the USAF, positioned so that the UK could maintain a strong awareness of tactical cyber developments in the US military. In the same year, the government also introduced an updated Data Protection Act,[19] mandating formal governance over all personal information held on electronic systems in the UK.

Further information security support was provided by the Joint Security Co-ordination Centre (JSyCC) at MOD headquarters in London. This organization provided information security threat assessments and security incident investigations. It also established the nation's first Warning, Advice, and Reporting Centre (WARP) structure that was later adopted across the UK to assist in the protection of the Critical National Infrastructure.[20]

The formation of the DCSA and creation of a central MOD Directorate for the procurement of all Information Systems created the conditions to standardize the Department's information architecture and provide both the efficiencies and operational benefits of common service management. These benefits also included improved and more direct accountability for cyber security. Significant defense programs delivered the foundational defense cyber architecture. These comprised the Defence Information Infrastructure (DII),[21] which brought nearly all MOD computer users onto a single service-managed infrastructure; Skynet 5, which provided cutting-edge military satellite capabilities under a Private Finance Initiative contract;[22] and the Defence Fixed Telecommunications System (DFTS), which replaced nineteen existing telecommunications networks to provide the fixed telecommunications infrastructure.[23] It was the UK MOD way of delivering the spirit

---

19   An Act to make new provision for the regulation of the processing of information relating to individuals, including the obtaining, holding, use, or disclosure of such information - July 1998.
20   A description of the WARP and how it applies to the Critical National Infrastructure can be found at: Center for the Protection of National Infrastructure. "WARP Background."
21   Details of the DII contract can be found at: Atlas Consortium, "About the DII Programme."
22   Skynet 5 is contracted for availability and provides satellite services for military users world-wide. It is delivered by Paradigm Services, with deployed manpower provided by the military. Paradigm Services by Astrium, "Skynet 5 Has the World Covered with Secure, Flexible, and Pinpoint Accurate Communications."
23   Baddeley, "DFTS: a Defence-Wide System."

of the 1996 US Clinger Cohen Act,[24] but without the formality of national legislation and stringent congressional/governmental oversight.[25]

As the DCIRT began to assert its influence, it became clear just how many disparate information system architectures existed across the MOD and its connected civilian partners. With the growth of the public Internet and the increasing need routinely to access both webpages and commercial email from the military desktop, the military/government infosphere was extending far beyond its previous borders. It therefore became vital to fully understand the vulnerabilities presented end-to-end across the military intranet. A major initiative entitled "Establish the Baseline" was launched across the MoD to discover the configuration of defense networks and the connectivity that existed to other systems. The early results were sobering, reflecting the piecemeal development of information capabilities over nearly two decades of devolved budgetary responsibility and precious little central governance. Additionally, it highlighted the need to pay significant attention not just to external threats, but to the behaviors and practices of the MOD's own users and service providers.

The threat posed by the product of system vulnerability and the capability and intent of adversaries at last began to appear as risks on military and government risk registers. Accordingly, this improved focus on cyber security was further enhanced by the appointment of a MOD Chief Information Officer (CIO), Mr. John Taylor, as both the Chief of Defence Staff's Chief Information Advisor and Senior Information Risk Owner (SIRO). CIOs were created across government departments, and communities of interest were generated to share their growing knowledge and experience. These contacts also extended to the "5-eyes" military community of the US, Canada, Australia, the UK, and New Zealand, enabling improved interoperability, information sharing and the opportunity to accelerate the understanding of cyber issues.

The mission to operate and defend UK MOD networks was given a military commander, vested with the authority to take action to balance the needs of the Military's operational activity against the cyber threat.

A key issue of coordination, particularly if any nation intends to do more than just defend its networks, is cyber equities. For example, an agency wishing to exploit a vulnerability in a network to undertake intelligence operations is potentially denying the opportunity

---

24 The Clinger-Cohen Act (CCA) of 1996, also known as the Information Technology Management Reform Act, established in law the posts of Chief Information Officers (CIOs) for all Federal Agencies. CIOs were made responsible for developing, maintaining, and implementing sound and integrated IT architectures. The CCA introduced congressional governance to the efficiency and interoperability of existing and future IT investment. "The Clinger-Cohen Act (CCA) of 1996."

25 Government Ministers are accountable to Parliament for the performance and activities within their ministry. In addition, the National Audit Office provides financial scrutiny of MOD procurement.

for defenders to correct vulnerabilities in their own networks. The reverse-engineering of security updates highlights vulnerabilities that may or may not have previously been understood. With this knowledge, there is a balance to be struck between securing vulnerabilities and allowing them to remain for potential exploitation. This is a problem made much more complex when making the assessment at a national level and across a broad critical national infrastructure. In 2005, the MOD set up an equities forum with GCHQ to investigate how such assessments could be made and to provide the basis for any necessary coordination. Such discussions and the development of frameworks for risk assessment would become important elements of future national and international collaboration efforts.

Shaping the Cyber Awakening - the Importance of the Most Unremarkable of Incidents!

Britain is quite happy to learn its lessons vicariously, hence the attention it pays to the pioneering efforts of its closest allies. Policymakers have closely observed events such as the Titan Rain exfiltration of data from the US NIPRNET; the GhostNet infiltrations of Western systems; Estonia in 2007 suffering Distributed Denial of Service (DDOS) attacks from Russian "patriot hackers," Georgia in 2008, and the use of the Stuxnet Worm to attack precisely-targeted SCADA systems in Iranian nuclear facilities. These events demonstrate the increasing sophistication and depth of penetration possible with cyber attack. However, it is also becoming clear that while the character of conflict in cyberspace changes with sophistication and encourages some observers to make extraordinary claims about the catastrophic potential of cyber power, the essential nature of conflict is the same, whether it be in cyberspace or any other domain.[26] A prudent response to the evolving story of cyber conflict would therefore involve critical observation, openness, and the ability to discern the new from the familiar. Nevertheless, several cyber-related incidents in the UK have pricked the consciousnesses of the policy elite, and a few of these will be discussed below.

A prescient reminder that the design and therefore vulnerabilities of the Internet are man-made came in the guise of the "Y2K bug." As revelers celebrated the passing of the Millennium, Information and Communications Technology (ICT) providers, the UK military, and critical infrastructure providers were rather nervously attending to their networks and services, to ensure that suspected anomalies with computer clock functions did not result in embarrassing, or worse-yet, catastrophic system failures as the clocks ticked past midnight. The new Millennium passed without any of the feared issues arising,[27] but several salutary lessons were learned. The first was the need for a better understanding of the physical and logical architecture of our information systems, their vulnerabilities,

---

26   For an excellent description of the objective nature of war, see Gray, Another Bloody Century: Future Warfare, 291-330.
27   "Y2K Bug Fails to Bite."

and how network risks manifested themselves within a system of systems. The second was the need to identify and organize business continuity efforts across the government, the military, and what became defined as the Critical National Infrastructure. Thirdly, it directed attention to the differences in age, operating systems, configuration, and patch status (and by implication, quality of husbandry) across information systems supporting key UK functions. Ironically, the Y2K experience also served to increase the skepticism of business leaders and heads of government concerning their IT departments and to increase the profile of the CIO on the governing boards of both government and industry.

In early 2003, as the Lovgate computer virus spread across the globe, [28] a number of MOD systems were infected. Lovgate spread rapidly. It reproduced by sending email messages which masqueraded as a reply to the victim and by copying itself to shared network folders. MOD technicians spent more than four weeks isolating and cleaning computer systems across 30 sites. The report on the incident concluded that the worm was probably introduced onto its systems by a single user, who infected an MOD computer by inserting a floppy disc.[29] The Lovgate virus presented a low-level risk and although there was no operational impact and no mission-critical systems were affected, this was the first major infection to be spotted and responded to by the DCIRT. It was a wake-up-call for the leadership. Senior officers were alarmed by the apparent vulnerability of a MOD system. But the response of the DCIRT provided the organization with added credibility. The incident also resulted in questions in Parliament and a focus on the ability of the National Infrastructure Security Co-ordination Centre to protect the Nation's Critical National Infrastructure.

One morning in May 2005, rumors circulated within the UK Permanent Joint Headquarters that the computers in MOD HQ had crashed due to an "Amarillo Virus" spreading across its primary computer system. With Britain supporting concurrent missions in Iraq and Afghanistan, the inability to exchange data such as emails with MOD HQ was of immediate concern and prompted swift investigation. What transpired was not a virus. The mail server had crashed due to a funny video attachment to an email that was "going viral" around the staff of the HQ, as it was being sent between friends and colleagues.[30] The actions of the MOD's own staff had in-effect created a self-imposed denial of service attack on the email system. Once it was understood what was happening, it took very little time to restore the system to normal functioning, but several key lessons resulted.

The description of this incident as a virus attack implied a cyber attack. Although it clearly had nothing to do with malevolent software or an attack from an outside "threat vector,"

---

28   See Symantec, Report on Lovgate.
29   "Single User Costs MoD £10 million after allowing Worm onto the Network."
30   "Amarillo Video Crashes MoD PCs."

the effect on service availability was essentially the same. The system managers blocked the video clip from email messages and moved it to an intranet website, so that users could see it without affecting the overall performance of the system. Had there had been a facility for the user to save the file as a video clip on a military website and then send a hyperlink in the email (and not the document itself), the email servers would not have been overloaded, and the incident could have been avoided. This underlined the importance of robust information management for cyber operations and the need both to provide more facilities to users and to educate them on how to avoid practices that could disrupt information services. The infamous military sense of humor was both demonstrated and tested that day: additionally, cyber incidents and information management were shown to be unusual but unavoidable bedfellows.

On 9 January 2008, a Royal Navy recruiter's laptop was stolen from the trunk of his car parked in Birmingham, England. Though the device did not contain any classified information, it held the unencrypted personal details of more than 600,000 people. Regrettably, this was not the first embarrassing loss of UK government data. Sir Edmund Burton was commissioned to report on the circumstances surrounding the incident and to recommend appropriate action. Though the incident investigation focused on a lack of adherence to the Data Protection Act, the report criticized the MOD for failing to treat information as a strategic asset and asked probing questions about the governance of information risk.[31]

In January 2009 and despite the repeated issue of warnings to update system software patches, the MOD, and the RAF in particular, was hit by the Conficker virus.[32] The response required the deployment of technicians from the Royal Air Force 90 Signals Unit to the affected units and the expenditure of an estimated 10,000 hours of technical effort.[33] Governance systems and warning information remained up-to-date throughout, and importantly, no mission critical systems were infected. But the incident underlined the potential disruption that could result from even the most simple of infections, the importance of rigorous standards of system management, and the necessity to retain expertise in depth and to surge it to problem areas where needed.

The thread of continuity that runs through these incidents is the personnel involved. A small cadre of engineers, police, policymakers, intelligence analysts, and procurement officers were learning these lessons under the purview of an increasingly interested senior leadership team. These same personnel are now in the Cabinet Office, GOSCC, DCIRT (now called the Joint Cyber Unit (JCU) in Corsham), the Defence Cyber Operations

31   Burton, "Report into the Loss of MOD Personal Data."
32   Willsher, "French Fighter Planes Grounded by Computer Virus."
33   Interview between the author and the Commanding Officer, 90 Signals Unit, RAF 23, March 2012.

Group in MOD HQ, exchange posts with the US Armed Forces, CIO functions, and service provider organizations across the Government.

Who is in Charge Now? Central Government Steps Up

The absence of a "cyber Pearl Harbor" in the UK may well have contributed to the relatively piecemeal development of its early capabilities and structure, but it has also allowed the dominant narrative of cyberspace in the UK to be one of economic growth and social communication (on the upside) and of organized crime (on the downside). The 2009 Cyber Security Strategy[34] established the Office of Cyber Security (OCS)

> *The absence of a "cyber Pearl Harbor" in the UK may well have contributed to the relatively piecemeal development of its early capabilities and structure, but it has also allowed the dominant narrative of cyberspace in the UK to be one of economic growth and social communication ...*

at the heart of the UK Government's power (within the UK Cabinet Office). Its early objectives were to secure the UK's advantage in cyberspace by reducing the risks of usage, exploiting opportunities, and improving knowledge capabilities and decision making. Strategic leadership and maintaining cross-governmental coherence were the tasks of the OCS. Another organization, the Cyber Security Operations Centre (CSOC), was established to conduct national monitoring and assessment, and to provide outreach across government departments to the nine sectors defined as forming the Critical National Infrastructure (CNI), as well as more broadly to industry. A 2011 Chatham House Report on *Cyber Security and the UK's Critical National Infrastructure*[35] criticized the government for the lack of productive coordination that had developed between government and the elements of the CNI since the crafting of the strategy. Most worryingly, the report's research reflected high levels of ignorance and even an unwillingness to engage, among a significant proportion of the CNI organizations canvassed. The OCS continued to take the threat seriously and in November 2011, it issued a renewed Cyber Security Strategy that went beyond the establishment of organizations to the appointing of specific lead agents and to implementing actions across government departments.[36] In a perfect reflection of the awakening that occurred at the MOD, the OCS also recognized the same umbilical connection between cyber security and the strategic value of information. Hence, the OCS re-named itself the Office of Cyber Security and Information Assurance (OCSIA). Importantly, the OCSIA was appointed as the national strategy lead for cyber, and also was handed the responsibility both to understand and to balance the opportunities and threats presented by cyberspace.

---

34 Cabinet Office, Cyber Security Strategy of the United Kingdom.
35 Cornish, et al., Cyber Security and the UK's Critical National Infrastructure.
36 *Ibid.*

The OCSIA has the task of allocating the £650 million of new money that the government has provided for the nation's cyber security to 2015. This and a fast-track route to the agenda of the National Security Council provide it with considerable political power. It has set itself four objectives to achieve by 2015: to tackle cyber crime and for the UK to be one of the most secure places in the world to do business in cyberspace; for the UK to be more resilient to cyber attacks and better able to protect its interests in cyberspace; for the UK to have helped shape an open, stable, and vibrant cyberspace, which the UK public can use safely and that supports open societies; and for the UK to have the cross-cutting knowledge, skills, and capability it needs to underpin all of its cyber security objectives.[37]

The Accelerating Challenges of Future Cyberspace

With organizations, structures, and governance processes established under the apex of central government and with the cadre of UK cyber professionals improving their ability to make sense of and determine a path through the current cyber maze, Britain has established its cyber foundations. However, it has yet to have its pedigree tested by a major disruptive cyber attack. Exercises provide an opportunity to improve cross-domain collaboration. These need to be extended where possible to the CNI and beyond. The planning and execution of pivotal national events, such as the London 2012 Olympics and Paralympics have provided ideal opportunities to develop norms of behavior, set standards, and learn lessons. The knowledge gained can be shared with the CNI, industry, and the public using mechanisms such as the UK's Cyber Security Hub.[38]

Britain has established its cyber foundations. However, it has yet to have its pedigree tested by a major disruptive cyber attack.

Meanwhile, the constitution and uses of the Internet will continue to develop at break-neck speed. Many of the future innovations of cyberspace will be unanticipated. However, it is also possible to see significant challenges looming from the developments that are already apparent, though these are in their infancy. Mobile working is likely to increase significantly over the coming years, demanding ever-more wireless connectivity and raising questions about issues such as wireless encryption, identity management, and attribution. The current trend towards cloud computing represents a potentially significant challenge in the area of data protection and integrity. What has become known in some circles as the "Internet of things" poses a number of security issues, as uses of many items in the physical domain rely on cyberspace for their core functionality. For example, the government must understand and be able to legislate over the difference between a smart meter that controls the gas and electricity in a home and the potential functionality that such a device might

---

37   *Ibid.*
38   *Ibid.*, 28.

afford as a cross-domain weapon. New and more sophisticated computing devices and technologies, such as bio-computing and nanotechnology, might not only revolutionize existing processes and capabilities, but also spawn completely new technologies and capabilities.

One of the themes of this chapter is the broadening of skills and experience needed to craft an appropriate strategy for cyberspace. Polymath expertise may be desirable, but it is clear that the basic mix of ingredients in any cyber policy unit now includes people with engineering, police, legal, finance, and business expertise; members from academia and training experts; military strategists; and even social anthropologists. Bringing this breadth of talent to bear on the issue of cyber strategy is a challenge akin to managing the creative explosion accomplished under the Medicis in Renaissance Florence.

The legal maze surrounding cyberspace only adds to the policy maker's woes. Legislation has tended to lag behind technology's advancements, and the UK government has espoused an ambition to make illegal on-line what is illegal off-line. Nonetheless, the power of any nation to take action against wrongdoers has its primacy in law. Where there is a time lag between the technical opportunity presented by cyberspace technology and the legal rules with which to govern that, undesirable behavior should be expected. Careful prioritization of the legislative effort and the development of a framework that allows technological opportunity to be balanced with the need to ensure that formal justice can be applied to malevolent cyber behaviour, are likely to remain core functions of governance in cyberspace.

Meanwhile, the gaps between cyber capability and legislation, and the continued low costs of entry will mean that the threat of cyber crime is only likely to worsen in the coming years. Thus, the relative importance of organizations such as the Police Electronic Crime Unit (PECU) and the Serious Organised Crime Agency (SOCA) is sure to grow, especially regarding their ability to operate and collaborate across national borders. Progress made on security and governance within sovereign borders is only likely to be as effective as the measures that can be put into place internationally to encompass the whole domain. The UK Foreign and Commonwealth Office (FCO) has also taken steps to provide international leadership in cyber issues. In November 2011, the FCO hosted an international conference in London[39] aimed at promoting and protecting the positive benefits of the Internet for all. As an originator and signatory of the Council of Europe's Budapest Convention on Cybercrime, the FCO has been shaping the agenda for the 2012 Budapest Conference, entitled "With Trust and Security for Freedom and Prosperity." The Convention aims to promote capacity development, security, and the free use of cyberspace

---

39   UK Foreign and Commonwealth Office, "Cyberspace: Cyber Security."

through close and practical cooperation between the private sector and government, as well as through more efficient cooperation between regional organizations.[40]

Conclusion

The UK has developed a strong pedigree in cyberspace. Some of what UK experts know of this new medium, they have learned from the inventions of the Industrial Revolution and the necessities of war. Amid the rapid expansion of the Internet, international e-commerce, and cybered events beyond its borders, Britain is also learning from the experiences of others. But the nation's long history of developing information technologies and applying them innovatively to national problems in financial austerity has shaped the attitudes and approach taken by its policymakers. The UK's curious mix of engineering, police, military, bureaucratic, business, intelligence, legal, and political talent has wrestled against its own "stovepipes of excellence," and has developed a vision of cyberspace that it is both absent of the rhetoric of "cybergeddon" and balanced between the perceived benefits of cyber's use and the vulnerabilities this creates.

> *Our vision is for the UK in 2015 to derive huge economic and social value from a vibrant, resilient and secure cyberspace, where our actions, guided by our core values of liberty, fairness, transparency and the rule of law, enhance prosperity, national security and a strong society.*[41]

As Britain ventures increasingly into the new domain of cyberspace, another history is in the making—one that must be charted, questioned, interpreted, and assimilated. But time is the least forgiving dimension of strategy,[42] and the race to a cyber future is already well underway. The nefarious users of cyberspace appear to have stolen a lead. We broadly understand who is on the same team, but struggle to understand or even to see the competition. The rules by which we play are understood, but they certainly are not followed by all. Maybe genuine proactivity is too much to ask of our governments at this stage, but working together is not. Ultimately, we need to ask what it is to "win" in cyberspace and to ensure that we act so as to remain in the race. Perfection is the enemy of "good enough." While we may know just how far we have come, we still have to discover what "good enough" really means.

---

40   "Budapest Conference on Cyberspace 2012."

41   Cabinet Office, The UK Cyber Security Strategy: Protecting and Promoting, 8.

42   Gray, Fighting Talk: Forty Maxims on War, Peace and Strategy, 70-73.

Part 6: Concluding Assessment

"Pointing the Finger" – National Responsibility For Cyber Conflicts

Jason Healey

What nations are behind these cyber conflicts? It may be too early to apply the judgment of history, but not so early for the judgment of this particular historian.

This chapter applies the ten-point "spectrum of state responsibility" from the Atlantic Council (see Table 3 on page 50) to help determine which nation bears the national responsibility for initiating three of the cyber conflicts in this book: Estonia, Georgia, and Stuxnet.[1]

Attribution of cyber attacks has been the most difficult, yet the most important, aspect of cyber defense. However, remember one of the key lessons of history: the more strategically significant the conflict, the more similar it is to conflicts in the other domains. Attribution, which usually starts at the most technical level before working up to the people and organizations responsible, usually is not a helpful approach for such strategically important cyber conflicts.[2] There will always be analysts who say, "you cannot prove that" or "the source of the attacks might be faked." These small technical truths have for too long obscured the larger truths of which nation was responsible.

So rather than this bottom-up, technical analysis, this chapter will employ a non-technical, top-down analysis, far more likely to aid decision-makers. The key question they need to answer is not "who did this?" but "what nation, if any, is responsible?"

Attack more likely to be non-state-sponsored if:

- Not traced to nation
- Not traced to state organizations
- Attacks not written or coordinated in national language
- Low state control over the Internet
- Low technical sophistication
- Low targeting sophistication
- Broad popular anger at target
- Direct commercial benefit
- No state support of hackers
- Public statements from hackers
- Openness and cooperation with the investigation
- Little correlation with national policy
- Many other nations or groups that benefit
- Not correlated or integrated with physical force

---

1   See Healey, "Beyond Attribution: Seeking National Responsibility for Cyber Attacks."

2   A typical attribution chain of analysis will typically go something like this: find the computers most directly involved -> find the computers controlling those computers, the command and control (C2) -> find the identity controlling the C2 computers -> determine which person is associated with that identity -> find links between that person and an organization -> look for evidence that the organization is under formal state control. Each next step in the chain becomes progressively more difficult.

Analyzing National Responsibility

This spectrum shows a full range of how nations can be responsible for attacks by ignoring, abetting, or conducting cyber attacks. At levels one and two, the nation will stop the attack if they can. At levels three and four, the nation is ignoring or encouraging the attack but not truly "sponsoring" it. At levels five and six, the nation is clearly the sponsor, as the group is getting very active support. Above that, from levels seven to ten, the nation itself is in *de facto* control over the attack. Any non-states involved are direct proxies, under the control of the state, and the attacks are state-sponsored.

Too often, technical tools and methodologies are unable to determine where an attack lies on the spectrum.[3] Fortunately, there's a rich tradition of analysis in the technical disciplines—as well as in the intelligence, law enforcement, and legal professions—which can guide us.

Fourteen key elements (see the text boxes on this page and the next) appear to have been central in analyzing attribution for attacks and attack campaigns over the past decade. Many are particularly helpful to analyze attacks that purport to be from "patriot hackers."

Few of these elements have strong attribution power on their own, or can be relied upon to attribute an attack with little or no other evidence relating to other identifying categories. But taken together, they can provide a compelling case. Analysts can make better, more confident assessments when we have strong evidence, corroborated from multiple sources, across many independent categories.

The strongest elements are attacks technically traced to state organizations, statements from national leadership ("Yes, we did it."), direct support of hackers, and attacks correlated or integrated with physical force. The weakest elements are attacks traced to the nation as a location of origin and assessments of the

Attack more likely to be state-sponsored if:

- Traced to nation
- Traced to state organizations
- Attacks written or coordinated in national language
- State control over the Internet
- Technical sophistication
- Targeting sophistication
- Little popular anger at target
- No direct commercial benefit
- Direct state support of hackers
- Strong correlation with statements from national leadership
- Lack of openness and cooperation
- Strong correlation with national policy
- Lack of any other nation or group that benefits
- Correlated or integrated with physical force

---

3   Verizon has found that of two-thirds of the incidents they investigated in 2009 were untraceable to a specific identity, other than an IP address, even when they were working with law enforcement. See the excellent Verizon Data Breach Report for 2008 (p.18) for this percentage and other hard data, which were incorporated in their updated 2009 report. Amazingly, the highly sophisticated attacks led to 95 percent of the total compromised data records. The 2008 report can be found at: http://www.verizonbusiness.com/resources/security/databreachreport.pdf. The 2009 report is here: http://www.verizonbusiness.com/resources/security/reports/2009_databreach_rp.pdf.

nation's technical sophistication.

Unfortunately, a common analytical mistake in the past has been to "connect the dots" for an attribution—meaning to develop a plausible attribution based on only one or a few (and usually the weakest) elements. These "just-so stories" could be one possible attribution, but often do not look across all the elements, and/or they ignore exculpatory evidence. This can lead to mistaken attribution and lack of credibility for the decision-makers.

Attacks are more likely to be proven state-sponsored if analysts can develop solid evidence across each the following elements:

- **Attack traced to a nation.** Though attacks routinely are routed through or originate from third countries, many large-scale attacks do indeed seem to be tied to their apparent national origin. The attack source information can be faked, but patriotic hackers often do not bother. Still, this element is only a weak link to state sponsorship.

  - Examples: the Hainan Island Incident, 2001;[4] Estonia, 2007;[5] Georgia, 2008.[6] Many attacks against the US, Estonia, and Georgia were traced to China and Russia, which corroborated other analytical elements to help attribute the attack.

- **Attack traced to state organizations**. Only rarely do analysts find this kind of evidence, but it provides a very strong link—especially if the state organization has a law enforcement or security role.

  - Examples: Falun Gong, 1999. After a crackdown in China, a Falun Gong website in Canada was attacked by a denial-of-service, which persisted even when the site was mirrored in the US. Some (but not all) of the attacks traced directly to China's Ministry of Public Security, which was, as now, under pressure to crack down on the group.[7]

- **Attacks written or coordinated in national language**. Though they may be written to misdirect and confound defenders, malicious codes usually at some level contain language clues or other cultural artifacts. Similarly, coordination of larger, denial-of-service attacks often takes place over the Internet and in a particular language which can be applied to attribution.

4　The US was attacked with a wave of defacement attacks after a Chinese interceptor collided with a US EP-3 reconnaissance aircraft, which subsequently crash-landed on Hainan Island, China.

5　Eniken, Kaska, and Vihul. "International Cyber Incidents: Legal Considerations," 23. Ethnic Russians protested in Estonia and conducted cyber attacks due to the removal of a statue of a WWII Russian soldier.

6　Bumgarner and Borg, "Overview by the US-CCU of the Cyber Campaign against Georgia in August of 2008," 2. Russian military forces invaded Georgia, and the physical invasion was accompanied by cyberattacks, after months of international tension.

7　Details on this largely forgotten state-sponsored attack can be found in Chase and Mulvenon, You've Got Dissent, 71-76.

- • Examples: GhostNet, 2009; Georgia, 2008. The GhostNet intruders used a Chinese-coded remote access control tool.[8] The discussions coordinating the Georgian attacks of 2008 took place over social networking sites, and all but one were in the Russian language.[9]

- **State control over the Internet**. Attacks coming from a country which keeps tight reins over the Internet are slightly more likely to be state-sponsored, since those governments have more options to control information traversing their networks.

  - • Examples: the Hainan Island incident, 2001. China has always tried to maintain tight limits on the use of the Internet by its citizens; that control is also believed to exist in Russia and other nations of the Shanghai Cooperation Organization. So, the defacement and denial-of-service attacks coming from China in 2001 were more likely to be state-sponsored than similar attacks from more liberal nations.

- **More technical sophistication than normal**. This analytical element too often misleads, as most analysts mistakenly assume that only nations have the ability to create sophisticated attack tools. Moreover, the reverse is also true: nations may use an unsophisticated tool, if it will still do the job. Indeed, some analysts felt BUCKSHOT YANKEE could not be state-sponsored because Agent.btz was so simple.

  The most incriminating technical sophistication is often not the technical tool itself, but any use of insiders, supply chain intervention, and other patient and resource-intensive methods of access. Therefore, be exceptionally cautious and skeptical when attributing using this analytical element.

  - • Examples: Stuxnet. This malware was so sophisticated that it is far more likely to be from a nation. It exploited multiple high-value, previously unknown vulnerabilities, was designed to be under tight control, and targeted a very rare industrial control system, requiring extensive testing on similar equipment.[10] Such an operation is beyond all but the most committed non-state groups.

- **More targeting sophistication than normal**. Attacks are less likely to be state-sponsored if they are against public webpages of organizations unrelated to a current conflict or without strategic purpose. State-sponsored attacks are more likely to be narrowly aimed toward targets supporting the military or government, critical infrastructure control systems, and related targets. Supporting evidence can come from knowing the extent of targeted organizations or discovering attack vectors crafted to

---

8   Information Warfare Monitor, "Tracking GhostNet: Investigating a Cyber Espionage Network," 46. The report reveals an extensive cyber espionage network with many links to China.

9   Bumgarner and Borg, "Overview by the US-CCU of the Cyber Campaign against Georgia in August of 2008," 3.

10 See the chapter by Chris Morton on Stuxnet in this book.

attack only specific targets of choice.

- Examples: GhostNet, 2009; Stuxnet. The GhostNet intruders used attack tools which were narrowly and individually crafted against the organization supporting the Dalai Lama.[11] This implicates the Chinese government, which accuses him of feeding separatism in Tibet.[12] Stuxnet was even more narrowly targeted to only disrupt a system configuration that existed in one place in the world, Iranian nuclear facilities.

- **There is only narrow government anger** (rather than broad societal fury) at the target. This category is helpful to distinguish state attacks posing as patriotic hacking.

  - Examples: Chinese Embassy Bombed in Belgrade, 1999; China's anger at Falun Gong, 2000; the Hainan Island incident, 2001; GhostNet, 2009. These examples highlight how the depth of public anger can help to determine national responsibility. Both after NATO bombs accidentally destroyed the Beijing embassy in Belgrade[13] and the Hainan Island incident, Chinese cities were rocked with angry demonstrations, fed by genuine public anger. The resulting defacements and denial-of-service attacks were easily attributed to patriotic hackers[14] (though perhaps encouraged or assisted by Chinese leadership).

    On the other hand, the similar attacks against the Falun Gong[15] are not so easily attributed to patriotic hackers, as the populace does not seem to share the Chinese leadership's prominent concern about this religious group. Some Chinese citizens do feel strongly about Tibet and Taiwan being integral parts of China, so GhostNet fits neatly between the first two examples.

- **No direct commercial benefit.** Verizon has found that 55 percent of the incidents they investigated over four years affected the retail or food and beverage sectors[16] with payment records (e.g., credit card data) accounting for 84 percent of the total records compromised.[17] Groups driven by criminal motives are far more likely than most nations to target this kind of data, so these are less likely to be state-sponsored. Incidents targeting military research and development, political decision making, and other less commercial interests are more likely to have a state-sponsored link.

---

11   Information Warfare Monitor, "Investigating GhostNet," 20.
12   Information Warfare Monitor, "Investigating GhostNet," 42-43.
13   See the BBC summary "1999: Chinese Anger at Embassy Bombing."
14   The National Infrastructure Protection Center (housed at the Federal Bureau of Investigation) warned US companies to prepare for a wave of Chinese patriotic hacking. For a summary of the events, see Hulme, "NIPC Warns of Chinese Hacktivism."
15   Several cases from 1999 onward are discussed in Chase and Mulvenon, You've Got Dissent, 1-44.
16   Verizon Business Risk Team. "Verizon Data Breach Report 2008," 8.
17   Verizon Business Risk Team. "Verizon Data Breach Report 2008," 21.

- • Examples: GhostNet, 2009; Koobface, 2010. The GhostNet attackers compromised NATO SHAPE headquarters, embassies, foreign ministries, and the office of the Dalai Lama.[18] As none of these were likely to lead to direct financial gain, it helps add weight to a state-sponsored attribution. By contrast, the gang behind Koobface were only interested in money, which they collected on a grand scale through fraud, though pennies at a time. Such crime might be ignored or encouraged by governments, but it is less likely to be the government itself.[19]

- **Direct support of hackers**. Evidence of direct government support of attacking groups would be particularly damning evidence, though it is rare to find. Governments usually try to keep their involvement covert; officials acting without official cover will be similarly slippery. When determining national responsibility, analysts cannot simply infer such support from related evidence. To qualify for this category, evidence should be suitably straightforward. Circumstantial evidence is not enough.

  - • Examples: Georgia, 2008. Some analysts who investigated the attacks on Georgia assessed that the cyber attackers had been tipped off about impending Russian military operations: "the signal [to attack specific targets] had to have been sent before the news media and general public were aware of what was happening militarily."[20]

- **Attack correlated with public statements**. Public statements are the most easily collected pieces of evidence, as they are found online or in that nation's media. Hackers will often boast of their participation in defacement or denial-of-service attacks, while national leadership can make public statements encouraging or discouraging attacks. When they seem to encourage attacks, these statements make the nation more responsible for the resulting attacks (even if they are actually undertaken by patriotic hackers). Conversely, statements from leadership calling for restraint and promising prosecution of hackers make it less likely.

  - • Examples: Chinese Embassy Bombed in Belgrade, 1999; Estonia, 2007; US Patriot Hacking, 2003. After the NATO bombing of the Chinese Embassy in Belgrade, the Chinese national leadership was enraged at the US, and their comments helped fuel the physical and cyber attacks against the US. Chinese hacker groups like l10n and HUC operated openly, with seemingly little fear of punishment from China.[21] Only after the protests had lasted for several days did the Chinese

---

18   Information Warfare Monitor, "Tracking GhostNet," 42–43.
19   Villeneuve, "Koobface: Inside a Crimeware Network."
20   Bumgarner and Borg, "Overview by the US-CCU of the Cyber Campaign against Georgia in August of 2008," 3.
21   See the chapter by Jon Diamond on patriotic hacking in this book.

leadership start making statements to restrain the attackers.[22]

During the Estonia attacks, the Russian government made no calls for restraint. Indeed, the Russian First Vice Prime Minister called for a boycott against Estonia, and the President criticized the Estonian decision to move the statue, appearing to give a green light for physical and cyber protests.[23]

In comparison, before the invasion of Iraq in 2003, the US warned US hackers that hacking "is illegal and punishable as a felony … The US government does not condone so-called 'patriot hacking' on its behalf." Any attacks against Iraq were less likely to be patriotic hackers and more likely to be US state-sponsored attacks (especially as the media has since reported the US was in fact planning state-conducted attacks). [24]

- **Lack of state cooperation during investigation.** This is a common, but subjective, element of the analysis which can be incriminating or exculpatory.

  - Examples: Estonia, 2007; Operation Physh Phry, 2009. The Russian government was implicated by their rejection of Estonian requests for assistance and information during the attack campaign against their country.[25] A more positive example is the cooperation between the US and the Egyptian governments in the 2009 arrest of a large number of hackers in both countries, a compelling indication that the attacks were not sponsored by either nation.[26]

- **Attack correlated with specific national policy.** National policy can be discerned most easily from publicly released documents, research and development priorities, industrial policy, and national security objectives. Through collection of secret intelligence, analysts may be able to add to their understanding of other nations' intelligence collection priorities and other key details. Identifying a nation's intelligence priorities can be particularly helpful when attributing penetrations which steal sensitive research and development information.

  - Example: GhostNet, 2009; Stuxnet. China has made it clear for decades that Taiwan and Tibet are "inalienable part[s] of the Chinese territory …"[27] Given the number of Tibetan and Taiwanese targets in GhostNet,[28] this makes it slightly

---

22 Rosenthal, "Crisis in the Balkans, China: More Protests in Beijing as Officials Study Bombing Errors."
23 See the chapter by Andreas Schmidt on the Estonian attacks in this book.
24 Shanker and Markoff, "Halted '03 Iraq Plan Illustrates U.S. Fear of Cyberwar Risk."
25 Eniken, Kaska, and Vihul. "International Cyber Incidents: Legal Considerations," 29.
26 FBI Los Angeles, "One Hundred Linked to International Computer Hacking Rin
27 This is a routine Chinese official statement. For the statement about Tibet, see "China's Top Legislature Slams EU Parliament for Tibet Resolution." For a good summary of the event, see "China, Taiwan, Tibet: Fraying at the Edges."
28 Information Warfare Monitor, "Tracking GhostNet," 42-43.

more likely that the GhostNet attacks are state-sponsored. The United States and Israel were clearly aligned strongly against the Iranian nuclear enrichment program, making them more obvious culprits once Stuxnet was discovered.

- ***Cui bono?*** (Latin for "who benefits?") Often, there are only a few nations or groups that benefit from the attack, making them the plausible candidates to be behind the attack.
  - Example: Estonia; Georgia; Stuxnet. In the Estonian and Georgian cyber conflicts, only Russia was involved in a national security crisis with those two nations. So, while some of the attacks in those conflicts traced to the United States, it is still more likely (barring other lines of evidence) that Russia was more responsible than the United States. Likewise, few nations other than the United States and Israel would benefit from destruction of Iranian nuclear enrichment gear.

- **Attack strongly correlated or even integrated with physical force**.
  - Example: Chinese Embassy Bombed in Belgrade, 1999; Georgia, 2008. As noted earlier, the denial-of-service and defacement attacks from China in 1999 corresponded with an outpouring of anger and physical violence against American embassies and consulates across China. Likewise, in Georgia the cyber attacks occurred against the backdrop of a physical invasion of that country by Russia. In both cases, most attacks were easily attributable to China and Russia, respectively, so the task for analysts was to further examine the evidence looking for explicit state support.[29]

Application: Responsibility for Estonia, Georgia, and Stuxnet

This methodology is most useful for disruptive attacks, when there is usually more public information available. It would be extremely difficult, for example, to examine responsibility for BUCKSHOT YANKEE, as there is little information, and what exists has been released or leaked from only one source, the US military itself. Fortunately, there is more than enough information for three other conflicts, Estonia, Georgia, and Stuxnet.

The following table shows an analytical assessment for each of the elements introduced above concerning the cyber attacks on Estonia in 2007.[30]

---

29 For a very structured analysis on Georgia by the US-CCU and Bumgarner, see Bumgarner and Borg, "Overview by the US-CCU of the Cyber Campaign against Georgia in August of 2008."

30 Please note, this analysis is this author's own, and may differ from the assessment of each of the chapter authors. While analysts may rightly argue about these individual and collective judgments, having a transparent analytical framework makes it much easier to assess how the evidence is assessed.

Table 4: Analysis of the Estonian Cyber Attacks of 2007

Analytical Element	Assessment
Attack Traced to Nation	Many traced to Russia[31]
Attack Traced to State Organizations	Some traced to Russian state institutions[32]
Attack Tools or Coordination in National Language	In Russian[33]
State Control over the Internet	Partial but growing[34]
Technically Sophisticated Attack	Not particularly sophisticated[35]
Sophisticated Targeting	Not particularly sophisticated[36]
Popular Anger	Strong[37]
Direct Commercial Benefit	Low[38]
Direct Support of Hackers	No evidence
Correlation with Public Statements	Comments by both government and individuals[39]
Lack of State Cooperation	Russia refused to cooperate[40]
Cui Bono?	High: Russia[41]
Correlation with National Policy	Strong[42]
Correlation with Physical Force	Moderate[43]

---

31   NATO CCDCOE Report, "International Cyber Incidents: Legal Considerations," 23

32   Ibid., 23.

33   Ibid., 15.

34   For example, see Zigfield, "Re-Imposing Totalitarian Information Control in Russia."

35   Ibid., 18-20. The attacks were mostly simple denial-of-service, defacements, and spam, though there were some more sophisticated attacks on DNS servers.

36   Ibid., 20. "Notably, traditional critical infrastructure targets, such as information systems supporting transportation and energy systems, were not targets."

37   In Estonia, there were strong pro-Russian protests, with one person killed and hundreds injured and arrested: "Tallinn Tense after Deadly Riots."

38   Though commercial targets (like banks) were taken offline for some time during the attacks, there was little chance for commercial gain. However, since the purpose of the attack was disruption, not taking data, this should not weigh heavily for our attribution.

39   A "commissar" of Nashi, a pro-Kremlin patriotic youth group, claimed credit for the attacks, in an interview with Charles Clover. Clover, "Kremlin-Backed Group Behind Estonia Cyber Blitz." During the conflict, Russian President Putin seemed to egg on attackers with comments like, "Acts of mockery of the heroes and victims of war give rise to anger and indignation." "Putin in Veiled Attack on Estonia."

40   NATO CCDDCOE Report, "International Cyber Incidents: Legal Considerations," 29.

41   There were no other nations or groups that obviously benefited from attacking Estonia or were in an existing crisis.

42   For example, the Russian Parliament threatened to impose sanctions. Sheeter, "Russia Slams Estonia Statue Move."

43   As noted above, the cyber attacks coincided with violent protests by ethnic Russians; however, there was no physical invasion or other use of overt force by Russia.

This analysis demonstrates that Russia's responsibility is somewhere in the middle of the spectrum of state responsibility. With no evidence of direction or coordination, the attacks are not obviously state-sponsored. But clearly, the Russian government is not without responsibility. Here are a few possible assignments from the spectrum of state responsibility:

3.   State-ignored. The national government knows about the third-party attack but is unwilling to take any official action.

4.   State-encouraged. Third parties control and conduct the attack, but the national government encourages them as a matter of policy.

5.   State-shaped. Third parties control and conduct the attack, but the state provides some support.

6.   State-coordinated. The government coordinates third-party attackers, such as by "suggesting" operational details.

There is no available evidence supporting any nations providing "active assistance" for the attack. However, Russia does not escape all responsibility: there were clear statements from the highest levels of the Russian government, a lack of cooperation with the investigation, a clear correlation with Russian official policy, and complete failure of the government to rein in the attacks. There is an accordingly **high confidence** that the attacks on Estonia **were** *at least encouraged* by the Russian government. The attacks were possibly also shaped by Russia, but other than links to the Nashi youth group, there simply is not enough solid evidence.

For the 2008 attacks against Georgia, the analysis looks similar, though more damning for Russia.

Table 5: Analysis of the Georgian Cyber Attacks of 2007

Analytical Element	Assessment
Attack Traced to Nation	Many traced to Russia (and in particular to Russian organized crime)[44]
Attack Traced to State Organizations	No strong evidence[45]
Attack Tools or Coordination in National Language	In Russian[46]
State Control over the Internet	Partial but growing[47]
Technically Sophisticated Attack	Yes[48]
Sophisticated Targeting	No[49]
Popular Anger	Broad anger within Russia
Direct Commercial Benefit	Low (but inconclusive)[50]
Direct Support of Hackers	None[51]
Correlation with Public Statements	Strong[52]
Lack of State Cooperation	Russia did not cooperate
Cui Bono?	High: Russia[53]
Correlation with National Policy	Very strong[54]
Correlation with Physical Force	Very strong[55]

44   Bumgarner and Borg, "Overview by the US-CCU of the Cyber Campaign against Georgia in August of 2008," 3.
45   *Ibid.*, 2: "… little or no direct involvement on the part of the Russian government or military."
46   *Ibid.*, 3.
47   Zigfield, "Re-Imposing Totalitarian Information Control in Russia."
48   Bumgarner and Borg, "Overview by the US-CCU of the Cyber Campaign against Georgia in August of 2008," 4: "The types of cyber attacks used against Georgia were … carried out in a very sophisticated manner."
49   *Ibid.*, 4: "The types of cyber attacks … were limited to denials-of-service and website defacements…"
50   As with Estonia, though commercial targets were attacked, there was little chance for commercial gain, though this should not weigh heavily in our attribution.
51   After researching Russian hacker sites, Project Grey Goose was unable to find any evidence for Russian state support or assistance. Greylogic. "Project Grey Goose Phase I Report.
52   The Russian government made repeated public statements (as part of their invasion). Hackers also left a public chain of comments where they exchanged target lists.
53   There were no other nations or groups that obviously benefited from attacking Georgia or were in an existing crisis.
54   The Russian government made their policy clear when they invaded and did not try to restrain any cyber attacks.
55   *Ibid.*, 3. Most importantly, there was a direct military invention, but also the "…organizers of the cyber attacks had advance notice of Russian military intentions."

For this analysis of Georgia, here are a few analytical elements from the middle of the spectrum of state responsibility:

4.   State-encouraged. Third parties control and conduct the attack, but the national government encourages them as a matter of policy.

5.   State-shaped. Third parties control and conduct the attack, but the state provides some support.

6.   State-coordinated. The government coordinates third-party attackers, such as by "suggesting" operational details.

7.   State-ordered. The state directs third-party proxies to conduct the attack on its behalf.

There is weighty evidence in several categories that implies the Russian state provided active assistance. Thus, the attack was clearly not just encouraged but directly supported. One analyst, through direct access to the relevant log files and interviews, concluded that the cyber attackers were tipped off before the military operation, and that "the primary objective of the cyber campaign was to support the Russian invasion..."[56] This implies enough connection with the attackers for the government to suggest targets and timing.

However, there seems to be little evidence that the groups involved were under *direct* orders regarding what to attack and when, so the attacks were likely not state-ordered. Accordingly, the evidence suggests with ***moderate confidence* that the attacks on Georgia were *state-shaped or state-coordinated* by the Russian government.** There is not enough reliable evidence at this point to say the attacks were fully state-ordered.

---

56   Bumgarner and Borg, "Overview by the US-CCU of the Cyber Campaign against Georgia in August of 2008," 3 and 6.

Here is the comparable analysis for Stuxnet:

Table 6: Analysis of the Stuxnet Cyber Attacks	
Analytical Element	**Assessment**
Attack Traced to Nation	Not applicable[56]
Attack Traced to State Organizations	Not applicable [57]
Attack Tools or Coordination in National Language	Partial[58]
State Control over the Internet	Not applicable[60]
Technically Sophisticated Attack	Highly[61]
Sophisticated Targeting	Highly[62]
Popular Anger	Low[63]
Direct Commercial Benefit	Low[64]
Direct Support of Hackers	Not applicable[65]
Correlation with Public Statements	Very High: US and Israel[66]
Lack of State Cooperation	Possible: US[67]
Cui Bono?	High: US, Israel[68]
Correlation with National Policy	High: US, Israel[69]
Correlation with Physical Force	Moderate: US, Israel[70]

---

57 Because Stuxnet was inserted by removable media, there was no clear trace, as there is for Internet-based disruptive attacks.

58 Again, there was no traceable network path.

59 More important than language, there were cultural artifacts perhaps pointing to Israel. However, sometimes such artifacts can be misleading and support confirmation bias. For example, a string of numbers can be assigned some cultural significance if, for example, they correspond to a date, which happens to support the analyst's existing theory.

60 There were no external networks involved, so network control is not applicable.

61 Multiple sources (see the chapter on Stuxnet in this book) describe in great detail the sophistication of Stuxnet, which used several zero-day vulnerabilities with code to target Siemens industrial control systems and required extensive testing.

62 As above, see the chapter on Stuxnet for examples of how tightly targeted Stuxnet had to be to only disrupt Iranian nuclear enrichment and nothing else.

63 Some citizens may be upset at Iran's enrichment plans, but none possessed the needed capability.

64 Theoretically, a competitor of Siemens or a consultant, seeking hefty fees to fix the Iranian's malfunctioning centrifuges, might have a commercial motive, but this is a thin theory, given the tool's capability.

65 Stuxnet was too sophisticated to be a hacker attack, so any nation's support of hackers is not applicable.

66 The disruption of the Iranian program was a critical foreign policy goal of these two countries—and few others. In addition, detailed press reports described in great detail the US and Israeli involvement. These were stories which demonstrated clear access to senior officials and were denied by both countries.

67 Anecdotally, the author has heard that the US government had asked US cybersecurity companies to ignore Stuxnet as much as they could.

68 The disruption of the Iranian program was a critical foreign policy goal of these two countries—and few others. Few other nations would benefit anywhere near as much.

69 It was such a priority that both nations had publicly considered military options, such as military strikes to delay the program, as Stuxnet did.

70 There was no ongoing physical crisis, but as noted above, both Israel and the United States had discussed plans for military strikes to delay the Iranian program.

The extremely high sophistication of the tool, and the precision and select targeting help to rule out the theory that rogue state actors or non-state adversaries were responsible, even with government help. The attack seems with high confidence to be state-executed: a state conducts the attack using cyber forces under their direct control.

Using a similar analytical process as used for the Estonian and Georgian assaults, and a preponderance of evidence, it is difficult to come to any other conclusion than that there is *medium confidence* **that Stuxnet was a *state-executed attack* by the United States and/or Israel**. And indeed, press reports, not refuted by either government, implicate both. Some analysts pointed the finger at other nations, including Russia and China, but these seem to be "just-so stories," grasping at a few straws of evidence but ignoring the weight of other evidence.

This assessment is not "high" confidence. Senior US officials in off-the-record discussions with the author have made comments hinting that analysts "should not believe everything they believe in the media," suggesting that the evidence implicating the United States is not as credible as it may seem. If so, then US officials should be clear in order to clear the historical record.

There is only twenty-five years of the history of cyber conflict, yet this is enough to identify clear lessons and emerging norms. In time, the interpretations presented here will be either reinforced or possibly refuted. But the world needs more historians, more researchers, and analysts of all types to join in and examine this history, to make their own discoveries and identify their own lessons.

Assessment Summary

Estonia:

* High confidence that the attacks on Estonia were at least encouraged by the Russian government

Georgia:

* High confidence that the attacks on Georgia were at least ignored by the Russian government

* Moderate confidence they were state-shaped or state-coordinated by the Russian government

Stuxnet:

* Medium confidence that Stuxnet was a state-executed attack by the United States and/or Israel

JJH

Appendices

Appendix 1: Glossary

- **Advanced Persistent Threat**: A group, often but not always tied to a government, with the intent and capacity, backed by very significant resources, to effectively and consistently target a specific entity. The APT knows what it wants and has resources to keep going after it from multiple directions, compared to typical hacker groups which only target poorly defended targets. The APT was first well described publicly in the 1991 report, Computers at Risk, by the US National Academies of Science as the "high-grade threat."

- **Advanced Research Projects Agency Network** (ARPANet): An operational packet switching network that was created in 1969 with funding from US military's Advanced Research Project Agency. It was the precursor to the modern Internet.

- **Botnet**: A collection of computers which have been taken over by a malicious attacker (after an *intrusion*) who controls their collective actions with another set of computers, called "botnet herders" or "command and control servers. Botnets can be rented out to raise money for the attacker or can be used to send spam, engage in fraud, or conduct *DDoS attacks*.

- **Comprehensive National Cyber Initiative** (CNCI): The still-classified CNCI was established by National Security Presidential Directive 54/Homeland Security Presidential Directive 23 by President Bush in January 2008 to focus efforts on 12 initiatives, largely focused on defending US government networks.

- **Computer Emergency Response Team** (CERT): A team of people to respond to computer or network outages on behalf of their organization or country. Their exact duties and structure vary between organizations, but typically a CERT will look for threats and patch *vulnerabilities*, develop plans to deal with outages or malicious attacks, and coordinate the response. The first CERT was created in November 1988 at Carnegie Mellon University at the behest of DARPA as a result of the *Morris Worm*.

- **Computer Network Attack** (CNA): A term from the US Department of Defense for an attack done through a network of computers that either disrupts, denies, degrades, or destroys another computer's information or the computers or networks themselves. The term does not include espionage or theft of information (which would be CNE) so long as no information or systems are destroyed.

- **Computer Network Defense** (CND): A term from the US Department of Defense for actions taken to resist attempts to steal, copy, infiltrate, read, disrupt, deny, degrade, or destroy information on computers or the computers or networks themselves.

- **Computer Network Exploitation** (CNE): A term from the US Department of Defense for a variety of actions for gathering intelligence from the adversary's computers and networks. This can be crime, outright espionage, or reconnaissance for a future attack but does not include disrupting or destroying the information or systems, which would be *CNA*.

- **Computer Network Operations** (CNO): A term from the US Department of Defense to encompass all cyber operations: *CNA*, *CND*, and *CNE*.

- **Critical Infrastructure Assurance Office** (CIAO): CIAO was created by PDD-63 in 1998 within the Department of Commerce to analyze the security for physical and cyber critical infrastructure. Its functions were folded into the *Department of Homeland Security*.

- **Critical Infrastructure Protection** (CIP): Actions taken to protect a nation's critical infrastructure. *PDD-63* was the first American CIP policy, issued in 1998, while Europe has a similar version in the European Programme for Critical Infrastructure Protection (EPCIP).

- **Cyber**: Originally an adjective (as in "cyberspace" or "cyber attack"), now cyber is becoming its own standalone noun to indicate anything having to do with cyberspace or, more specifically, *cybersecurity*.

- **Cyber attack**: Different communities have different definitions, but generally using a computer or network to maliciously affect other computers and networks. Law enforcement officials see this as a crime; military officers consider it a potential act of war; and technologists see it as a misuse of common resource. Attacks require a *vulnerability* and *exploit*, combined with access to the target.

- **Cyber conflict**: When nations and non-state groups use offensive or defensive cyber capabilities to attack, defend, and spy on each other, typically for political or other national security purposes. Generally does not include cyber crime, but inclusive of cyber war.

- **Cyber Command**: See *US Cyber Command*

- **Cyber crime**: A criminal act that is mediated through cyberspace, in which computers or networks play an instrumental role, such as DDoS, intrusions or worms.

- **Cyberspace**: Interconnected information technology. There are more complex definitions, but generally if it stores or processes any information and is connected to a network, it can be considered part of cyberspace. Specific definitions of cyberspace are often outdated as soon as they are written, whereas descriptions tend to be longer lasting and more useful. Originally described by William Gibson, a science fiction author, in 1982 as a "consensual hallucination."

- **Cybersecurity**: Also used interchangeably as two words: cyber security. Generally means all actions to protect computers and networks from attacks on their confidentiality, integrity and availability. However, as the "cyber" field expands, cybersecurity is most associated with the most technical aspects of defense. Someone that knows cybersecurity, for example, may not be an expert in cyber conflict and vice versa.

- **Cyber war**: Actions by a nation-state to damage or disrupt another nation's computers or networks, which are heavily damaging and destructive—similar to the effects achieved with traditional military force—and so are considered to be an armed attack. A nation in a cyber war is, in fact, in an actual war meaning it can use lethal force in response. There has not, as of 2012, been a cyber war though there have been many cyber conflicts.

- **Defense Industrial Base**: The system of manufacturing, logistics, research and development, infrastructure, and services that support military acquisition and operations. Major weapons manufacturers (such as Lockheed Martin or BAE) are the most typical kind of DIB company, but it also encompasses electricity providers, small and medium size enterprises, and other non-traditional companies.

- **Defense Science Board (DSB)**: A committee of civilian experts founded in 1956 that advises the DoD on scientific and technical matters. The DSB has issued several important reports on information warfare and cyber security.

- **Directorate for National Protection and Programs** (NPPD): The element that oversees most cyber efforts of the United States at the *Department of Homeland Security*, overseeing the *Office of Cybersecurity and Communications* (CS&C).

- **Distributed Denial of Service Attack** (DDoS): A cyber attack in which multiple systems flood a targeted system, disrupting it to make it unusable. DDoS attacks can work by flooding a target's network connection (so it is unreachable) or overwhelming the target computer's processor (so it is reachable but unable to respond). In 2012, most DDoS attacks are conducted using botnets.

- **Exploit**: Malware that takes advantage of a *vulnerability* to abet a cyber attack. Until someone writes an exploit, a vulnerability is useless. For example, imagine a computer will break if someone presses the "a" key one hundred times, followed by the number

"1" and then "a" another thousand times. This obscure vulnerability is of no use until someone can figure out how to exploit it.

- **Hacktivists**: Hacker-activists who conduct their activities on behalf of an ideology. This started with groups like EDT or Cult of the Dead Cow in the 1990s but is most associated today with Anonymous.

- **Homeland Security Presidential Directive 7** (HSPD-7): Established on 17 December 2003 by President Bush, HSPD-7 was the United States' policy for identifying and prioritizing protection for critical infrastructure, with different sectors covered by different government departments. Updated *PDD-63*.

- **Information Operations**: The US military doctrine, now largely defunct, which sought to engage adversaries in operations in the information domain. It became exceptionally popular after the 1991 Persian Gulf War and encompassed cyber operations and also included influence operations (such as public affairs and psychological operations), information technology, and other uses of information. It still has some adherents in 2012 and the US military still occasionally uses it or similar terms, such as the Navy's Information Dominance Corps, created in 2009. Descended from the functionally similar term of *information warfare*.

- **Information Operations Technology Center** (IOTC): Activated in 1997 at the *National Security Agency*, this Center brought together many cyber elements of the military and Intelligence Community to provide advice and develop techniques.

- **Information Sharing and Analysis Center** (ISAC): Non-profit groups called for in PDD-63 to assist critical infrastructure sectors to share information and analysis on cyber and (sometimes) physical threats.

- **Information Warfare**: See *information operations*.

- **Intrusion**: A cyber attack which is a deliberate and illegal entry into a computer system, such as to exfiltrate (steal) information or conduct a later disruptive attack. Intrusions can turn computers into botnets which can be used for another kind of cyber attack, DDoS.

- **Joint Functional Component Command – Network Warfare** (JFCC-NW): was a subordinate component of United States Strategic Command (USSTRATCOM) that operated out of Fort Meade in 2005-2010 and focused on offensive cyber plans and operations. It was merged into *USCYBERCOM* in October 2010.

- **Joint Task Force for Computer Network Defense** (JTF-CND): The first joint cyber command, this unit was stood up in December 1998 to be in command when the US Department of Defense was under attacks that were particularly widespread or intense. Originally it reported directly to the Secretary of Defense, but later was assigned to *US Space Command*. It later assumed responsibility for the DoD's computer network attack mission to became the *JTF-CNO* in the fall of 2000.

- **Joint Task Force for Computer Network Operations** (JTF-CNO): After being assigned the offense, as well as defense mission, the *JTF-CND* developed into the JTF-CNO in the fall of 2000. It later was also assigned responsibility for managing DoD networks and further developed into the *JTF-GNO*.

- **Joint Task Force-Global Network Operations** (JTF-GNO): After being assigned the network management mission (in addition to defense and offense) the *JTF-CNO* developed into JTF-GNO, assigned to US Strategic Command. Along with *JFCC-NW*, it was incorporated into *USCYBERCOM* in late 2010.

- **Joint Worldwide Intelligence Communications System** (JWICS): The most highly classified US government large network. Run by the Intelligence Community, it is used to carry very sensitive intelligence and military communications. Compared to *NIPRNET* and *SIPRNET*, JWICS carries the most classified information and is best protected.

- **Malware**: Malicious software, such as (*viruses, worms*, or an *exploit*) used for *cyber attacks*.

- **Military Network** (MILNET): A part of the *ARPANet* that was used for unclassified DoD traffic. It later split off and became the Defense Data Network and *NIPRNET*.

- **National Computer Security Center** (NCSC): Established in 1981 as a part of the *NSA*, this group was responsible for testing computer equipment and evaluating it for use in high security and confidential applications.

- **National Cybersecurity and Communications Integration Center** (NCCIC): The operational arm of the DHS cyber mission, NCCIC works with federal, state, and local authorities along with the private sector to respond to cyber incidents and distribute information on new *vulnerabilities*.

- **National Cyber Security Division** (NCSD): This is a division of the *Office of Cyber Security & Communications* within the *Department of Homeland Security's Directorate for National Protection and Programs*. It was in 2003 to have the national lead to cooperate with the private sector, the government, military, and intelligence stakeholders to conduct risk assessment and lessen vulnerabilities and threats to IT assets and activities affecting the state and private-sector cyber critical infrastructure.

- **National Infrastructure Protection Center** (NIPC): Created, with the *CIAO*, from *PDD-63* in 1998, the NIPC was housed in the FBI and worked with the private sector to safeguard infrastructure networks and systems from cyber and physical attack. Like CIAO, it was folded into the newly created DHS.

- **National Security Agency** (NSA): The US intelligence agency with the primary role to collect and analyze foreign information and foreign signals intelligence while improving the nation's information security and encryption. In the 1990s, this mission overlapped significantly with new networks, attracting many signals intelligence professionals into *information warfare* and *cyber* operations. NSA is widely regarded to be the best cyber organization in the world, leading *US Cyber Command* to be co-located with it.

- **Nonsecure Internet Protocol Router Network** (NIPRNET): Successor to the original *MILNET*, this is private US government network carries unclassified information. Compare to *JWICS* and *SIPRNET*, which both carry classified information and are accordingly more highly secured.

- **Office of Cyber Security & Communications**: A sub-component of the *DHS' Directorate for National Protection and Programs*, that has the mission of assuring the security, has the mission of assuring the security, resiliency, and reliability of the nation's cyber and communications infrastructure.

- **Patching**: The process of closing *vulnerabilities* in an organization's computers and networks, often overseen by the *CERT*.

- **President's Commission on Critical Infrastructure Protection** (PCCIP): A commission established as an interagency Presidential advisory commission by Executive Order 13010 dated 15 July 1996. It created a game-plan for protecting critical infrastructure which was largely implemented in *PDD-63*.

- **Presidential Decision Directive 63** (PDD-63): The first major policy on *Critical Infrastructure Protection*, enacted in the United States by President Clinton on 22 May 1998. It established *ISACs* and the *CIAO* and *NIPC*.

- **Secret Internet Protocol Router Network** (SIPRNET): A critical US military network to carry Secret-level communications critical to military plans and operations. Compare to *NIPRNET* and *JWICS*.

- **US Cyber Command** (USCYBERCOM): A sub-unified command, subordinate to *USSTRATCOM*. It was set up in 2009 to run the military's networks and defend the nation from cyber attacks. It assumed the responsibilities of both the *JTF-GNO* and the *JFCC-NW*. It is co-located with *NSA* and, as of 2012, the same general leads both organizations.

- **US Space Command** (USSPACECOM): This Unified Combatant Command was created in 1985 to institutionalize how the US military accessed and used outer space. Though it was considered to have played a major role in the 1991 Persian Gulf War, the command was later merged into *USSTRATCOM*. USSPACECOM was the DoD lead for cyber issues from 2000 until the merger.

- **US Strategic Command** (USSTRATCOM): USSTRATCOM is one of nine Unified Combatant Commands and was formed from the earlier Strategic Air Command, SAC, to bring together missions for global strike and supporting missions. This includes control over America's nuclear weapon inventory, along with space operations and cyber offense and defense. *USCYBERCOM* is one of its primary operational units.

- **Virus**: A malicious computer program that replicates itself from one computer to another. Unlike a *worm*, a virus needs the user to take action, such as clicking on a link or opening a document. Also used as a generic term for any *malware*.

- **Vulnerability**: A flow in software that allows a malicious attacker to bypass controls to take advantage of the computer, usually by gaining control over it or disrupting its operation. To make use of a known vulnerability, an attacker must first have an *exploit* for it and have access to the target.

- **Worm**: *Malware* which, like a virus, replicates itself from one computer to another, though a worm does not requires user intervention as it is able to spread automatically due to vulnerabilities in the software of its hosts. The Morris Worm of 1988 caught the Internet community by surprise.

- **Zero-Day** (or 0day): A *vulnerability* that is unknown to cyber defenders, who only learn of it after it is used against them. Once the cyber defense community learns of a new vulnerability, they start the clock, so a 1-day vulnerability was discovered yesterday and a 30-day last month. Best practice is to *patch* vulnerabilities with days of being discovered, so a 0day can command high prices by attackers as it guarantees access to a target.

Appendix 2: Works Cited

Part 1: A Brief History of US Cyber Conflict

Preface and Introduction

Army Cyber Command. "Army Cyber Command Update." *AFCEA Belvoir Chapter*. March 8, 2012. Accessed March 19, 2013. http://www.afceabelvoir.org/images/uploaded/AFCEABelvoir_ARCYBERCommandBrief_COLSchilling_23APR12.pdf.

Shelton, William. Commander Air Force Space Command. Remarks at Air Force Association, CyberFutures Conference, National Harbor, MD, March 22, 2012. Accessed March 19, 2013. Audio available at http://www.afa.org/events/CyberFutures/2012/postCyber/default.asp (quote around 14:47).

Valeriano, Brandon and Ryan Maness. "The Fog of Cyberwar." Foreign Affairs. November 21, 2012. Accessed January 19, 2013. http://www.foreignaffairs.com/articles/138443/brandon-valeriano-and-ryan-maness/the-fog-of-cyberwar.

The Beginning: Realization (to 1998)

"Air Force Information Warfare Center." Air Intelligence Agency Almanac. August 1997. Accessed March 19, 2013. http://www.fas.org/irp/agency/aia/cyberspokesman/97aug/afiwc.htm.

"Appendix E." In Computers at Risk: Safe Computing in the Information Age, 283-285. Washington, DC: The National Academies Press, 1991. Accessed March 27, 2013. http://www.nap.edu/openbook.php?record_id=1581&page=283.

Arkin, William M. "A Mouse That Roars?" *Washington Post*, June 7, 1999. Accessed May 25, 2012. http://www.washingtonpost.com/wp-srv/national/dotmil/arkin060799.htm.

Baker, Wade, et al. "2011 Data Breach Investigations Report." Verizon. 2011. Accessed March 19, 2013. http://www.verizonbusiness.com/resources/reports/rp_data-breach-investigations-report-2011_en_xg.pdf.

"Bletchley's code-cracking Colossus." BBC.co.uk. February 2, 2010. Accessed March 19, 2013. http://news.bbc.co.uk/2/hi/technology/8492762.stmhttp://news.bbc.co.uk/2/hi/technology/8492762.stm.

Brock, Jack L. "Computer Security: Hackers Penetrate DOD." US Government Accountability Office. 1991. Accessed April 20, 2012. http://www.gao.gov/assets/110/104234.pdf.

CERT Coordination Center. "About Us." Carnegie Mellon University. Accessed April 19, 2012. http://www.cert.org/meet_cert/.

Cult of the Dead Cow. "Hactivismo." Cultdeadcow.com. July 17, 2000. Accessed November 1, 2012. http://w3.cultdeadcow.com/cms/2000/07/hacktivismo.html. http://w3.cultdeadcow.com/cms/2000/07/hacktivismo.html.

Department of the Air Force, "609 IWS: A Brief History, Oct 1995—Jun 1999." Securitycritics.org. Accessed April 24, 2013. http://securitycritics.org/wp-content/uploads/2006/03/hist-609.pdf

Eichen, Mark W. and Jon A. Rochlis. "An Analysis of the Internet Worm of November 1988." Massachusetts: MIT, February 9, 1989. Accessed March 27, 2013. https://www.utd.edu/~edsha/security/internet-worm-MIT.pdf.

Eichin, Mark W. and Jon A. Rochlis. "With Microscope and Tweezers: An Analysis of the Internet Virus of November 1988." Massachusetts Institute of Technology. 1988. Accessed April 19, 2012. http://www.mit.edu/~eichin/virus/main.html.

Field, Tom. "The Influencers: Steve Katz." Bankofsecurity.com. February 4, 2010. Accessed November 1, 2012. http://www.bankinfosecurity.com/influencers-steve-katz-a-2164.

Fogleman, Ronald, and Sheila Widnall. "Cornerstones of Information Warfare." C4i.org. 1997. Accessed May 25, 2012. http://www.c4i.org/cornerstones.html.

Fredericks, Brian. "Information Warfare: The Organizational Dimension." US Army War College Paper. February 7, 1996. Accessed March 27, 2013. http://www.dtic.mil/cgi-bin/GetTRDoc?AD=ADA309782.

Greely, A.W. "The Military Telegraph." In The Photographic History of the Civil War: Soldier Life, Secret Service, edited by Francis Trevelyan Miller and Robert Sampson Lanier, 342-368. Springfield: Patriot Publishing Co., 1911.

Joint Chiefs of Staff. "Joint Vision 2010." Dtic.mil. 1996. Accessed April 18, 2012. http://

www.dtic.mil/jv2010/jv2010.pdf.

"L0pht on Hackers." (Transcript.) PBS.org. May 8, 1998. Accessed April 19, 2012. http://www.pbs.org/newshour/bb/cyberspace/jan-june98/l0pht_hackers.html.

Madsen, Wayne. "Intelligence Agency Threats to Computer Security." International Journal of Intelligence and Counter-Intelligence 6 (Winter 1993): 412-488.

Markoff, John. "Computer Intruder Is Put on Probation and Fined $10,000." New York Times, May 5, 1990. Accessed April 19, 2012. http://www.nytimes.com/1990/05/05/us/computer-intruder-is-put-on-probation-and-fined-10000.html.

Markoff, John. "Dutch Computer Rogues Infiltrate American Systems with Impunity." New York Times, April 21, 1991. Accessed March 27, 2013. http://www.nytimes.com/1991/04/21/us/dutch-computer-rogues-infiltrate-american-systems-with-impunity.html.

"Notable Hacks." PBS.org. 2001. Accessed November 1, 2012. http://www.pbs.org/wgbh/pages/frontline/shows/hackers/whoare/notable.html.

"Official DEFCON FAQ v0.95." DEFCON.org. Accessed April 19, 2012. https://www.defcon.org/html/links/dc-faq/dc-faq.html.

President's Commission on Critical Infrastructure Protection, The. "Critical Foundations: Thinking Differently." IWar.org. 1997. Accessed March 27, 2013. http://www.iwar.org.uk/cip/resources/pccip/summary.pdf.

Reed, Thomas. At the Abyss: An Insider's History of the Cold War. New York: Presidio Press, 1995.

Rhoads, Walter "Dusty." "Lessons from Our Cyber Past, The First Military Cyber Units." (Also known as "First Cyber Commanders.") Audio transcript of the Atlantic Council's Cyber Statecraft Initiative Workshop, in Washington, D.C., March 5, 2012. Accessed March 28, 2013. http://www.acus.org/event/lessons-our-cyber-past-first-military-cyber-units.

Rhodes, Keith A. "Information Security: Code Red, Code Red II, and SirCam Attacks Highlight Need for Proactive Measures." US Government Accountability Office. August 2001. Accessed April 19, 2012. http://www.gao.gov/new.items/d011073t.pdf.

Schell, Roger. "Computer Security, the Achilles' Heel of the Electronic Air Force?" Air

University Review (January–February 1979). Accessed April 20, 2012. http://www. airpower.maxwell.af.mil/airchronicles/aureview/1979/jan-feb/schell.html.

Schwartau, Winn. *Information Warfare: Chaos on the Electronic Superhighway*. New York: Thunder's Mouth Press, 1994.

Schwiezer, Peter. *Friendly Spies: How America's Allies are Using Economic Espionage to Steal Our Secrets*. New York: Atlantic Monthly Press, 1993.

Spafford, Eugene H. "The Internet Worm Program: An Analysis." Purdue University, December 8, 1988. Accessed April 19, 2012. http://spaf.cerias.purdue.edu/tech-reps/823.pdf.

Sterling, Bruce. *Hacker Crackdown: Law and Disorder on the Electronic Frontier*. New York: Bantam Books, 1994.

Stoll, Clifford. *Cuckoo's Egg*. New York: Pocket Books, 1989.

Stoll, Clifford. "Stalking the Wily Hacker." Communications of the ACM 31, 5 (May 1988): 484–497.

System Security Study Committee, Commission on Physical Sciences, Mathematics, and Applications National Research Council. "Why the Security Market Has Not Worked Well." In Computers at Risk: Safe Computing in the Information Age, 143–178. Washington, DC: The National Academies Press, 1991.

"The Internet." In The Role of NSF's Support of Engineering in Enabling Technological Innovation, edited by SRI International, 1997. Accessed April 12, 2012. http://www. nsf.gov/pubs/1997/nsf9756/nsf9756.htm?org=ENG.

Thomas, Julie L. C. "The Ethics of Hactivism." Hacker Culture. January 12, 2001. Accessed April 18, 2012. http://www.dvara.net/HK/Ethics-Hacktivism.asp.http:// www.dvara.net/HK/Ethics-Hacktivism.asp.

Toffler, Alvin and Heidi Adelaide Toffler. *War and Anti-War: Making Sense of Today's Global Chaos*. New York: Warner Books, 1993.

Tuchman, Barbara. *The Zimmermann Telegram*. New York: Ballantine Books, 1956.

Ungoed-Thomas, Jonathan. "How Datastream Cowboy Took U.S. to the Brink of War." *The Toronto Star*, April 12, 1998. Accessed April 18, 2012. http://www.mail-archive. com/pen-l@galaxy.csuchico.edu/msg25434.html.

US General Accounting Office. "Computer Security: Virus Highlights Need for

Improved Internet Management." GAO/IMTEC-89-57. Washington, DC. June 1989. Accessed October 9, 2012. http://www.gao.gov/assets/150/147892.pdf.

US Senate Permanent Committee on Investigations. "Appendix B. The Case Study: Rome Laboratory, Griffiss Air Force Base, NY Intrusion." In Security in Cyberspace Staff Statement U.S. Senate Permanent Subcommittee on Investigations (Minority Staff). Hearings on June 5, 1996. Accessed April 20, 2012. http://www.fas.org/irp/congress/1996_hr/s960605b.htm.

"U.S. vs. Robert Tappan Morris." 928 F.2d 504 (1991). No. 774, Docket 90-1336. United States Court of Appeals, Second Circuit. Accessed April 19, 2012. http://scholar.google.com/scholar_case?case=551386241451639668.

Ware, Willis H. Security Controls for Computer Systems: Report of Defense Science Board Task Force on Computer Security (1979). Defense Science Board. October 10, 1979. Accessed April 19, 2012. http://www.rand.org/pubs/reports/R609-1/index2.html.

Warner, Michael. "Cybersecurity—A Prehistory." Intelligence and National Security Vol. 27, Issue 5 (2012): 781-799. Accessed March 27, 2013. http://www.tandfonline.com/doi/pdf/10.1080/02684527.2012.708530.

"Wikileaks Infowar not the first online protest action." Medialternatives (blog). December 15, 2012. Accessed April 19, 2012. http://medialternatives.blogetery.com/2010/12/15/intervasion-supports-anonymous/.

Yanalitis, Mark. "Cuckoo's Egg Prequel or Perfect Storm." AFCEA.org. 2012. Accessed March 27, 2013. http://www.afcea.org/committees/cyber/documents/ImpactofBNDProjectRAHABandCCContheFutureofComputer-NetworkMediatedEspionage-CuckoosEggPreque.pdf.

Maturing Organizations and Concepts: Take-Off (1998-2003)

"About the FS-ISAC." FS-ISAC. Accessed October 19, 2012. http://www.fsisac.com/about/.

Adams, James. "Virtual Defense." Foreign Affairs. May/June 2001. Accessed March 27, 2013. http://www.foreignaffairs.com/articles/57037/james-adams/virtual-defense.

Anderson, Kevin. "US fears Chinese hack attack." BBC.co.uk. April 28, 2001. Accessed March 27, 2013. http://news.bbc.co.uk/2/hi/americas/1301327.stm.

Arkin, William M. "A Mouse That Roars?" *Washington Post*, June 7, 1999. Accessed May 25, 2012. http://www.washingtonpost.com/wp-srv/national/dotmil/arkin060799.htm.

Barr, Stephen. "Anti-NATO Hackers Sabotage 3 Web Sites." *Washington Post*, May 12, 1999. Accessed March 27, 2013. http://www.washingtonpost.com/wp-srv/inatl/longterm/balkans/stories/hackers051299.htm.

"Bio, Mr. Peiter 'Mudge' Zatko." DARPA. Accessed October 19, 2012. http://www.darpa.mil/Our_Work/I2O/Personnel/Mr_Peiter_Zatko.aspx.

Campbell, John. "Lessons from Our Cyber Past: The First Military Cyber Units." (Also known as "First Cyber Commanders.") Audio transcript of the Atlantic Council's Cyber Statecraft Initiative Workshop, in Washington, D.C., March 5, 2012. Accessed March 28, 2013. http://www.acus.org/event/lessons-our-cyber-past-first-military-cyber-units.

Chase, Michael S. and James C. Mulvenon. *You've Got Dissent: Chinese Dissident Use of the Internet and Beijing's Counter-Strategies.* RAND. 2002. Accessed November 1, 2012. http://www.rand.org/content/dam/rand/pubs/monograph_reports/MR1543/MR1543.ch2.pdf.

"Chinese Embassy Bombing Belgrade: News Reports of the Protests in China and World Wide." InformationWar.org Accessed April 9, 2001. http://web.archive.org/web/20010202182600/http://www.informationwar.org/china/china1.htm.

"Critical Infrastructure Protection: PDD-63." Federation of American Scientists. May 22, 1998. Accessed October 19, 2012. http://www.fas.org/irp/offdocs/pdd/pdd-63.htm.

"Cyber Security "Wake-Up Calls" for the Federal Government" CTO Vision. Accessed April 18, 2012. http://ctovision.com/cyber-security-wake-up-calls-for-the-federal-government/.

Drogin, Bob. "Russians Seem To Be Hacking into Pentagon / Sensitive information taken—but nothing top secret." *Los Angeles Times,* October 7, 1999. Accessed May 18, 2012. http://www.sfgate.com/news/article/Russians-Seem-To-Be-Hacking-Into-Pentagon-2903309.php.

"Eligible Receiver." Global Security.org. 2011. Accessed October 15, 2011. http://www.globalsecurity.org/military/ops/eligible-receiver.htm.

"Filipinos told: Exercise restraint amid cyber attacks." *Sun Star Manila,* April 22, 2012. Accessed April 18, 2012. http://www.sunstar.com.ph/manila/local-news/2012/04/22/filipinos-told-exercise-restraint-amid-cyber-attacks-217599.

"Government websites 'attacked by Chinese hackers'." *Sun Star Manila*, April 23, 2012. Accessed April 20, 2012. http://www.sunstar.com.ph/manila/local-news/2012/04/23/government-websites-attacked-chinese-hackers-217792.

Graham, Bradley. "US Studies a New Threat: Cyber Attack." *Washington Post*, May 24, 1998. Accessed March 27, 2013. http://www.washingtonpost.com/wp-srv/washtech/daily/may98/cyberattack052498.htm.

"Hackers attack U.S. government Web sites in protest of Chinese Embassy bombing." CNN.com. May 10, 1999. Accessed March 27, 2013. http://www.cnn.com/TECH/computing/9905/10/hack.attack/index.html?_s=PM:TECH.

"Hackers Testifying at the United States Senate, May 19, 1998 (L0pht Heavy Industries)." YouTube video, 59:04. Accessed October 19, 2012. http://www.youtube.com/watch?v=VVJldn_MmMY.

Healey, Jason. "Beyond Attribution: Seeking National Responsibility in Cyberspace." Atlantic Council Issue Brief. 2012. Accessed May 18, 2012. http://www.acus.org/publication/beyond-attribution-seeking-national-responsibility-cyberspace.

Hildreth, Steven. "Cyberwarfare." *Congressional Research Service*. June 19, 2001. Accessed October 15, 2011. http://www.fas.org/irp/crs/RL30735.pdf.

Joint Chiefs of Staff. "No-Notice Interoperability Exercise Program." Dtic.mil. March 21, 2008. Accessed October 15, 2011. http://www.dtic.mil/cjcs_directives/cdata/unlimit/3510_01.pdf.

Johnson, Ian and Thom Shanker. "Beijing Mixes Messages over Anti-Japan Protests." *Washington Post*, September 16, 2012. Accessed May 25, 2012. http://www.nytimes.com/2012/09/17/world/asia/anti-japanese-protests-over-disputed-islands-continue-in-china.html?ref=world.

Kimery, Anthony. "Moonlight Maze." Infowar. December 3, 1999. Accessed May 18, 2000. http://web.archive.org/web/20020803211533/http://www.infowar.com/class_2/99/class2_120399b_j.shtml.

"Kosovo cyberwar intensifies Chinese hackers targeting U.S. sites, government says." CNN.com. May 12, 1999. Accessed March 27, 2013. http://www.cnn.com/TECH/computing/9905/12/cyberwar.idg/index.html?_s=PM:TECH.

Lemos, Robert. "Web worm targets White House." CNET.com. July 19, 2001. Accessed

November 1, 2012. http://news.cnet.com/2100-1001-270272.html.

"Lessons from Our Cyber Past: The First Cyber Cops." Transcript of the event hosted by the Atlantic Council's Cyber Statecraft Initiative, in Washington, D.C., May 16, 2012. Accessed March 19, 2013. http://www.acus.org/event/lessons-our-cyber-past-first-cyber-cops; and http://www.acus.org/event/lessons-our-cyber-past-first-cyber-cops/transcript.

Leyden, John. "US Gov. warns script kiddies to stay out of cyberwar." *The Register*, February 13, 2003. Accessed April 18, 2012. http://www.theregister.co.uk/2003/02/13/us_gov_warns_script_kiddies/print.html.

Madsen, Wayne. "Code Red: A Red Herring." July 30, 2001. Accessed November 1, 2012. http://cryptome.org/yell-fire.htm.

"Next Generation FS/ISAC: Frequently Asked Questions." *Financial Services ISAC.* Accessed October 19, 2012. http://www.aba.com/Solutions/Documents/7c5d7be861b74258bc6467d189d825c1FAQISAC.pdf.

Poulsen, Kevin. "Video: Solar Sunrise, the Best FBI-Produced Hacker Flick Ever." *Wired.* September 23, 2008. Accessed April 20, 2012. http://www.wired.com/threatlevel/2008/09/video-solar-sun/.

"Presidential Decision Directive/NSC-63." Federation of American Scientists. May 22, 1998. Accessed April 20, 2012. http://www.fas.org/irp/offdocs/pdd/pdd-63.htm.

"Program Information." *National Communications System.* Accessed October 19, 2012. http://www.ncs.gov/ncc/program_info.html.

"Sci/Tech: Kosovo info warfare spreads." BBC.co.uk. April 1, 1999. Accessed April 18, 2012. http://news.bbc.co.uk/2/hi/science/nature/308788.stm.

Stephen, Justin. "The Changing Face of Distributed Denial of Service Mitigation." *SANS Institute.* 2001. Accessed April 21, 2012. http://www.sans.org/reading_room/whitepapers/threats/changing-face-distributed-denial-service-mitigation_462.

Suro, Roberto. "FBI Lagging Behind on Cyber Crime." *Washington Post*, 7 October 1999. Accessed March 27, 2013. http://www.washingtonpost.com/wp-srv/national/daily/oct99/cyber7.htm.

Tang, Rose. "China-U.S. cyber war escalates." CNN.com. May 1, 2001. Accessed March 19, 2013. http://archives.cnn.com/2001/WORLD/asiapcf/east/04/27/china.hackers/index.html.

Verton, Dan. "DOD: Change Passwords." *Federal Computer Week*. 8 August 1998. Accessed March 19, 2013. http://fcw.com/articles/1999/08/08/dod-change-passwords. aspxhttp://fcw.com/articles/1999/08/08/dod-change-passwords.aspx.

Weiss, Todd. "FBI Warns of More Cyberattacks." *Computer World*. May 14, 2001. Accessed April 18, 2012.http://www.computerworld.com/s/article/60501/FBI_Warns_of_ More_Cyberattacks.

"WikiLeaks backlash: The first global cyber war has begun, claim hackers." *The Guardian*, December 11, 2010. Accessed March 27, 2013. http://www.guardian.co.uk/ media/2010/dec/11/wikileaks-backlash-cyber-war.

Yesterday's Problems Today: Militarization (2003 to today)

Barnes, Julian. "Pentagon computer networks attacked." *Los Angeles Times*, November 28, 2008. Accessed April 19, 2012. http://articles.latimes.com/2008/nov/28/nation/na-cyberattack28.

Bryan, David. "Lessons from Our Cyber Past: The First Military Cyber Units." (Also known as "First Cyber Commanders.") Audio transcript of the Atlantic Council's Cyber Statecraft Initiative Workshop, in Washington, D.C., March 5, 2012. Accessed March 28, 2013. http://www.acus.org/event/lessons-our-cyber-past-first-military-cyber-units.

Carrol, Ward. "Israel's Cyber Shot at Syria." Defense Tech. November 26, 2007. Accessed January 19, 2013. http://defensetech.org/2007/11/26/israels-cyber-shot-at-syria/.

Chabrow, Eric. "White House Partly Lifts CNCI Secrecy." Govinfosecurity.com. March 2, 2010. Accessed April 18, 2012. http://www.govinfosecurity.com/white-house-partly-lifts-cnci-secrecy-a-2257.

"Chronology of cyber incidents since 2006." The Center for Strategic and International Studies. Washington, D.C. May 4, 2012. Accessed March 27, 2013. http://csis.org/ files/publication/120504_Significant_Cyber_Incidents_Since_2006.pdf.

Clarke, Richard and Robert Knake. *Cyber War: The Next Threat to National Security and What To Do about It*. New York: Harper Collins Publisher, 2010.

Clayton, Mark. "Stuxnet malware is 'weapon' out to destroy ... Iran's Bushehr nuclear plant?" *Christian Science Monitor*, 21 September 2010. Accessed April 28, 2012. http://www.csmonitor.com/USA/2010/0921/Stuxnet-malware-is-weapon-out-to-destroy-Iran-s-Bushehr-nuclear-plant.

"Conficker Working Group: Lessons Learned." Confickerworkinggroup.org. June 2010. Accessed April 18, 2012. http://www.confickerworkinggroup.org/wiki/uploads/ Conficker_Working_Group_Lessons_Learned_17_June_2010_final.pdf.

Denning, Dorothy. "Terrors Web: How the Internet Is Transforming Terrorism." To appear in *Handbook on Internet Crimes*, edited by Y. Jewkes and M. Yar. Willan Publishing. 2009. Accessed November 1, 2012. http://faculty.nps.edu/dedennin/publications/ Denning-TerrorsWeb.pdf.

Eltringham, Scott. "Prosecuting Cyber Crimes." *US Department of Justice Cyber Crimes Manual*. Office of Legal Education Executive Office for United States Attorneys, 2010. Accessed April 19, 2012. http://www.justice.gov/criminal/cybercrime/docs/ ccmanual.pdf.

Graham, Bradley. "Hackers Attack via Chinese Web Sites." *Washington Post*, August 25, 2005. Accessed March 27, 2013. http://www.washingtonpost.com/wp-dyn/ content/article/2005/08/24/AR2005082402318.html.

Gross, Joseph. "Enter the Cyber Dragon." *Vanity Fair*. September 2001. Accessed May 25, 2012. http://www.vanityfair.com/culture/features/2011/09/chinese-hacking-201109.

"International Strategy for Cyberspace." White House. May 2011. Accessed March 19, 2013. http://www.whitehouse.gov/sites/default/files/rss_viewer/international_ strategy_for_cyberspace.pdf.

Korns, Stephen W. and Joshua E. Kastenberg. "Georgia's Cyber Left Hook." Parameters XXXVIII, No. 4 (2009): 60-76. Accessed March 27, 2013. http://www.carlisle.army. mil/USAWC/parameters/Articles/08winter/korns.pdf.

Krebs, Brian. "Experts Warn of New Windows Shortcut Flaw." Krebs on Security (blog). Last updated July 16, 2010. Accessed March 19. 2013. http://krebsonsecurity. com/2010/07/experts-warn-of-new-windows-shortcut-flaw/.

"Lessons from Our Cyber Past: The First Cyber Cops." Transcript of the event hosted by the Atlantic Council's Cyber Statecraft Initiative, in Washington, D.C., May 16, 2012. Accessed March 19, 2013. http://www.acus.org/event/lessons-our-cyber-past-first-cyber-cops; and http://www.acus.org/event/lessons-our-cyber-past-first-cyber-cops/transcript.

Leyden, John. "NSA Top Spook Blames China for RSA Hack." *The Register*. March

29, 2012. Accessed January 19, 2013. http://www.theregister.co.uk/2012/03/29/ nsa_blames_china_rsa_hack/.

Lynn, William. "Defending a New Domain." *Foreign Affairs*. September/October 2010. Accessed March 27, 2013. http://www.foreignaffairs.com/articles/66552/william-j-lynn-iii/defending-a-new-domain.

"Malware Affecting Siemens WinCC and PCS7 Products (Stuxnet)." Siemens. July 19, 2010. Accessed May 18, 2012. http://www.automation.siemens.com/WW/forum/ guests/PostShow.aspx?PageIndex=1&PostID=225690.

Markoff, John. "Computer Experts Unite to Hunt Worm." *New York Times*, March 18, 2009. Accessed April 18, 2012. http://www.nytimes.com/2009/03/19/ technology/19worm.html?_r=1.

Markoff, John and Thom Shanker. "Halted '03 Iraq Plan Illustrates U.S. Fear of Cyberwar Risk." *New York Times*, August 1, 2009. Accessed May 24, 2012. http://www.nytimes. com/2009/08/02/us/politics/02cyber.html.

Mills, Elinor. "Microsoft offers $250,000 reward for Conficker arrest." CNET.com. February 12, 2009. Accessed April 18, 2012. http://news.cnet.com/microsoft-offers-$250000-reward-for-conficker-arrest/.

Nakashima, Ellen. "Dismantling of Saudi-CIA Web site illustrates need for clearer cyberwar policies." *Washington Post*, March 19, 2010. Accessed April 18, 2012. http://www.washingtonpost.com/wp-dyn/content/article/2010/03/18/ AR2010031805464.html.

Nakashima, Ellen, Greg Miller and Julie Tate. "U.S., Israel developed Flame computer virus to slow Iranian nuclear efforts, officials say." *Washington Post*, June 19, 2012. Accessed April 18, 2012. http://www.washingtonpost.com/world/national-security/ us-israel-developed-computer-virus-to-slow-iranian-nuclear-efforts-officials-say/2012/06/19/gJQA6xBPoV_story.html.

"National Cybersecurity Awareness Month." South Georgia College. Accessed October 19, 2012. http://www.sgc.edu/president/departments/IIT/NCSAM.html.

Norton, Quinn. "How Anonymous Picks Targets, Launches Attacks, and Takes Powerful Organizations Down." *Wired*. July 3, 2012. Accessed April 19, 2012. http://www. wired.com/threatlevel/2012/07/ff_anonymous/all/.

"Operation Buckshot Yankee: Key players and networks infected." *Washington Post*, December 8, 2011. Accessed April 19, 2012. http://www.washingtonpost.com/

world/national-security/key-players-in-operation-buckshot-yankee/2011/12/08/
gIQASJaSgO_story.html.

FBI Los Angeles. "One Hundred Linked to International Computer Hacking Ring
Charged by United States and Egypt in Operation Phish Phry." FBI.gov. October 7,
2009.http://www.fbi.gov/losangeles/press-releases/2009/la100709-1.htm

"Overview of the US-CCU of the Cyber Campaign against Georgia in August of 2008."
US Cyber Consequences Unit. August 2009. Accessed March 27, 2013. http://
www.registan.net/wp-content/uploads/2009/08/US-CCU-Georgia-Cyber-
Campaign-Overview.pdf.

"Paper Cuts." The Economist. October 27, 2012. Accessed November 1, 2012. http://
www.economist.com/news/international/21565146-paperless-polling-stations-are-
unfashionable-internet-voting-its-way-paper-cuts.

Perloty, Nicole. "In Cyberattack on Saudi Firm, U.S. Sees Iran Firing Back." New York
Times, October 23, 2012. Accessed November 1, 2012. http://www.nytimes.
com/2012/10/24/business/global/cyberattack-on-saudi-oil-firm-disquiets-us.
html?pagewanted=all.

Priisalu, Jaan. "Building a Secure Cyber Future: Attacks on Estonia, Five Years On."
Transcript of the event hosted by the Atlantic Council, in Washington, D.C., May 23,
2012. Accessed May 23, 2012. http://www.acus.org/event/building-secure-cyber-
future-attacks-estonia-five-years/transcript; Audio transcript, http://www.acus.org/
event/building-secure-cyber-future-attacks-estonia-five-years.

Rumsfeld, Donald. "Memorandum on Assignment and Delegation of Authority to
Director." Defense Information Systems Agency (DISA). June 18, 2004.

Sanger, David. "Obama Order Sped Up Wave of Cyberattacks against Iran." New
York Times, June 1, 2012. Accessed May 24, 2012. http://www.nytimes.
com/2012/06/01/world/middleeast/obama-ordered-wave-of-cyberattacks-against-
iran.html?pagewanted=all.

Shanker, Thom and David Sanger. "U.S. Suspects Iran Was Behind a Wave of
Cyberattacks." New York Times, October 13, 2012. Accessed October 19, 2012.
http://www.nytimes.com/2012/10/14/world/middleeast/us-suspects-iranians-
were-behind-a-wave-of-cyberattacks.html?pagewanted=all.

Shmitt, Eric and Thom Shanker. "U.S. Debated Cyberwarfare in Attack Plan on Libya." *New York Times*, October 17, 2011. Accessed April 18, 2012. http://www.nytimes. com/2011/10/18/world/africa/cyber-warfare-against-libya-was-debated-by-us. html.

Smithson, S. "Cyber Command combines offense, defense in planning." *The Washington Times*, February 22, 2012. Accessed October 9, 2012. http://www.washingtontimes. com/news/2012/feb/22/cyber-command-combines-offense-defense-in-planning/?page=all.

"Text of Speech by Defense U.S. Secretary Leon Panetta." *Defense News*. October 12, 2012. Accessed October 19, 2012. http://www.defensenews.com/article/20121012/ DEFREG02/310120001/Text-Speech-by-Defense-U-S-Secretary-Leon-Panetta.

Tikk, Eneken, Kadri Kaska, Kristel Rünnimeri, Mari Kert, Anna-Maria Talihärm, and Liis Vihul. "Cyber Attacks Against Georgia: Legal Lessons Identified." *Cooperative Cyber Defence Centre of Excellence*. November 2008. Accessed *April 15, 2012*. www. carlisle.army.mil/DIME/documents/Georgia%201%200.pdf.

Tikk, Eneken, Kadri Kasha, and Liis Vihul. "International Cyber Incidents: Legal Considerations." CCD-COE Publications, 2010. Accessed March 27, 2013. http:// www.ccdcoe.org/publications/books/legalconsiderations.pdf.

"US and Israel were behind Stuxnet claims researcher." BBC.co.uk. March 4, 2011. Accessed May 18, 2012. http://www.bbc.co.uk/news/technology-12633240.

"US Finance Sector Warned of Cyber Attacks." *Security Week*. September 19, 2012. Accessed October 19, 2012.http://www.securityweek.com/us-finance-sector-warned-cyber-attacks.

Woodcock, Bill. "Building a Secure Cyber Future: Attacks on Estonia, Five Years On." Transcript of the event hosted by the Atlantic Council, in Washington, D.C., May 23, 2012. Accessed May 23, 2012. http://www.acus.org/event/building-secure-cyber-future-attacks-estonia-five-years/transcript; Audio transcript, http://www.acus.org/ event/building-secure-cyber-future-attacks-estonia-five-years.

Zetter, Kim. "Google Hack Attack Was Ultra Sophisticated, New Details Show." *Wired*. June 14, 2010. Accessed April 18, 2012. http://www.wired.com/ threatlevel/2010/01/operation-aurora/.

Conclusion

Nakashima, Ellen. "Pentagon proposes more robust role for its cyber-specialists."
     Washington Post, August 9, 2012. Accessed September 13, 2012. http://www.
     washingtonpost.com/world/national-security/pentagon-proposes-more-robust-role-
     for-its-cyber-specialists/2012/08/09/1e3478ca-db15-11e1-9745-d9ae6098d493_
     story.html.

Shalal-Esa, Andrea. "Ex-U.S. general urges frank talk on cyber weapons." *Reuters*, June 6,
     2011. Accessed April 18, 2012. http://www.reuters.com/article/2011/11/06/us-
     cyber-cartwright-idUSTRE7A514C20111106.

Part 2: Realization

Cuckoo's Egg: Stalking the Wily Hacker

Beals, E., D. Busing, W. Graves, and Clifford Stoll. "Improving VMS security: Overlooked ways to tighten your system." In "Session Notes," *DECUS Fall Meeting* in Anaheim, California, December 7-11. Digital Equipment User's Society. Boston: 1987.

Bednarek, M. "Re: Important Notice (Distrust Software from People Breaking into Computers)." Paper presented at the Internet Info-Vax Conference, August 4, 1987.

Boing, W. and B. Kirchberg. "L'Utilisation de Systemes Experts dans l'Audit Informatique in *Congress Programme, Securicom 88.*" Paper presented at the 6th World Congress on Computer Security, in Paris, France, March 17, 1988.

California State Legislature. "Computer crime law." *California Penal Code* S. 502, 1986. (Revised 1987).

Carpenter, B. "Malicious Hackers." *CERN Computer Newsletter* ser. 185. September 1986.

Clark, David D. and David R. Wilson. "A Comparison of Commercial and Military Computer Security Policies." In *Proceedings of the IEEE Symposium on Security and Privacy in Oakland, California on April 27–29*, 184–194. New York: IEEE Press, 1987.

Hartman, W. "The Privacy Dilemma." Paper presented at the "International Conference on Computers and Law" in Santa Monica, California, February 1988. Available from Erasamus Universiteit, Rotterdam.

Israel, H. "Computer viruses: Myth or reality." In *Proceedings of the 10th National Computer Security Conference in Baltimore, on September 21-24, 1987.*

Kneale, D. "It Takes a Hacker." *Wall Street Journal,* November 3, 1987.

Landau, Susan. "Zero Knowledge and the Department of Defense." *Notices of the American Mathematical Society 35* (January 1988): 5–12.

Latham, D. "Guidance and Program Direction Applicable to the Defense Data Network." *DDN Protocol Handbook*, NIC 50004. vol. 1. Washington, DC, December 1985.

Lehmann, F. "Computer Break-Ins." *Communications of the ACM* 30, 7 (July 1987): 584–585.

Metz, S. J. "Computer Break-Ins." *Communications of the ACM* 30, 7 (July 1987): 584.

Markoff, John. "Computer Sleuths Hunt a Brilliant Hacker." *San Francisco Examiner,* October 3, 1986.

McDonald, Chris. "Computer Security Blunders." In *Proceedings of the DOE 10th Computer Security Group Conference* in Albuquerque, NM, May 5–7, 35–46. Washington, D.C.: Department of Energy, 1987.

Morris, R. H. and K. Thompson. "Password security: A Case History." *Unix Programmer's Manual.* AT&T Bell Laboratories, 1984.

Morshedian, D. "How to fight password pirates." *Computer* 19 (January 1, 1986).

Omond, G. "Important notice [on widespread attacks into VMS systems]." Paper presented at Internet Info-Vax Conference, July 31, 1987.

Proceedings of *the Intrusion Detection Expert Systems* Conference, November 17, 1987.

Reid, Brian. "Reflections on Some Recent Widespread Computer Break-Ins." *Communications of the ACM* 30, 2 (February 1987): 30.

Schmemann, Serge. "West German Computer Hobbyists Rummaged NASA'sFfiles." *New York Times,* September 16, 1987.

Slind-Flor, Victoria. "Hackers Access Tough New Penalties." *The Recorder: Bay Area Legal Newspaper,* January 6, 1988.

Stallman, Richard. *Gnu-Emacs Text Editor Source Code.*

Stevens, D. "Who goes there? A Dialog of Questions and Answers about Benign hacking." In *Proceedings of the Computer Measurement Group* in December 1987.

Stoll, Clifford. "What Do You Feed a Trojan Horse?" In *Proceedings of the 10th National Computer Security Conference in Baltimore on September 21-24, 1987.*

U.S. Congress. "The Federal Computer Crime Statute." 18 U.S.C.A. 1030. Washington, D.C.: U.S. Congress, 1986.

Whitten, Ian H. "Computer (in)security: Infiltrating Open Systems." Summer 1987.

Morris Worm: Virus Highlights

NSF Network News. No. 5. NSF Network Service Center. October 1988.

Part 3: Take Off

SOLAR SUNRISE: Cyber Attack from Iraq?

Burrough, Bryan. "Invisible Enemies." *Vanity Fair*. June 2000. Accessed March 19, 2013. http://www.vanityfair.com/culture/features/2000/06/web-hackers-200006.

CERT. "CERT Advisory CA-1996-09 Vulnerability in rpc.statd." CERT.org. 1997. Accessed March 19, 2013. http://www.cert.org/advisories/CA-1996-09.html.

Chabinsky, Steve. "Lessons from Our Cyber Past: The First Cyber Cops." Transcript of the event hosted by the Atlantic Council's Cyber Statecraft Initiative, in Washington, D.C., May 16, 2012. Accessed March 19, 2013. http://www.acus.org/event/lessons-our-cyber-past-first-cyber-cops; and http://www.acus.org/event/lessons-our-cyber-past-first-cyber-cops/transcript.

Dick, Ronald L. "Testimony before the House Energy and Commerce Committee, Oversight and Investigation Subcommittee." FBI.gov. April 5, 2001. Accessed March 19, 2013. http://www.fbi.gov/news/testimony/issue-of-intrusions-into-government-computer-networks.

Donelly, John and Vince Crawley. "Hamre to Hill: 'We're in a Cyberwar'." *Defense Week*. March 1, 1999. Accessed March 19, 2013. http://articles.latimes.com/print/1998/apr/27/news/mn-43491.

"FBI Eyes Teens in Pentagon 'Attacks,'." *Wired*. February 27, 1998. Accessed March 19, 2013. www.wired.com/science/discoveries/news/1998/02/10594.

GPO. "Critical Information Infrastructure Protection: The Threat is Real." GPO.gov. October 6, 1999. Accessed October 25, 2012. http://www.gpo.gov/fdsys/pkg/CHRG-106shrg68563/html/CHRG-106shrg68563.htm.

"Hackers tap into Pentagon Computers." Toledo Blade, 26 February 1998. Accessed March 19, 2013. http://news.google.com/newspapers?nid=1350&dat=19980226&id=X8gwAAAAI-BAJ&sjid=kAMEAAAAIBAJ&pg=2405,3527994.

Hildreth, Steven A. "Cyberwarfare." CRS Report for Congress. June 19, 2001. Accessed March 19, 2013. http://www.fas.org/irp/crs/RL30735.pdf.

Lardner, Richard and Pamela Hess. "Pentagon Looks for Answers to Massive Computer Attack." Defense Electronics and Electronics Report. February 13, 1998. Accessed March 19, 2013. www.ntk.net/hacks.

Nichols, Arthur. "A Perspective on Threats in the Risk Analysis Process." SANS Institute. 2002. Accessed March 19, 2013. http://www.sans.org/reading_room/whitepapers/auditing/perspective-threats-risk-analysis-process_63.

Panorama. "CYBER ATTACK." BBC Video transcript. BBC.co.uk. March 7, 2000. Accessed October 25, 2012. http://news.bbc.co.uk/hi/english/static/audio_video/programmes/panorama/transcripts/transcript_03_07_00.txt.

Poulson, Kevin. "Solar Sunrise Hacker 'Analyzer' Escapes Jail." The Register, June 15, 2001. Accessed March 19, 2013. http://www.theregister.co.uk/2001/06/15/solar_sunrise_hacker_analyzer_escapes/.

Poulson, Kevin. "Video: 'Solar Sunrise,' The Best FBI Produced Hacker Flick Ever." Wired. September 23, 2008. Accessed March 19, 2013. http://www.wired.com/threatlevel/2008/09/video-solar-sun/.

Power, Richard. "Joy-Riders: Mischief that Leads to Mayhem." Informit.com. October 30, 2000. Accessed March 19, 2013. http://www.informit.com/articles/article.aspx?p=19603&seqNum=4.

Prados, Alfred B. "Iraq: Post-War Challenges and US Responses 1991-1998." CRS Report for Congress. March 31, 1999. Accessed March 19, 2013. http://www.fas.org/man/crs/98-386.pdf.

Reed, Dan and Dan L. Wilson. "Whiz-Kid Hacker Caught." San Jose Mercury News, March 19, 1998. Accessed March 19, 2013. http://web.archive.org/web/20001007150311/http://www.mercurycenter.com/archives/reprints/hacker110698.htm.

Serabian, Jr., John A. "Cyber Threats and the US Economy." CIA.gov. February 23, 2000. Accessed March 19, 2013. https://www.cia.gov/news-information/speeches-testimony/2000/cyberthreats_022300.html.

"Teen Hacker with Access to Arms." The Baltimore Sun, 5 March 5, 1998. Accessed March 19, 2013. http://articles.baltimoresun.com/1998-03-05/news/1998064095_1_cyber-pals-cloverdale-livermore-national-laboratories.

Trounson, Rebecca. "Hacker Case Taps into Fame, Fury." Los Angeles Times, 27 April 1998. Accessed March 19, 2013. http://articles.latimes.com/print/1998/apr/27/news/mn-43491.

United Nations Security Council resolution S/RES/1194, September 9, 1998.

United Nations Security Council resolution S/RES/1205, November 5, 1998.

United Nations Security Council resolution S/RES/1115, June 21, 1997.

United Nations Security Council Presidential Statement S/PRST/1997/49, October 29, 1997.

United Nations Security Council Presidential Statement S/PRST/1997/51, November 13, 1997.

United Nations Security Council Presidential Statement S/PRST/1998/1, January 14, 1998.

United Nations Security Council Presidential Statement S/PRST/1998/11, May 14, 1998.

Zetter, Kim. "Israeli Hacker 'The Analyzer' Suspected of Hacking Again." *Wired*. September 5, 2008. Accessed March 19, 2013. http://www.wired.com/threatlevel/2008/09/the-analyzer-su/.

Zetter, Kim. "'The Analyzer' Gets Time Served for Million-Dollar Bank Heist." *Wired*. July 5, 2012. Accessed March 19, 2013. http://www.wired.com/threatlevel/2012/07/tenenbaum-sentenced/.

Early Patriotic Hacking

Ackerman, Gwen. "Government sites under cyber-attack." *The Jerusalem Post*, October 25, 2000. Accessed March 19, 2013. http://seclists.org/isn/2000/Oct/128.

Allen, Patrick, and Chris Demchak. "The Israeli-Palestinian Cyber War." Military Review, March–April 2003.

Andrews, Allan R. "The First Internet War." Monitor.net. April 9, 1999. Accessed March 19, 2013. http://www.monitor.net/monitor/9904a/copyright/internetwar.html.

Arquilla, John and David Ronfeldt. "Cyberwar is Coming!" Comparative Strategy 12 (1993): 141–165.

Briscoe, David. "No Winner in Kosovo Propaganda War." Associated Press, May 17, 1999. Accessed March 19, 2013. http://www.apnewsarchive.com/1999/No-Winner-in-

Kosovo-Propaganda-War/id-d198b8d8a2411c6577639d4e0d1063cd.

Brown, Andrew. "Invasion of the cyber-Members." *The Independent* (London), March 20, 1995. Accessed March 19, 2013. http://www.independent.co.uk/life-style/invasion-of-the-cybermembers-1612022.html.

CERT. "CERT Advisory CA-1999-04 Melissa Macro Virus." CERT.org. Last updated March 31, 1999. Accessed March 19, 2013. http://www.cert.org/advisories/CA-1999-04.html.

CERT. "CERT Advisory CA-2001-11 sadmind/IIS Worm." CERT.org. May 10, 2001. Accessed March 27, 2013. http://www.cert.org/advisories/CA-2001-11.html.

Cha, Ariana Eunjung. "Chinese Suspected of Hacking U.S. Sites; Anger Over Plane Collision Produces Calls for Revenge, Advice on Web Attacks." *Washington Post*, April 13, 2001. Accessed March 27, 2013. http://www.infosecnews.org/hypermail/0104/3905.html.

"China warns of massive hack attacks." CNN.com. May 3, 2001. Accessed March 19, 2013. http://articles.cnn.com/2001-05-03/world/china.hack_1_cyber-war-chinese-cyber-chinese-hackers?_s=PM:asiapcf.

"Chinese Hackers Halt Web War, Say 1,000 U.S. sites defaced." *The Globe and Mail* (Canada), May 10, 2001. Accessed March 28, 2013. http://www.theglobeandmail.com/news/world/chinese-hackers-halt-web-war-say-1000-us-sites-defaced/article4147621/.

"Chinese poker." *The Economist*. April 17, 2001. Accessed March 19, 2013. http://www.economist.com/node/576103?story_id=E1_VSGTDP.

"Chinese, US hackers' cyber battle goes global." *The New Zealand Herald*, May 4, 2001. Accessed March 27, 2013. http://www.nzherald.co.nz/world/news/article.cfm?c_id=2&objectid=186936.

Clausewitz, Carl von. *On War*. Translated by Michael Howard and Peter Paret. Princeton, NJ: Princeton University Press, 1989.

Denning, Dorothy E. "Cyber Conflict as an Emergent Social Phenomenon." In Corporate Hacking and Technology-Driven Crime: Social Dynamics and Implications, edited by Thomas Hold and Bernadette Schell, 170-186. Hershey, PA: IGI Global, 2011. Accessed March 27, 2013. http://faculty.nps.edu/dedennin/publications/CyberConflict-EmergentSocialPhenomenon-final.pdf.

Dunn, Ashley. "Battle Spilling Over onto the Internet." Los Angeles Times, April 3, 1999.

Accessed March 19, 2013. http://articles.latimes.com/1999/apr/03/news/mn-23851.

Evers, Joris. "Feds Warn of May Day Hack Attacks." PC World. April 27, 2001. Accessed March 19, 2013. http://www.pcworld.com/article/48624/feds_warn_of_may_day_hack_attacks.html.

Geers, Kenneth. "Cyberspace and the Changing Nature of Warfare." *SC Magazine*. August 27, 2008. Accessed March 19, 2013. http://www.scmagazine.com/cyberspace-and-the-changing-nature-of-warfare/article/115929/.

Gentile, Carmen. "Israeli Hackers Vow to Defend." *Wired*. November 15, 2000. Accessed March 19, 2013. http://seclists.org/isn/2000/Nov/94.

Grier, Peter. "Preparing for 21st Century Information Warfare." Government Executive. August 1995.

"Hackers Deface Website of U.S. Justice Department." *Los Angeles Times*, August 18, 1996. Accessed March 19, 2013. http://articles.latimes.com/1996-08-18/news/mn-35440_1_justice-department-officials.

Harrison, Ann. "NATO Web site holds off cyberattacks." Computer World. April 6, 1999. Accessed March 19, 2013. http://www.computerworld.com.au/article/6089/nato_web_site_holds_off_cyberattacks/.

Hellaby, David. "Sadmind Worm Daubs Anti-US Slogans Globally." *The Australian*, May 15, 2001. Accessed March 19, 2013. http://www.lexisnexis.com/hottopics/lnacademic.

Henderson, Scott J. *The Dark Visitor: Inside the World of Chinese Hackers*. Fort Leavenworth, KS: Foreign Military Studies Office, 2007.

Hess, Pamela. "China prevented repeat cyber attack on the US." UPI.com. October 29, 2002. Accessed March 19, 2013. http://www.upi.com/Business_News/Security-Industry/2002/10/29/China-prevented-repeat-cyber-attack-on-US/UPI-51011035913195/.

iDefense. "Israeli-Palestinian Cyber Conflict (IPCC) Report v2.0PR." Fairfax, VA: Intelligence Services Report, 2001.

Jones, Andy, Gerald L. Kovacich, and Perry G. Luzwick. Global Information Warfare: How Businesses, Governments, and Others Achieve Objectives and Attain Competitive Advantage. New York: Auerbach Publications, 2002.

Joseph, Manu. "Both Sides Hacked Over Kashmir." *Wired*. December 23,

2000. Accessed March 19, 2013. http://www.wired.com/politics/law/news/2000/12/40789?currentPage=all.

Karatzogianna, Athina. *The Politics of Cyberconflict.* New York: Routledge, 2006.

Kellan, Ann. "Hackers hit government Web sites after China embassy bombing." CNN.com. May 11, 1999. Accessed March 19, 2013. http://www.cnn.com/TECH/computing/9905/10/hack.attack.02/index.html.

"Korea Hit in US, China Crossfire." *The Australian*, May 22, 2001. Accessed March 19, 2013. http://www.lexisnexis.com/hottopics/lnacademic.

"Kosovo Crisis Creates New Roles For Internet Firms." Newsbytes, April 5, 1999. Accessed March 19, 2013. www.lexisnexis.com/hottopics/lnacademic.

Krebs, Brian. "Chinese Hackers Step Up Attacks On US Web Sites." Newsbytes, May 4, 2001. Accessed March 19, 2013. www.lexisnexis.com/hottopics/lnacademic.

Legard, David. "Web Site Defacements Hit All-Time High." PC World. September 30, 2002. Accessed March 19, 2013. http://www.pcworld.com/article/105498/web_site_defacements_hit_alltime_high.html.

Lynch, April. "Kosovo Being Called First Internet War / Web personalizes it with images, communications." *San Francisco Gate*, April 15, 1999. Accessed March 19, 2013. http://www.sfgate.com/news/article/Kosovo-Being-Called-First-Internet-War-Web-2936299.php.

McCullagh, Declan. "Did Russians Get Whitehouse.gov?" *Wired.* March 29, 1999. Accessed March 19, 2013. http://www.wired.com/politics/law/news/1999/03/18787.

Nanjappa, Vicky. "Cyber wars: Pak has an advantage over India." Rediff.com. August 16, 2010. Accessed March 19, 2013. http://www.rediff.com/news/report/indo-pak-cyber-war-set-to-escalate/20100816.htm.

Nuttall, Chris. "Net warfare over Kosovo." BBC.co.uk. October 23, 1998. Accessed March 19, 2013. http://news.bbc.co.uk/2/hi/science/nature/200069.stm.

Paget, François. "Hacktivism." McAfee White Paper. 2012. Accessed March 19, 2013. http://www.mcafee.com/us/resources/white-papers/wp-hacktivism.pdf.

Pollock, Ellen Joan and Andrea Petersen. "Serbs take offensive in first cyberwar, bombing America." *The Wall Street Journal,* April 18, 1999. Accessed March 19, 2013. http://www.deseretnews.com/article/690283/Serbs-take-offensive-in-the-first-cyberwar-bombing-America.html?pg=all.

"Pro-Pakistan hackers invade Indian website, post anti-India messages." *Deutsche Presse-Agentur,* August 17, 2000. Accessed March 19, 2013. www.lexisnexis.com/hottopics/lnacademic.

Raiu, Costin. "One Sad Mind." Kaspersky Labs. Accessed March 19, 2013. http://www.noh.ro/craiu.com/papers/papers/sadmind.html.

Satchell, Michael. "Captain Dragan's Serbian Cybercorps: How Milosevic took the Internet battlefield." *US News & World Report,* May 2, 1999. Accessed March 19, 2013. http://www.usnews.com/usnews/news/articles/990510/archive_000954.htm.

"Serb Hackers Reportedly Disrupt US Military Computer." BBC Monitoring Europe - Political Supplied by BBC Worldwide Monitoring. March 29, 1999. Accessed March 19, 2013. www.lexisnexis.com/hottopics/lnacademic.

Shaikh, Risadullah. "The futility of Indo-Pak cyber wars." Dawn.com. July 28, 2011. Accessed March 19, 2013. http://dawn.com/2011/07/28/the-futility-of-indo-pak-cyber-wars/.

Sheehan, Maeve. "Serbs hackers fight cyber war." *The Australian,* August 17, 1999. Accessed March 19, 2013. www.lexisnexis.com/hottopics/lnacademic.

Stenger, Richard. "FBI probes pro-China attacks on U.S. Web sites." CNN.com. April 17, 2001. Accessed March 19, 2013. http://asia.cnn.com/2001/TECH/internet/04/16/china.hacking/index.html.

Stoll, Clifford. *The Cuckoo's Egg: Tracking a Spy Through the Maze of Computer Espionage.* New York: Pocket Books, 2000.

"Timeline: A 40-year history of hacking." CNN.com. November 19, 2001. Accessed March 19, 2013. http://articles.cnn.com/2001-11-19/tech/hack.history.idg_1_phone-phreaks-chaos-computer-club-emmanuel-goldstein/2?_s=PM:TECH.

"Timeline of Major Events in Internet Security." Symantec.com. February 2006. Accessed March 19, 2013. http://www.symantec.com/about/news/resources/press_kits/securityintelligence/media/SSR-Timeline.pdf.

"Virus alert in Hacker War." *The Herald Sun,* April 23, 2001. Accessed March 19, 2013. http://www.lexisnexis.com/hottopics/lnacademic.

"Vision Of Warfare Future As Us And China Swap Cyber Attacks." *Birmingham Post,* May

8, 2001. Accessed March 19, 2013. www.lexisnexis.com/hottopics/lnacademic.

Wagstaff, Jeremy. "The Internet Could Be the Site of the Next China-U.S. Standoff." *Wall Street Journal*, April 30, 2001. Accessed March 19, 2013. http://online.wsj.com/article/SB98856633376453558.html.

"White House Web Site Hacked By Anti NATO Hactivists?" Newsbytes, March 30, 1999. Accessed March 19, 2013. www.lexisnexis.com/hottopics/lnacademic.

"Wikileaks Infowar not the first online protest action." Medialternatives (blog). December 12, 2010. Accessed March 19, 2013. http://medialternatives.blogetery.com/2010/12/15/intervasion-supports-anonymous/.

Moonlight Maze

Abreu, Elinor. "Cyber Attack Reveals Cracks in US Defense." PC World. May 9, 2001. Accessed March 19, 2013. http://www.pcworld.com/article/49563/cyberattack_reveals_cracks_in_us_defense.html.

Adams, James. "Virtual Defense." *Foreign Affairs* Vol. 80, No. 3, May/June 2001. Accessed March 27, 2013. http://www.foreignaffairs.com/articles/57037/james-adams/virtual-defense.

Armistead, Leigh. *Information Operations: The Hard Reality of Soft Power.* Dulles: Brassey's, Inc., 2004.

Arquilla, John and David Ronfeldt. "Cyberwar is Coming!" Comparative Strategy 12 (1993): 141–165.

Bayuk, Jennifer L., Jason Healey, Paul Rohmeyer, Marcus H. Sacks, Jeffrey Schmidt, and Joseph Weiss. *Cyber Security Policy Handbook.* Hoboken: Wiley, 2012.

Cordesman, Anthony H. *Cyber Threats, Information Warfare, and Critical Infrastructure Protection: Defending the US Homeland.* Washington, D.C.: Center for Strategic and International Studies, 2002.

"Cyberwar!" PBS Frontline. April 24, 2003. Accessed March 19, 2013. http://www.pbs.org/wgbh/pages/frontline/shows/cyberwar/warnings/#maze.

Defense Science Board. "Protecting the Homeland." Report of the Defense Science Board on Defensive Information Operations. 2000 Summer Study Vol. II. March 2001

Drogin, Bob. "Russians Seem to Be Hacking Into Pentagon." *Los Angeles Times*, October 7, 1999. Accessed March 19, 2013. http://www.sfgate.com/news/article/Russians-Seem-To-Be-Hacking-Into-Pentagon-2903309.php.

Gelinas, Ryan. "Cyberdeterrence and the Problem of Attribution." MA Thesis, Georgetown University, 2012.

Gourley, Bob. "JTF-CND to JTF-CND to Cybercom." CTO Vision. September 8, 2010. Accessed March 19, 2013. http://ctovision.com/2010/09/jtf-cnd-to-jtf-cno-to-jtf-gno-to-cybercom/.

Gourley, Bob. "The Maginot Line of Information Security." CTOVision.com. July 15, 2011. Accessed March 19, 2013. http://ctovision.com/2011/07/the-maginot-line-of-information-systems-security/.

Government Accountability Office. "Information Security: Challenges to Improving DOD's Incident Response Capabilities." Report to the Chairman, Committee on Armed Services, House of Representatives. March 2001.

Hamre, John. Interviewed in "Cyberwar!" PBS Frontline. February 18, 2003. Accessed March 28, 2013. http://www.pbs.org/wgbh/pages/frontline/shows/cyberwar/interviews/hamre.html.

Joyner, Christopher C. and Catherine Lotrionte. "Information Warfare as International Coercion: Elements of a Legal Framework." In European Journal of International Law, Vol. 12, No. 5, 825-865. New York: EJIL, 2001. Accessed March 27, 2013. http://www.ejil.org/pdfs/12/5/1552.pdf.

Kimery, Anthony. "Russian Hackers Get Into DOD in the US." Insight. November 3, 2002.

Kitfield, James. "CIA, FBI, and Pentagon Team to Fight Terrorism." National Journal, September 19, 2000. Accessed March 19, 2013. http://www.govexec.com/federal-news/2000/09/cia-fbi-and-pentagon-team-to-fight-terrorism/7073/.

Loeb, Vernon. "Pentagon Computers Under Assault." *Washington Post*, May 7, 2001. Accessed March 27, 2013. http://www.infosecnews.org/hypermail/0105/4047.html.

Nakashima, Ellen. "An Army of Tech-Savvy Warriors Has Been Fighting Its Battle in Cyberspace." *Washington Post*, September 23, 2010. Accessed March 27, 2013. http://www.washingtonpost.com/wp-dyn/content/article/2010/09/23/AR2010092303000.html.

Suro, Roberto. "FBI Lagging Behind on Cyber Crime." *Washington Post*, October 7, 1999.

Accessed March 19, 2013. http://www.washingtonpost.com/wp-srv/national/daily/ oct99/cyber7.htm.

Thomas, Timothy L. "Nation-State Cyber Strategies." In Cyberpower and International Security, edited by Franklin D. Kramer, Stuart H. Starr, and Larry K. Wentz, 476-477. Washington, D.C.: National Defense University Press, 2009.

Verton, Daniel. "Russia Hacking Stories Refuted." *Federal Computer Week.* September 27, 1999. Accessed March 19, 2013. http://fcw.com/articles/1999/09/27/russia-hacking-stories-refuted.aspx.

Vistica, Gregory. "We're in the Middle of a Cyber War." Newsweek. September 19, 1999. Accessed March 19, 2013. http://www.thedailybeast.com/newsweek/1999/09/19/ we-re-in-the-middle-of-a-cyerwar.html.

Part 4: Militarization

From TITAN RAIN to BYZANTINE HADES: Chinese Cyber Espionage

Alperovich, Dmitri. "Revealed: Operation Shady Rat." McAfee White Paper. August 2011. Accessed March 19, 2013. http://www.mcafee.com/us/resources/white-papers/wp-operation-shady-rat.pdf.

Barboza, David. "Hacking Inquiry Puts China's Elite in New Light." *New York Times*, February 21, 2010. Accessed March 27, 2013. http://www.nytimes.com/2010/02/22/technology/22cyber.html?_r=0.

"China Denies Government Links to Cyber Attacks on Google." Gov.cn. February 24, 2010. Accessed March 19, 2013. http://www.gov.cn/misc/2010-02/24/content_1540196.htm.

"Comprehensive National Cybersecurity Initiative, The." Washington, D.C.; White House, March 2010. Accessed March 19, 2013. http://www.whitehouse.gov/cybersecurity/comprehensive-national-cybersecurity-initiative.

"Cyber Attacks against China Remain Severe." Xinhua, March 19, 2012. Accessed March 19, 2013. http://news.xinhuanet.com/english/china/2012-03/19/c_131476422.htm.

"Cyber-attack Malware Identified." Yomuri Shimbun, January 4, 2013. Accessed March 19, 2013. http://www.yomiuri.co.jp/dy/national/T130103003334.htm.

FireWare Malware Intelligence Lab. "CFR Watering Hole Attack Details." Fireeye.com (blog). December 28, 2012. Accessed March 19, 2013. http://blog.fireeye.com/research/2012/12/council-foreign-relations-water-hole-attack-details.html.

Fulghum, David, Bill Sweetman, and Amy Butler. "China's Role in Spiraling JSF Costs." Aviation Week. February 3, 2012.

Goel, Vindu. "McAfee Says Microsoft Flaw Was a Factor in Cyberattacks." *New York Times*, January 14, 2010. Accessed March 19, 2013. http://bits.blogs.nytimes.com/2010/01/14/mcafee-cites-microsoft-flaw-in-cyberattacks/.

Goodrich, Jimmy. "Chinese Civilian Cybersecurity: Stakeholders, Strategies, and Policy." *In China and Cybersecurity: Political, Economic, and Strategic Dimensions*, edited by Jon Lindsay, 5-8. University of California, San Diego Workshop Report, April 2012.

Google. "A New Approach to China." Google. Official Blog. January 12, 2010. Accessed March 19, 2013. http://googleblog.blogspot.com/2010/01/new-approach-to-china. html.

Gorman, Siobhan, August Cole, and Yochi Dreazen. "Computer Spies Breach Fighter-Jet Project." Wall Street Journal, April 21, 2009. Accessed March 19, 2013. http://online. wsj.com/article/SB124027491029837401.html.

Graham, Bradley. "Hackers Attack Via Chinese Web Sites." *Washington Post*, August 25, 2005. Accessed March 27, 2013. http://www.washingtonpost.com/wp-dyn/content/ article/2005/08/24/AR2005082402318.html.

Greenert, Jonathan W. "Cooperation from Strength: The U.S., China and the South China Sea." Washington, D.C.: Center for a New American Security, January 11, 2012. Accessed March 19, 2013. http://www.cnas.org/node/7668.

Gross, Michael Joseph. "Enter the Cyber-dragon." *Vanity Fair*. September 2011. Accessed March 19, 2013. http://www.vanityfair.com/culture/features/2011/09/chinese-hacking-201109.

Gross, Michael Joseph. "Exclusive: Operation Shady RAT Unprecedented Cyber-espionage Campaign and Intellectual-Property Bonanza." *Vanity Fair*. August 2, 2011. Accessed March 19, 2013. http://www.vanityfair.com/culture/features/2011/09/ operation-shady-rat-201109.

Grow, Brian and Mark Hosenball. "Special report: In cyberspy vs. cyberspy, China has the edge." Reuters, April 14, 2011. Accessed March 19, 2013. http://www.reuters.com/ article/2011/04/14/us-china-usa-cyberespionage-idUSTRE73D24220110414.

Information Warfare Monitor. "Tracking Ghostnet: Investigating a Cyber Espionage Network." March 29, 2009. Accessed March 19, 2013. http://www.scribd.com/ doc/13731776/Tracking-GhostNet-Investigating-a-Cyber-Espionage-Network.

Information Warfare Monitor and Shadowserver Foundation. "Shadows in the Cloud: Investigating Cyber Espionage 2.0." April 6, 2010. Accessed March 19, 2013. http:// www.scribd.com/doc/29435784/SHADOWS-IN-THE-CLOUD-Investigating-Cyber-Espionage-2-0.

Krekel, Bryan, Patton Adams, and George Bakos. "Occupying the Information High Ground: Chinese Capabilities for Computer Network Operations and Cyber Espionage." Paper prepared for the U.S.-China Economic and Security Review Commission, Northrop Grumman Corp, March 2012. Accessed March 19, 2013. http://www.

uscc.gov/RFP/2012/USCC%20Report_Chinese_CapabilitiesforComputer_
NetworkOperationsandCyberEspionage.pdf.

Lynn, III, William J. Remarks on the Department of Defense Cyber Strategy, at National
Defense University, Washington, D.C., Thursday, July 14, 2011. Accessed March 19,
2013. http://www.defense.gov/speeches/speech.aspx?speechid=1593.

Mandiant. "APT 1: Exposing one of China's Cyber Espionage Units." Mandiant.com.
February 18, 2013. Accessed April 24, 2013. http://intelreport.mandiant.com/
Mandiant_APT1_Report.pdf

Markoff, John. "SecurID Company Suffers a Breach of Data Security." New York Times,
March 18, 2011. Accessed March 19, 2013. http://www.nytimes.com/2011/03/18/
technology/18secure.html.

Markoff, John and David Barboza. "2 China Schools Said to Be Tied to Online Attacks."
New York Times, February 18, 2010. Accessed March 19, 2013. http://www.nytimes.
com/2010/02/19/technology/19china.html.

Nakashima, Ellen. "Google China Cyberattack Part of Vast Espionage Campaign, Experts
Say." Washington Post, January 14, 2010. Accessed March 19, 2013. http://www.
washingtonpost.com/wp-dyn/content/article/2010/01/13/AR2010011300359.
html.

Nakashima, Ellen. "Google to enlist NSA to help it ward off cyberattacks." Washington Post,
February 4, 2010. Accessed March 19, 2013. http://www.washingtonpost.com/wp-
dyn/content/article/2010/02/03/AR2010020304057.html.

Nakashima, Ellen. "Report on 'Operation Shady RAT' Identifies Widespread Cyber-
spying." Washington Post, August 3 2011. Accessed March 19, 2013. http://www.
washingtonpost.com/national/national-security/report-identifies-widespread-cyber-
spying/2011/07/29/gIQAoTUmqI_story.html?hpid=z2.

Nakashima, Ellen. "US Plans to Issue Protest to China over Attacks on Google." Washington
Post, January 16, 2010. Accessed March 27, 2013. http://articles.washingtonpost.
com/2010-01-16/news/36816400_1_chinese-search-engine-internet-freedom-
chinese-government.

Norton-Taylor, Richard. "Titan Rain - How Chinese Hackers Targeted Whitehall." The
Guardian, September 4, 2007. Accessed March 27, 2013. http://www.guardian.co.uk/
uk/2007/sep/05/topstories3.politics.

Office of the National Counterintelligence Executive. "Foreign Spies Stealing US Economic Secrets in Cyberspace." NCIX.gov. October 2011. Accessed March 19, 2013. http://www.ncix.gov/publications/reports/fecie_all/Foreign_Economic_ Collection_2011.pdf.

"Pentagon's Cyber Pilot Dropout Rate Signals Trouble Ahead." Nextgov.com. October 25, 2012. Accessed March 19, 2013. http://www.nextgov.com/cybersecurity/ cybersecurity-report/2012/10/pentagons-cyber-pilot-dropout-rate-signals-trouble- ahead/59041/.

Peter, Tom A. "How Bad Was the Cyber Attack on Lockheed Martin?" The Christian Science Monitor, May 29. 2011. Accessed March 19, 2013. http://www.csmonitor. com/World/terrorism-security/2011/0529/How-bad-was-the-cyber-attack-on- Lockheed-Martin.

Pollpeter, Kevin. "Controlling the Information Domain: Space, Cyber, and Electronic Warfare." In Strategic Asia 2012-13: China's Military Challenge, edited by Tellis, Ashley and Tanner Travis. Seattle, Washington: National Bureau of Asian Research, October 2012.

Raasch, Chuck and Kevin Johnson, "Think Tanks Hit by Hackers from China, Other Nations," USA Today, October 4, 2012. Accessed March 19, 2013. http://www. usatoday.com/story/news/nation/2012/10/04/think-tanks-cyberattacks-china- hacking/1600269/.

Riley, Michael and Dune Lawrence. "Hackers Linked to China's Army Seen from EU to D.C." Bloomberg.com. July 26, 2012. Accessed March 19, 2013. http://www. bloomberg.com/news/2012-07-26/china-hackers-hit-eu-point-man-and-d-c-with- byzantine-candor.html.

Riley, Michael and John Walcott. "China-Based Hacking of 760 Companies Shows Cyber Cold War." Bloomberg.com. December 14, 2011. Accessed March 19, 2013. http:// www.bloomberg.com/news/2011-12-13/china-based-hacking-of-760-companies- reflects-undeclared-global-cyber-war.html.

Rogers, Mike. "Opening Statement Open Hearing: Cyber Threats and Ongoing Efforts to Protect the Nation." House Permanent Select Committee on Intelligence. October 4, 2011. Accessed March 19, 2013. http://intelligence.house.gov/sites/intelligence. house.gov/files/documents/100411CyberHearingRogers.pdf.

Rogin, Josh. "NSA Chief: Cybercrime constitutes the 'greatest transfer of wealth in history'." The Cable, July 9 2012. Accessed March 19, 2013. http://thecable.foreignpolicy.com/posts/2012/07/09/nsa_chief_cybercrime_constitutes_the_greatest_transfer_of_wealth_in_history.

Segal, Adam. "Chinese Computer Games." *Foreign Affairs* Vol. 91, no 2 (March/April 2012). Accessed March 27, 2013. http://www.foreignaffairs.com/articles/137244/adam-segal/chinese-computer-games.

Stokes, Mark and L.C. Russell Hsiao. "Countering Chinese Cyber Operations: Opportunities and Challenges for U.S. Interests." Project 2049 Institute. October 2012. Accessed March 19, 2013. http://project2049.net/documents/countering_chinese_cyber_operations_stokes_hsiao.pdf.

Thornburgh, Nathan. "Inside the Chinese Hack Attack." *Time.* August 25, 2005. Accessed March 27, 2013. http://www.time.com/time/nation/article/0,8599,1098371,00.html.

Tyson, Ann Scot and Dana Hedgpeth, "Officials Say Hackers Didn't Steal Critical Data About New Fighter Jet," *Washington Post*, April 22, 2009. Accessed March 19, 2013. http://www.washingtonpost.com/wp-dyn/content/article/2009/04/21/AR2009042103938.html.

The Estonian Cyberattacks

Aarelaid, Hillar. "Overview of Recent Incidents." Presentation given at the ENISA/ CERT CC Workshop on Mitigation of Massive Cyberattacks in Porto, Portugal, September 19, 2007. Accessed November 8, 2010. http://www.enisa.europa.eu/act/cert/events/files/ENISA_overview_of_recent_incidents_Aareleid.pdf.

Adomaitis, Nerious. "Estonia Calm after Red Army Site Riots, Russia Angry." Reuters, April 28, 2007. Accessed October 15, 2012. http://www.reuters.com/article/2007/04/28/us-estonia-russia-idUSL2873034620070428/.

Alas, Joe. "May 9 Protestors Call for Removing Bronze Soldier Statue." *Baltic Times*, May 10, 2006. Accessed March 19, 2013. http://www.baltictimes.com/news/articles/15345/.

Alas, Joe. "Reformists Pull Off Surprise Victory, Consider Dumping Centrists." *Baltic Times*, February 21, 2007. Accessed October 15, 2012. http://www.baltictimes.com/news/articles/17358/.

Alas, Joe. "Soldier Fails to Sway Elections." *Baltic Times*, February 21, 2007. Accessed October 15, 2012. http://www.baltictimes.com/news/articles/17358/.

Arbor Networks. Protecting IP Services from the Latest Trends in Botnet and DDoS Attacks. Burlington, MA: Arbor Network, 2012.

Arnold, Chloe. "Russian Group's Claims Reopen Debate on Estonian Cyberattacks." Radio Free Europe / Radio Liberty. 2009. Accessed March 19, 2013. http://www.rferl.org/articleprintview/1564694.html.

Ashmore, William C. "Impact of Alleged Russian Cyber Attacks." Baltic Security & Defence Review 11 (2009): 4-40. Accessed March 19, 2013. http://www.bdcol.ee/files/files/documents/Research/BSDR2009/1_%20Ashmore%20-%20Impact%20of%20Alleged%20Russian%20Cyber%20Attacks%20.pdf.

Berendson, Risto. "Küberrünnakute Taga Seisavad Profid." *Postimees*, May 3, 2007. Accessed March 19, 2013. http://www.tarbija24.ee/120507/esileht/siseuudised/258409.php.

Blank, Stephen. "Web War I: Is Europe's First Information War a New Kind of War?" Comparative Strategy 27, no. 3 (2008): 227-247. Accessed March 19, 2013. http://www.tandfonline.com/doi/pdf/10.1080/01495930802185312.

Bumgarner, John and Scott Borg. "Overview by the US-CCU of the Cyber Campaign against Georgia in August of 2008." US-CCU Special Report, U.S. Cyber Consequences Unit, August 2009. Accessed March 27, 2013. http://www.registan.net/wp-content/uploads/2009/08/US-CCU-Georgia-Cyber-Campaign-Overview.pdf.

Clover, Charles. "Kremlin-backed Group Behind Estonia Cyber Blitz." *Financial Times*, March 11, 2009. Accessed March 19, 2013. http://www.ft.com/intl/cms/s/0/57536d5a-0ddc-11de-8ea3-0000779fd2ac.html.

Danckworth, Till-Gneomar. "Estlands Außenpolitik nach dem Beitritt zur Europäischen Union: Handlungsoptionen eines Kleinstaates." Dissertation zur Erlangung des akademischen Grades doctor philosophiae (Dr. phil.), vorgelegt der Philosophischen Fakultät der Technischen Universität Chemnitz, 2007.

Eesti Statistika, *Statistical Yearbook of Estonia 2009*. Talinn: Statistics Estonia, 2009. Accessed April 24, 2013. http://www.stat.ee/publication-download-pdf?publication_id=18269

Eesti Statistika, *Statistical Yearbook of Estonia* 2010. Talinn: Statistics Estonia, 2009. Accessed April 24, 2013. http://www.stat.ee/publication-download-pdf?publication_id=19991

"Estland Im Visler: Ist Ein Internetangriff Der Ernstfall?" Frankfurter

Allgemeine Zeitung, June 18, 2007. Accessed November 4, 2010. http://www.faz.net/s/RubDDBDABB9457A437BAA85A49C26FB23A0/Doc~E7CCF88CEFB6F467BB8D75A400C07B959~ATpl~Ecommon~Scontent.html.

"Estonian DDoS - a Final Analysis." The H Security. May 31, 2007. Accessed March 19, 2013.   http://www.h-online.com/security/news/item/Estonian-DDoS-a-final-analysis-732971.html.

"Estonia Hit by Moscow Cyber War." BBC.co.uk. May 17, 2007. Accessed March 19, 2013. http://news.bbc.co.uk/2/hi/europe/6665145.stm.

"Estonian PM, justice minister insist that cyber attacks came from Kremlin computers" Baltic Times, June 8, 2007. Accessed April 24, 2013. http://www.baltictimes.com/news/articles/18038/

Evron, Gadi, Hillar Aarelaid. "Estonia: Information Warfare and Lessons Leaned." YouTube video, 56:40, posted by "Christiaan008," August 2007, http://www.youtube.com/watch?v=jxfinNdO-uc

Evron, Gadi. "Authoritatively, Who Was Behind the Estonian Attacks?" Darkreading.com. May 17, 2009. Accessed March 19, 2013. http://www.darkreading.com/security/news/227700882/authoritatively-who-was-behind-the-estonian-attacks.html.

Evron, Gadi. "Battling Botnets and Online Mobs. Estonia's Defence Efforts During the Internet War." Georgetown Journal of International Affairs 9, no. 1 (2008): 121-126. Accessed March 19, 2013.http://ec.europa.eu/information_society/policy/nis/docs/largescaleattacksdocs/s5_gadi_evron.pdf.

Evron, Gadi. "[NANOG] An account of the Estonian Internet War." Ge@linuxbox.org. May 20, 2008. Accessed January 2011. http://mailman.nanog.org/pipermail/nanog/2008-May/000676.html.

Finn, Peter. "Cyber Assaults on Estonia Typify a New Battle Tactic." Washington Post, May 19, 2007. Accessed March 19, 2013. http://www.washingtonpost.com/wpdyn.content/article/2007/05/18/AR2007051802122.html.

Goodman, W. "Cyber Deterrence - Tougher in Theory Than in Practice?" Strategic Studies (Fall 2010): 102-135. Accessed March 27, 2013. http://www.au.af.mil/au/ssq/2010/fall/goodman.pdf.

Grant, Rebecca. "Victory in Cyberspace." Special Report, Air Force Association. Arlington, VA: Air Force Association, October 2007. Accessed March 27, 2013. http://www.afa.

org/media/reports/victorycyberspace.pdf.

Hansabank Group. "Annual Report of Hansabank Group 2007." Tallinn: Hansabank, 2008. Accessed March 27, 2013. https://www.swedbank.ee/static/pdf/about/finance/reports/info_annual-report-2007_eng.pdf.

"Hansapanka Tabas Küberrünne." *Postimees*, May 10, 2007. Accessed March 19, 2013. http://www.tarbija24.ee/180507/esileht/majandus/259920.php.

Healey, Jason. "Beyond Attribution: Seeking National Responsibility for Cyber Attacks." Atlantic Council Issue Brief. January 2012. Accessed March 19, 2013. http://www.acus.org/publication/beyond-attribution-seeking-national-responsibility-cyberspace.

"Here We Go Again." *Baltic Times*, April 4, 2007. Accessed March 19, 2013. http://www.baltictimes.com/news/articles/17635/.

Hosking, Geoffrey. Rulers and Victims: The Russians in the Soviet Union. Cambridge: Belknap Press, 2009. Hyppönen, Mikko. "Unrest in Estonia." F-Secure Weblog. April 2007. Accessed March 19, 2013. http://www.f-secure.com/weblog/archives/00001181.html.

Hyppönen, Mikko. "Update on the Estonian DDoS Attacks." F-Secure.com (blog). April 30, 2007. Accessed March 19, 2013. http://f-secure.com/weblog/archives/00001183.html.

Johnson, Bobby. "Nokia Crisis Highlights Internal Struggle." BBC.co.uk. February 10, 2011. Accessed February 10, 2011. http://www.bbc.com/news/technology-12414595.

Kaeo, Merike. "Cyber Attacks on Estonia: Short Synopsis." Presentation at NANOG40, in Bellvue, WA, June 3-6, 2007. Accessed March 19, 2013. http://doubleshotsecurity.com/pdf/NANOG-eesti.pdf.

Kash, Wyatt. "Lessons from the Cyberattack on Estonia. Interview with Lauri Almann, Estonia's Permanent Undersecretary of Defence." Government Computer News. June 2008. Accessed March 19, 2013. http://gcn.com/Articles/2008/06/13/Lauri-Almann--Lessons-from-the-cyberattacks-on-Estonia.aspx?p=1.

Kershaw, Ian. Hitler: 1889-1936 Hubris. New York: W. W. Norton and Company, 2000.

Kosachev, Konstatin. "An Insult to Our War Dead." *The Guardian*, March 5, 2007. Accessed March 19, 2013. http://www.guardian.co.uk/commentisfree/2007/mar/06/comment.secondworldwar.

Landler, Mark; Markoff, John. "In Estonia, what may be the first war in cyberspace," *New York Times*, May 28, 2007. Accessed April 24, 2013. http://www.nytimes.com/2007/05/28/business/worldbusiness/28iht-cyberwar.4.5901141.html?pagewanted=all

Marsan, Carolyn Duffy. "How Close Is World War 3.0? Examining the Reality of Cyberwar in Wake of Estonian Attacks." Network World, August 22, 2007. Accessed March 19, 2013. http://www.networkworld.com/news/2007/082207-cyberwar.html.

Miller, Robert A., and Daniel T. Kuehl. "Cyberspace and the 'First Battle' in 21st-century War." In Support to Civil Authorities: Protecting the Homeland Newsletter. Fort Levenworth, Kansas: Center for Army Lessons Learned (2009): 117-126. Accessed March 27, 2013. http://usacac.army.mil/cac2/call/docs/10-52/10-52.pdf.

Mützenich, Rolf. "Die Nutzung Neuer Medien Als Instrument Russischer Außenpolitik in Seinem 'Nahen Ausland'." Website of German MP R. Mützenich. 2009. Accessed March 19, 2013. http://www.rolfmuetzenich.de/texte_und_reden/veroeffentlichungen/Muetzenich_SF.pdf.

Myers, Stephen Lee. "Debate Renewed: Did Moscow Free Estonia or Occupy It?" *New York Times*, January 25, 2007. Accessed March 19, 2013. http://www.nytimes.com/2007/01/25/world/europe/25tallinn.html.

"NATO Sees Recent Cyber Attacks on Estonia As Security Issue." DW-World.de. May 26, 2007. Accessed March 19, 2013. http://www.dw-world.de/dw/article/0,,2558579,00.html.

Poulsen, Kevin "'Cyberwar' and Estonia's Panic Attack." *Wired*. August 22, 2007. Accessed November 10, 2010. http://www.wired.com/threatlevel/2007/08/cyber-war-and-e/.

Nazario, José. "Estonian DDoS Attacks - A summary to date." Arbornetworks.com. May 17, 2007. Accessed March 19, 2013. http://asert.arbornetworks.com/2007/05/estonian-ddos-attacks-a-summary-to-date/.

Ottis, Rain. "Conflicts in Cyberspace: Evgeny Morozov on Cyber Myths." Conflictsincyberspace (blog). June 26, 2009. Accessed December 12, 2011. http://conflictsincyberspace.blogspot.com/2009/06/evgeny-morozov-on-cyber-myths.html.

Rantanen, Miiska. "Virtual Harassment, but for Real." Helsingin Sanomat International Edition, May 8, 2007. Accessed March 19, 2013. http://www.hs.fi/english/article/Virtual+harassment+but+for+real+/1135227099868.

Segura,V. and J. Lahuerta. "Modeling the Economic Incentives of DDoS Attacks: Femtocell Case Study." *In Economics of Information Security and Privacy*, edited by Tyler Moore, David J. Pym, and Christos Ioannidis, 107-119. New York: Springer, 2010.

Sietmann, Richard. "22C3: Pro Und Kontra E-Voting." Heise.de. December 29, 2005. Accessed January 15, 2011. http://www.heise.de/newsticker/meldung/22C3-Pro-und-Kontra-e-Voting-161678.html.

Socor, Vladimir. "Moscow Stung by Estonian Ban on Totalitarianism's Symbols." Eurasia Daily Monitor,The Jamestown Foundation, January 26, 2007. Accessed March 19, 2013. http://www.jamestown.org/programs/edm/single/?tx_ttnews[tt_news]=32427&tx_ttnews[backPid]=171&no_cache=1.

Thomson, Iain. "Russia 'hired Botnets' for Estonia Cyber-war - Russian Authorities Accused of Collusion with Botnet Owners." Computing.co.uk. 2007. Accessed March 19, 2013. http://www.computing.co.uk/vnunet/news/2191082/claims-russia-hired-botnets.

"US Embassy Cables: Germany Behind NATO Proposal for Baltic States." *The Guardian*, December 6, 2010. Accessed March 19, 2013. http://www.guardian.co.uk/world/us-embassy-cables-documents/240187.

"Venemaa Keeldub Endiselt Koostööst Küberrünnakute Uurimisel." ERR UUDISED, December 13, 2008. Accessed April 24, 2013. http://uudised.err.ee/index. php?06147571

"Was It Worth It?" *Baltic Times*, May 1, 2008. Accessed October 23, 2012. http://www. baltictimes.com/news/articles/20360/.

"What We Do - EU Agency for Large-scale IT Systems." European Commission - Home Affairs. March 5, 2013. Accessed March 27, 2012. http://ec.europa.eu/dgs/home-affairs/what-we-do/policies/borders-and-visas/agency/index_en.htm.

Woodcock, Bill. "Building a Secure Cyber Future: Attacks on Estonia, Five Years On." Transcript of the event hosted by the Atlantic Council, in Washington, D.C., May 23, 2012. Accessed May 23, 2012. http://www.acus.org/event/building-secure-cyber-future-attacks-estonia-five-years/transcript; Audio transcript, http://www.acus.org/event/building-secure-cyber-future-attacks-estonia-five-years.

The Russo-Georgian War 2008

"1999: Chinese Anger at Embassy Bombing." BBC.co.uk. May 9, 1999. Accessed March 19, 2013. http://news.bbc.co.uk/onthisday/hi/dates/stories/may/9/ newsid_2519000/2519271.stm.

Berryman, John. "Russia, NATO Enlargement, and 'Regions of Privileged Interests'." In *Russian Foreign Policy in the 21st Century*, edited by Roger E. Kanet, 228-245. New York: Palgrave Macmillian, 2011.

Bumgarner, John and Scott Borg. "Overview by the US-CCU of the Cyber Campaign against Georgia in August of 2008." US-CCU Special Report, U.S. Cyber Consequences Unit. August 2009. Accessed March 27, 2013. http://www.registan.net/wp-content/ uploads/2009/08/US-CCU-Georgia-Cyber-Campaign-Overview.pdf.

Burton, Fred and Dan Burges. "Russian Organized Crime." Stratfor.com. November 14, 2007. Accessed September 23, 2012. http://www.stratfor.com/weekly/russian_ organized_crime.

Carr, Jeffrey. *Inside Cyber Warfare: Mapping the Cyber Underworld*. Sebastopol, CA: O'Reilley Media Inc., 2012.

Chase, Michael S. and James C. Mulvenon. *You've Got Dissent: Chinese Dissident Use of the Internet and Beijing's Counter-Strategies*. Santa Monica, CA: RAND, 2002.

"China, Taiwan, Tibet: Fraying at the Edges." *The Economist*. July 10, 2008. Accessed March 19, 2013. http://www.economist.com/opinion/displayStory.cfm?story_ id=11707478.

"China's Top Legislature Slams EU Parliament for Tibet Resolution." Xinhua, March 13, 2009. Accessed October 17, 2009. http://news.xinhuanet.com/english/2009-03/13/ content_11007789.htm.

Clarke, Richard and Robert Knake. *Cyber War: The Next Threat to National Security and What To Do About It*. New York: Harper Collins Publisher, 2010.

Clover, Charles. "Kremlin-Backed Group behind Estonia Cyber Blitz." *Financial Times*, March 11, 2009. Accessed March 19, 2013. http://www.ft.com/cms/s/0/57536d5a- 0ddc-11de-8ea3-0000779fd2ac.html?nclick_check=1.

Cornell, Svante and Frederick Starr. *The Guns of August 2008: Russia's War in Georgia*. New York: Central Asia-Caucasus Institute, 2009.

Danchev, Dancho. "Coordinated Russia vs. Georgia cyber attack Cyber Attack in progress." ZD Net.com. August 11, 2008. Accessed October 30, 2012. http://www.zdnet.com/

blog/security/coordinated-russia-vs-georgia-cyber-attack-in-progress/1670.

Danchev, Dancho. "Georgia President's web site under DDoS attack from Russian hackers." ZD Net.com (blog). July 22, 2008. Accessed April 15, 2012. http://www.zdnet.com/blog/security/georgia-presidents-web-site-under-ddos-attack-from-russian-hackers/1533.

Espiner, Tom. "Georgia accuses Russia of coordinated cyberattack." C-Net.com. August 11, 2008. Accessed April 17, 2012. http://news.cnet.com/8301-1009_3-10014150-83.html.

George, Julia A. *The Politics of Ethnic Separatism in Russia and Georgia*. New York: Palgrave Macmillian, 2009.

Goodin, Dan. "Georgian cyber attacks launched Cyber Attacks Launched by Russian Crime Gangs." The Register, August 18, 2009. Accessed April 22, 2012. http://www.theregister.co.uk/2009/08/18/georgian_cyber_attacks/.

Gorman, Siobhan. "Hackers Stole IDs for Attacks." *The Wall Street Journal*, August 17, 2009. Accessed August 17, 2009. http://online.wsj.com/article/SB125046431841935299.html.

Greylogic. "Project Grey Goose Phase I Report: The evolving state of cyber warfare." Scribd.com. March 20, 2009. Accessed September 23, 2012. http//: www.scribd.com/doc/6967393/Project-Grey-Goose-Phase-I-Report.

Greylogic. "Project Grey Goose Phase II Report: The evolving state of cyber warfare." Scribd.com. March 20, 2009. Accessed September 23, 2012. http://www.scribd.com/doc/13442963/Project-Grey-Goose-Phase-II-Report.

Harding, Luka. "WikiLeaks cables: Russian government 'using mafia dirty work'." *The Guardian*, December 1, 2010. Accessed April 22, 2012. http://www.guardian.co.uk/world/2010/dec/01/wikileaks-cable-spain-russian-mafia.

Healey, Jason. "Beyond Attribution: Seeking National Responsibility for Cyber Attacks." Atlantic Council issue brief. February 22, 2012. Accessed March 19, 2013. http://www.acus.org/publication/beyond-attribution-seeking-national-responsibility-cyberspace.

"High Profile Foreign Sites." Attrition.org. November 30, 2000. Accessed March 27, 2013. http://attrition.org/security/commentary/hp-foreign-01.html.

Hollis, David. "Cyberwar Case Study: Georgia 2008." Small Wars Journal, January 6, 2011.

Accessed *April 15, 2012.* http://smallwarsjournal.com/blog/journal/docs-temp/639-hollis.pdf.

Hulme, George V. "NIPC Warns of Chinese Hacktivism." Information Week. April 27, 2001. Accessed October 16, 2009. http://www.informationweek.com/nipc-warns-of-chinese-hacktivism/6505353.

Information Warfare Monitor. "Tracking GhostNet: Investigating a Cyber Espionage Network." March 29, 2009. Accessed March 29, 2013. http://www.scribd.com/doc/13731776/Tracking-GhostNet-Investigating-a-Cyber-Espionage-Network.

Keizer, Gregg. "Russian Hacker 'Militia' Mobilizes to Attack Georgia." Network World. August 13, 2008. Accessed April 21, 2012. http://www.networkworld.com/news/2008/081208-russian-hacker-militia-mobilizes-to.html.

Korns, Stephen W. and Joshua E. Kastenberg. "Georgia's Cyber Left Hook." Parameters Vol. XXXVIII, No. 4 (2009): 60-76. Accessed March 27, 2013. http://www.carlisle.army.mil/USAWC/parameters/Articles/08winter/korns.pdf.

Krebs, Brian. "Report: Russian Hacker Forums Fueled Georgia Cyber Attacks." *Washington Post*, October 16, 2008. Accessed March 27, 2013. http://voices.washingtonpost.com/securityfix/2008/10/report_russian_hacker_forums_f.html.

Markoff, John. "Before the Gunfire, Cyberattacks." *New York Times*, August 12, 2008. Accessed April 15, 2012. http://www.nytimes.com/2008/08/13/technology/13cyber.html?_r=1.

Melikishvili, Alexander. "The Cyber Dimension of Russia's Attack on Georgia." The Jamestown Foundation. September 12, 2008. Accessed April 21, 2012. http://www.jamestown.org/single/?no_cache=1&tx_ttnews%5Btt_news%5D=33936.

Menn, Joseph. "Expert: Cyber-attacks on Georgia websites tied to mob, Russian government." *Los Angeles Times,* August 13, 2008. Accessed April 15, 2012. http://latimesblogs.latimes.com/technology/2008/08/experts-debate.html.

Nazario, José. "Georgia On My Mind – Political DDoS." DDoS and Security Reports: The Arbor Networks Security Blog. July 20, 2008. Accessed October 30, 2012. http://ddos.arbornetworks.com/2008/07/georgia-on-my-mind-political-ddos/.

Nichol, Jim. "Russia-Georgia Conflict in August 2008: Context and Implications for U.S. Interests." Congressional Research Service. March 3, 2009. Accessed *April 15, 2012.* http://www.fas.org/sgp/crs/row/RL34618.pdf.

"North Korea May Be Behind Wave of Cyber Attacks." Foxnews.com. July 8, 2009. Accessed October 17, 2009. http://www.foxnews.com/story/0,2933,530645,00. html

"One Hundred Linked to International Computer Hacking Ring Charged by United States and Egypt in Operation Phish Phry." FBI – Los Angeles. October 7, 2009. Accessed October 16, 2009.. http://losangeles.fbi.gov/pressrel/2009/la100709.htm.

"Putin in Veiled Attack on Estonia." BBC.co.uk. May 9, 2007. Accessed October 18, 2009. http://news.bbc.co.uk/2/hi/europe/6638029.stm.

Rhodes, Ron. Cyber Meltdown. Eugene: Harvest House Publishers, 2011.

Rosenthal, Elisabeth. "Crisis in the Balkans, China: More Protests in Beijing as Officials Study Bombing Errors." New York Times, May 10, 1999. Accessed October 16, 2009. http://www.nytimes.com/1999/05/10/world/crisis-balkans-china-more-anti-us-protests-beijing-officials-study-bombing-error.html.

"Russia-Georgia conflict: Why both sides have valid points." The Christian Science Monitor. August 19, 2008. Accessed April 14, 2012. http://www.csmonitor.com/World/Europe/2008/0819/p12s01-woeu.html.

Schönbohm, Arne. Germany's Security - Cyber Crime and Cyber War. Münster: MV-Verlag, 2012.

Shanker, Thom and John Markoff. "Halted '03 Iraq Plan Illustrates U.S. Fear of Cyberwar Risk." New York Times, August 1, 2009. Accessed October 16, 2009. http://www.nytimes.com/2009/08/02/us/politics/02cyber.html.

Sheeter, Laura. "Russia Slams Estonia Statue Move." BBC.co.uk. January 17, 2007. Accessed October 17, 2009. http://news.bbc.co.uk/2/hi/europe/6273117.stm.

"Tallinn Tense after Deadly Riots." BBC.co.uk. April 28, 2007. Accessed October 17, 2009. http://news.bbc.co.uk/2/hi/europe/6602171.stm.

Tikk, Eneken, Kadri Kaska, Kristel Rünnimeri, Mari Kert, Anna-Maria Talihärm, and Liis Vihul. "Cyber Attacks against Georgia: Legal Lessons Identified." Cooperative Cyber Defence Centre of Excellence. November 2008. Accessed April 15, 2012. www.carlisle.army.mil/DIME/documents/Georgia%201%200.pdf.

Tikk, Eneken, Kadri Kasha, and Liis Vihul. "International Cyber Incidents: Legal Considerations." CCD COE Publications, 2010. Accessed March 27, 2013. http://www.ccdcoe.org/publications/books/legalconsiderations.pdf.

Verizon Business Risk Team, The. "Verizon Data Breach Report for 2008." Verizon. Accessed March 19, 2013. http://www.verizonbusiness.com/resources/security/ databreachreport.pdf.

Weitz, Richard. *Global Security Watch Russia: A Reference Handbook.* Santa Barbara: Praeger Security International, 2010.

Wentworth, Travis. "You've Got Malice." Newsweek: The Daily Beast, August 22, 2008. Accessed April 15, 2012. http://www.thedailybeast.com/newsweek/2008/08/22/ you-ve-got-malice.html.

Ziegler, Charles E. "Russia, Central Asia, and the Caucasus after the Georgia Conflict." In *Russian Foreign Policy in the 21st century*, edited by Roger E. Kanet, 155-180. New York: Palgrave Macmillian, 2011.

Zigfield, Kim. "Re-Imposing Totalitarian Information Control in Russia." American Thinker. September 30, 2009. Accessed March 19, 2013. http://www.americanthinker. com/2009/09/reimposing_totalitarian_inform.html.

Opetation BUCKSHOT YANKEE

Alexander, Keith. Interviewed by the House Armed Subcommittee (transcript). Cyberspace Operations Testimony. Washington, D.C. 2010. Accessed March 19, 2013. http://www. defense.gov/home/features/2011/0411_cyberstrategy/docs/House%20Armed%20 Services%20Subcommittee%20Cyberspace%20Operations%20Testimony%20 20100923.pdf.

Anderson, Brian and Barbara Anderson. *Seven Deadliest USB Attacks.* Burlington, MA: Elsevier, 2010.

Barnes, Julian E. "Pentagon computer networks attacked." *Los Angeles Times*, November 28, 2008. Accessed November 1, 2012. http://articles.latimes.com/2008/nov/28/nation/ na-cyberattack28/2.

Lynn III, William J. "Defending a New Domain: The Pentagon's Cyberstrategy." *Foreign Affairs.* September/October 2010. Accessed November 1, 2012. http://www. foreignaffairs.com/articles/66552/william-j-lynn-iii/defending-a-new-domain.

Nakashima, Ellen. "Cyber-intruder sparks massive federal response – and debate over dealing with threats." *Washington Post*, December 8, 2011. Accessed November 1, 2012. http://www.washingtonpost.com/national/national-security/cyber-intruder-sparks-response-debate/2011/12/06/gIQAxLuFgO_print.html.

Shachtman, Noah. "Hackers, Troops Rejoice: Pentagon Lifts Thumb-Drive Ban (Updated)." *Wired*. February 18, 2010. Accessed November 1, 2012. http://www.wired.com/ dangerroom/2010/02/hackers-troops-rejoice-pentagon-lifts-thumb-drive-ban/.

Shachtman, Noah. "Under Worm Assault, Military Bans Disks, USB Drives." *Wired*. November 19, 2008. Accessed November 1, 2012. http://www.wired.com/ dangerroom/2008/11/army-bans-usb-d/.

Steward, Phil and Jim Wolf. "Old worm won't die after 2008 attack on U.S. military." Reuters, June 16, 2011. Accessed November 1, 2012. http://www.reuters.com/ article/2011/06/17/us-usa-cybersecurity-worm-idUSTRE75F5TB20110617.

"W32.SillyFDC." Symantec.com. February 27, 2007. Accessed November 1, 2012. http:// www.symantec.com/security_response/writeup.jsp?docid=2006-071111-0646-99.

Stuxnet, Flame, and Duqu – the OLYMPIC GAMES

Albright, David and Paul Brannan. "IAEA Iran Safeguards Report: Iran Degrading Safeguards Effectiveness; Low Enriched Uranium Production Holds Steady." Institute for Science and International Security. September 6, 2010. Accessed September 9, 2012. http://isis-online.org/uploads/isis-reports/documents/ISIS_Analysis_IAEA_ Iran_Report_September_2010.pdf.

Albright, David, Paul Brannan, and Christina Walrond. "Stuxnet Malware and Natanz: Update of ISIS 22 December, 2010 Report." *Washington Post*, February 15, 2011. Accessed March 24, 2011. http://media.washingtonpost.com/wp-srv/world/ documents/stuxnet_update_15Feb2011.pdf.

Barnes, Ed. "Mystery Surrounds Cyber Missile That Crippled Iran's Nuclear Weapons Ambitions." Foxnews.com. November 26, 2012. Accessed March 23, 2011. http:// www.foxnews.com/scitech/2010/11/26/secret-agent-crippled-irans-nuclear- ambitions/.

Berkow, Jameson. "Iranian Cyber Attacks Against 'Enemies': Report." *Financial Post*, March 14, 2011. Accessed April 6, 2011. http://business.financialpost.com/2011/03/14/ iranian-military-launches-cyber-attacks-against-enemies-report/#more-34277.

Broad, William J., John Markoff, and David E. Sanger. "Israeli Test on Worm Called Crucial in Iran Nuclear Delay." *New York Times*, January 15, 2011. Accessed March 25, 2011.

http://www.nytimes.com/2011/01/16/world/middleeast/16stuxnet.html?hp.

Bruno, Greg. "Iran's Balistic Missile Program." CFR.org. July 23, 2012. Accessed March 23, 2011. http://www.cfr.org/iran/irans-ballistic-missile-program/p20425.

Bruno, Greg. "Iran's Nuclear Program." CFR.org. March 2012. Accessed March 23, 2011. http://www.cfr.org/iran/irans-nuclear-program/p16811.

Bush, George W. "President Delivers State of the Union Address." White House. January 29, 2002. Accessed March 2011. http://georgewbush-whitehouse.archives.gov/news/releases/2002/01/20020129-11.html.

Central Intelligence Agency. "Special National Intelligence Estimate." GWU.edu. August 1974. Accessed March 23, 2011. http://www.gwu.edu/%7Ensarchiv/NSAEBB/NSAEBB240/snie.pdf.

Clarke, Richard and Robert K. Knake. *Cyber War: The Next Threat to National Security and What to Do About It.* New York, NY: Harper-Collins Publishers, 2010.

Clayton, Mark. "Stuxnet: Ahmadinejad Admits Cyberweapon Hit Iran Nuclear Program." *Christian Science Monitor*, November 30, 2012. Accessed March 23, 2011. http://www.csmonitor.com/USA/2010/1130/Stuxnet-Ahmadinejad-admits-cyberweapon-hit-Iran-nuclear-program.

Couts, Andrew. "Iran Accused of Attempted Cyber-Attack on Google, Yahoo, Skype." Digital Trends. March 25, 2011. Accessed April 6, 2011. http://www.digitaltrends.com/computing/iran-accused-of-cyber-attack-on-google-yahoo-skype/.

Dunn, John E. "Iran's Orwellian Cyber-Police Target Dissent." CSO Online, January 25, 2011. Accessed April 6, 2011. http://www.csoonline.com/article/657702/iran-s-orwellian-cyber-police-target-dissent.

Erdbrink, Thomas. "Iran Confirms Attack by Virus That Collects Information." *New York Times*, May 29, 2012. Accessed September 14, 2012. http://www.nytimes.com/2012/05/30/world/middleeast/iran-confirms-cyber-attack-by-new-virus-called-flame.html.

Falliere, Nicolas, Liam O. Murchu, and Eric Chien. "The Stuxnet Worm." Symantec.com. February 2011. Accessed March 23, 2011. http://www.symantec.com/business/outbreak/index.jsp?id=stuxnet.

Fildes, Jonathan. "Stuxnet virus targets and spread revealed." BBC.co.uk. February 15, 2011. Accessed March 25, 2011. http://www.bbc.co.uk/news/technology-12465688.

Fogarty, Kevin. "Iran Responds to Stuxnet by Cyberwar Militia." IT World. January 12, 2011. Accessed April 6, 2011. http://www.itworld.com/security/133469/iran-responds-stuxnet-expanding-cyberwar-militia.

Ghajar, Shayan. "Iran Cites Western Experts to Blame Israel for Stuxnet Virus." Inside Iran.org. September 27, 2010. Accessed March 25, 2011. http://www.insideiran.org/media-analysis/iran-cites-western-experts-to-blame-israel-for-stuxnet-virus/.

Gross, Michael Joseph. "Stuxnet Worm. A Declaration of Cyber-War." *Vanity Fair*. April 2011. Accessed March 24, 2011. http://www.vanityfair.com/culture/features/2011/04/stuxnet-201104?currentPage=1.

Jackson, William. "Stuxnet Shut Down by its Own Kill Switch." Government Computer News, June 26, 2012. Accessed September 5, 2012. http://gcn.com/articles/2012/06/26/stuxnet-demise-expiration-date.aspx.

Jaseb, Hossein and Fredrik Dahl. "Ahmadinejad says Israel will 'Disappear'." Reuters, June 3, 2008. Accessed March 24, 2011. http://www.reuters.com/article/2008/06/03/us-iran-israel-usa-idUSL0261250620080603.

Kaspersky Lab. "Kaspersky Lab and ITU Research Reveals New Advanced Cyber Threat." Kaspersky.com. May 28, 2012. Accessed September 14, 2012. http://www.kaspersky.com/about/news/virus/2012/Kaspersky_Lab_and_ITU_Research_Reveals_New_Advanced_Cyber_Threat.

Keizer, Gregg. "Stuxnet worm can re-infect scrubbed PCs." ComputerWorld. September 27, 2010. Accessed April 6, 2011. http://www.computerworld.com/s/article/9188238/Stuxnet_worm_can_re_infect_scrubbed_PCs.

Kessler, Carol. "Nuclear Nonproliferation – Does Iran Want a Nuclear Weapon?" Pacific Northwest Center for Global Security. July 21, 2009. Accessed March 23, 2011. http://pnwcgs.pnl.gov/pdfs/WhyIran.pdf.

Langner, Ralph. "Ralph Langner: Cracking Stuxnet, a 21st-century Cyber Weapon." TED Talks. March 2011. Accessed April 6, 2011. http://www.ted.com/talks/ralph_langner_cracking_stuxnet_a_21st_century_cyberweapon.html.

Lappin, Yaakov. "US under secretary of state: We Won't Allow Nuclear Iran." YNet News, January 21, 2007. Accessed April 4, 2011. http://www.ynetnews.com/articles/0,7340,L-3355144,00.html.

Markhoff, John. "Malware Aimed at Iran Hit Five Sites, Report Says." *New York Times*, February 11, 2011. Accessed April 6, 2011. http://www.nytimes.com/2011/02/13/

science/13stuxnet.html?_r=1&scp=1&sq=Malware%20Aimed%20At%20Iran%20
Hit%20Five%20Sites,%20Report%20Says&st=cse.

Markoff, John and David E. Sanger. "In a Computer Worm, a Possible Biblical Clue."
New York Times, September 29, 2010. Accessed March 25, 2011. http://www.nytimes.
com/2010/09/30/world/middleeast/30worm.html?pagewanted=1&_r=3&hpw.

McConnell, Michael. "McConnell Cites 'Overwhelming Evidence of Iran's Support for
Iraqi Insurgents." Council on Foreign Relations. June 28, 2007. Accessed March 24,
2011.   http://www.cfr.org/intelligence/mcconnell-cites-overwhelming-evidence-
irans-support-iraqi-insurgents/p13692.

Nakashima, Ellen. "Defense Official Discloses Cyberattack." *Washington Post*, August 25,
2010. Accessed September 14, 2012. http://www.washingtonpost.com/wpdyn/
content/article/2010/08/24/AR2010082406528.html.

Nakashima, Ellen, Greg Miller, and Julie Tate. "U.S., Israel Developed Flame Computer
Virus to Slow Iranian Nuclear Efforts, Officials Say." *Washington Post*, June 19, 2012.
Accessed September 7, 2012. http://www.washingtonpost.com/world/national-
security/us-israel-developed-computer-virus-to-slow-iranian-nuclear-efforts-
officials-say/2012/06/19/gJQA6xBPoV_story.html.

Neff, Donald. "Israel Bombs Iraq's Osirak Nuclear Research Facility." Washington Report
on Middle East Affairs. June 1995. Accessed March 24, 2011. http://www.wrmea.
com/component/content/article/162-1995-june/7823-israel-bombs-iraqs-osirak-
nuclear-research-facility.html.

"Report: Iran's Nuclear Capacity Unharmed, Contrary to U.S. Assessment." Reuters, January
22, 2011. Accessed April 6, 2011. http://www.haaretz.com/news/international/
report-iran-s-nuclear-capacity-unharmed-contrary-to-u-s-assessment-1.338522.

Sanger, David E. "Obama Order Sped Up Wave of Cyberattacks against Iran." *New
York Times*, June 1, 2012. Accessed September 7, 2012. http://www.nytimes.
com/2012/06/01/world/middleeast/obama-ordered-wave-of-cyberattacks-against-
iran.html?pagewanted=all.

Sanger, David E. "U.S. Rejected Aid for Israeli Raid on Iranian Nuclear Site." *New York Times*,
January 10, 2009. Accessed March 25, 2011. http://www.nytimes.com/2009/01/11/
washington/11iran.html?pagewanted=1&_r=3&sq=israel%20iran&st=cse&scp=1.

Sarif, M. Javad. "Tackling the Iran-US Crisis." Journal of International Affairs 60, no. 2
(Spring/Summer 2007): 73-94.

"Siemens Industry Online Support." Siemens.com. November 3, 2011. Accessed September 5, 2012. http://support.automation.siemens.com/WW/llisapi.dll?func=cslib.csinfo&-objid=43876783&nodeid0=10805583&caller=view&lang=en&siteid=cseus&akt-prim=0&objaction=csopen&extranet=standard&viewreg=WW.

Skow, John. "The Long Ordeal of the Hostages." *Time.* January 26, 1981. Accessed March 24, 2011. http://www.time.com/time/magazine/article/0,9171,954605-1,00.html.

Toor, Amar. "Ahmadinejad Says Iran's Nuclear Facilities Were Hit by Stuxnet Worm." Switched. November 30, 2011. Accessed April 6, 2011. http://www.switched.com/2010/11/30/mahmoud-ahmadinejad-iran-nuclear-stuxnet-worm/.

Venere, Guilherme and Peter Szor. "The Day of the Golden Jackal – The Next Tale in the Stuxnet Files: Duqu Updated." McAfee.com (blog). October 18, 2011. Accessed September 14, 2012. http://blogs.mcafee.com/mcafee-labs/the-day-of-the-golden-jackal---further-tales-of-the-stuxnet-files.

"W32.Duqu: The Precursor to the Next Stuxnet" Symantec.com. October 24, 2011. Accessed September 7, 2012. http://www.symantec.com/connect/w32_duqu_precursor_next_stuxnet.

"War in the Fifth Domain." *The Economist.* July 1, 2010. Accessed September 14, 2012. http://www.economist.com/node/16478792.

Weiss, Stanley A. "Israel and Iran: The Bonds that Tie Persians and Jews." *New York Times,* July 10, 2006. Accessed March 24, 2011. http://www.nytimes.com/2006/07/10/opinion/10iht-edweiss.2165689.html.

Williams, Christopher. "Israeli security chief celebrates Stuxnet cyber attack." *The Telegraph,* February 16, 2011. Accessed March 25, 2011. http://www.telegraph.co.uk/technology/news/8326274/Israeli-security-chief-celebrates-Stuxnet-cyber-attack.html.

Yoong, Sean. "Ahmadinejad: Destroy Israel, End Crisis." *Washington Post,* August 3, 2006. Accessed September 23, 2012. http://www.washingtonpost.com/wp-dyn/content/article/2006/08/03/AR2006080300629.html.

Part 5: Other National Perspectives

Japan's Cyber Security History

"About JPCERT." JPCERT. 2012. Accessed March 19, 2013. http://www.jpcert.or.jp/english/about/.

"An Overview of ISMS Conformity Assessment Scheme in Japan." Information Management System Promotion Center. Last updated May 20, 2010. Accessed March 19, 2013. http://www.isms.jipdec.jp/en/about/index.html.

"Arrests and Consultations of Cybercrime in 2003." National Police Agency. 2003. Accessed March 19, 2013. http://www.npa.go.jp/cyber/english/statics/2003.htm.

Baker, Stewart. "Decoding OECD Guidelines for Information Security Policy." International Law Journal 31 (1997): 729.

Baker, Stewart. "Japan Enters the Crypto Wars." *Wired*. September 1996. Accessed March 19, 2013. http://www.wired.com/wired/archive/4.09/es.crypto.html.

Bar, Francois and Emily Murase. "The Potential for Transatlantic Cooperation in Telecommunications Service Trade in Asia." Berkeley Roundtable on the International Economy. November 1997. Accessed March 19, 2013. http://brie.berkeley.edu/econ/publications/wp/wp108.html.

"Chinese hackers deface Yasukuni Shrine website...again." Thedarkvisistor.com. January 1, 2009. Accessed March 27, 2013. http://www.thedarkvisitor.com/2009/01/chinese-hackers-deface-yasukuni-shrine-websiteagain/.

Computer Fraud and Abuse Act, The, 18 U.S.C. Section 1030 (e)(2). Accessed March 28, 2013. http://www.columbia.edu/~mr2651/ecommerce3/2nd/statutes/ComputerFraudAbuseAct.pdf.

"Cyber-attacks target 20 ministries, agencies." Asahi Shimbun, October 10 2011. Accessed February 20, 2013. http://ajw.asahi.com/article/behind_news/social_affairs/AJ2011103116185.

"Cyber Force Center." FIRST.org. Accessed August 23, 2012. http://www.first.org/members/teams/cfc.

"Dell to Supply Defense Agency PCs." *Japan Times*, April 15, 2006. Accessed February 20, 2013. http://www.japantimes.co.jp/news/2006/04/15/business/dell-to-supply-defense-agency-pcs/

Eguchi, Masahiro. "How Have ECOM Guidlelines for the Protection of Personal Information Evolved?" 2008. Accessed February 20, 2013. http://www.jipdec.or.jp/archives/ecom/journal/2008e/topics/top2.html.

Electronic Network Consortium. "Privacy Protection in Japan." PowerPoint presentation by the Electronic Network Consortium, New York, NY, June 2000. Accessed March 19, 2013. pics.enc.or.jp/privacy/download/documents/pi(privacy_jpn).ppt.

Gladstone, Julia Alpert. "Does the EC Council Directive No. 95/46/EC Mandate the Use of Anonymous Digital Currency?" Fordham International Law Journal 22, 5 (1998): 1907-1923.

Handerhan, Ryan. "Japanese and American Computer Crime Policy." Dietrich College Honor Thesis. Paper 69. 2010. Accessed March 27, 2013. http://repository.cmu.edu/hsshonors/69/.

Hiramatsu, Tsuyoshi. "Protecting Telecommunications Privacy in Japan." Communications of the ACM 36, 8 (August 1993): 74-77.

Hongo, Jun. "File-Sharing: Handle Winny at your own Risk." *Japan Times*, October 27, 2009. Accessed March 19, 2013. http://www.japantimes.co.jp/text/nn2009102711.html.

"Information Security." Japanese Ministry of Economy, Trade and Industry. Accessed March 19, 2013. http://www.meti.go.jp/english/information/data/IT-policy/securityl.htm.

Information Technology Promotion Agency, "Reporting Status of Vulnerability-related Information about Software Products and Websites." December 2012. Accessed April 24, 2013. http://www.ipa.go.jp/security/vuln/report/vuln2012q4-e.pdf.

Ito, Yurie. "Making the Internet Clean, Safe and Reliable." Paper presented at the Second Worldwide Cybersecurity Summit (WCS), London, June 2011. Accessed March 27, 2013. https://dl.dropbox.com/u/869038/Papers2011/Ito.pdf.

Iwashita, Naoyuki. "Business Needs for Cryptographic Technology in Japan's Financial Industry." Bank of Japan. March 1, 1999. Accessed March 19, 2013. http://www.imes.boj.or.jp/research/papers/japanese/h9903.pdf.

"Japan defense firm Mitsubishi Heavy in cyber attack." BBC.co.uk. September 20, 2011. Accessed March 19, 2013. http://www.bbc.co.uk/news/world-asia-pacific-14982906.

"Japan: Organized Chinese hackers hit official Japan sites." *The Japan Times*, August 7, 2004. Accessed March 27, 2013. http://www.asiamedia.ucla.edu/article.asp?parentid=13424.

"Japan Textbook Angers Neighbors." BBC.co.uk. April 3, 2001. Accessed March 27, 2013. http://news.bbc.co.uk/2/hi/asia-pacific/1257835.stm.

"Japanese Government's Efforts to Address Information Security Issues: Focusing on the Cabinet Secretariat's Efforts." Japan National Information Security Center. September 2006. Accessed March 19, 2013. http://unpan1.un.org/intradoc/groups/public/documents/apcity/unpan027267.pdf.

Kamata, Keisuke. "JPCERT/CC Activities for Critical Infrastructure Protection." JPCERT/CC, August 29, 2007. Accessed February 20, 2013. http://www.itu.int/ITU-D/cyb/events/2007/hanoi/docs/kamata-jpcertcc-hanoi-29-aug-07.pdf.

Kamata, Keisuke and Miyagawa, Yuichi. "Threats of P2P File Sharing Software." JPCERT/CC, June 25, 2006. Accessed February 20, 2013. http://www.first.org/conference/2006/papers/kamata-keisuke-slides.pdf.

Kitahara, Munenori. "Information Society Law in Japan." US – China Law Review, 8, 21 (2011): 21-40.

Krebs, Brian. "Talking Bots with Japan's Cyber Clean Center." Krebs on Security (blog). March 2010. Accessed March 19, 2013. http://krebsonsecurity.com/2010/03/talking-bots-with-japans-cyber-clean-center.

Kubota, Yoko. "Military data possibly stolen in Mitsubishi Heavy hacking: Asahi." Reuters, Oct. 23, 2011. Accessed March 19, 2013. http://www.reuters.com/article/2011/10/23/us-mitsubishi-heavy-cyberattack-idUSTRE79M3XS20111023.

"Legal Framework." Privacy International, 2012. Accessed February 20, 2013. https://www.privacyinternational.org/reports/japan/i-legal-framework.

Lewis, James A. and Katrina Timlin. "Cybersecurity and Cyberwarfare." UNIDIR.org. Accessed March 19, 2013. http://www.unidir.org/pdf/ouvrages/pdf-1-92-9045-011-J-en.pdf.

Leyden, John. "Japan's biggest defense contractor hit by hackers," The Register. September

19, 2011. Accessed February 20, 2003. http://www.theregister.co.uk/2011/09/19/mitsubishi_malware_attack/.

Matsubara, Mihoko. "What the LDP Victory Means for Japan's Cybersecurity Policy." CFR. org, Dec. 20, 2012. Accessed February 20, 2013. http://blogs.cfr.org/asia/2012/12/20/mihoko-matsubara-what-the-ldp-victory-means-for-japans-cybersecurity-policy/.

Microsoft, "Microsoft Security Intelligence Report," Vols. 9 and 11. 2010, 2011. Accessed February 20, 2013. http://www.microsoft.com/security/sir/default.aspx.

McMillan, Graeme. "Japan Criminalizes Cybercrime: Make a Virus, Get Three Years in Jail." Techland Time. June 17, 2011. Accessed March 19, 2013. http://techland.time.com/2011/06/17/japan-criminalizes-cybercrime-make-a-virus-get-three-years-in-jail/.

"Ministry to Establish Cyberdefense Unit." Yomiuri Shimbun, September 8, 2012. Accessed February 20, 2013. http://www.yomiuri.co.jp/dy/national/T120907004328.htm.

National Information Security Center, "Information Security 2012." July 4, 2012. Accessed February 20, 2013. http://www.nisc.go.jp/eng/pdf/is2012_eng.pdf.

"NTT Encryption Archive List." NTT Secure Platform Laboratories Information Security Project. Accessed March 19, 2013. http://info.isl.ntt.co.jp/crypt/eng/archive/.

Organization for Economic Cooperation and Development. Privacy Online: OECD Guidance on Policy and Practice. OECD Publishing, 2008. Accessed February 20, 2013. http://books.google.com/books?hl=en&lr=&id=84vib2TslVcC&oi=fnd&pg=PA9&dq=Privacy+Online:+OECD+Guidance+on+Policy+and+Practice&ots=p5h-8zjkkE&sig=C4gs5qPUKrRKyzOSootkAera28E.

Osawa, Jun. "Japan Faces New Cyberwar Era." Institute for International Policy Studies. 2011. Accessed February 20, 2013. http://www.iips.org/iips_perspectives/oosawa01.pdf.

Preatoni, Robert. "Japanese Fight against Cybercrime." Zone-h.org. May 27, 2006. Accessed March 19, 2013. http://www.zone-h.org/news/id/4357.

Purcell, Richard, ed. OECD Privacy Guidelines: Thirty Years in the Public Sector. The Privacy Projects. December 1, 2010. Accessed March 27, 2013. http://theprivacyprojects.org/wp-content/uploads/2009/08/FINAL-OECD-PRIVACY-GUIDELINES-PUBLIC-SECTOR.pdf.

"Register Search." International Register of ISMS Certificates. August 2012. Accessed

March 19, 2013. http://www.iso27001certificates.com/Register%20Search.htm.

"Remarks by President Obama and Prime Minister Noda of Japan at Joint Press Conference." Whitehouse.gov. April 30, 2012. Accessed March 19, 2013. http://www.whitehouse.gov/the-press-office/2012/04/30/remarks-president-obama-and-prime-minister-noda-japan-joint-press-confer.

"Researcher Details: Tsutomu Matsumoto." Yokohama National University. Last updated March 4, 2013. Accessed March 19, 2013. http://er-web.jmk.ynu.ac.jp/html/MATSUMOTO_Tsutomu/ja.html.

Saka, Akira. "Unauthorized Computer Access Law." Japan National Police Agency. June 21, 2003. Accessed February 20, 2013. http://saka.jp/lecture/SAKA-1v2.ppt

Scherrer, Amandine. *G8 Against Transnational Organized Crime*. Surrey: Ashgate, 2009.

"Second National Strategy on Information Security, The." NISC. February 3, 2009. Accessed March 27, 2013. http://www.nisc.go.jp/eng/pdf/national_strategy_002_eng.pdf.

Segal, Adam. "Coming this Weekend: A Sino-Japanese Hacking War?" Council on Foreign Relations. September 17, 2010. Accessed March 19, 2013. http://blogs.cfr.org/asia/2010/09/17/coming-this-weekend-a-sino-japanese-hacking-war/.

"Tallinn, Japan to Strengthen Military Co-Operation." New Europe Online, April 22, 2012. Accessed March 19, 2013. http://www.neurope.eu/article/tallinn-japan-strengthen-military-co-operation.

Tsuchiya, Motohiro. "Patriotic Geeks Wanted to Counter a Cyber Militia." AJISS-Commentary. February 17, 2012. Accessed March 19, 2013. http://www.jiia.or.jp/en_commentary/201202/17-1.html.

"Unauthorized Computer Access Law." Government of Japan, Law No. 128 of 1999. Accessed March 19, 2013. http://www.npa.go.jp/cyber/english/legislation/ucalaw.html.

UNESCO. "The Council of Europe Convention on Cyber Crime, Before Its Entry into Force." UNESCO.org. March 2004. Accessed March 19, 2013. http://portal.unesco.org/culture/en/ev.php-URL_ID=19556&URL_DO=DO_TOPIC&URL_SECTION=201.html.

"What is Clean Cyber Center?" Clean Cyber Center. 2011. Accessed March 27, 2013. https://www.ccc.go.jp/en_ccc/.

Yamada, Yasuhide, Atsuhiro Yamagishi, and Ben T. Katsumi. "A Comparative Study of the Information Security Policies of Japan and the United States." Journal of National Security Law and Policy 4 (2010): 217-232.

Unglamorous Awakenings: How the UK Developed Its Approach to Cyber

"1945 Proposal by Arthur C. Clarke for Geostationary Satellite Communications, The." Lakdiva.org. Accessed October 11, 2012. http://lakdiva.org/clarke/1945ww/.

Aldrich, Richard. GCHQ: The Uncensored Story of Britain's Most Secret Intelligence Agency. New York: Harpercollins, 2010.

A Strong Britain in the Age of Uncertainty: The National Security Strategy. Government of the United Kingdom. London: The Stationery Office, October 2010. Accessed March 19, 2013. http://www.direct.gov.uk/prod_consum_dg/ groups/dg_digitalassets/@dg/@en/documents/digitalasset/dg_191639. pdf?CID=PDF&PLA=furl&CRE=nationalsecuritystrategy.

Atlas Consortium "About the DII Programme." Accessed March 19, 2013. http://web. archive.org/web/20110318092813/http://www.atlasconsortium.info/what-is-dii. aspx.htm.

"'Amarillo' Video Crashes MoD PCs." BBC.co.uk. May 17, 2005. Accessed September 5, 2012. http://news.bbc.co.uk/1/hi/uk/4554083.stm.

Baddeley, Adam. "DFTS: a Defence-Wide System." Defence Management Journal 31 (December 2005). Accessed March 19, 2013. http://www.defencemanagement.com/ article.asp?id=200&content_name=Communications&article=5142.

"Budapest Conference on Cyberspace 2012." Hungarian Government Ministry of Foreign Affairs. August 9, 2012. Accessed September 10, 2012. http://www.kormany.hu/en/ ministry-of-foreign-affairs/news/budapest-conference-on-cyberspace-2012.

Burton, Edmund. "Report into the Loss of MOD Personal Data." Ministry of Defence. April 30, 2008. Accessed March 19, 2013. http://www.mod.uk/NR/rdonlyres/3E756D20-E762-4FC1-BAB0-08C68FDC2383/0/burton_review_rpt20080430.pdf.

Cabinet Office. Cyber Security Strategy of the United Kingdom: Safety, Security and

Resilience in Cyber Space. London: The Stationery Office, 2009. Accessed March 19, 2013. http://webarchive.nationalarchives.gov.uk/+/http://www.cabinetoffice.gov.uk/media/216620/css0906.pdf.

Cabinet Office. The UK Cyber Security Strategy: Protecting and Promoting the UK in a Digital World. November 2011. Accessed March 19, 2013. http://web.archive.org/web/20120531125811/http://www.cabinetoffice.gov.uk/sites/default/files/resources/uk-cyber-security-strategy-final.pdf.

Center for the Protection of National Infrastructure. "WARP Background." Warp.gov.uk. Accessed March 19, 2013. http://www.warp.gov.uk/background.html.

"Clinger-Cohen Act (CCA) of 1996, The." DoD CIO Desk Reference: Volume 1 Foundation Documents. Department of

Defense Chief Information Office. August 2006. Accessed March 19, 2013. http://dodcio.defense.gov/Portals/0/Documents/ciodesrefvolone.pdf.

"Colossus Rebuild Project." Bletchlypark.org. Accessed March 19, 2013. http://www.bletchleypark.org.uk/content/visit/whattosee/ColossusRebuildProject.rhtm.

Cornish, Paul, David Livingstone, David Clemente, and Claire Yorke. Cyber Security and the UK's Critical National Infrastructure. London: Chatham House, 2011.

"Cyberspace: Cyber Security." UK Foreign and Commonwealth Office. Accessed October 28, 2012. http://web.archive.org/web/20121028152523/http://www.fco.gov.uk/en/global-issues/cyber-space/005-cyber-security/.

Gray, Colin S. Another Bloody Century: Future Warfare. London: Phoenix, 2005.

Gray, Colin S. Fighting Talk: Forty Maxims on War, Peace and Strategy. Washington D.C: Potomac Books, 2009.

Luttwack, Edward N. Strategy: the Logic of War and Peace. Cambridge, MA: Harvard University Press, 1987.

Michell, Simon. "A History of Networks." In NEC: Understanding Network Enabled Capability, edited by Simon Michell, 42-45. London: Newsdesk Communications, Ltd., 2009. Accessed March 27, 2013. http://www.newsdeskmedia.com/files/NEC%202009.pdf.

"Privatisation of British Telecom (1984), The." In The "S" Factors: Lessons from IFG's policy success reunion, edited by Jill Rutter, Edward Marshall, and Sam Sims, 45-59.

Institute for Government. January 2012. Accessed October 11, 2012. http://www. instituteforgovernment.org.uk/sites/default/files/british_telecom_privatisation.pdf.

Securing Britain in an Age of Uncertainty: The Strategic Defence and Security Review. Government of the United Kingdom. London: The Stationary Office, October 2010. Accessed March 19, 2013. http://www.direct.gov.uk/prod_consum_dg/groups/dg_digitalassets/@ dg/@en/documents/digitalasset/dg_191634.pdf.

"Single User Costs MoD £10 million after allowing Worm onto the Network." Computer Weekly. June 8, 2004. Accessed May 26, 2009. http://www.computerweekly.com/ feature/Single-user-costs-MoD-10m-after-allowing-worm-onto-the-network.

"Skynet 5 Has the World Covered with Secure, Flexible, and Pinpoint Accurate Communications." Paradigmsecure.com. Accessed March 19, 2013. https://www. paradigmsecure.com/our_services/skynet5.

"Strategic Defence Report." Presented to Parliament by the Secretary of State for Defence by Command of Her Majesty, July 1998. Accessed March 19, 2013. http://www. mod.uk/NR/rdonlyres/65F3D7AC-4340-4119-93A2-20825848E50E/0/sdr1998_ complete.pdf.

Symantec, Report on Lovgate. Accessed April 24, 2013. http://www.symantec.com/ security_response/writeup.jsp?docid=2003-022411-2431-99

Taylor, Claire. "The Defence White Paper." Research Paper 04/71. House of Commons Library. September 17, 2004. Accessed March 19, 2013. http://www.parliament.uk/ documents/commons/lib/research/rp2004/rp04-071.pdf.

Toffler, Alvin and Heidi Toffler. *War and Anti-War: Survival at the Dawn of the 21st Century.* New York: Little Brown & Co., 1993.

UK Cyber Security Strategy: Protecting and Promoting the UK in a Digital World, The. London: Cabinet Office, November 25, 2011. Accessed March 27, 2013. https://www.gov. uk/government/uploads/system/uploads/attachment_data/file/60961/uk-cyber- security-strategy-final.pdf.

"W32.HLLW.LOVEGATE.C@MM." Symantec.com. Updated February 13, 2007. Accessed March 19, 2013. http://www.symantec.com/security_response/writeup. jsp?docid=2003-022411-2431-99.

Willsher, Kim. "French Fighter Planes Grounded by Computer Virus." *The Telegraph,* February 7, 2009. Accessed March 19, 2013. http://www.telegraph.co.uk/news/ worldnews/europe/france/4547649/French-fighter-planes-grounded-by-computer-virus.html.

"Y2K Bug Fails to Bite." BBC.co.uk. January 1, 2000. Accessed March 19, 2013. http://news.bbc.co.uk/1/hi/sci/tech/585013.stm.

Part 6: Concluding Assesment

Concluding Assessment: "Pointing the Finger" - National Responsibility for Cyber Conflicts

"1999: Chinese Anger at Embassy Bombing." BBC.co.uk. May 9, 1999. Accessed March 19, 2013. http://news.bbc.co.uk/onthisday/hi/dates/stories/may/9/newsid_2519000/2519271.stm.

Bumgarner, John and Scott Borg. "Overview by the US-CCU of the Cyber Campaign against Georgia in August of 2008." US-CCU Special Report, U.S. Cyber Consequences Unit. August 2009. Accessed March 27, 2013. http://www.registan.net/wp-content/uploads/2009/08/US-CCU-Georgia-Cyber-Campaign-Overview.pdf

Chase, Michael S. and James C. Mulvenon. *You've Got Dissent: Chinese Dissident Use of the Internet and Beijing's Counter-Strategies.* Santa Monica, CA: RAND, 2002.

"China's Top Legislature Slams EU Parliament for Tibet Resolution." Xinhua, March 13, 2009. Accessed October 17, 2009. http://news.xinhuanet.com/english/2009-03/13/content_11007789.htm.

"China, Taiwan, Tibet: Fraying at the Edges." *The Economist.* July 10, 2008. Accessed March 19, 2013. http://www.economist.com/opinion/displayStory.cfm?story_id=11707478.

Clover, Charles. "Kremlin-Backed Group Behind Estonia Cyber Blitz." *Financial Times,* March 11, 2009. Accessed March 19, 2013. http://www.ft.com/cms/s/0/57536d5a-0ddc-11de-8ea3-0000779fd2ac.html?nclick_check=1.

FBI Los Angeles. "One Hundred Linked to International Computer Hacking Ring Charged by United States and Egypt in Operation Phish Phry." FBI.gov. October 7, 2009. http://www.fbi.gov/losangeles/press-releases/2009/la100709-1.htm

Greylogic. "Project Grey Goose Phase II Report: The evolving state of cyber warfare." Scribd.com. March 20, 2009. Accessed September 23, 2012. http://www.scribd.com/doc/13442963/Project-Grey-Goose-Phase-II-Report.

Healey, Jason. "Beyond Attribution: Seeking National Responsibility for Cyber Attacks." Atlantic Council Issue Brief. February 22, 2012. Accessed March 19, 2013. http://www.acus.org/publication/beyond-attribution-seeking-national-responsibility-cyberspace.

Hulme, George V. "NIPC Warns of Chinese Hacktivism." Information Week. April 27, 2001. Accessed October 16, 2009. http://www.informationweek.com/nipc-warns-of-chinese-hacktivism/6505353.

Information Warfare Monitor. "Tracking GhostNet: Investigating a Cyber Espionage Network." March 29, 2009. Accessed March 19, 2013. http://www.scribd.com/doc/13731776/Tracking-GhostNet-Investigating-a-Cyber-Espionage-Network.

"Putin in Veiled Attack on Estonia." BBC.co.uk. May 9, 2007. Accessed October 18, 2009. http://news.bbc.co.uk/2/hi/europe/6638029.stm.

Rosenthal, Elisabeth. "Crisis in the Balkans, China: More Protests in Beijing as Officials Study Bombing Errors." New York Times, May 10, 1999. Accessed October 16, 2009. http://www.nytimes.com/1999/05/10/world/crisis-balkans-china-more-anti-us-protests-beijing-officials-study-bombing-error.html.

Shanker, Thom and John Markoff. "Halted '03 Iraq Plan Illustrates U.S. Fear of Cyberwar Risk." New York Times, August 1, 2009. Accessed October 16, 2009. http://www.nytimes.com/2009/08/02/us/politics/02cyber.html.

Sheeter, Laura. "Russia Slams Estonia Statue Move." BBC.co.uk. January 17, 2007. Accessed October 17, 2009. http://news.bbc.co.uk/2/hi/europe/6273117.stm.

"Tallinn Tense after Deadly Riots." BBC.co.uk. April 28, 2007. Accessed October 17, 2009. http://news.bbc.co.uk/2/hi/europe/6602171.stm.

Tikk, Eneken, Kadri Kaska, and Liis Vihul. "International Cyber Incidents: Legal Considerations." Tallinn, Estonia: NATO Cooperative Cyber Defense Center of Excellence, 2010. Accessed March 27, 2013. http://www.ccdcoe.org/publications/books/legalconsiderations.pdf.

Verizon Business Risk Team. "Verizon Data Breach Report for 2008." Verizon. Accessed March 19, 2013. http://www.verizonbusiness.com/resources/security/databreachreport.pdf.

Verizon Business Risk Team. "Verizon Data Breach Report for 2009." Verizon. Accessed March 19, 2013. http://www.verizonbusiness.com/resources/security/reports/2009_databreach_rp.pdf.

Villeneuve, Nart. "Koobface: Inside a Crimeware Network." InfoWar Monitor. 2010. Accessed March 19, 2013. http://www.infowar-monitor.net/reports/iwm-koobface.pdf.

Zigfield, Kim. "Re-Imposing Totalitarian Information Control in Russia." American Thinker, September 30, 2009. Accessed March 19, 2013. http://www.americanthinker.com/2009/09/reimposing_totalitarian_inform.html.

Appendix 3: Timeline

Cyber Conflict History Timeline Appendix

11 February 1970	Ware Report released. This Defense Science Board report, Security Controls for Computer Systems, outlined security controls, many of which remain familiar today.
August 1986	Cuckoo's Egg intrusions, the first recognizable cyber conflict begins. West German hacker Markus Hess, was recruited by the KGB to intrude into Lawrence Berkley National Labs and other US networks to steal US military information. Hess was discovered about a year into his sphying by Clifford Stoll whose efforts to track and capture Hess were later outlined in the popular book the Cuckoo's Egg. Hess was arrested on 2 March 1989.
2 November 1988	Morris Worm was released by Robert Tappan Morris, then a graduate student at Cornell. This piece of malicious software, the first significant worm, unintentionally took down a considerable portion of the Internet. There was no central group to coordinate the response to incidents like this, so DoD quickly funded the creation of the world's first Computer Emergency Response Team at Carnegie Mellon University.
April 1990 – May 1991	Dutch Hackers intruded into the networks of over 30 US military installations during the lead up to the first Gulf War. Using fairly unsophisticated methods, the teenage hackers from the Netherlands were searching for information on missiles, nuclear weapons, and DESERT SHIELD.
3 March 1995	Citibank Hacks: Russian hacker Vladimir Levin is arrested in London for hacking Citibank for tens of millions of dollars in losses. This led Citibank to create the first Chief Information Security Officer to oversee the security of its networks, a position now common worldwide.
28 September 1995	US Air Force's 609th Information Warfare Squadron was established, probably the first true offense-defense combat cyber unit in the world.

21 December 1995	Strano Network implements first denial of service attack. The Strano Network is considered the first hacktivist group, and targeted ten agencies of the French government for its ongoing nuclear testing in the Pacific. It was the first mass participation of a virtual sit in and demonstrated the potential of cyber hacktivism.
June 1997	ELIGIBLE RECEIVER (ER97), a cyber "red team" exercise, conducted by the Chairman of the Joint Chiefs of Staff of the US military. This exercise received extremely high-level attention as it highlighted US vulnerability to cyber attacks.
15 July 1997	President's Commission on Critical Infrastructure Protection established by Bill Clinton through Executive Order 13010. This influential advisory commission was the first to delve deeply into infrastructure protection and cyber issues. It reported only a few months later, on 13 October 1997 with recommendations largely incorporated into PDD-63 the following year.
1-26 February 1998	SOLAR SUNRISE series of attacks against DoD unclassified systems. The intrusions came soon after ER97 and were initially thought to be the precursors of a cyber war from Saddam Hussein's Iraq. Even though the cuprits were two California teenagers with an Israeli mentor, the attacks were a wakeup call to DoD, which rushed to create the JTF-CND to command during such incidents.
March 1998 to ???	MOONLIGHT MAZE, a still largely classified cyber espionage case, was investigated by the JTF-CND and FBI. A huge wake up call for the DoD, MAZE included hundreds of related intrusions into computers at NASA, the Pentagon, other governmental agencies, universities, and research laboratories.
22 May 1998	Presidential Decision Directive 63 (PDD 63) issued by President Clinton, based on the recommendations of the PCCIP report. It was the first of several major presidential strategies on infrastructure protection and cyber and created the National Infrastructure Protection Center (NIPC) and called on the private sector to create Infrastructure Sharing and Analysis Centers. Like its successor strategies, it has helped create new organizations and programs, though cyber problems have only gotten worse.

9 September 1998	Electronic Disturbance Theater (EDT) conducted a 'FloodNet' denial of service attack against the Pentagon in support of the Zapatista rebels in Mexico. This incident generated headlines when a defensive tactic by the DoD caused problems for the attacking computers due to a programming flaw in FloodNet.
30 December 1998	Joint Task Force for Computer Network Defense (JTF-CND) was created by the DoD as a lesson learned from ER97 and SOLAR SUNRISE. With barely more than twenty staff, the JTF-CND was the first joint warfighting cyber command, the precursor of today's US Cyber Command. The command did not reach full operating capability until June 1999.
26 March 1999	Melissa strikes. This virus spread through email and infected and shut down many email addresses. It caught the public's attention and highlighted the insecurity of cyberspace.
March to June 1999	ALLIED FORCE and Attacks on NATO: The Alliance began this operation on 24 March to evict Yugoslav forces from Kosovo. On 26 March, the NATO web server was unavailable as a result of denial or service attacks. Many other attacks on NATO and member militaries followed, mostly conducted by patriotic hackers from Yugoslavia or Russia.
7 May 1999	During Operation Allied Force, US bombed the Belgrade Chinese Embassy. This lead to large Chinese patriot hacktivism on US DoD information systems and marked the emergence of the notorious Red Hackers Alliance.
1 April 2001	JTF-CND became the Joint Task Force for Computer Network Operations (JTF-CNO) adding cyber offense to its existing defense mission. In October 2002 the unit switched reporting from US Space Command to US Strategic Command.
18 September 2001	The computer worm NIMDA affected millions of computers worldwide in just 22 minutes. As the worm came just a week after the 9/11 terrorist attacks, it causing concern that it was the first act of cyber terrorism.

24 January 2003	The Department of Homeland Security officially begins operations, incorporating the NIPC and other cyber functions handled by Commerce, Defense, and other agencies.
25 January 2003	SQL Slammer Worm was released, causing massive denial of service attacks on certain Internet host and slowed down Internet traffic.
18 June 2004	Joint Task Force for Global Network Operations (JTF-GNO) was created from the existing JTF-CNO, giving the command authority for network management, not just defense and offense.
17 December 2003	HSPD-7 was signed by President George W. Bush, the first major update to PDD-63. This established the United States' policy for identifying and prioritizing protection for critical infrastructure, with different sectors covered by varying government organizations. Along with the National Strategy to Secure Cyberspace, signed 14 February 2003, these remained the heart of cyber policy for a decade.
2005 to 2010	Joint Functional Component Command – Network Warfare: JFCC-NW operated as a subordinate command to US Strategic Command to handle offensive operations. This had been the mission of JTF-CNO; the JFCC-NW was a sister unit to JTF-GNO until both were folded into US Cyber Command.
27 April to 23 May 2007	Estonia Cyber Conflict: Estonia was subjugated to several weeks of DDoS attacks, website defacements, and other attacks during a national security crisis with Russia. Ultimately, the event was a strategic and tactical defeat for Russia, as the patriotic hacking did not coerce Estonia which is know renowned for cyber expertise.

5–9 August 2008	Georgia Cyber Attacks: During Georgia's war with Russia over South Ossetia, it suffered a large campaign of denial of service attacks and defacements. Whereas the Estonian attacks the year before were clearly patriotic hacking, the attacks on Georgia bore more even fingerprints of Russian government policy. On August 9th, the Georgian government declared a state of war, and suspended electronic banking services through August 16th.
October 2008	BUCKSHOT YANKEE: The DoD discovered a large-scale intrusion in US Central Command, then engaged in combat operations in Iraq and Afghanistan. The intrusion was particularly serious because DoD is convinced it was from a foreign intelligence service (most likely from Russia) and penetrated into the classified SIPRNET network. The response, called Operation BUCKSHOT YANKEE, was well publicized as it banned USB thumb drives throughout the military.
November 2008 to mid-2009	Conficker infected computers around the world to create a mysterious botnet with no clear purpose. The private sector Conficker Working Group was the first truly successful collaboration effort, and created the first all-hands-on-deck crisis for cyber defenders worldwide.
29 March 2009	Ghostnet was reported by the Information Warfare Monitor after a 10-month investigation. These intruders had compromised NATO SHAPE headquarters, embassies, foreign ministers, the office of the Dali Lama, and other targets. in over 100 countries with China being the very obvious suspect.
12 January 2010	Operation Aurora – Google publicly discloses the Aurora attacks against them and other private sector corporations by hackers they associate with the Chinese government.

21 May 2010	US Cyber Command reaches initial operating capability as a sub-unified command under US Strategic Command. It absorbed JTF-GNO and JFCC-NW on 7 September 2010 and reached full operational capability on 31 October 2010. Though far larger and more capable, US Cyber Command is essentially a direct descendent of the JTF-CND created in December 1998.
16 July 2010	Stuxnet was discovered by VirusBlokAda, an anti-virus company based in Belarus. Stuxnet is the most sophisticated piece of malware software ever found, a quantum leap in complexity and audacity in cyber conflict and intended to disrupt Iran's uranium enrichment propgram at Natanz. On 1 June 2012, the NY Times reported Stuxnet was part of a joint US-Israeli operation called OLYMPIC GAMES.
17 March 2011	RSA Secure ID Hacks – RSA disclosed that its SecureID system has been hacked. SecureID and other RSA technologies are centerpieces of the defenses of countless companies and nations. Leveraging the information stolen, it appears Chinese hackers were subsequently able to gain access to other companies, including to steal the plans for the F-35 Joint Strike Fighter from Lockheed Martin.
28 May 2012	Flame malware was reported by Iran CERT. Flame operated undiscovered for more than two years before it was found and revealed and linked to Stuxnet and OLYMPIC GAMES.

Appendix 4: Index

Symbols

A

B

C

D

E

G

CPSIA information can be obtained
at www.ICGtesting.com
Printed in the USA
LVOW04*0238120416

483176LV00002B/2/P